Colección Támesis

SERIE A: MONOGRAFÍAS, 259

A COMPANION TO PABLO NERUDA

EVALUATING NERUDA'S POETRY

JASON WILSON

A COMPANION TO PABLO NERUDA

EVALUATING NERUDA'S POETRY

TAMESIS

First published 2008 by Tamesis, Woodbridge

ISBN 978–1–85566–167–7

Tamesis is an imprint of Boydell & Brewer Ltd
PO Box 9, Woodbridge, Suffolk IP12 3DF, UK
and of Boydell & Brewer Inc.
668 Mt Hope Avenue, Rochester, NY 14620, USA
website: www.boydellandbrewer.com

A CIP catalogue record for this book is available
from the British Library

This publication is printed on acid-free paper

Printed in Great Britain by
CPI Antony Rowe, Chippenham, Wiltshire

CONTENTS

To Andrea

PREFACE

I quote Neruda because nowhere in contemporary poetry have I read such a powerful visceral description of the bombing of civilians.
                                    Harold Pinter, Nobel Lecture, 'Art, Truth & Politics'

I have benefited from countless chats with Neruda scholars and critics, from the late Robert Pring-Mill to his biographer in English, Adam Feinstein. Over many years, I have taught classes on all aspects of Neruda, but concentrating on the Neruda I still read with enthusiasm, the great and dark poems up to the 1940s. Jean Franco set me on my way when I was an undergraduate, as did reading Neruda in translation in *Evergreen Review*. I heard Neruda recite his poems on two occasions in London so I can follow his voice while I read his later work. I bumped into him, conversing with Octavio Paz in a private hotel in Sloane Square, London, even though they were still not speaking to each other, and later visited Isla Negra.

My triple aim is to introduce Neruda to new readers, to rescue him from his complete works and to debate with more skilled and critical readers, aware that there is a Neruda *claque*, to which I do not belong, and that the secondary writing on him is massive. I tend to agree with Ilan Stavans that 'little is actually readable' and realise that my interpretative prose may jar with the poems. To write about a great poet in another language and culture, however well I may know Spanish and Hispanic poetry, is an added risk, so I have added my own literal translations of the poems cited, while including an appendix on Neruda's translations into English, with the odd comments on the quality of translation throughout my text. When his and his critics' prose is literal, I have translated it without too much loss. I have inserted abbreviated bibliographic details in the footnotes and full ones in the bibliography, unless the citation is local and then it is full in the note.

I would like to thank the Fundación Pablo Neruda for permission to cite from his works, Professor Stephen Hart for suggesting the book, and Ellie Ferguson and the publishers for their careful tidying of my typescript.

JW, London

Introduction

Pablo Neruda was a great love poet. Love poems form the core of his abundant output and he wrote his love poems from the start to the end of his career as a poet.[1] In 1971 he told a Mexican interviewer that love was his main theme: 'I have written ten books about love.' To the next question about politics, he denied that it was essential to his poetry: 'What is essential? It is to discover what one truly feels at every moment of life.'[2] This ambition can be located at the very start of Neruda's career as a poet when, in his poem 'Sensación autobiográfica' [Autobiographic sensation], he asserted his version of that male life-ambition of planting a tree, writing a book and having a child with a woman: 'Haber amado a una mujer y haber escrito / un libro' [To have loved a woman and to have written a book].[3] In 1965 he told Mario Vargas Llosa that his advice to a young poet was to 'continue writing poems to his lover', for poetry begins as communication between lovers. Throughout this *Companion*, I will argue that the lover as destinee of a poem creates the illusion of intimacy for later readers. He dedicated a copy of his *Cien sonetos de amor* to Vargas Llosa's wife so that the poems could be read aloud to her. A secondary underpinning of this book is how Neruda's poetry stresses the need to voice a poem. Voice enriches text, emotionalises and humanises it.[4]

Neruda was also a love poet in a less Romantic mode, with poems dealing with love for his *patria*, for his continent, its fauna and flora and geology; he wrote love poems about his fellow poets, his beloved Chileans and all working-class Latin Americans. He also celebrated, as a kind of tepid love poem, the simple things of life. Despite, then, the love poems to his party, to

---

[1]   See Oscar Hahn, *Poemas de amor de Pablo Neruda*, 1994, which includes poems from *Crepusculario* to *Memorial de Isla Negra*. See also the bestselling Pablo Neruda, *Love*, 1995, a parallel text of poems from the film *Il Postino*. Two further anthologies focus on the love poetry: *Canto corporal. Antología de poemas de amor* (Zaragoza: Olifante, 2004) and *Los mejores poemas de amor* (Barcelona: Lumen, 2006).

[2]   Pablo Neruda, 'Pablo Neruda se confiesa', *Siempre*, p. 36: 'he escrito diez libros sobre el amor'; 'Qué es lo esencial? Es descubrir lo que verdaderamente se siente en cada instante de la existencia.'

[3]   Pablo Neruda, *Cuadernos de Temuco*, p. 181. Henceforth, CT and page number in text.

[4]   Mario Vargas Llosa, *Diccionario*, pp. 253–4.

fellow communists and friends, it is essentially as a Romantic love poet that he survives and will be read and learnt by heart. The other side of the coin is that he is also a fierce hater and was involved, poetically and biographically, in countless scandals and feuds. In 2006 Loyola noted that attacking Neruda had become a 'national sport'.[5] So intensities of love and hate form the axis of his work.

Like many prolific writers, Neruda wrote constantly throughout his life as a daily discipline. You could say that he organised his life around his desire and need to write. The experience of loneliness and lovelessness at the core of his early years merge with the solitude necessary for any kind of writing. Neruda's life as a poet had to balance this need to be alone at a desk and write and yet not suffer a sense of abandonment. This theme and experience of alone-ness diminished with age, as he surrounded himself with friends and admirers, so that his later work is less intense, more communal and communicative. He noted this change himself:

> The young writer cannot write without that thrill of loneliness, even if it is fictitious, in the same way that the mature writer cannot do anything without the taste of human company, of society.[6]

Indeed, much of his work from the politicised 1940s onwards is flawed, as we will see, and yet contains some nugget of sound and meaning, some insight that confirms that he was in contact with his earthy muses. However, Neruda's powerful literary personality dominated views on his work. His posthumous memoirs, his adventurous life, his many lovers and love poems have led to countless biographic interpretations, and rightly so as he wrote the work he signed. Despite this inevitable biographic approach, I intend to focus on how Neruda recreated himself and the world inside his poems and then projected this 'persona' on to readers – what Selden Rodman called his 'capacity to project his own personality' over his readers and critics.[7] This approach avoids acquiescing with Neruda's own powerful control of meaning. Because he has overplayed his anti-bookishness from the vantage point of his emotional Marxism, I am keen to look into his literariness, his debts and conversations with other poets, living and dead, inside his poems. I am fascinated by what Neruda read, the implicit 'library' within his work.

---

5   Hernán Loyola, *Neruda*, 2006, p. 11.

6   Pablo Neruda, *Confieso que he vivido. Memorias*, p. 127: 'El escritor joven no puede escribir sin ese estremecimiento de soledad, aunque sea ficticio, así como el escritor maduro no hará nada sin el sabor de la compañía humana, de sociedad.'

7   Selden Rodman, *South America of the Poets*, p. 230.

He has alluded to his early 'literary voracity', to his 'greed for reading'; he called himself an 'ostrich, I swallowed without discriminating'.[8]

The metaphor behind his reading is often 'digestive', as it was to Rita Guibert in 1974: 'I was a hungry and thirsty reader' (PN5 1154). Strangely, few critics have alluded to such abundant reading, let alone explored the 'digestive' metaphor and its excremental end result. One is Enrico Mario Santí in his *Pablo Neruda: the Poetics of Prophecy*, 1982, where he argued for a Borgesian Neruda, challenging the 'anti-intellectual image that Neruda himself fostered'.[9] Another is Darío Oses who has compiled an anthology of explicit references to poets in Neruda's work.[10] Mario Vargas Llosa told an interviewer in 2004 that behind Neruda's anti-intellectual pose there was 'a rigorous, deep reader, very familiar with all the great modern literature'.[11] A good analogy for the way Neruda read is with how the painter Francis Bacon conceived of the work of art 'without the brain interfering with the inevitability of the image', which the critic Julian Bell translated as 'an ideal of painting that makes a radically direct impact on the viewer, bypassing all rationally organized procedures for recording appearance'.[12]

Neruda himself at the end of his *Canto general* bequeathed his old books to the future poets of America. He asked them to love his favourite authors from his select library in 1948:

> Que amen como yo amé mi Manrique, mi Góngora,
> mi Garcilaso, mi Quevedo:
> fueron
> titánicos guardianes, armaduras
> de platino y nevada transparencia,
> que me enseñaron el rigor, y busquen
> en mi Lautréamont viejos lamentos
> entre pestilenciales agonías.
> Que en Mayakovski vean cómo ascendió la estrella
> y cómo de sus rayos nacieron las espigas   (PN1 833)

> [Let them love like I loved my Manrique, mi Góngora, / my Garcilaso, my Quevedo:/ They were / titanic guardians, armour / of platinum and snowy transparency / who taught me rigour and

---

8   Neruda, *Confieso*, pp. 30–1: 'voracidad literaria', 'avidez de lectura'; 'avestruz, yo tragaba sin discriminar'.

9   Enrico Mario Santí, *Pablo Neruda. The Poetics of Prophecy*, p. 17.

10   See also his 'Pablo Neruda bibliófilo y lector, el amor por la vida y el amor por los libros', *Atenea*, 489, 2004, pp. 51–62.

11   Manuel Toledo, interview with Mario Vargas Llosa, BBC Mundo on <news.bbc.co/uk/hi/spanish/specials/2004>: 'un lector riguroso, profundo y muy familiarizado … con la gran literatura moderna'.

12   Julian Bell, 'The Cunning of Francis Bacon', p. 6.

let them seek / in my Lautréamont old laments / amongst pestilen-
tial death throes. / Let them see in Mayakovsky how the star rose
/ and how ears of wheat were born from its rays.]

Neruda avowed his peninsular Spanish roots with 'his' Quevedo, despite
having despised Góngora earlier, as an exercise in rhetorical 'rigour'. Quevedo,
as we will see, always kept his 'pasión genital' alive. Neruda discovered
Quevedo in Madrid in 1935, delighted to find that both he and Quevedo had
come to a similar verbal discovery with the expression 'una familia de oro'
[a family of gold], which Neruda had coined in his poem 'Alianza' [Alliance]
and Quevedo in his 'Retrato de Lisi' [Portrait of Lisi].[13] When he read him
in 1935 Neruda claimed that 'Quevedo has been for me not a reading, but a
lived experience, with all the rumorous matter of life'.[14] Bellini considered
that Neruda's continuous use of 'polvo' [dust], 'ceniza' [ash] and 'hueso'
[bone] in the 1930s derives from Quevedo. However, when it comes to 'mi'
Góngora, Neruda elsewhere admitted disliking Góngora's 'frozen beauty',
and found traces of 'gongorine opulence' in all later Spanish poetry.[15] Not
for nothing were the great Spanish poets of the 1920s – Lorca, Cernuda,
Alberti, Guillén, Salinas etc. – called the generation of 1927 in honour of the
tricentenary of Góngora's death. Neruda's acute critique is grounded in his
belief in sincerity as the source of poetry.

He rescued the Uruguayan-born Isidore Ducasse (the father of Parisian
surrealism) who wrote under the pseudonym Comte de Lautréamont (1846–
70). Later, he would write a long and excellent poem 'Lautréamont recon-
quistado' [Lautréamont reconquered] where he personalised his reading into
a meeting with Ducasse, and turned him into an 'americano' (PN2 1071) who
wrote his cantos (*Les Chants de Maldoror*, 1869) on horseback, 'galopando /
entre la dura hierba' [galloping / among the hard grass], for both Ducasse and
Neruda loved galloping along deserted beaches. Lautréamont was killed by
Paris itself, Neruda claimed, and was, like him, a 'joven desdichado' [young
and lovesick] (PN2 1072), a 'niño feroz' [ferocious child] and an 'indómito
uruguayo' [indomitable Uruguayan]. Neruda would often invoke Lautréamont's example. In his essay on Quevedo, he repeated that Lautréamont was
'American, Uruguayan, Chilean, Colombian, ours' (PN4 455); he was the
'bloodthirsty hero of the dark depths of our America', despite writing in
French. He had been inspired not by the Seine, but by the Amazon, by America's 'geographic environment of gigantic exploration'. This Uruguayan still
incites readers, his 'ravings still set fire to the world's poetry' (PN5 247).

13   Amado Alonso, cited in Giuseppe Bellini, *Quevedo*, p. 59.
14   'Quevedo ha sido para mí no una lectura, sino una experiencia viva, con toda la rumorosa materia de la vida,' in Bellini, *Quevedo*, p. 61.
15   Neruda, *Confieso*, p. 356.

He uses the word 'desdichado' (PN5 177) to sum him up (as we will see, a crucial term borrowed from Nerval that equally characterises early Neruda). Neruda influenced Lorca's views on Lautréamont; Lorca agreed about this 'never French count of Lautréamont'.[16] Neruda first read about Lautréamont in Rubén Darío's essay on him in Los raros [The Odd Ones], 1896 and, translated into Spanish, in Díez-Canedo's 1913 anthology.[17] But the main point in Neruda's reclaiming Lautréamont as South American was to counter André Breton's inclusion of him in the inner core of surrealist models in the second surrealist manifesto of 1929.[18]

But, in his bequeathed library, Neruda gives pride of place to the Russian Vladimir Mayakovsky, as poet of rebirth, forgetting his suicide in 1930. The lines cited about Mayakovsky end with that Utopian socialist promise, the cliché of 'espiga' [ear of wheat], the future bread for the proletariat. Neruda jettisoned the French influences (Ducasse is really a Latin American who wrote in French), and ended with a Russian Communist poet endorsed by Stalin as 'the best and most talented poet of our Soviet epoch'.[19] But there is no sense in Neruda that Stalin, in Deutscher's words, 'allowed the lights of its [Soviet] language and literature to be so thoroughly blacked out'. Deutscher summarised Stalin's attitude to literary culture as a 'distrust of intellectual and artistic originality: for in that he always scented unorthodoxy'. So Yesenin and Mayakovsky, 'the most original poets of contemporary Russia', killed themselves.[20] I turn to Deutscher as a writer making sense of Stalin contemporaneous with Neruda, before Stalin died. Neruda toed the party line, avoiding any enquiry, any deeper curiosity. To rub in how conventionally Stalinist Neruda was over Mayakovsky, a brief comparison with what César Vallejo wrote in 1930 in his acute essay 'El caso Maiakovski', after he had met him in Moscow, will suffice. Vallejo pinpointed Mayakovsky's dilemma as 'acute moral crisis', unable to transform his work into anything more than Bolshevik pose. His petit-bourgeois past survived 'tenacious and irreducible', and he was unable to swap his Futurist vest for the revolutionary blouse. So Mayakovsky's inner life was in open conflict with his revolutionary duties, with the result that he became a simple versifier, 'un retórico hueco' [hollow rhetorician]. His poetry was reduced to formulae, lacked deep heat, was just 'central heating', a declamatory, nullified art that betrayed his true self.[21] Vallejo had winkled out why a poet might kill himself.

This biased library skips over his actual literary debts and passions.

16 Federico García Lorca, Obra completa, p. 148: 'nunca francés conde de Lautréamont'.
17 Enrique Díez-Canedo, La poesía francesa ..., pp. 183–91.
18 André Breton, Manifestes du surréalisme, pp. 184, 210.
19 Margaret Drabble (ed.), The Oxford Companion to English Literature, p. 656.
20 Isaac Deutscher, Stalin, pp. 367–9.
21 César Vallejo, El arte y la revolución, pp. 104–10.

Margarita Aguirre, once his secretary and an early biographer, outlined his collection of first editions. It included Rimbaud's 1873 *Une Saison en enfer*, Darío's *Azul*, 1888, books by Huidobro, López Velarde, Verlaine, Baudelaire and countless dedicated ones that he donated to the University of Chile's library.[22]

Yet again, in the opening poem of *Cantos ceremoniales*, 1961, titled 'El sobrino de Occidente' [Nephew of the West], Neruda revived his adolescent reading when his uncle Manuel gave him *Sindbad the Sailor* as a present (these are tales added to *The Arabian Nights*). Neruda recalled his reaction to the book: 'y supe de pronto / que más allá de la lluvia estaba el mundo' [and I knew at once / that beyond the rain lay the world] (PN2 1019). Reading these folktales set in motion his desire to know the world, and travel away from rainy home in Temuco. A book, he claimed, was a door that then vanished like Pascal, or Dumas or Lautréamont, leaving the house empty. For Neruda, to read was to know himself beyond narcissism: 'Y cuando abres la puerta hay un espejo / en que te ves entero y te da frío' [And when you open the door there's a mirror / in which you see yourself completely and feel cold] (PN2 1020).

How can reading a book reveal a sobering self-image? I hazard that Neruda read books as provocations to himself, as a prompt, as if the author was his enemy. My emphasis so far on Neruda as a reader is that reading comes before writing. There are many circumstantial and even genetic reasons why a child becomes a poet; an essential one is the thrill of reading to reveal another self and then wanting to participate, become that self and write. Susan Sontag put it as 'reading usually precedes writing. And the impulse to write is almost always fired by reading. Reading, the love of reading, is what makes you dream of becoming a writer.'[23]

I hinted that Neruda viewed his past as a poet and reader negatively from a present as a poet and militant Communist. Given this implicit self-critique, can we talk of a radical change in Neruda's poetry and life, and thus of two Nerudas? The answer is obviously yes, if we read Neruda politically, for much that he wrote from the Spanish Civil War on, when his poetry 'changed', is politicised, a Cold War, Stalinist polemic. When did Neruda discard his earlier work and change? There is no one date. Some critics, with Robert Pring-Mill at the forefront, deem it to be his Spanish Civil War poems of 1936–7. The change lies within his poetry. There's a shift from an intense, tortured lyrical subjectivity, beyond circumstances of place and outside time, to being more 'anecdotal and prosaic', even 'militantly prosaic' in J. M. Alonso's words.[24] Other critics, like Emir Rodríguez Monegal, cite

---

[22] Margarita Aguirre, *Las vidas de Pablo Neruda*, pp. 82–91.
[23] Susan Sontag, *Where the Stress Falls. Essays* (London: Cape, 2002), p. 265.
[24] J. M. Alonso, *Review*, p. 33.

Neruda's 1943 visit to Machu Picchu to suggest that the conversion was not sudden but gradual. Yet another critic has argued that the change appears in his poem 'Reunión bajo las nuevas banderas' [Reunion under new flags], first published in 1940, with his 'para que junte mis pasos de lobo / a los pasos del hombre' [so that I join my wolf's steps / with those of man] (PN1 365).[25] The self-images are obvious; the lone wolf has joined the pack, an individual merges with the collectivity. Neruda himself saw his public reading at La Vega Central market in Santiago in 1938, where workers wept over his Spanish Civil War poems, as the moment of change: 'I began then to think not only of social poetry. I felt that I was in debt to my country, to my people.'[26] What happened at this market reading was Neruda's awareness that voice took the poem out of the book (and bookshops) to touch illiterate readers, the *pueblo*. This discovery of the power of oral poetry is linked with the creation of the persona Pablo Neruda, so that readers knew him from his voiced poems, to the point that he almost no longer had a private life.

But up until around 1938, Neruda was simply the greatest avant-garde writer in Spanish who explored love, time and destruction and loneliness in all their varieties. The Uruguyan critic and poet Eduardo Milán put this case bluntly: 'Neruda is, at the least, two: the author of *Residencia en la tierra* and the author of the rest of his work.' His later work showed a 'fatal fall in its aesthetic temperature'. Milán lamented that critics had done no more than celebrate Neruda, for his work constituted one of the great critical dilemmas of twentieth-century Latin American poetry.[27] I cite Milán because I share his verdict. At an anecdotal level even photographs confirm that there were two Nerudas: a thin and then a tubby, later one; a self-tortured one and then a contented one. By his marriage in 1930 Neruda was putting on weight; in a letter to his sister Laura he claimed that he had reached 80 kilos in Batavia.[28] However, this will not be a study of Neruda's shape in relation to his poetics, though there is a link. Looked at poetically, there may be two Nerudas, but the core Neruda remained a Romantic, through whose sensibility life was filtered and crafted into words and rhythms and sounds. Direct sensual experience formed the basis of his writing. The Chilean poet Enrique Lihn intimated this Romantic core:

25 Mario Rodríguez Fernandez, '*Reunión bajo las nuevas banderas* o de la conversión poética de Pablo Neruda', in Angel Flores (ed.), *Aproximaciones a Pablo Neruda*, pp.149–64.

26 From Neruda's 'Algo sobre mi poesía y mi vida', 1954, cited by J. Valdivieso, 'Neruda', p. 102: 'Comencé entonces a pensar no sólo en la poesía social. Sentí que estaba en deuda con mi país, con mi pueblo.'

27 Eduardo Milán, *Una cierta mirada. Crónica de poesía*, pp. 149–50: 'Neruda es, por lo menos, dos: el autor de *Residencia en la tierra* y el autor del resto de su obra'; 'descenso fatal en su temperatura estética'.

28 Neruda, *Cartas a Laura*, p. 53.

Neruda continued to be, despite himself, after joining Marxist rationalism, a neo-romantic, more intimately linked to magic rather than logic, to myth rather than reality, to fragmentary and chaotic subjectivity, rather than the collective self.[29]

In 1926 Neruda wrote a laconic manifesto as a prologue to his only narration *El habitante y su esperanza* [The Inhabitant and his Hope]: 'I have a dramatic concept of life, and a Romantic one; what doesn't deeply touch my sensibility means nothing to me.'[30] What touches him deeply could be anything from love for a woman to a book of poems. His self-awareness as a Romantic poet testing life through feelings and sensations is our guide-line. Saúl Yurkievich is the critic who best summarised this Romantic filiation:

from *Crepusculario* to *Residencia,* Neruda's poetics will be a progressive attempt to free his imagination from rational controls, from cultural complexes, from history, from literature, from society.[31]

Neruda was also a great nature poet, an urban outsider who recreated the inner rhythms and sounds of the howling wind, the incessant, cold rain and the hostile ocean waves that invaded his imagination as he grew up around Temuco and Puerto Saavedra in southern Chile. He affirmed: 'Whoever does not know the Chilean woods does not know this planet,' clarifying that his micro region symbolised the macro system.[32] At the kernel of his work lies a great nature myth, that he saw himself as an organic or telluric poet in direct contact with the natural world, rather than with poems and books and culture. The word 'nature' is perhaps too abstract, for Neruda alludes to the specific wet and temperate forests of southern Chile. Again, he understood, even mythified this link: 'From those lands, from that mud, that silence, I left

---

[29] Enrique Lihn, 'Momentos esenciales de la poesía chilena', p. 252: 'Neruda siguió siendo, a pesar suyo, después de su adhesión al racionalismo marxista, un neorromántico íntimamente más ligado a la magia que a la lógica, al mito que a la realidad, al subjectivismo fragmentario y caótico, que al yo colectivo.'

[30] Pablo Neruda, *Obras completas 1. De 'Crepusculario' a 'Las uvas y el viento', 1923–1954,* p. 217: 'Yo tengo un concepto dramático de la vida, y romántico; no me corresponde lo que no llega profundamente a mi sensibilidad.' Henceforth, I will cite from these complete works as PN1 or 2 or 3 etc. and page number in the text.

[31] Saúl Yurkievich, *Fundadores de la nueva poesía latinoamericana,* p. 141: 'desde *Crepusculario* hasta *Residencia* la poética de Neruda será un progresivo intento de liberar su imaginación de los controles racionales, de todo complejo cultural, de la historia, de la literatura, de la sociedad'.

[32] Neruda: 'Quien no conoce el bosque chileno, no conoce este planeta', cited by Loyola, 2006, p. 43.

to walk and sing around the world.'[33] A prose piece, 'Provincia de la infancia' [Province of Infancy] from his *Anillos* [Rings], 1926, ends by stressing the wet, the isolation and unknown-ness as a poetic manifesto:

> El niño que encaró la tempestad y crió debajo de sus alas amargas la boca, ahora te sustenta, país húmedo y callado, como a un gran árbol después de la tormenta. Provincia de la infancia deslizada de horas secretas, que nadie conoció. Región de soledad, acostado sobre unos andamios mojados por la lluvia reciente, te propongo a mi destino como refugio de regreso.
>
> (PN1 244)

> [The child who confronted the storm and raised his mouth under its bitter wings, now sustains you, wet and silent country, like a great tree after the storm. Province of infancy slipped out from secret hours, that nobody knew. Region of loneliness, leaning on soaked scaffoldings by recent rain, I propose you as my destiny as a refuge for return]

Another prose piece, 'Imperial del sur' [Imperial South] from *Anillos*, is even more specific in naming this 'place' by a river ('Imperial') and a village ('Carahue'):

> Muelles de Carahue, donde amarran las gruesas espigas y desembarcan los viajeros; cuánto y cuánto conozco tus tablones deshechos, recuerdo días de infancia a la sombra del maderamen mojado, donde lame y revuelve el agua verde y negra. (PN1 241)

> [Wharves of Carahue, where the great mastheads moor and travellers disembark; how well, how well I know your broken planks, I remember days of infancy in the shadow of soaked timber, where the green and black water lick and turn over]

Jorge Edwards, who knew Neruda intimately from 1952 to his death, said that this nature was the 'essential contact' behind his work.[34] Neruda once wrote: 'I was some ten years old, but was already a poet. I did not write verse, but was attracted to birds, beetles, partridge eggs.'[35] He affirmed that 'as a child and older I walked more among birds and along rivers than in libraries and with writers'.[36] Note how immersion in nature functions as his

---

[33] Neruda 'De aquellas tierras, de aquel barro, de aquel silencio, he salido y a andar, a cantar por el mundo', *Confieso que he vivido*, p. 12.

[34] Jorge Edwards, 'Un adiós a muchas cosas', in Arturo Fontaine (ed.), *Estudios Públicos*, p. 296: 'resorte esencial'.

[35] PN4 929: 'Yo tendría unos diez años, pero ya era poeta. No escribía versos, pero me atraían los pájaros, los escarabajos, los huevos de perdiz.'

[36] Pablo Neruda, *Para nacer he nacido*, p. 142: 'de niño y de grande anduve más entre ríos y pájaros que entre bibliotecas y escritores'.

guide and generates the self-myth about the growth of a poet. In 1950 in his *Canto general* he boasted that 'no escribo para que otros libros me aprisionen' [I do not write to be imprisoned by other books] (PN1 829). In 1954, in his light-hearted 'Oda al libro' [Ode to the book], Neruda confirmed that 'mis poemas / no han comido poemas / devoran apasionados acontecimientos' [my poems / have not eaten poems / they devour passionate happenings] (112). This ode tells 'books' to return to the 'library', while he, the poet, will wander the streets. In 'Así es mi vida' [Such is my life] from *Canción de gesta* [Song of protest], 1961, he defined his post-war relationship with books: 'Soy el hombre del pan y del pescado / y no me encontrarán entre los libros' [I am a man of bread and fish / and you won't find me among books] (PN2 943). Scorn for books by a book-writer itself has a tradition and is Romantic, epitomised in William Wordsworth's lovely poem 'The Tables Turned', which opens 'Up! Up! My Friend and quit your books', for we should enjoy the natural world of sun and woodland linnet. The poet laments: 'Books! 'tis a dull and endless strife' and tells his reader, like Neruda, 'Let Nature be your Teacher'. Wordsworth's criminal is 'our meddling intellect' for 'We murder to dissect'.[37] Like Neruda, Wordsworth brooded over his deep contact with the natural world and thus 'had small need of books'.[38] If Neruda never read Wordsworth, he did imbibe Whitman who also criticised books: 'You shall no longer take things at second or third hand, nor look through the eyes of the dead, nor feed on the spectres in books,' for books imply a vicarious experience.[39] Whitman's example is a flower: 'A morning-glory at my window satisfies me more than the metaphysics of books.'[40] But there's also an anti-bookish streak to surrealism and the avant-garde in general. Saúl Yurkievich aptly compared Neruda with André Breton: both tried to 'free themselves of a bookish overweight and rhetorical worries', and both 'pursued a naturalizing regression that allowed them to recover the integrity of the beginning [...]'.[41]

Nevertheless, I will argue that to write a poem you must have read many poems. Writing and becoming a poet are not natural acts, but cultural desires. It is better to approach Neruda as a proto-philosopher or at least a thinker, dealing with existentialist anguishes, exploring sound as the pulse of life and creating a home in his words along Heideggerian lines, and insidiously and

---

[37] William Wordsworth, *Selected Poems*, p. 355.
[38] Wordsworth, 'The Wanderer', from *The Excursion*, p. 464.
[39] Walt Whitman, *Leaves of Grass*, p. 50.
[40] Whitman, *Leaves of Grass*, p. 68.
[41] Yurkievich, 'Pablo Neruda: persona, palabra, mundo', p. 25: 'despojarse de sobrecarga libresca y de prurito retórico', and 'persiguen la regresión naturalizante que les permita recobrar la integridad del comienzo [...]'.

insistently lamenting his lost Beatrice. Indeed, the Scottish poet and critic G. S. Fraser, who visited Neruda in 1947 in Chile, noted acutely that

> the thought in Neruda's poetry could perhaps be described as existential – in so far as one thinks of the existentialist as the person, who, instead of sitting back and formulating a metaphysics, immerses himself in actual metaphysical experience.[42]

Fraser's apt phrase sticks to Neruda: immersed in actual metaphysical experience. Neruda shared this attitude to philosophy with one of his mentors, the poet Francisco Quevedo: 'For Quevedo, metaphysics is immensely physical.'[43] For Neruda too, thinking begins with the body, with sensations. In an early 1935 review of *Residencia en la tierra* [Residence on Earth], the Chilean critic Alone (Hernán Díaz Arrieta) charged Neruda with what would become a repeated accusation: 'There are no ideas, no synthesis available to a formula [...].'[44] Along similar lines, Octavio Paz opined that Neruda was 'a man of few ideas and governed by passions'.[45] Thus, contrary to received opinion, I will explore Neruda as a gut thinker, inside his poems. He played down what he dismissed as 'masticating theories'; he wrote little critical prose (unlike Paz or Borges or Lezama Lima or Huidobro). He told Alardo Prats in 1935 that 'for me the poet is the supreme anti-intellectual' (PN5 1054). He asserted in a prologue to a Portuguese translation of his work: 'I am now 53 years old and have never known what poetry is nor to define what I do not know.' He detested treatises on poetry and never read them.[46] He worked at deeper levels than that shared rationality that underscores criticism and differentiates its coherence from poetry. Critics have to take care that their rational interpretations do not exclude exactly what Neruda meant by poetry, that is, deep, emotional vibrations, tapping the pulse or root (one of his favoured words) of life. I liked Dominic Moran's version of Nerudan thinking:

> ... in these poems he was seeking to convey thought and sensation in the raw, with a minimum of interference from his own organizing but inevitably distorting consciousness, and from conspicuously 'poetic' embellishment.[47]

---

[42] G. S. Fraser, *News from South America*, p. 120.

[43] PN5 457: 'Para Quevedo la metafísica es inmensamente física.'

[44] The review is reproduced by Nicolás Salerno in *Estudios Públicos*, 2004, p. 317: 'No hay ideas, no hay síntesis accesibles a la fórmula [...].'

[45] Octavio Paz, *Sombras de obras*, pp. 51–2: 'un hombre de pocas ideas y gobernado por pasiones'.

[46] Neruda, *Para nacer he nacido*, p. 142.

[47] Dominic Moran, *Veinte poemas*, p. 25.

In terms of 'thinking-within-the-poems', there is a critical strand in Neruda studies that has isolated a material poetics grounded in Marxism, best formulated by Concha, Loyola and Sicard, who shared political allegiances with Neruda. In 2006 Loyola defined this way of characterising Neruda's philosophy:

> The secret resides in that *what is personal* for Neruda is not just his subjectivity, his intimate ego, but also, in a constant and inextricable way, his Circumstance, the world. In other words, Neruda's poetry is the dialectical 'account'...[48]

An excellent article by Russell Salmon and Julia Lesage on the Neruda of the 1960s adopted this version of dialectical materialism, that 'constant interchange with matter', as Neruda's philosophy (and their debt to Concha). The world is seen by the poet as a 'complex of interdependent processes', with all things 'both interconnected and changing' in a flux of matter. They assert that Neruda is 'truly dialectical'. There is no doubt that the poet tests his thoughts, his words, with the material world, that he scorns interiority, but it all seems vague and would describe any poet, rather than establishing that the world is inside the poet as language and perceptions. In a footnote Salmon and Lesage wonder what version of Marxism Neruda would have read, and cite Stalin's *Dialectical and Historical Materialism* as possible source. I doubt if Neruda bothered with Stalin's works, though Stalin was also a published poet who could recite Whitman by heart.[49] Instead, I return to Enrique Lihn's insight about Neruda's deeper romanticism, discarding theory and understanding through sensations, especially hearing.[50]

This *Companion* will follow Neruda's main collections as chapters and subheadings so that a reader will be able to grasp the outline of his output. I will insist on the question of the value of his work, at what I believe is essential. René de Costa was one of the first critics to argue for 'an agreement on the literary significance of the major works by examining them in detail in an effort to point out just why they are, or were, major'.[51] In asides I will also deal with the polemical way Neruda participated as a spokesperson in the debates about art in the terrible twentieth century, as well as focusing on key words in the way that his best early critic. Amado Alonso, did with his rational close-reading of symbols like 'rosas, palomas, mariposas, abejas, peces, sal, trigo, vino, espadas, [...] piedra, tierra, lana, fuego, marfil, cuero,

---

[48] Loyola, 2006, p. 9.
[49] Simon Sebag Montefiore, 'Before the Terror', *Review*, *Guardian*, 19 May 2007, p. 22. He wrote his poems under the name Soselo, before assuming the name Stalin in 1912.
[50] Russell Salmon and Julia Lesage, *Hispania*, pp. 224–6, 241.
[51] René de Costa, *The Poetry of Pablo Neruda*, p. ix.

uvas, lluvia, guitarra ...' [roses, doves, butterflies, bees, fish, salt, wheat, wine, swords ... stone, earth, wool, fire, ivory, leather, grapes, rain, guitar].[52] My aim is to rescue Neruda from his complete works (the latest in five volumes with some 6000 pages), from being mummified and thus not read.[53] Every critic has to face up to the prestige of a poet like Neruda, even take on board opinions like Clayton Eshleman's that 'Neruda is one of the most over-rated poets of this century.'[54] The English poet and translator Charles Tomlinson put this critical problem in a nutshell: 'Pablo Neruda has written some of the best and worst poems of our era.'[55]

Pablo and Neruda

In Isabel Allende's first novel, *La casa de los espíritus* [The House of the Spirits]. 1982, a family saga embodying Chilean history, Pablo Neruda is simply called 'El Poeta'. The public identification of Neruda with Poet is exactly what he himself sought. From early on, he wanted to become a poet, and becoming a poet meant more than just writing poems. It was a social role, a lifestyle and a glamorous dream (the prestige of the poet was quite different in Chile then to what it is in Britain today). Neruda dressed as a poet when he first arrived in Santiago (a 24-hour train journey from the south) to study to become a teacher of French in March 1921, with black cape and wide-brimmed black hat, imitating a dreamed-up nineteenth-century French image of a *poète maudit* [cursed poet], a term coined by Verlaine in 1884. Poets then, and perhaps still, signalled sartorially what they did. Being a poet ensured a social niche, with many advantages, including getting paid work with free time to write. This social desire to become a poet emerges from his chosen pen name, Pablo Neruda.

There are many reasons why anybody would want to write with a pseudonym: to avoid public scrutiny, out of shame, as a kind of spy. Biographers focus on Neruda's hostile relationship with his father, a 'conductor de un tren lastrero' [driver of a ballast train] (PN4 915), who died in 1938 and who thought poets were cissies. Certainly, the insidious *¿qué dirán?* [what will people say], which ruled Hispanic life, is a factor. In a shame-culture, you are what others think of you. However, to move beyond the banalities of social psychology, I return to what choosing 'Pablo Neruda' meant for

---

52 Amado Alonso, *Poesía*, p. 243 and in detail, pp. 244–89.

53 In Buenos Aires I came across a 1952 anthology of Neruda's titled *Poemas*, which shrunk him down to 32 pages, but it excludes all the *Residencia* poems and in its anonymous prologue praises Stalin.

54 Eshleman, *Review*, p. 41.

55 Charles Tomlinson, 'Overdoing the Generosity', p. 286.

the young poet Ricardo Eliever Neftalí Reyes Basoalto. He was known as
Neftalí Reyes at work, in his documents and in his first published poems in
1918. He signed letters to his 'novia' Albertina Azócar as 'Ricardo'. As late
as March 1939 he was known officially as 'Sr Neftalí Ricardo Reyes'.[56] In
fact, he only legally adopted the name 'Pablo Neruda' on 28 December 1946,
years after his father's death. Loyola recalled seeing a school notebook with
'Pablo Neruda' written on it from October 1920.[57] I begin with a tradition of
pen names in Latin America.

An influence on his early development as a poet was the Chilean poet
Gabriela Mistral, who was appointed Head of the Liceo de Niñas [Girls'
School] in Temuco in 1919. She was awarded the Nobel Prize in 1945 and
was a great educationalist. In a brief encounter in Temuco, she insisted that
Neruda read the grand nineteenth-century Russian writers. There is little
common ground between them as poets, but both chose melodious surnames.
Lucila Godoy Alcayaga (1889–1957) picked on a minor French poet who won
the Nobel Prize and who wrote in the *Langue d'Oc*, a provincial outsider (like
her) called Frédéric Mistral (1830–1914), who also chose his pseudonym.
The 'mistral' is the great wind of southern France and wind is a venerable
symbol of inspiration. Equally important in Neruda's assumption of a pen
name was the great *mestizo* poet from Nicaragua, Rubén Darío (1867–1916),
who led the *modernistas* out of provincial Latin America into the anguishes
and crises of modernity, adapting French poetic fashions, that 'mental Galli-
cism' that shocked the Spanish critic Juan Valera. Darío published his first
influential collection (mainly poetic prose), *Azul* [Blue], 1888, in Santiago
de Chile where he had landed in 1887, seeking a wider horizon and working
his way as a poet on the bread-line to the cultural centres of his world, Paris
and Buenos Aires. Many of Darío's poems were learnt by young 'Neruda' (I
should write Reyes) by heart, especially his erotic poems. Darío's worship of
Paul Verlaine ('Oh lyrical Socrates of an impossible time!' and 'the greatest
poet of this century') also reverberated in Neruda's memory.[58] Darío – it has
'río' there, the river of inspiration – was a pen-name obscuring his birth name
of Félix Rubén García Sarmiento (1867–1916). A third example of choosing
a pen name comes from one of Neruda's fellow students at Temuco's Liceo
de Hombres [Boys' School], Gilberto Concha Riffo, who became a well-
known poet of the provinces, with the telling name of Juvencio Valle [valley]
(1900–99). As we will see, Mistral, Darío, Valle and Neruda shared a similar
journey out of provincial roots through their gifts as poets. As Darío noted
in 1896, despite having Indian blood and being a 'mestizo' [mixed blood],

---

56 Pablo Neruda, *Epistolario viajero*, p. 243.
57 Loyola, *Neruda*, 2006, p. 78.
58 Rubén Darío, 'Paul Verlaine', *Los raros*, p. 46: '¡Oh lírico Sócrates de un tiempo
imposible!' and 'el más grande de los poetas de este siglo'.

he was a natural 'marquis' through the use of his hand, as a writer.[59] If we just stay with Chilean poets and pen names, we also find that the avant-garde friend of Neruda's, Juan Emar ('our Kafka'),[60] was really baptised Alvaro Yáñez Bianchi (1893–1964) and adopted his surname as a corruption of 'j'en ai marre' [I'm fed up]. Neruda's vicious literary rival in Chile, the poet Pablo de Rokha, was born Carlos Ignacio Díaz Loyola (1894–1968). The 'roca' [rock] lurking in 'rokha' (the 'h' is silent) could reinforce his theme of being the hard 'macho'. Neruda's attempt to marry one of de Rokha's sisters was frustrated by the father. Another contemporary Chilean poet, dedicated to a surrealist interiority, was Rosamel del Valle (1901–63), which binds 'rosa' with 'miel' and 'valle' (rose/honey/valley) and whose real name was Moisés Gutiérrez.

So inventing a pen name was common, but why did Neftalí Reyes choose the surname 'Neruda'? The poet himself explained that as a fourteen-year-old (more likely, a sixteen-year-old) he had loved a short story by the Czech writer Jan Neruda (1834–91), author of 'Vampire', published in 1920 in a magazine, and so took the name to hide his dream of becoming a poet 'to protect myself from my father's anger' (PN4 936). But nobody seems to have found this source. Adam Feinstein, in his biography, unearthed a concert violinist with that same name, who might have caught Neruda's attention in Temuco.[61] More recently, Loyola has pointed out that there is a Neruda in the Sherlock Holmes novel *A Study in Scarlet*, 1887, translated into Spanish in 1908. Less convincingly, Loyola follows up on previous research to find a musical score dedicated to a frau Norman-Neruda by a Pablo de Sarasate where both Pablo and Neruda figure on the same page (but in Berlin).[62] I like to think that hidden behind 'Neruda' is a literary debt, the French Romantic Gérard de Nerval; the letters NERA in common. Nerval too was an adopted name – he was Gérard Labrunie (1808–55). Juan Larrea, a Spanish poet who wrote in French and published Neruda in Paris in 1926, first suggested this filiation: 'the curious, manifest affinity between Ner-val and Ner-uda in the choice of pseudonyms'.[63] Neruda identified deeply with Nerval. The latter's errant life, his literary work, his travels to the East, his times in prison, his hashish smoking, his insanity, his hopeless love for the actress Jenny Colon, his taking a lobster for a stroll, his final hanging himself from a railing (possibly murdered) are all Romantic marks, the legend that young Neruda

[59] Darío: '¿Hay en mi sangre alguna gota de sangre de Africa, o de indio chorotega o nagrandano? Pudiera ser, a despecho de mis manos de marqués...,' from 'Palabras liminares', *Prosas profanas*, p. 10.
[60] Pablo Neruda, 'J.E.', in Juan Emar, *Diez*, p. 10.
[61] Adam Feinstein, *Pablo Neruda. A Passion for Life*, p. 23.
[62] Loyola reproduces the cover of the musical score in his *Neruda*, 2006, p. 80.
[63] Juan Larrea, *Del surrealismo a Machupicchu*, p. 83.

fed off in Temuco.[64] Nerval's 1853 self-portrait. with the title in Spanish, 'El desdichado' [Ill-fated], the opening poem of *Les chimères* [Chimera], became Neruda's own secret portrait, as we will underline. But first, note the Spanish in 'El desdichado' (in manuscript Nerval had written 'Le Destin'); he copied it from an inscription on Ivanhoe's shield from Walter Scott's 1819 novel. This is the man whose 'dicha' (happiness) has run out, who is cursed and lovesick. This Spanish-titled poem leads to the core drama of Neruda's *Veinte poemas de amor y una canción desesperada* [Twenty love poems and a song of despair] 1924, published just before he reached twenty years of age. He was 'el desdichado', unlucky in love. Nerval's poem opens:

> Je suis le ténébreux, – le veuf, – l'inconsolé
> Le prince d'Aquitaine à la tour abolie:
> Ma seule *étoile* est morte, – et mon luth constellé
> Porte le *Soleil noir* de la *Mélancolie*[65]

> [I'm the gloomy man, the widower, the unconsolable / The Prince of Aquitaine in the doomed tower: / My only star is dead and my constellated luth / bears the black Sun of Melancholy]

Neruda often saw himself within his earlier poems as the 'viudo' [widower], the *veuf*, abandoned by his lover, by love itself. Much of his early poetry projected the image of a Hamlet, a poet dressed in black, doomed and cursed by melancholia, a state of creative depression and despair (Nerval knew Dürer's print 'Melencolia' well). That was his debt to Nerval, surely the epitome of the Romantic poet. But there is more, for this sonnet is about winning and losing a lover. The last tercet states:

> Suis-je Amour ou Phoebus? ... Lusignan ou Biron?
> Mon front est rouge encor du baiser de la Reine;
> J'ai rêvé dans la Grotte où nage la Syrène ...

> [Am I Love or Phoebus ? ... Lusignan or Byron ? / My forehead is red from the queen's kiss, / I have dreamed in the cave where the siren swims]

Alejandro Bekes noted that the first line is about doubting self-identity. He also explained that 'Lusignan' harks back to the fairy Mélusine ('Mère Lusignan') who was 'betrayed' by her husband when he spied on her while bathing. Mélusine became a surrealist myth when André Breton's lover Nadja associated herself with Mélusine; Octavio Paz would take up this story of

---

64 See Gérard de Nerval, *Poesía*, versión, prólogo y notas de Alejandro Bekes.
65 Gérard de Nerval, *Les chimères*, translated by William Stone, p. 28.

woman spied on by man in his long poem *Piedra de sol* [Sun Stone] in 1957, with its epigraph from Nerval: 'I saw your atrocious scales / Melusina shine green at dawn...'[66] Nerval's closing line is the confession that day-dreaming about love, its loss, is at the core of poetry.

Juan Larrea made a further crucial point about the place of Nerval in the surrealist genealogy, the 'patron saint' of surrealism.[67] Much has been written about Breton's debt in dream research to Freud, but Larrea saw Nerval as the axial thinker about dreams and reality in his *Aurélia ou le rêve et la vie* [Aurélia or Dream and Life], 1855. Breton, in his 1924 *Manifeste du surréalisme*, did recognise that 'Nerval possessed to a marvellous degree the *spirit* which we reclaim' and then cited two long passages about Nerval's 'Supernaturalisme'.[68] Larrea developed this subversive insight about the origins of surrealism: that it 'springs up from Nerval'. He wrote that Nerval was the 'unconscious promoter of surrealism'.[69]

Later, we will argue that Neruda's exploration of dreams is surrealist because of its links with Nerval, the forgotten source of dream-work. Nerval opened his *Aurélia*, part autobiography and part prose poem, with a famous sentence: 'Le rêve es une seconde vie' [The dream is a second life]. In this book he analysed what he called 'outpourings of the dream in real life', as did Neruda in his poems up to the late 1930s.[70] The Mexican poet Xavier Villaurrutia, born a year before Neruda in 1903, confirmed Nerval as the source of modern poetry in his living out tragically the 'deep anxieties of German romanticism'.[71] He too recognised the role of André Breton in discovering how 'modern' Nerval was in his dream research and emphasis on travel. In Villaurrutia's cogent words, 'to leave is to mature a bit. Nobody matures if they do not travel. Inside or outside a bedroom, what matters is to move, to lose yourself, to find yourself: to travel.'[72] He translated Nerval's foundational sonnet 'El desdichado' and summarised what can be learnt from Nerval:

> With its allusions charged with mystery, with its symbolic character, with its secret symmetries, it reveals fragments of a world into which the poet

66 Octavio Paz, *Poemas (1935–1975)*, p. 267: 'Yo vi tu atroz escama, / Melusina, brillar verdosa al alba ...' See also Jason Wilson, *Octavio Paz* (Boston: Twayne, 1986), pp. 96–7.

67 A. Alvarez, *Night. An Exploration of Night Life, Night Language, Sleep and Dreams* (London: Vintage, 1996), p. 204.

68 Breton, *Manifestes du surréalisme*, p. 39.

69 Juan Larrea, *Del surrealismo*, pp. 70–5.

70 Gérard de Nerval, *Aurélia ou le rêve et la vie*, p. 2 and 'l'épanchement du songe dans la vie réelle', p. 10.

71 Xavier Villaurrutia, *Obras*: 'profundas inquietudes del romanticismo alemán', p. 895.

72 Villaurrutia, *Obras*: 'partir es madurar un poco. No madura quien no viaja. Dentro o afuera de la alcoba, lo que importa es trasladarse, perderse, encontrarse: viajar,' p. 898.

has been able to descend, with Orpheus, in search of Eurydice, to a real and profound hell.[73]

That is, the hell of love and loss, the deep theme of all Neruda's early Nervalian verse.

The last point to make about Neruda's chosen poet's name is the actual sound of it – NERUDA, with the stress on the middle 'u', a lugubrious vowel, accompanied by the equally voiced 'e' and 'a'. Vowel sounds in Spanish are unique in being constant, unlike French or English where the five vowels shift about in their voicing. Neruda just *sounds* right. As a poet, Neruda identified with the magical sound of words. He wrote to Albertina: 'Now I like the word *apple*. APPLE.'[74] The sound of a word is part of its reality, making it more than mere literal reference, and voicing words in rhythmic poems was Neruda's gift to the reader.

Now we come to the seemingly innocuous 'Pablo'. If we translate this Christian name into French we get 'Paul'. Emir Rodríguez Monegal suggested that 'Paul' was Neruda's homage to Paul Verlaine. There is no doubt about his complete identification with Verlaine. The sheer miracle of Verlaine's verbal music, his breaking with bourgeois conventions, especially his affair with and shooting of Arthur Rimbaud and coining of the term *poète maudit*, resurface in Neruda's rebellious attitudes. Darío's master was also Paul Verlaine, and, as noted, in his 1896 *Prosas profanas* [Profane Prose] penned the sonnet 'Responso' [Prayer for the dead], an obituary to his recently deceased mentor. Verlaine was one of Darío's *Los raros*. Strangely, Verlaine's first published poem was signed as 'Pablo' Verlaine.[75] In a 1920 uncollected poem with a French title, 'La chair est triste, hélas!' [Flesh is sad, alas], Neruda saw his poetry as 'untando mis dolores con versos de Verlaine' [anointing my pains with lines from Verlaine] (PN4 169).[76] He read Verlaine to alleviate lovesickness. Both poets felt they were ugly and failed with women, and both built their work on sincerity, on being themselves.[77]

But there is a further homage in 'Paul' to another famous literary lover,

---

[73] Villaurrutia, *Obras*: 'Con sus alusiones cargadas de misterio, con su carácter simbólico, con sus secretas simetrías, nos descubren fragmentos de un mundo al que el poeta ha podido descender, con Orfeo, en busca de una perdida Eurídice, a un infierno real y profundo,' p. 900. Villaurrutia wrote a prologue to Agustín Lazo's translation of Nerval's *Aurelia* in 1942.

[74] Sergio Fernández Larraía, *Cartas de amor de Pablo Neruda*, p. 181. 'Ahora me gusta la palabra *manzana*. MANZANA.'

[75] Paul Verlaine, *Oeuvres poétiques complètes*, p. xvii.

[76] Victor Farías transcribed this line as 'juntando mis dolores con versos de Verlaine', Neruda, *Cuadernos*, p. 191. If we follow Loyola's 'untando' we would have 'anointing my pains with Verlaine's verse' as opposed to Farías's 'joining my pains...'

[77] See Francis Carco, *Verlaine* (Paris: Editions de la Nouvelle Revue Critique, 1939), pp. 3–30 and Verlaine's advice: 'L'art, mes enfants, c'est d'être absolument soi-même,' p. 170.

if we translate Pablo into Italian, Paolo. When did Neruda read and digest Dante's *Commedia*? Certainly as a teenager. In his poem 'Ivresse' [Drunkenness], with its French title, from his first collection *Crepusculario*, 1923, Neruda pictured his desired self in the present tense as he wrote this opening couplet:

> Hoy que danza en mi cuerpo la pasión de Paolo
> y ebrio de un sueño alegre mi corazón se agita: (PN1 114)
>
> [Today, Paolo's passion dances in my body / And drunk with a happy dream, my heart gets upset]

As Paolo in canto V, he begs his dream lover to enchant him with her 'senos locos' [mad breasts], drunk with her youth. The poem is archly literary, the woman-muse a 'pulpa blanca de poma' ('white flesh of apple'; the archaic 'poma' is perhaps a Gongorine term, forced by the rhyme 'loma') to close with the desire: 'Oh Francesca, hacia dónde te llevarán mis alas!' [Oh Francesca, where will my wings take you]. The whole poem is derivative of his reading of another poem. Even a line like 'en el azul paremos nuestras blancas escalas' [in the blue let us stand our white stopping places] recalls Darío's obsession with 'azul' in *Azul*. The line that echoes the title in French, 'Bebamos. Nunca dejamos de beber' [Let us drink. Let us never stop drinking], hints at Baudelaire's recommendation to all poets: 'Il faut être toujours ivre' [One must be always drunk], but here, awkwardly, the poet will drink from the wine glasses of her breasts. Obviously, the image comes from the shape of a breast. However, Neruda could have read the same image in Lugones' prose poem 'Oda a la desnudez' [Ode to nakedness] (from *Las montañas de oro* [Gold Mountains], 1897): 'dame tus pechos, – cálices del ritual de nuestra misa – de amor; dame tus uñas, dagas de oro – para sufrir tu posesión maldita' [give me your breasts – chalices of the ritual of our mass of love; give me your fingernails, golden daggers, to suffer your cursed possession].[78] However, he modified Lugones's camp *modernismo* from chalice to down-to-earth wine glass for breasts. Neruda's implicit critique of such verbal excess is part of his innovation. So to drink wine / milk is to be drunk on love and poetry and to be free. There is even a hidden allusion to Tagore's 'gardener' (more on this later), here with 'Sembremos la llanura antes de arar la loma' [Let us sow the plain before ploughing the earth]. No doubt that young Neruda is in love with reading and dreaming of becoming a Temucan Paolo. In an unpublished poem from *Album Teresa*, 1923, the poet writes 'PAOLO / TERESA' in wet sand (PN4 274). Paolo and Francesca appeared in the fifth canto of *Inferno* as the eternally punished adulterers. Dante and

---

[78] Leopoldo Lugones, *Obras*, p. 62.

his guide Virgil listen to Francesca tell her tale. She was reading with Paolo, her brother-in-law, about how Lancelot of *Lancelot du lac* was kissed, adulterously, by Guinevere, King Arthur's wife, and how suddenly Paolo, equally adulterously, kissed her on the mouth: 'la bocca mi bació tutto tremante' ['he kissed my mouth all quivering' in Steve Ellis's version].[79] What we have in this collusion between Neruda and Paolo and Francesca is illicit love, that passion only exists outside matrimony and convention. It is a passion that in this poem remains a fantasy. Equally important, the lovers were reading a *book* together. Sharing love poems for lovers, like adapting a Tagore poem for Albertina Azócar (in his *Veinte poemas*), is an exciting erotic ritual for a poet, and for readers. Did Neruda read about Paolo and Francesca directly in Dante or in his beloved Gustavo Adolfo Bécquer? *Rima XXIX's* epigraph is that same line from Dante's canto V, in Italian, but with 'bocca' misspelled as 'boca'. Bécquer's poem re-enacts two unnamed lovers, with the book open on a lap, her curls on his cheek, in deep lover's silence (in deep reader's silence). All the poet could hear was her 'aliento' [breath] and then they kissed. Bécquer then asks his lover: do you see how a whole poem fits into one line? Bécquer: 'Y ella respondió encendida: / –¡Ya lo comprendo!' [And she answered with passion / I now understand it].[80] Here is the clue: lovers *reading* about lovers – what more potent way to read poetry? – and all poetry shrunk to one line, even one word 'tremante'.[81] The late Spanish Romantic poet Bécquer suggests a Romantic reading of Dante that Neruda shared: stealing one kiss and the hell of love. Years later, in 1936, Neruda published a homage to the centenary of Bécquer's birth in 1836 in his poetry magazine *Caballo verde para la poesía* [Green Horse for Poetry], extolling Bécquer's melancholy and sentimentalism. It concluded: 'Sol desdichado, señor de las lluvias!' [Unfortunate sun, lord of the rains] (PN4 385), blending himself with Bécquer as lovers, with the rain of Temuco and Bécquer's northern poems. The 'sol desdichado' echoes Nerval's sonnet with its 'melancholic sun' and its title 'el desdichado'. Despite his avant-garde leanings of the 1930s, Neruda's homage confirms his early keen reading of the Sevillan poet.

The title 'Ivresse' itself is a compressed manifesto of debts, particularly to Baudelaire's 'Le spleen de Paris' where the poet decides that art must rule life, that the artist must remain 'drunk' on inspiration: 'You must always be drunk (*ivre*). Everything is there [...] Not to feel the horrible burden of time

---

[79] Dante, *La Divina Commedia, Inferno. Purgatorio. Paradiso*, p. 56. *Hell*, p. 140.

[80] Gustavo Adolfo Bécquer, *Rimas*, pp. 61–2.

[81] Humberto Núñez-Faraco explored this key word in Borges's debts to Dante in his *Borges and Dante. Echoes of a Literary Friendship*, tracing the use of 'tremante' back to 1919, see pp. 124–5, 136–7.

[...] With wine, with poetry or with virtue, as you like. But get drunk.'[82] Later, in 1967, Neruda would publish his translation of Baudelaire's sonnet 'El enemigo' [The enemy] ('L'ennemi'), which curiously evoked Neruda's own youth in the rain and storms of Chile. It opens:

> Ma jeunesse ne fut qu'un ténébreux orage,
> Traversé çà et là par de brillants soleils;
> Le tonnerre et la pluie ont fait un tel ravage,
> Qu'il reste en mon jardin bien peu de fruits vermeils.

> [My youth was but a sombre storm / crossed here and there by brilliant suns; /Thunder and rain have made such havoc / that in my garden few vermilion fruit remain]

The sonnet closes with the cry of pain about passing time lodged in the heart:

> – O douleur! O douleur! Le Temps mange la vie,
> Et l'obscur Ennemi qui nous ronge le coeur
> Du sang que nous perdons croît et se fortifie.

> [Oh pain! Oh pain! Time eats life / and the obscure enemy who gnaws the heart / grows and gets strong on the blood we lose][83]

Through reading poetry that revealed his ungraspable, enemy self, Neruda could escape humdrum social life, enter a state of ecstasy. Baudelaire had ended his opening poem dedicated to the reader ('Au lecteur') with his apt '– Hypocrite lecteur, – mon semblable, – mon frère!' [Hypocritical reader, my fellow, my brother].[84]

Unhappy love suggests one last 'Paul' and that is the hero of *Paul et Virginie* (in Spanish *Pablo y Virginia*), the idealised story of ill-fated lovers, written by Jacques-Henri Bernardin de Saint-Pierre in 1787. It became an international bestseller, and Neruda read 'the delirious love of Pablo y de Virginia' and sobbed.[85] In his lecture 'Infancia y poesía' [Infancy and Poetry] he reiterated this reading: 'and I cry with love with Bernardino de Saint-Pierre' (PN4 925). Paul and Virginie are brought up as siblings in the woods on a hill above Port Louis in tropical Ile de France, today's Mauritius. At puberty,

---

[82] Robert Gibson, *Modern French Poets and Poetry*, p. 55: 'Il faut être toujours ivre. Tout est là [...] Pour ne pas sentir l'horrible fardeau du temps [...] De vin, de poésie ou du vertu, à votre guise. Mais enivrez-vous.'

[83] Charles Baudelaire, *Les Fleurs du mal*, p. 17.

[84] Baudelaire, *Les Fleurs*, p. 4.

[85] Pablo Neruda and Nicanor Parra, *Discursos*, p. 79: 'el delirante amor de Pablo y de Virginia'.

their idyll is broken because Virginie is sent back to Paris to be 'educated'. She never stops loving Paul. On her return, as her sailing ship nears the tropical island, a storm sinks it on the reefs and Virginia drowns because she refuses to be saved (touched) by a sailor. Paul then kills himself. Albert Camus found this love story a 'really heart-breaking book [that] makes no concessions to consolation'.[86] Neruda felt the same. Most of his poetry up to 1935 was written from the pain and suffering of a penniless, jilted lover, a Paul in hell. In letter 14 to Albertina Azócar, collected as *Cartas de amor* [Love Letters], we read: 'think of the ill-fated life of your Pablo, without a home, without money, without you'. In letter 18, the name is not even translated into Spanish, 'to your Paul'.[87] Bernardin de Saint-Pierre's Paul was equally poor, left behind on the island with his single mother, ostracised, without a proper home. No doubt about Neruda's identification with this quasi-orphaned tropical 'Paul'. J. M. Alonso defined this journey towards the creation and projection of a 'persona':

> with great and exhausting care, he [Neruda] continued to try to create what he called 'the obligatory essence' of a poet, by which he meant a style that was uniquely and unmistakably his. That is to say, a voice of his own, a *persona*.

To recapitulate, the chosen name 'Pablo Neruda' reveals associations that betray Neruda's literary ambitions. Behind all that has been written here lies Neruda's rejection of the national Chilean poetic tradition, as Gabriela Mistral brilliantly noted in 1936: 'Pablo Neruda in this work has no relation at all with Chilean lyric poetry.'[88]

The early, uncollected work

Victor Farías outlined the history of Neruda's early manuscripts. They were kept by his sister Laura, then lost, and ended up being sold at Sotheby's anonymously. Photocopies were found and published as *Cuadernos de Temuco* [Temuco Notebook].[89] Most of the poems were written in 1919–20 when Neruda, at the time Reyes, was 15 and 16 years old. Some thirteen poems were published in magazines and newspapers (the earliest on April 1918) and

---

[86] See my introduction to Jacques-Henri Bernardin de Saint-Pierre, *Journey to Mauritius*, pp. 1–51.

[87] Sergio Fernández Larraín, *Cartas de amor de Pablo Neruda,* pp. 220, 223.

[88] Gabriela Mistral, 'Recado sobre Pablo Neruda', p. 19: 'Pablo Neruda de esta obra no tiene relación alguna con la lírica chilena.'

[89] Farías, 'Prólogo', in Pablo Neruda, *Cuadernos de Temuco*, pp. 22–3.

three entered his first book, *Crepusculario*, though Loyola later unearthed his first publication (18 July 1917) in prose 'Entusiasmo y perseverancia' [Enthusiasm and perseverance].[90]

These poetic exercises reveal important literary desires in the teenage poet's journey to becoming Pablo Neruda. I will inspect these desires under three brief headings: the poetics of the provinces, cultural references, and deeper poetic models.

Neruda was born as a poet during a continental reaction to Rubén Darío's acolytes, to a style mocked as *rubendarismo*. This reaction would generate Antonio Machado's best work by eliminating Darío's exaggerations and would sharpen Jorge Luis Borges's views of being a poet by focusing on the image and quiet backstreets. In 1936, Gabriela Mistral noted how Neruda had derided this style:

> It is necessary to remember the cloying linguistic store house of 'bulbuls', 'sendals' and 'roses' in which second-rate modernismo left us stuck in order to grasp that brine-like, marine squall with which Pablo Neruda cleaned the air ...[91]

Literary historians once labelled this reaction *posmodernismo* for justifying a poetics antagonistic to Darío's cosmopolitan, erotic and cultural avidities. Against the cosmopolitan city, these younger poets like Neruda proposed the Latin American provinces as a place of poetic meditation, a *locus amoenus*. Neruda churned out lines that evoked this desire about 'la dulzura tranquila / de la aldea en la noche' [sweet peace of the village at night] (CT 36) or 'la dulzura de la mansedumbre' [sweetness of the quiet] and the 'quietud de las cosas' [quietness of things] (CT 29). He eulogised the 'paz campesina' [peasant peace] (CT 36), and gently mocked 'lo mismo' [sameness], the monotony. A title refers to 'los pueblos humildes' [humble villages] and the 'emoción sencilla' [simple emotion] that flourished there. The words 'humilde' and 'dulce' recur. In another poem, Neruda criticised a fellow poet: 'no supiste cantar la vida provinciana' [You did not know how to sing about provincial life] (CT 127), while he at least tried. The word 'provinces', of course, signals Neruda's rural origins in Temuco, but enters poetry across the Americas, from Ramón López Velarde in Mexico to César Vallejo in Peru and Leopoldo Lugones in Argentina. It is as if 'provinces' better spoke for the American experience as marginal, far-off from urban imperial centres. A similar reac-

---

90 Loyola, 2006, p. 54.
91 Gabriela Mistral, 'Recado sobre Pablo Neruda', p. 21: 'Es preciso recordar el empalagoso almacén lingüístico de "bulbules", "cendales", y "rosas" en que nos dejó atollados el modernismo segundón, para entender esta ráfaga marina asalmuerada con que Pablo Neruda limpia su atmósfera ...'

tion had been happening in provincial France concerning the dominance of
Paris and decadent art through poets like Samain and Mistral. The Mexican
poet Enrique González Martínez (1871–1952), in a famous sonnet from *Los
senderos ocultos* [Hidden Paths], 1901, whose very title promoted a poetics
of humility and innerness, wrote: 'Tuércele el cuello al cisne de engañoso
plumaje' [Wring the swan's neck, with its deceitful feathers]. For this swan,
so associated with Darío, does not feel 'el alma de las cosas ni la voz del
paisaje' [The soul of things nor the voice of the landscape]. To capture
'la vida profunda' [deep life], González Martínez proposed an alternative
bird, the 'buho' [owl]. Just to track the adverb 'humildemente' across these
provincial rebels would link Neruda with Ramón López Velarde's *La sangre
devota*, 1916, where poems like 'Viaje al terruño' [Journey to home ground],
'Domingos de provincia' [Sundays in the provinces] and 'A la gracia primitiva
de las aldeanas' [To the primitive grace of village girls] suggest a relief from
the turbulence of Mexico City as López Velarde dreams of his muse 'Fuen-
santa', miles away in his village Jerez.[92] 'La suave patria' [Gentle fatherland],
1921, became a legendary, civic poem across the Americas, redefining local
mestizo values against European ones. In 1963 Neruda called him an 'essential poet of our extensive America'. He once rented López Velarde's house in
Coyoacán in Mexico City, with its abandoned garden and old swimming pool.
Neruda felt a friendship for the Mexican poet that he had never felt before,
soaked in his poems. He evoked this civic poet's 'purísimo patriotismo' [very
pure patriotism]. Finally, he called him 'the most provincial of poets'. He was
Neruda's 'final master'.[93] He treasured a book of López Velarde's (listed by
Aguirre).

There are some explicit cultural references that reveal what Neruda was
reading and how over these crucial years he would slowly and then suddenly
become 'modern'. Two literary thinkers are cited: Schopenhauer and Nietzsche
(both read in French). One musician is named, Chopin. Several writers are
cited, some from French like Verlaine, Mallarmé and Jean Lorrain, and some
from Spanish like Berceo, Valle-Inclán and Felipe Trigo. I have no idea what
unites these disparate writers except that Neruda chanced upon them. Some
of them were modern and decadent. Felipe Trigo (1864–1916), for example,
was a Spanish writer who between 1901 and his suicide in 1916 made a
fortune through writing pornographic novels that were a 'scandalous success',
according to Martín Muelas Herraiz.[94] Borges also read Trigo (*Las ingenuas*)
and told Bioy Casares that he was 'better than others' and was erotic and

---

92 Ramón López Velarde, *Obras*, pp. 86–92.
93 Pablo Neruda, 'RLV', in Juan Loveluck, 'Neruda ante la poesía hispanoamericana', pp. 70–2.
94 Martín Muelas Herraiz's thesis 'La obra narrativa de Felipe Trigo' can be read on <www.cervantesvirtual.com>.

sad.[95] Or Jean Lorrain (Neruda called him Juan) (1855–1906), a homosexual dandy who once fought a duel with Proust. Valle-Inclán was equally decadent and dangerous, and references to 'satanismo' are probably Baudelaire filtered through his 'sonatas'. So, though Neruda was writing poems about the monotonous provinces, he was fleeing the provinces through reading. What is obvious is that Neruda had not yet read Huidobro or any avant-garde works.

At a deeper level, I detect that Neruda read Antonio Machado, who reacted to Darío's verbal excesses by excising whatever did not fit his own direct experience of provincial Soria in the second edition of *Soledades, galerías y otros poemas* [Solitudes, Galleries and other Poems], 1907. Neruda's poem 'Ensoñación perdida' [Lost daydream] mimics Machado's own emphasis on bitter day-dreaming, like in his 'Yo voy soñando caminos / de la tarde ...' [I go dreaming paths / in the evening].[96] The poem 'Lo mismo' [The same] echoes Machado's loveless poet's song 'La calle en sombra' [The street in shadow], where sunset, streets, anguish, pain, a portrait and the lack of a woman cross from one poet to the other. Neruda opens:

> Por estas calles tristes en este atardecer
> paseando mi cansancio de chiquillo precoz,
> un sentir en los labios, en los ojos y en
> el recuerdo del retrato de la estéril visión.

> [Along these sad streets on this evening / walking my weariness of precocious little boy / a feeling on my lips, in my eyes and in / the memory of the sterile vision's portrait]

Antonio Machado has:

> La calle en sombra. Ocultan los altos caserones
> el sol que muere; hay ecos de luz en los balcones
> ...
> La imagen, tras el vidrio, de equívoco reflejo
> surge o se apaga como daguerrotipo viejo

> [The street in shadows. The high houses hide / the dying sun; there are echoes of light on the balconies /The image, behind glass, of equivocal reflection, surges or dies out like an old daguerrotype]

and ends: '¡Oh, angustia! Pesa y duele el corazón ...' [Oh anguish. My heart weighs and pains me].[97] Neruda's main divergence lies in his projecting

---

[95] Adolfo Bioy Casares, *Borges*, edición al cuidado de Daniel Martino (Buenos Aires: Destino, 2006), p. 587.

[96] Antonio Machado, *Obras. Poesía y prosa*, p. 71.

[97] Machado, *Obras*, p. 75.

himself as the precocious little boy. In another poem about a class in his
'liceo' titled 'Sensación de clase de química' [Sensation of a chemistry class],
we have the same rain on the glass, the same 'thinking', and the inevitable
'angustia' as in Machado's 'Es una tarde cenicienta y mustia' [It's an ashen,
gloomy afternoon], though rain in school could be an archetype of class-
room boredom. Neruda closes with 'Angustia! Fastidio, fastidio, fastidio!'
[Anguish. Tedium, tedium, tedium] (CT 192), merging Darío's and Machado's exploration of 'angustia'. In this poem, Neruda wrote:

> La lluvia en los vidrios deja sus rosetas
> y yo pienso, pienso tal como un poeta
> que a veces detesto y a veces ... envidio ... (CT 192)

> [The rain leaves its little roses on the glass and I think, I think like
> a poet who at times I detest and at times ... envy]

The ellipsis about which poet Neruda is thinking of surely refers to an
unnamed 'Antonio Machado', the epitome of poet-thinker in Spain.

What we can say about these early poems is that Neruda wakes up to
poetry as a *posmodernista*, but cannot find his own voice, his poetic unique-
ness. There are signs that his ambition is greater than echoing sweet poems
about humble lives. One poem reveals this desire:

> Volcarme todo en un poema
> y en él vibrar, vibrar, vibrar
> con todas estas voces plenas
> nacidas en la soledad. (CT 124)

> [To throw myself into a poem and in it vibrate, vibrate, vibrate
> with all those full voices born from solitude]

For Neruda to *live* the poem, a Romantic and later surrealist dream of fusing
life and art, meant abandoning the dull provinces and becoming a poem in
a Dionysiac way, where poem and ecstasy are analogical spaces embodied
in the verb 'vibrar'. From these provinces, it was as if only living intensely
inside a poem, in the writing and then reading of it, mattered. And the only
source of this orgasmic desire is 'soledad'. Here's the seed of why he left
the provinces and set off to live in loneliness in order to become 'Pablo
Neruda'.

1

The 1920s: from *Crepusculario* to *Veinte poemas de amor y una canción desesperada*

Crepusculario, 1923

Neruda published his first book of poems in 1923, at his own expense (selling, for example, his father's gold watch, a parting present) in order to afford the 180-paged, but not paginated, *Crepusculario*. The second edition appeared in 1926, with a third in 1937, confirming its popularity. The earliest poem in this anthology of his early work, divided into five sections, dates from 1919 when he was 15 years old. Already at this early age, a critic, Raúl Silva Castro, had predicted the arrival of a talented poet.[1] Another of Chile's prominent critics, Alone, who helped Neruda with money to pay for the first edition, also praised the book for its 'magic of true poetry'.[2] So, as a poet, Neruda was born with this collection. It sounds a modern note from its title for that word 'crepusculario' does not exist in Spanish. It is made up of 'crepúsculo' [twilight] and, perhaps, 'poemario' [collection of poems]. There is an oblique homage to the Argentine *modernista* Leopoldo Lugones (1874–1938), whose outrageous collection, mocking the Romantics' allusions to 'moon', was titled *Lunario sentimental*, 1909, and whose earlier, equally ironic book was *Crepúsculos del jardín*, 1905; combining 'crepúsculo / lunario', we get, 'crepusculario'. In a letter to Héctor Eandi, Neruda praised Lugones as 'so denigrated, he seems to me in truth rich with gifts, his poetry nearly always poetic, that is, legitimate, although anachronic and baroque'.[3] However, the most direct transposition of 'crepúsculo' derives from Baudelaire's prose poem 'Le Crépuscule du soir' [Evening twilight], where he intones the area Neruda explores: 'O nuit! O rafraîchissants ténèbres! Vous êtes pour moi le signal

---

[1] Loyola, *Neruda*, 2006, reproduces the newspaper with Fernando Ossorio's (Silva Castro) review, p. 102.

[2] Alone's 1923 review complete in *Estudios Públicos*, p. 309: 'magia de la verdadera poesía'.

[3] Margarita Aguirre, *Pablo Neruda / Héctor Eandi. Correspondencia durante Residencia en la tierra*, p. 52: 'tan denigrado, me parece en verdad rico de dotes, su poesía casi siempre poética; es decir, legítima, aunque anacrónica y barroca'.

d'une fête intérieure, vous êtes la delivrance d'une angoisse' [Oh night! Oh refreshing darkness! You are for me the sign of an inner feast, you are deliverance from anguish].[4] Following this therapeutic twilight, no wonder the poem for the young Neruda becomes a space of nocturnal relief. He would have read Baudelaire's poem translated in Díez-Canedo's 1913 anthology.[5] As was his usual way of reading, Neruda identified directly with Baudelaire. There's also a resonance with Victor Hugo's *Les Chants du crépuscule* [Twilight Songs], 1835. This *modernista* word 'crepúsculo' continued as a key word in his *Veinte poemas* (in poems 2, 3, 6, 10 and 16). Twilight, then, is the nostalgic moment of the day, epitomised in Samain's 'Las vírgenes en el crepúsculo' [twilight virgins] from Díez-Canedo's 1913 anthology, which ends 'dulcemente sollozan en la noche infinita' [they sweetly sob in the infinite night].[6] Twilight is also the reading moment, after the day's work. In poem 10 of *Veinte poemas de amor* we read: 'Cayó el libro que siempre se toma en el crepúsculo' [The book that we always pick up at twilight fell from my hands]. That book that fell from his hands when he thinks of 'her' could have been by Baudelaire (to close the circle). There's also the hint that reading is an aid to daydreaming about the absent lover, another variant of the Paolo / Francesca syndrome. Dominic Moran defined the appeal that twilight held for Neruda well as 'a time of unique existencial intimacy, when the barriers between the physical and the spiritual, the material world and that of the poet's "reino interior" seem to melt away'.[7] Finally, as Baudelaire insinuated, twilight is 'ami du criminel' [friend of a criminal] or crime time, when the 'bête fauve' [wild beast] emerges, and, as noted, Neruda enjoyed the company of criminals.[8]

Neruda was early stimulated by that other poet prodigy, Arthur Rimbaud, who had written: 'Il faut être absolument moderne' [One must be absolutely modern].[9] How to assert this urge to be 'modern' from Temuco and then from Santiago shaped Neruda's poetic ambitions. Rimbaud was the sole poet cited by name in Neruda's Nobel acceptance speech in 1971, confirming his life-long attention to the rebel poet: 'a poor and splendid poet, the most atrocious of the despairing'.[10] Jorge Edwards deemed early Neruda as another Rimbaud, 'a precious genius of poetic writing', but unlike Rimbaud, who gave up writing for adventure in the Middle East, Neruda did not relinquish

---

4   Charles Baudelaire, *Petits poëmes en prose*, p. 77.
5   Enrique Díez-Canedo, 'El crepúsculo de la noche', in *La Poesía francesa del romanticismo al surrealismo*, p. 97.
6   Díez-Canedo, *La Poesía francesa*, p. 277.
7   Dominic Moran, *Veinte poemas*, p. 50.
8   Baudelaire, *Les Fleurs*, p. 105.
9   Arthur Rimbaud, 'Adieu', *Oeuvres complètes*, p. 116.
10 Nobel speech: 'un pobre y espléndido poeta, el más atroz de los desesperados'.

writing. Instead he turned to 'utilitarian poetry'.[11] In 1973, the Argentine poet Enrique Molina made a similar point that in *Residencia en la tierra* Neruda had touched the depths: 'it seemed impossible to go further', and compared this reaching a limit with Rimbaud's example of giving up writing poetry at the age of nineteen. Only 'Neruda did not remain silent' and, contrary to Rimbaud, moved on to write an optimistic, didactic poetry. Molina suggests that it was not the Spanish Civil War that changed Neruda, but that he could explore no further without repeating himself.[12] I share this view. Like Joyce or Picasso or his friend Federico García Lorca, Neruda did not want to repeat himself. His poetry *had* to change. At this early stage then, Neruda read works by poets like Rimbaud and Baudelaire that struck him so deeply that he wanted to emulate them as a poet.

How he obtained books in Temuco, an outpost of European immigration surrounded by vast deciduous forests and taciturn Mapuche culture and only founded in 1881, is itself an enigma. *Crepusculario* is the sole collection that leaves traces about his formative readings. Years later, Matilde Urrutia, his widow, remembered how he told her that he was a 'skinny, weak, introverted and silent boy' who when 'reading a book, sadness entered my soul and I cried alone, silently. I never had anybody by my side to share these intimate thoughts.'[13] No wonder, then, that reading for this solitary adolescent was so momentous. For that single reason, it is a crucial collection. Organised around a rite of passage, it combines a journey from twilight (with several references to 'crepúsculos' in the poems) to dawn. In his memoirs, Neruda recounted how he would sit on a balcony on the street in Santiago de Chile called Maruri 513 (noted in the poems) and watch the sun set, like his poetic mentor Tagore who called *The Gardener* 'my sunset songs'.[14] The last poem 'Final' (dated 1923) mentions 'alba' [dawn]. The secondary journey is therapeutic and narrates the transition from adolescence to adulthood and from being a non-poet (Reyes) to becoming a poet (Neruda). There is a third journey from love as the central existential solution to anguish, then to writing and remembering about it and finally just simply writing to discover his real identity. Night is the time when all these dilemmas emerge as he is free to be alone and write.

The modern tone of the collection derives from a clash between a colloquial and sincere idiom and diction and convoluted similes and high-flown, even baroque literary language. On one side we have self-images like 'Mi vida es

---

11 Jorge Edwards, 'Un adiós a muchas cosas', *Estudios Públicos*, p. 293.

12 Enrique Molina, 'Neruda de siempre', p. 8.

13 Matilde Urrutia, *Mi vida*, p. 62: 'flacucho, débil, introvertido y silencioso niño'; 'leyendo un libro, la pena entraba en mi alma y lloraba solo, callado. Nunca tuve a nadie al lado para compartir mis pensamientos íntimos.'

14 Rabindranath Tagore, *The Gardener*, p. 58.

un gran castillo sin ventanas y sin puertas' [My life is a great castle without windows or doors] (PN1 120), from 'El castillo maldito' [The cursed castle], where Neruda is no other than the French poet Nerval in 'El desdichado' that 'prince d'Acquitaine à la tour abolie' [Aquitaine prince of the abolished tower], the solitary, depressed prince in his locked-up castle waiting to be released. On the other hand, we have direct speech where we can hear the young poet speak aloud: 'Fui tuyo, fuiste mía. Qué más? ...' [I was yours, you were mine. What more?] (PN1 123) from 'Farewell', a conversational sequence that he later incorporated into his poem 20 of *Veinte poemas*: 'Yo la quise, y a veces ella también me quiso ... Eso es todo' [I loved her and sometimes she loved me ... That's all] (PN1 195–6). Neruda quickly learnt, by ear, how to prune this 'literary' air. Years later in 1973 Julio Cortázar picked on this simplifying process and gave it a Latin American frame: 'he pulled us out of a vague theory about loved ones and European muses to chuck us into the arms of an immediate and tangible woman [...] with the simple words of daily life'.[15]

I will examine some examples of this literary 'simplification', which forms part of a generational reaction against baroque *modernismo*. The word 'bruma' [mist], from the poem 'Los crepúsculos de Maruri' (that street in Santiago where he lived), is built up into a metaphor of 'plúmula trémula' [tremulous feathers]: lovely sounds, but baroque froth. The opening poem has 'rosas tremantes' [trembling roses], but 'tremante' does not exist in Spanish and is borrowed direct from Dante – that already mentioned 'la bocca mi bacciò tutto tremante' – spoken by Francesca in canto V.

Neruda would develop his colloquial modernity into avant-garde images in the later *Veinte poemas de amor*, like the startling closing couplet of poem 7:

> Galopa la noche en su yegua sombría
> desparramando espigas azules sobre el campo. (PN1 184)

> [Night gallops on its shadowy mare / scattering blue wheat ears over the land][16]

Or the closing of poem 10:

> Siempre, siempre te alejas en las tardes
> hacia donde el crepúsculo corre borrando estatuas. (PN1 186)

> [Always, always you you slip away in the evenings / towards where the twilight runs erasing statues]

---

[15] Julio Cortázar, *Obra crítica 3*, p. 66: 'nos arrancaba a la vaga teoría de las amadas y las musas europeas para echarnos en los brazos a una mujer inmediata y tangible [...] con las simples palabras del día'.

[16] Note that W. S. Merwin's translation has 'shedding blue tassels over the land', p. 23.

Or poem 13:

> Mi boca era una araña que cruzaba escondiéndose. (PN1 188)
>
> [My mouth was a spider that crossed hiding itself]

In all three cases, the images are striking as the nouns do not follow the verbs in any literal meaning. For example, the disturbing image of the mouth as a spider could derive from Tagore's *The Gardener* where 'Poets are weaving for you a web', where the poet is a spider. More specifically, the image elaborates on Rimbaud's simile where a 'petit baiser, comme une folle araignée, / Te courra par le cou' [little kiss, like a mad spider / will run along your neck] (where the kiss is a spider), but Neruda does not acknowledge Rimbaud.[17] Then, there is the spider as an artist, which Walt Whitman's poem 'A Noise-less Patient Spider' evokes. An isolated spider launches filaments 'out of itself' and 'connects' and catches prey just as the artist brings forth his art, his threads, out of himself and connects with the world.[18] Mallarmé, in a letter of 1866, saw himself as an 'arraignée sacrée' [sacred spider], on a web issuing from his mind as he weaves his work (his poem).[19] That a spider somehow stands for Neruda's poetic identity emerges in an early poem of 1918 'No te ocultes, araña' [Don't hide yourself, spider] where he addresses himself as the spider, begging him to come out of his hole (PN4 58–9). The Peruvian poet José Santos Chocano addresses his lover in 'El amor de las selvas' [Love for the jungles] as a humble spider who would like to knot himself in her hair, like exploring a mountain. Yet, despite these poetic echoes, the mouth as a spider remains bizarre, modern.

Explicit traces of Neruda's readings in this first collection include the already mentioned self-identification with Dante's lovers Paolo and Francesca from the poem 'Ivresse'. Neruda cites Ronsard (Pierre de Ronsard, 1524–85) in his 'El nuevo soneto a Helena', that *carpe diem* theme of 'cueillez, cueillez votre jeunesse / comme à cette fleur, la viellesse / fera ternir votre beauté' [Pick, pick your youth / like that flower, old age / will dull your beauty]. But he focuses more directly, as a modern ('El nuevo ...'), on the sexual nature of this 'flower'. The Renaissance topos of 'rose' clearly mutates into the rose-like vagina where Neruda tells his 'niña' [girl] that if she doesn't bed him quickly 'tendrás los senos tristes de amamantar tus hijos' [you will have sad breasts from feeding your children] (PN1 113). Clearly, he does not want 'her' as a mother of his child, for he yearns to abandon home. The

17 Rimbaud, *Oeuvres complètes*, p. 32.
18 Whitman, *Leaves of Grass*, pp. 347–8.
19 Robert Gibson, *Modern French Poets on Poetry*, p. 83.

topos of 'leaving home' ('partir' is crucial in both this collection and the *Veinte poemas de amor*) confirms that Neruda knew he had to travel abroad to become a real poet. The Ronsard-naming sonnet closes with this prediction: 'y porque aunque me llames yo estaré tan lejano' [and because even if you call me I will be far off]. By the writing of this sonnet, he had already abandoned Temuco for the far-off capital city Santiago. The last writer named in this collection is the Portuguese novelist Eça de Queiroz. The poet admits that he had to look up the word 'saudade' in a dictionary and then gives us his poet's definition of this term, its sweetness 'obsesses' him, 'como una mariposa de cuerpo extraño y fino / siempre lejos – tan lejos! – de mis tranquilas redes' [like a strange and delicate bodied butterfly / always far – so far from my tranquil nets] (PN1 136). He defines 'saudade' as a white word that, like a fish, escapes his grasp. The whole poem 'Saudade' is about the deep, emotional resonances of an exotic word picked up from a novel. What I derive from this poem is how the music of foreign words, especially French ones, seems to promise something.

But more crucial than the explicit citations are the secret, sometimes obvious links, with poets. An overarching self-image, which leaps forward to his next collection *Veinte poemas de amor*, is that of the 'gardener', who sows his seeds ('semillas') into furrows ('surcos'). Neruda so loved reading Tagore that he borrowed this role, though he never worked as a 'jardinero'. Tagore's gardener asks to be the servant of the Queen, to serve 'your idle days'. Again, what Neruda makes of his reading reveals his creativity. He does not repeat, but elaborates. His gardener is obviously a metaphor for male sexuality, his animality, sowing his seed into the furrow of his lover's vagina. The opening poem 'Inicial' from the section 'Helios y las canciones' (Greek for 'sun') has this poet-gardener 'laborando en silencio mis jardines ausentes' [ploughing in silence my absent gardens] and chucks his seeds of 'pulpa ardiente' (sperm) into roses. This poem about desire, even masturbation, is a 15-year-old's lament 'de un desconsolado jardín adolescente' [of a disconsolate adolescent garden] (PN1 111). Reading Tagore in Spanish translation prompted him to evoke his sexual urges more fully than the gentle erotic association of Tagore's Queen's flower garden. The critic Jaime Concha quoted from a journalistic piece that Neruda wrote in 1921 called 'Sexo' where the poet wrote about himself in the third person: 'The burning flame of sex runs through his arteries in electrical tremors. Pleasure has now been discovered and attracts him as the simplest and most marvellous thing that he has ever been shown' (in fact, this piece enumerates the stages of a boy's sexual development from masturbation to love for a sister, then a woman and brothels, cursing societal taboos).[20] The words 'semillas' and 'surco' become part of his private sexual vocabulary and the rewriting of Tagore stretches to the next collection, *Veinte poemas de amor y una canción desesperada*.

Tagore's poem 3 opens: 'In the morning I cast my net into the sea. I dragged up from the dark abyss things of strange aspect and strange beauty – some shone like a smile, some glistened lilke tears...'[21] Tagore can also link his art with a net: 'I have caught you and wrapt you, my love, in the net of my music.'[22] Neruda rewrote this in his poem 7 of *Veinte poemas*, as one of the key images of the collection:

> Inclinado en las tardes tiro mis tristes redes
> a tus ojos océanicos
> ...
> Sólo guardas tinieblas, hembra distante y mía,
> de tu mirada emerge a veces la costa del espanto (PN1 183–4)

> [Leaning into the afternoons I cast my sad nets / into your oceanic eyes /.../ You only keep darkness, distant female and mine, / from your look emerges at times the coast of dread]

The differences between Tagore and Neruda are as revealing as the borrowings (cast / net / abyss), for Neruda adds pathos with his 'triste', an obsessive and telling adjective, and 'her' inner self evades him as distant and dark. Tagore's translated text triggers Neruda's response; he becomes himself through reading Tagore. The noun 'redes' [net] stands for the poem and Neruda's frustrations that the poem does not bring her back to love him, unlike Tagore in poem 30, the one plagiarised by Neruda: 'I have caught you and wrapt you, my love, in the net of my music' (translated by Zenobia Camprubi as 'En la red de mi música te tengo presa, amor mío').[23] Neruda is more allusive, 'net' as poem, as music is suggested, not stated, and it fails. Of course, hunting a woman with a net harks back to Ovid's *Ars amatoria*: '... a mistress / Won't drop out of the sky at your feet. A hunter's skilled where to spread his nets for the stag, senses / in which glen the wild boar lurks.'[24] The metaphor of the 'net' suggests that Neruda cast his poem to catch his elusive lover.

[20]   Jaime Concha, *Neruda*, p. 186: 'La llamarada ardiente del sexo corre por sus arterias en sacudimientos eléctricos. El goce ya ha sido descubierto y lo atrae como la cosa más simple y maravillosa que le hubiera mostrado.' Collected in PN4 224–5.

[21]   Tagore, *The Gardener*, p. 7. Zeonobia Camprubí's translation reads: 'Con el alba eché mi red al mar, y robé al abismo oscuro raras cosas de belleza extraña'; in Rabindranath Tagore, *El jardinero*, traducción de Zenobia Camprubí de Jiménez (no publisher, Madrid, 1917), p. 21.

[22]   Tagore, *The Gardener*, p. 59.

[23]   Tagore, *The Gardener*, p. 59 and *El jardinero*, pp. 73–4.

[24]   Ovid, *The Erotic Poems*, p. 167.

Another echo of Tagore in Neruda concerns the 'Canción desesperada' and Neruda's paradoxical need to be free of love in order to be a poet. Tagore's prose poem 48 opens:

> Free me from the bonds of your sweetness, my love! No more of
>   this wine of kisses.
> This mist of heavy incense stifles my heart.
> …
> Free me from your spells, and give me back the manhood to
>   offer you my freed heart.[25]

Being in love has somehow robbed Tagore of his manhood. Neruda elaborated on this and substituted manhood for 'becoming a poet'. Poem 63 turns Tagore into the 'traveller' who must leave home: 'Traveller, we are helpless to keep you. We have only our tears.'[26] Neruda's love-suffering and rejection turn him too into the 'traveller'. The early uncollected poem 'Comunión ideal' (of 1919) invokes the poet as 'el viajero' (and Neruda hid behind the pseudonym Kundalini – it means 'serpent's power', a psychic energy that rises up the backbone – in the Temuco newspaper, PN4 78–80).[27] The crucial insight in *Veinte poemas de amor* picked up in Tagore concerns writing as therapy to loss of a lover. Tagore writes: 'Peace, my heart, let the time for the parting be sweet. / Let it not be a death but completeness. / Let love melt into memory and pain into songs.'[28] Disconsolate love is the source of song.

It is curious that, across the Andes, Victoria Ocampo also became fascinated with Tagore. She came across his work through André Gide's translation. When Tagore visited Buenos Aires in 1924, it fell to Victoria Ocampo to look after him during an illness and lodge him in a house in San Isidro. She cited lines from his work that could have equally appealed to Neruda, as if that generation in the *cono sur* read him the same way. She quoted from Tagore's English: '"Your questioning eyes are sad. They seek to know my meaning as the moon would fathom the sea,"' lines that are similar to the evocation of woman's enigmatic eyes in Neruda's love songs. Tagore wrote that 'el amor es el misterio sin fin', and again Ocampo and Neruda develop the mystery of love as means of grasping the meaning of life.[29] Later, their paths diverged and Neruda publicly mocked her.

Returning to literary echoes in *Crepusculario*, we can trace debts to

    [25] Tagore, *The Gardener*, p. 85.

    [26] Tagore, *The Gardener*, p. 105. Zenobia Camprubí translated 'traveller' as 'caminante', p. 124.

    [27] Georg Feuerstein, *Encyclopedic Dictionary of Yoga* (London: Unwin, 1990), pp. 189–91.

    [28] Tagore, *The Gardener*, p. 102.

    [29] Victoria Ocampo, *Tagore*, pp. 25–8. Most of this book is anecdotal.

Rubén Darío, so conspicuous that de Rokha argued that 'in *Crepúsculo* the little lines from Darío's *Prosas profanas* predominate'.[30] The poem 'Helios' invokes Darío's similarly named poem from *Cantos de vida y esperanza* [Songs of Life and Hope], 1905, where Darío's longing for art to solve life's problems is phrased as: '¡Helios! Porta estandarte de Dios, padre del Arte ... y de la melodía del crepúsculo' [Sun! Standard-bearer of God, father of art and melody of twilight], anticipating the title of Neruda's collection.[31] The delightful poem 'Morena, la besadora' [Dark girl, the kisser] is a litany of 'her' body parts (Neruda is irreductibly heterosexual). The list starts with 'cabellera' [head of hair], moves to 'uñas' [fingernails], the 'comba del vientre' [bulge of her belly], the 'dulce rodilla' [sweet knee], 'pelo' [hair], 'senos' [breasts] and her mark in bed to the 'palabras locas' [mad words] that burst out of this body-part-naming through the similes. The poem ends, like Darío's erotic poem 'Ite Missa Est', as a blasphemy, 'Amén', and the poet asking that she 'kiss' him 'now', that 'now' the moment of the actual writing (and reading) of the poem when he is thinking of 'her', absent, but present in his mind (PN1 115–16). Concerning the debt to Rubén Darío, master poet of the previous generation, the decisive influence emerges from Verlaine's differentiation between 'poetry' and 'literature', between a sincere language that corresponded to feelings and experience and a professional writer's rhetorical skill. Verlaine's closing of his 'Art poétique' – 'Et tout le reste est littérature' [And all the rest is literature] – defined for Darío and later for Neruda modern poetry's authenticity as not belonging to the genres of literature. The term that flows from this stricture is 'sincerity'. Darío evoked Verlaine – 'sin literatura' – in this stanza that is the generational poetics of *modernismo*:

> todo ansia, todo ardor, sensación pura
> y vigor natural; y sin falsía,
> y sin comedia y sin literatura ...
> si hay un alma sincera, esa es la mía.[32]

> [All anxiety, all ardour, pure sensation / And natural vigour; and without falsity / And without acting and without literature ... / If there's a sincere soul, it's mine]

Years later, in one of his scant essays on poetry, Neruda emphasised this term: 'Sincerity, in that so modest, so old-fashioned, so stepped on and scorned word lies perhaps the definition of my constant action.'[33] He would also sever

---

30 Faride Zerán, *La guerrilla literaria*, p. 223.
31 Rubén Darío, *Cantos de vida y esperanza*, pp. 40–2.
32 Darío, *Cantos*, p. 28.
33 Neruda y Parra, *Discursos*, p. 73: 'Sinceridad, en esta palabra tan modesta, tan atrasada,

poetry from literature, from prose and journalism, and write from his vital
'sincerity'. *The New Encyclopedia of Poetry and Poetics* defined sincerity as
'the absence of duplicity or dissimulation' and located its apogee with the
Romantics as a 'congruence between the poet's emotion and the poet's utterance', undermined in the twentieth century by irony. Emphasis on this term
ties Neruda into Romantic poetics.[34]

In Neruda's poem 'Tengo miedo' [I'm frightened] we have this couplet
'Tiene mi corazón un llanto de princesa / olvidada en el fondo de un palacio
desierto' [My heart has a princess' sob / forgotten in the depths of a deserted
palace], which paraphrases the opening line from Darío's popular 'Sonatina'
from his 1896 *Prosas profanas*: 'La princesa está triste …, ¿qué tendrá la
princesa? / Los suspiros se escapan de su boca de fresa, / que ha perdido la
risa, que ha perdido el color. / La princesa está pálida …/ … ya no quiere
el palacio …' [The princess is sad. What's up with the princess? Her sighs
escape her strawberry mouth, / that has lost its laugh, its colour. / The princess is pale / no longer wants her palace].[35] The sacrilegious erotic provocations of Darío's 'Ite Missa Est', where the 'hostia' (host) is sexualised,
merge – 'su espíritu es la hostia de mi amorosa misa' [her spirit is the host of
my amorous mass] – with Heloise 'virgen como la nieve' [virgin like snow]
into the opening poem of Neruda's fifth section 'Melisanda' in another paraphrase: 'Su cuerpo es una hostia fina, mínima y leve. / Tiene azules los ojos
y las manos de nieve' [her body is a fine, minimal and light host. / She has
blue eyes and snowy hands] (PN1 148).[36]

There are briefer allusions to other poets. In a poem about gamblers, the
poet asserts that 'sé que la vida es triste' [I know that life is sad], which
echoes Mallarmé's opening line of 'Brise marine' [Sea breeze]: 'La chair est
triste, hélas! Et j'ai lu tous les livres' [Flesh is sad, alas. And I've read all the
books].[37] Mallarmé's totemic poem about the urge to travel far away into the
unknown was memorised by Neruda, who cited it by heart on 5 September
1931 in a letter from Java to his Argentine friend Héctor Eandi.[38] Neruda
exploited that Mallarmean disgust for books. The clue to his deep reading of
this Mallarmé poem emerges from an uncollected poem with that first line
as the title, kept in French, 'La chair est triste, hélas' (PN4 164–5), with its
closing line 'como en aquel doliente verso de Mallarmé' [like in that painful
line from Mallarmé].[39] Years later, in 1965, Neruda said about Mallarmé that

---

tan pisoteada y despreciada … está tal vez definida mi constante acción.'
[34] *The New Encyclopedia of Poetry and Poetics*, 'Sincerity', pp. 1153–4.
[35] Rubén Darío, *Prosas profanas*, pp. 25–6.
[36] Darío, *Prosas profanas*, p. 61.
[37] Stéphane Mallarmé, *Oeuvres complètes*, p. 38.
[38] Aguirre, *Neruda / Eandi*, p. 79.
[39] Loyola called this poem a 'documento testimonial de las lecturas de Neftalí', *Neruda*,

'I read his poetry constantly and constantly extract powerful lessions from it' (PN5 1097).

We can trace further allusions to Gustavo Adolfo Bécquer's *Rimas* in Neruda's short poem 'Si Dios está en mi verso' [If God is in my verse], which reads:

> Perro mío.
> Si Dios está en mi verso,
> Dios soy yo.
>
> Si Dios está en tus ojos doloridos,
> tú eres Dios.
>
> Y en este mundo inmenso nadie existe
> que se arrodille ante nosotros dos! (PN1 131–2)
>
> [Dog of mine. / If God is in my verse, / I am God. / If God is in
> your hurt eyes, / you are god / And in this immense world nobody
> exists / who would kneel in front of us two]

The same emotional intensity, the same direct lover's talk, comes in Bécquer's *Rima* XVII, which ends: 'hoy la he visto … la he visto y me ha mirado … / ¡Hoy creo en Dios!' [Today I saw her. I saw her and she looked at me / Today I believe in God][40] and the famous *Rima* XXI: '¿Qué es poesía? ¿Y tú me lo preguntas? / Poesía …¡ eres tú!' [What is poetry? And you ask me? Poetry is you!].[41] Bécquer's shadow reappears in the poem 'Playa del Sur' [Southern beach], the first of Neruda's many poems to the long Pacific Ocean that defines his Chilean identity. It opens with a metaphor of violence: 'La dentellada del mar muerde / la abierta pulpa de la costa / donde se estrella el agua verde / contra la tierra silenciosa' [The nip of the sea bites / the open pulp of the coast / where the green water smashes itself againt the silent coast] (PN1 144). This oceanic fury leads Neruda to beseech the wind to carry him off, 'arrástrame' [drag me off] and 'llévame' [take me], as in Bécquer's *Rima* LII where 'Olas gigantes que os rompéis bramando … / ¡llevadme con vosotras!' [gigantic waves that break bellowing / take me with you!]; a plea to be carried away – 'llévame' – by a passion that would obliterate his memory of her and thus pain ('… me arranque la memoria'), for Bécquer, the poet, confessed: '¡Tengo miedo de quedarme / con mi dolor a solas!' [I'm scared to remain alone with my pain].[42] Neruda's empathy for Bécquer's bitter posthumous love songs is natural; after Neruda's *Veinte poemas*, Bécquer's are the most read and learnt by heart in all Spanish poetry

2006, p. 69.
40 Gustavo Adolfo Bécquer, *Rimas*, p. 54.
41 Bécquer, *Rimas*, p. 56.
42 Bécquer, *Rimas*, p. 72.

and offer readers the same course in the contradictions of love and heart-break. Neruda would endorse his generation's recovery of Bécquer (found, for example, in the epigraphs of Rafael Alberti's avant-garde poems *Sobre los ángeles* [Concerning angels], 1929 and in Luis Cernuda's poetry). The poet critic who best articulated how modern poetry in Spanish begins with Bécquer is the Mexican Xavier Villaurrutia. He situated him as the source of 'autenticidad', as an 'ostra solitaria' [solitary oyster] in a 'sea of emptiness' until the arrival of the *modernista* precursors like Nájera, Silva and Casal and then, of course, Darío.[43]

Much of Neruda's formative reading was from French literature, and this is natural, part of his Latin American generation's inheritance of French as the language of culture. At school in Temuco (1914–20), he was initiated into French literature by his teacher, who had Neruda copying and learning poems by heart. He was not a good student, though his only mark of 'distinguido' [distinction] was in French.[44] He trained to be a teacher of French (before dropping out), and translated French poems. Like any reader starting from scratch, Neruda first read anthologies and translations, then the original French, stutteringly, with a dictionary. He has been completely silent about this hard-earned discipline of learning to read a foreign language. A word in a foreign language is intrinsically a poem, with an opaque meaning and a strange sound. Neruda actually studied French for four years in the Instituto Pedagógico of Santiago where he met Albertina, also a student of French. Of the French poets learnt by heart, most crucial was Arthur Rimbaud (as already noted), with allusions hidden in Neruda's longing to travel, be errant, abandon Chile and stay wild and uncultivated. In an early interview with his first critic, he boasted that he would write a 30-page essay on Rimbaud (PN5 1051). Further anecdotal confirmation comes from Jaime Valdivieso who interviewed an aged Neruda in bed. Neruda was 'curiously reluctant to talk about literature', but he also 'knows English and French poetry by heart'. Valdivieso tests him by citing some lines in poor French, when Neruda interrupted him: 'he says to me dryly, cuttingly; "Rimbaud, my son." '[45] In fact, they were lines from Rimbaud's early 1870 poem 'Sensation'. Another interviewer was asked by Neruda to guess the poet he had recited in French. After Cordal guessed that it was Rimbaud, Neruda told him: 'I know several stanzas of that poem by heart ['Le Bateau ivre'] that Rimbaud wrote to remember the sea.' Neruda's habit of learning Rimbaud by heart continued with his studying in the Instituto Pedagógico in Santiago.[46] Today, Rimbaud is canonical, but Enid Starkie reminds us that the critical reception of Rimbaud

---

[43] Villaurrutia, *Obras*, p. 873.
[44] Víctor Farías, in Neruda, *Cuadernos de Temuco*, p. 11.
[45] Jaime Valdivieso, "Neruda', pp. 100–1.
[46] Alfredo Cordal, 'Mi entrevista con Pablo Neruda', *Qué*, marzo–abril 2005, pp. 16–18.

from drunken lout to visionary poet took place with the surrealists in the 1920s. He was until then under Verlaine's shadow. The first book on Rimbaud in English, for example, was by Edgell Rickword in 1924. In that sense, for Neruda, Rimbaud was almost a contemporary.[47] Efraín Kristal makes the same point about contemporaneity through latish translations about Baudelaire and Vallejo: 'In Peru Baudelaire, discovered in the 1890s, became a contemporary of Darío.' A 1905 translation makes Baudelaire's sensibility closer to Vallejo than the French original.[48]

Neruda, like many of his generation, fed off Enrique Díez-Canedo and Fernando Fortún's 1913 anthology *La poesía simbolista francesa*, which he recalled in a 1971 interview without naming it: 'At that time there was a very beautiful anthology of French poetry' (PN5 1193). Loyola deemed it as 'fundamental' to him.[49] It contained translations from Verlaine, Rimbaud, Baudelaire, Lautréamont, Nerval, Samain and others. Neruda copied down two poems by Sully Prudhomme, three by Baudelaire, two by Verlaine and so on from this anthology.[50] An example of this generational reading of the Díez-Canedo anthology can be found in César Vallejo's prose poem 'LV' from *Trilce*, 1922. It opens: 'Samain diría el aire es quieto y de una contenida tristeza' [Samain would say the air is calm and of a contained sadness], straight from Samain's poem 'L'Automne' in the anthology. He then diverges: 'Vallejo dice hoy la Muerte está soldando cada lindero a cada hebra de cabello perdido ...' [Vallejo says today Death is soldering each limit to each strand of lost hair].[51] Vallejo's own modernity is highlighted by Samain's melancholic privacy. Neruda also tested himself against Samain, but less violently, and recalled 'the fugitive melancholy of Albert Samain' (PN4 1096). Neruda also translated from the French (Schwob, Rilke, France etc.). The translation of Rimbaud's 'El barco ebrio' [Drunken boat] ('Le Bateau ivre') from the Díez-Canedo anthology was also keenly read by Vallejo and Neruda, with lines from the poem appearing in Vallejo *Trilce* 'I' (archipelago / bird's excrement) and in Neruda's *Veinte poemas* (Red Indians / boat journey). For many young Latin American poets at the start of the twentieth century, this anthology was a source of novelties, of assuming modern poetry.

An explicit example of this French debt comes from the whole of the fifth section, 'Pelleas y Melisanda', of *Crepusculario*, which rewrites the stilted, archly literary but tragic love story *Pelléas et Mélisande* 1892, by Maurice Maeterlinck (1862–1949), who won the Nobel Prize in literature in 1911. This verse 'play' about adulterous love, fratricide and tragic death

---

47 Enid Starkie, 'Rimbaud in England', p. 7.
48 Kristal, 'Introduction' to Vallejo, *The Complete Poetry*, p. 7.
49 Loyola, *Neruda*, 2006, p. 96.
50 Listed by Loyola, *Neruda*, 2006, p. 96.
51 César Vallejo, *Poesías completas*, p. 482.

in wordless suggestions and an absence of explanations was swiftly turned into music by Fauré, by Sibelius and into an opera by Debussy (in 1902). Neruda obviously read Maeterlinck, as did all his generation. In Peru, for example, in 1918, Manuel González Prada informed César Vallejo about the new poetry: 'In it there's the influence of actual French decadentism – he tells me. And then savouring a pronounced feint of complacency, he adds, and of Maeterlinck.'[52]

Crepusculario is best viewed as a poetic laboratory, or 'crisol' [crucible] in Antonio Melis's term, where Neruda worked out his identity as a poet.[53] A reader can hear other voices in these poems that are integrated, sometimes cited, but derive from passionate reading, without the distancing filters of rational criticism. The closing poem 'Final' suggests this awareness. The poet states that the 'words' we have just read were created by himself, but also 'se mezclaron voces ajenas a las mías' [voices alien to mine were mixed into it]. He adds: 'así vinieron estas palabras extranjeras / a desatar la oscura ebriedad de mi alma' [thus came these foreign words / to undo the dark drunkeness of my soul] (PN1 154). This tribute to inspiration – alien words unknotting his dark self – is also his sense that reading other poets has helped him create himself. Alien words are also foreign words like 'caroussel', 'ivresse' and 'farewell' embedded in his Chilean Spanish. The love poem 'Farewell', with its English title, which encapsulates the theme of being abandonned of the later *Veinte poemas de amor*, summarises an affair and the poet's need to be off, like a sailor, and pays tribute to Shakespeare's love tragedy *Romeo and Juliet*, 1597. When did Neruda read this play and how good was his English? Later, in 1964, after five years in British colonies, he would translate *Romeo and Juliet* into Spanish. Suffice it to say that the title suggests he read the play as his own, less dramatic story. In the parting scene on the balcony, Romeo cries out 'Farewell, Farewell! One kiss and I'll descend.'[54] One kiss seals their love, but fate, in the form of murdering Juliet's cousin, banishes Romeo to Mantua. Neruda's poem recreates this 'parting', this *farewell*. Nothing had yet happened between Neruda and his lover, as she was as young as the 14-year-old Juliet: 'Ni la fiesta de amor que no tuvimos, / ni tus sollozos junto a la ventana' [Not the feast of love that we didn't have, / nor your weeping by the window] (PN1 121). But it was that same 'window' and balcony in Verona. Neruda's lover yearns to leave and not be bound by love: 'Yo me voy. Estoy triste: pero siempre estoy triste. / Vengo desde tus brazos. No sé hacia dónde voy' [I'm off. I'm sad, but I'm always sad. / I come from your arms.

52   Vallejo, *Obras completas*, tomo 2, Artículos y crónicas (1918–1939), p. 656: 'Hay en ella la influencia del decadentismo francés actual – me dice. Y después, saboreando un pronunciado finte de complacencia, agrega: y de Maeterlinck.'

53   Antonio Melis, 'Neruda y la poesía hispanoamericana: una presencia polémica', p. 18.

54   William Shakespeare, *Romeo and Juliet* (London: J. M. Dent, 1953), p. 278.

I don't know where I'm going]. It is Romeo speaking before the suicides. According to Neruda, his poem was known by heart by countless readers. Che Guevara claimed it was his favourite poem.[55]

These early poems also record the poet's growing up and becoming a poet. Part of the mood of the collection is the poet's disgust with his new urban surroundings where love has been commercialised into sex and his natural self contaminated by industrial and city artifice. Neruda wrote in 1970 that 'this book was written between two cities, Temuco y Santiago, [...] that monstrous city with a strange smell, with trams and conductors ...' (PN5 317). Some of the more powerful poems explore this new state of alienation from his country roots. The poem 'Oración' [Prayer] deals with 'putas' [whores] in 'estas ciudades del dolor' [these cities of pain], where the poet feels his 'carne doliente y machacada' [flesh suffering and battered]. On the straw mattress in the outskirts of the city, he suffers 'mal de amor' [love-sickness]. His spirit, his yearning for real love, flies off at that hour when 'las lilas / sacuden sus hojas tranquilas / para botar el polvo impuro' [lilacs shake off their tranquil leaves to bounce the impure dust], repeated twice, though what he means by 'botar' is not clear to me. 'Lila / lilac' is a crucial metaphor of poetry for Neruda as it is associated with his childhood in an early poem 'Sensación de olor' [Sensation of smell]: 'Fragancia / de lilas ... / oh dulces atardeceres de mi lejana infancia' [Fragrance of lilacs. Oh sweet afternoons of my distant infancy] (PN4 177). That impure dust from lilacs could be his wasted sperm in this bitter, onanistic poem (PN1 116–18).

The poem 'Barrio sin luz' [Suburb without light] encapsulates Neruda's anti-city attitude. The second stanza generalises:

> Las ciudades – hollines y venganzas –,
> la cochinada gris de los suburbios,
> la oficina que encorva las espaldas,
> el jefe de ojos turbios. (PN1 125–6)

> [Cities – soot and vengeance – / the grey filth of the suburbs, / the office that bends shoulders, / the boss with turbid eyes]

The rebel poet will always oppose work in offices to the poet's vocation; work kills the spirit, there's 'sangre sobre las calles y las plazas, / dolor de corazones rotos' [blood in the streets and squares / pain of broken hearts]. Way beyond the hellish city, there is 'el campo' [country], where oxen pant and men sweat, while the poet remains alone in the urban ruins. This anti-urban diatribe informs many later poems in *Residencia en la tierra*, as we will see, and confirms the primacy of the theme of his lost organic self. The

---

[55] Adam Feinstein, *Pablo Neruda*, p. 325.

futuristic poem 'Puentes' [Bridges] has this poet identify with the alien steel of bridges above water, with trains crossing over as a 'maldición' [curse], for the immobile steel's anguish 'se hunde más en la tierra y más la clava' [sinks more and more into the earth and nails it]. He is both that steel bridge and that anguish and senses its claws inside him (PN1 126–7). This same sense of inner metal harming him surfaces in a lovely poem 'Maestranzas de noche' [Machine shops of the night], which is one long-drawn metaphor of his soul lost in urban hell. These machines are screams of desolation and seem like crows that attack him as nerves 'o como la cuerda rota de un violín' [or like the snapped string of a violin]. Each machine stares at him and he hears 'pasos en los cuartos desiertos' [footsteps in the deserted rooms]. The poem ends with his sudden identification with the workers in this factory of hell:

> Y entre la noche negra – desesperadas – corren
> y sollozan las almas de los obreros muertos. (PN1 128)

> [And in the black night – desperate – run and sob the souls of the dead workers]

The poem 'El pueblo' has the simple country poet suffering the din of trams in the grey, sad town. There is 'un olor de almacén por tus calles' [a smell of shops in your streets] and the water of the wells is bitter, and the souls of its inhabitants ugly. For these cursed city dwellers 'no saben la belleza de un surtidor que canta' [ignore the beauty of a fountain that sings], and hate is born in him. The last line modifies all that has just been written before for only love redeems this urban hell: 'Pero ella vive aquí' [But she lives here] (PN1 147).

There are two one-line poems, almost haikus. The first is titled 'Mi alma' and goes: 'Mi alma es un carrousel vacío en el crepúsculo …' [My soul is an empty carousel in the twilight] (PN1 137). A French word – merry-go-round – is a self-image of inner vacuum at that nostalgic moment that is the title of the collection. Here is Neruda's take on Ramón Gómez de la Serna's very modern 'greguería', a clever image that, in his case, captures a moment of sincerity, of giddy loss of childhood's self. Neruda admired this Madrilenean avant-gardist as 'the Picasso of our maternal prose'.[56] He also called him 'the great figure of surrealism, anywhere in the world'.[57] In one of his prose notes about travelling to the East in 1927, Neruda described the twilight as a 'greguería misteriosa' (impossible to know what he meant).[58]

[56] Neruda, *Discursos*, p. 58.
[57] Pablo Neruda, *Para nacer he nacido*, p. 239: 'la gran figura del surrealismo, entre todos los países'.
[58] Cited by Enrique Anderson Imbert, 'La prosa vanguardista de Neruda', in *Simposio Pablo Neruda*, p. 299.

Equally, Neruda could have followed Apollinaire's suite. In *Alcools*, the poem 'Chantre' [Singer] is a one-liner: 'Et l'unique cordeau des trompettes marines' [And the unique rope of marine trumpets], a mysterious poem about sound.[59] Neruda once praised Apollinaire's 'telegraphic genius' and 'exact word'.[60]

The poem 'Farewell', derived from Shakespeare as already noted, captures Neruda as a poet-child, this 'niño triste' [sad child] who cherishes the idea of leaving home: 'Amo el amor de los marineros / que besan y se van. Dejan una promesa. / No vuelven nunca más' [I love the love of sailors who kiss and go. They leave a promise. Never come back]. Neruda identified with these 'sailors', with this constant parting of seafaring life. Love cannot hold him back. He must be free of love. He says simply: 'Fui tuyo, fuiste mía' [I was yours, you were mine], as he will in poem 20 of *Veinte poemas*. However, 'Farewell' is also a secret homage to Rimbaud's 'Adieu', the last prose poem of his 1873 *Une Saison en enfer* [A season in hell] (later Neruda owned a first edition). This too is a 'dawn' poem when the 'combat spirituel' is over and Rimbaud has seen through love for a woman:

> Un bel avantage, c'est que je puis rire des vieilles amours mensongères, et frapper de honte ces couples menteurs, – j'ai vu l'enfer des femmes là-bas; – et il me sera loisible de *posséder la vérité dans un âme et un corps*.[61]

> [One fine advantage, I can laugh at the old false loves, and strike shame into those lying couples – I have seen the hell of women over there – and it will now be permitted to me to *possess truth in a soul and a body*]

The crucial lesson learnt by Neruda in his own life and desire to be a poet, taken from his identification with Rimbaud, is that to be himself, to be a true poet, holding truth in his body and soul, meant *not* being trapped by love. But for Neruda, unlike Rimbaud, this inner decision was very difficult to carry out.

The whole of *Crepusculario*, and the following *Veinte poemas*, will underline this joy of 'departure' from love and woman. The poet who narrates this archetypal journey away from home is Charles Baudelaire, whom Neruda translated as a lad.[62] The closing couplet – 'Plonger au fond du gouffre, Enfer ou Ciel, qu'importe? / Au fond de l'Inconnu pour trouver du *nouveau*' [To dive into the depths of the abyss, Hell or Heaven, who cares? / Into the depths of the unknown to find the *new*] from his master-poem 'Le Voyage' – sets the scene.[63]

59 Guillaume Apollinaire, *Alcools*, p. 36.
60 Neruda, *Discursos*, p. 72: 'genio telegráfico' and 'palabra justa'.
61 Rimbaud, *Oeuvres complètes*, p. 117.
62 Pablo Neruda, *Confieso que he vivido*, p. 35.
63 Baudelaire, *Les Fleurs*, p. 158.

Neruda's own journey into the unknown is stated thus:

> Yo me voy. Estoy triste: pero siempre estoy triste.
> Vengo desde tus brazos. No sé hacia dónde voy.

> [I'm off. I'm sad. But I'm always sad. I come from your arms. I
> don't know where I'm going]

Equally, Neruda identified with Tagore's yearning to travel afar and his impotence at being tied down: 'I am restless. I am athirst for faraway things. / My soul goes out in a longing to touch the skirt of the dim distance. /O Great Beyond, O the keen call of thy flute!' Tagore's poet harbours an 'impossible hope' and is a 'wanderer in my heart'. We could call this the archetype of leaving home to gain experience and a more real self, perhaps a Prodigal Son re-enactment. To read Tagore's poem as his own is the act of appropriation and identification that is reading.[64] Famously, as Borges put it in a footnote, when you read a line by Shakespeare, you are Shakespeare.[65]

Veinte poemas de amor y una canción desesperada, 1924

Pablo Neruda was nearly twenty years old when this second collection was published in Santiago de Chile by Carlos Nascimento. It was a squat 96-paged book, without illustrations or page numbers. On the cover the 'Veinte poemas' was in green and larger print, while 'de amor y una canción deses-perada' was, aptly, in black. According to Edmundo Olivares, it received negative reviews, being called 'too rhetorical, too cerebral' by the early critic Mariano Latorre.[66] Alone, who supported Neruda's first book, also found this second one 'odder and less accessible'; it was dominated by a 'hesitant dryness'. Even in the famous opening poem number 1, Alone found Neruda's words 'disconcerting, lacking in meaning, disorientated'; the whole book was 'disparatado' [foolish].[67] Eight years later, in 1932, when the second edition appeared, the critic Raúl Silva Castro found the book 'worrying, disturbing'.[68] Today these puzzled comments tell us more about the critics' inability to grasp these new poems than anything about the poems (though many lines remain enigmatic). But the essential premise is that *Veinte poemas* was innovative and experimental. Neruda answered these early hostile critics in the Chilean newspaper *La Nación* on 20 August 1924. He defended his 'expression of my thought' and his complete 'sincerity', and claimed that

---

64 Tagore, *The Gardener*, pp. 12–13.
65 Cited in Wilson, *Jorge Luis Borges*, p. 5.
66 Edmundo B. Olivares, *Pablo Neruda: los caminos de Oriente*, p. 28.
67 Cited from Alone's 1924 review in *Estudios Públicos*, p. 313.
68 Schopf, 2003, p. 80.

these poems poured out, without rational control: 'libremente, inconteni-blemente, se me soltaron mis poemas' [freely, uncontainably, these poems freed themselves] (PN4 324). This vivid description of 'inspiration' ('se me soltaron') is close to surrealism's location of art in the dream world and the subconscious.

The second edition of *Veinte poemas* was not published until 1932, when Neruda returned to Chile after nearly five years in the Far East. In this edition he changed poem 9 to the one now known by heart by so many. Poem 9 opened with a ridiculous, *modernista* line: 'Fimbria rubia de un sol que no atardece nunca' [Fair border of a sun that never turns into evening]. But the great erotic poem he put there instead belongs to the *Residencia* cycle, as Juan Loveluck has convincingly shown (more on this later). Neruda admitted writing it in 1932, that is, ten years later than the rest of the poems.[69] From 1932 on then, *Veinte poemas* has been continuously in print, by far the best-selling book of poems written in Spanish. In 1961 it reached one million officially sold in Spanish, and in 1972 it passed the two million mark (sales are now some six million-plus, but it is hard to be precise owing to so many pirated and now Internet editions). In a reader's choice in the Madrid news-paper *El País* for the most popular poems in Spanish of the past millen-nium, Neruda's poem 20 ('Puedo escribir los versos más tristes esta noche') came first and his poem 15 ('Me gustas cuando callas porque estás como ausente') came third.[70] Rodríguez Monegal spoke for many male critics by blaming such success on women readers. However, the most acute insight into its continuing readability comes from Antonio Melis: 'Neruda's novelty consists, above all, in revealing the anatagonistic character of the loving rela-tionship [...] the other face of the erotic relationship.'[71]

A boost for Neruda's love poems came with the film *Il Postino*, 1994, taken from Antonio Skármeta's novel *Ardiente paciencia* [Ardent patience], 1985, itself taken from Neruda's politicised poem 'Quién muere?' [Who dies?]: 'Solamente la ardiente paciencia / hará que conquistemos una espléndida felicidad' [Only ardent patience / will ensure that we conquer a splendid happiness]. Neruda had lifted this phrase from his master Rimbaud – 'Armés d'une ardente patience, nous entrerons aux splendides villes' [Armed with an ardent patience, we will enter the splendid cities].[72] In his Nobel acceptance speech, he linked Rimbaud with his own roots:

[69] Juan Loveluck, 'El navío de Eros: *Veinte poemas de amor ... Número nueve*', in *Simposio Pablo Neruda*, pp. 220, 231.

[70] 'Lectores españoles y latinoamericanos eligen 50 poemas del milenio', *El País*, 9 de abril de 2001.

[71] Melis, 'Neruda', p. 22: 'La novedad de Neruda consiste, sobre todo, en la revelación del carácter antagónico de la relación amorosa [...] la otra cara de la relación erotica.'

[72] Rimbaud, *Oeuvres complètes*, p. 117.

I believe in that prophecy by the seer Rimbaud. I come from a dark province, from a country separated from others by a severe geography. I was the
most abandonded of poets, and my poetry was regional, sorrowful, steeped
in rain. But I always had confidence in man. I never lost hope.[73]

It exemplifies how Neruda changed Rimbaud for his own purposes. However,
director Michael Radford altered the film's title to focus on Neruda's postman
at Isla Negra, Chile during Pinochet's 1971 coup, with Neruda dying of prostate cancer, and he added in Neruda's illicit affair on Capri with Matilde
Urrutia. But certainly, the film and its accompanying poems contributed
to selling Neruda around the world in translation. What was fascinating in
the film was that Neruda helped the postman seduce his beloved by quoting
Neruda. This postman is caught out by his girl's mother, who in turn had
been seduced by her man citing Neruda. That is, Neruda's love poetry had
become oral, part of ordinary lover's talk, outside bookshops and high culture.
Skármeta's novel then had its title changed to that of the film, *El cartero de
Neruda* [Neruda's postman].

   The poet Carol Ann Duffy obviously saw this film. In her poem 'Dear
Norman' we have the newspaper boy turned into a diver for pearls, whom she
names 'Pablo'. I cite: 'Pablo laughs and shakes the seaweed from his hair. /
Translucent on his palm a pearl appears. He is reminded. / *Cuerpo de mujer,
blancas colinas, muslos blancos.* / I find this difficult, and then again easy,
/ as I watch him push his bike off in the rain.' This opening line of poem 1
of the *Veinte poemas* is not even translated, and Pablo just remains Pablo
without his surname as if everybody knows this line and Neruda has become
an image of exotic erotica. Many other poets have been inspired by these love
poems. One of the more radical critiques, within poetry, is Adrienne Rich's
Twenty-One Love Poems, published the same year as her extraordinary feminist text, *Of Woman Born*, 1975. There are no specific references to Neruda,
but the title is her answer to his 'macho' poems. Each poem begins, like Neruda's, with a number not a title, with a free-floating unnumbered poem corre-
sponding to the 'canción desesperada', which argues that 'whatever happens
with us, your body / will haunt mine', with the same stress on 'body'. The
word 'cuerpo' opens Neruda's *Veinte poemas*. The collection celebrated
Rich's 'coming-out' as lesbian lovers 'outside the law'.[74] One last anecdote
about Neruda's popularity concerns Germán Arciniegas who recounted how
once in Cali, Colombia, Neruda's plane broke down. A reading was organised
in the local Cali theatre, and it was packed out. Neruda began reciting 'Puedo
escribir los versos más tristes ...' and before the end of this famous line,
everybody in the theatre joined in. Neruda told Arciniegas that he had never

---

[73] Cited by Ilan Stavans, *The Poetry of Pablo Neruda*, p. 975.
[74] Adrienne Rich, *Adrioenne Rich's Poetry and Prose*, p. 121.

felt a more powerful emotion.[75] Hernán Loyola summarised such success by calling Neruda's collection a 'silencioso *best-seller* permanente' [silent, permanent bestseller] (PN1 1150).

How to account for such popularity? We can approach this topic from several angles, beginning with the title. The working title, according to a letter Neruda wrote in 1923 to Alone, the influential literary critic, was 'Poemas de una mujer y de un hombre' [Poems of a woman and of a man] (PN5 927). Not a book about two individuals, but about what lies behind each person, the generic woman and man (note how Neruda reversed the usual order), a kind of Eve and Adam, or how each person re-enacts archetypes, Paul et Virginie, Paolo y Francesca (note the usual order). As a whole, Neruda tends towards the generic, a city, not Santiago, and this allows the reader in, for she and he are also just a woman and a man. So the 'love' of the title suggests a universal experience, beyond what might have happened biographically to Neruda in Temuco in the 1910s as he grew up. But why 'twenty' poems? In another letter to Alone, Neruda opted for 'Doce poemas de amor y una canción desesperada' [Twelve poems ...] (PN5 929) as a possible title. In 1922 the Argentine avant-garde poet Oliverio Girondo had published *Veinte poemas para ser leídos en el tranvía* [Twenty poems to be read in a tram], but it was a limited edition in Paris (the second edition of 1924 in Buenos Aires was the popular one). Maybe there is a nod towards Blaise Cendrars' *Dix-neuf poèmes élastiques* [Nineteen elastic poems], 1919, a Swiss–French aventurer poet in the Apollinaire mould? Was the 'twenty' of the title then just arbitrary? Was it an allusion to his age or to his twenty writer's fingers?

The title also appears to oppose 'amor' [love] and 'desesperanza' [despair], as if love is a synonym for 'hope', for what might or will happen. Clearly, he envisioned Darío's 1905 collection *Cantos de vida y esperanza*, but negatively. Love then seems like a religion, an experience that ties you to life ('re-ligare' is the etymology for 'religion'). For Neruda, a Romantic, love twins with passion, and gives life its deep meaning. His question through the poems is whether life without passion is bearable. Love is thus 'opposed to mourning', as the French psychoanalyst André Green proposed.[76] But, there lurks a paradox at the heart of this collection for passion, etymologically, derives from the Latin 'passio', hence Christ's passion or suffering. And this collection is about learning from suffering, from passion. It is crucial to underline that such is the intensity of questioning passion that references to Chilean historical and political contexts are abolished – a 'notorious elision', in Loyola's words.[77]

[75] Germán Arciniegas, 'Encuentros con Pablo Neruda' in *América nació entre libros* (Bogotá: Biblioteca Familiar Presidencia de la república, 1996), p. 531.

[76] André Green and Gregorio Kohon, *Love and its Vicissitudes*, p. 15.

[77] Loyola, *Neruda*, 2006, p. 164.

Neruda's twenty-one poems both celebrate carnal, erotic love and lament its absence, leaving the poet lonely, in despair at his separation and even abandonment by 'her'. There is a history of this ambivalence about love. According to Green again 'love is unbearable ... It carries the possibility of betrayal,' for there is no such thing as unconditional love and love as passion dies out, undergoes 'sudden extinction', beyond reasonableness and promises.[78] So suffering is knotted into love, almost its synonym.

For complex, historical reasons, our current notion of 'passionate love' was born and codified by lyric poets called troubadours in twelfth-century Provence or Languedoc. This ritual was known as the *leys d'amor*. Love was linked to taboo-breaking adultery, probably because marriages excluded 'falling in love' as they were 'arranged', based on consolidating power and alliances and maintaining hierarchies. So passionate love was free-floating, could not be contained in the institution of marriage, and was outlawed. Against a notion of love as manageable, as compassion and companionship, passionate love was seen as dangerous, even heretical. Poets explored this 'courtly love' where the poor poet fell hopelessly in love – 'l'amour fou' / 'el loco amor' [mad love] – with a woman he could not attain but who obsessed him. If the social codes were broken, and adultery took place, the lovers, like Paolo and Francesca, were punished in hell. Courtly love poems play with this emotional and sexual paradox for the consequence of this ongoing desire for the forbidden woman was failure and despair. Hence, Neruda's 'canción desesperada', but despair, for a poet, is cognitive; there is a love-knowledge that the poet learns through suffering. In Neruda's case, he became a poet. This is what Denis de Rougement called the 'religion of love', the 'love of being in love', where the idealised woman lives on, torturing the poet in his mind, forever unattainable and absent.[79]

In Neruda, I can trace this 'amor cortés' to four strands:

1. Passionate love lies outside marriage; it is a natural force that transgresses the social and moral code. For a class rebel like Neruda, there is no other love. The poet is 'duro de pasiones' [hard with passions] (PN1 185), not hiding his phallic purpose. Poem 14 asserts a pagan sexual energy: 'Quiero hacer contigo / lo que la primavera hace con los cerezos' [I want to do with you what spring does with the cherry trees] (PN1).
2. Neruda inherits the religion of love, that life without passion is unbearably dull and alien. Separation is hell. This parodies a real religion, that life without God is unbearable etc.

[78] Green and Kohon, *Love and its Vicissitudes*, pp. 12, 15.
[79] Denis de Rougemont, *Passion and Society*, p. 41. The classic account of courtly love is C. S. Lewis's *The Allegory of Love*, 1936.

3. In the present tense of writing when Neruda sat down alone and wrote and when she was 'absent' but in his mind, passion and intensity become despair and self-knowledge. Mariana Alcaforado's 'I thank you from the bottom of my heart for the despair into which you have thrown me. Farewell: love me and make me suffer still more' could have been penned by Neruda.[80] Later, in a poem 'Tiranía' [Tyranny] from *Residencia en la tierra 1*, he invokes the lady, 'O dama sin corazón' [oh heartless lady], who tyranises the poet, for his ontological security depends on her. He confesses: 'Hay algo enemigo temblando en mi certidumbre' [There's some enemy trembling in my certainty] (PN1 271) and that 'algo', unanalysed, is her indifference.

4. Neruda develops the theme of 'parting as continuous suffering'. A summary of his love philosophy would be 'the further off I am the more I long for her'.[81] And 'she' is either in Temuco, has dropped him or loves another. 'She' is also deliberately generic – not to hide her real identity, but to increase the role she plays in the mind – for the image of 'her' is not the real person (in biographical fact, at least three women, but hard to separate in the poems).

De Rougemont defined passion as a 'rejection of satisfaction, an obsession of the imagination with a single image'.[82] According to Green, Freud insisted on 'always something lacking for complete discharge and satisfaction'. This sense of 'lack' can be traced, at least, back to Plato's *The Symposium* where Aristophanes famously argued that originally we were all androgynous, that is, triple sexed, a male, a female and an androgyne. But these mythic ancestors were cut in half by the angry gods and 'each half yearned for the half from which it had been separated'. Thus love 'restores' our wholeness and heals us from our solitary, abandoned state. Physical, erotic love is thus a desire for the 'whole' where the separated lovers 'melt into' each other to become 'one being instead of two'. However, this does not happen, so Socrates' summary is that 'one desires what one lacks', thus establishing 'lack' at the core of love, and Neruda's love-philosophy. Socrates had learnt from a woman called Diotoma that love is 'homeless', a spirit hunting out for lovers, yearning after knowledge and immortality.[83] A sharp summary of this love / suffering / art topos comes from Susan Sontag who claims that for two thousand years 'it has been spiritually fashionable to be in pain'. For her, the 'spiritual merits and benefits of suffering' are best found in the 'making

---

80 Rougemont, *Passion and Society*, p. 207.
81 Rougemont, *Passion and Society*, p. 87.
82 Rougemont, *Passion and Society*, p. 141.
83 Plato, *The Symposium*, pp. 61–93.

of works of art' and in 'sexual love'.[84] Octavio Paz concluded his study of love with a vast generalisation: 'the history of "courtly love" [...] is not only that of our art and our literature: it is the history of our sensibility [...] of Western civilization'.[85]

From Plato, it is clear that 'individuality is a curse', that love, in Erich Fromm's words, is the 'need to overcome separateness, to leave the prison of aloneness'.[86] But Neruda, at the end of the book, like Rimbaud's closing prose poem 'Adieu', wants to develop his individuality, his aloneness from women, so we can understand how suffering leads to 'poetry', for lovers would remain blissfully mute, without need for art. Neruda's *Veinte poemas de amor* is as much about love as it is about remaining painfully alone and becoming a poet; *soledad* [loneliness] drives creativity.

Another frame for exploring Neruda's power to continue to seduce his readers today emerges from the confusing versions of 'poet' that he mixed inside his 19-year-old's poems. In one sense, his provincial, third world upbringing sought out the best in western culture, following Darío and the *modernistas*, principally located in Paris. Neruda is eclectic and Gallic. Reading Tagore and Rimbaud in translation was deeply formative. The poet is a 'maker' but his prestige and social role antedate the written or 'made' poem because the poet belongs to the ancient bardic tradition as oral word-hoarder. This bardic tradition was still alive with the Mapuches around Temuco, but not alluded to explicitly by Neruda, who was 'European' in his thinking about poets and poetry. But his non-bookish roots suggest the power of the spoken voice, of orality. Already in *Crepusculario*, we hear the poet 'talking' to us, in direct speech rhythms. One crucial consequence of this bardic, oral tradition, when the poet had a well-defined social role, is how from this second book of 1924 Neruda reached out beyond the clique of poetry readers. As Federico Schopf noted: 'with this message, he wants to pass beyond literary people and critics' and 'reach a non-literary public', which he did.[87]

A second version of 'poet' was inherited from history, namely the Romantic nature poet. Neruda claimed that his poetry attempted to match natural sounds and rhythms, like rain falling on a tin roof, or waves breaking on the shore, or the cold Patagonian wind in pines. The heart and the body offer nodal metaphors for his direct link between the poet and nature. There is a curiously traditional side to even the most audacious poems. Neruda always admired 'los viejos poetas' [the old poets], meaning, I think, the great Romantic nature tradition. Critic Michael Wood put his finger on this issue:

---

84 Susan Sontag, *Where the Stress Falls. Essays*, pp. 47–8.
85 Paz, *La llama doble*, pp. 100–1.
86 Erich Fromm, *The Art of Loving*, p. 14.
87 Schopf, 2000, pp. 79–80.

In one sense, of course, Neruda is an old-fashioned poet, but this is because he prolongs traditions, not because he tries to sound archaic and lofty. Many of his favorite poetic strategies belong to the nineteenth-century [...] He prefers similes to metaphors; he likes to personify moods, conditions, landscapes; he is fond of operatic exclamations [...].[88]

However, Neruda also fused with the rebel tradition, the 'poeta maldito' [cursed poet] invented by Verlaine and picked up from his readings. The poet was an outsider, a bohemian, hostile to comfort and the bourgeois lifestyle. He dressed like a poet, wanted to be recognised as such in the street (his black 'cape' enters his poem 10). Neruda recounted years later how he arrived from his wet provinces at Santiago station: 'possessing a tinplate suitcase, with the indispensable black suit of the poet, skinny ...'. He added self-consciously that he went about town 'ritually dressed in black since very young, as *the true poets of the last century dressed*' (my italics).[89] This black uniform recalls Nerval, and Neruda's assumption of 'le veuf' [widower], in mourning. He created this Nervalian self clearly in poem 11: 'Hace una cruz de luto entre mis cejas' [It makes a mourning cross between my eyebrows] (PN1 187), and he is linked with a 'sol negro y ansioso' [a black, yearning sun] in poem 19 (viz. Nerval's 'Soleil noir de la Mélancolie' from 'El desdichado', again). Even his voice is Nervalian and black: 'mi voz viuda' [my widowed voice], he wrote in poem 16. He was perceived as dangerous to know, unpresentable by his *novias*. He owed this reputation to his absorption of Baudelaire, Nerval, Rimbaud and Verlaine, the 'true poets of the nineteenth century'. This kind of poet culminated in the daring, provocative avant-garde poet, outraging and defying his readers. In poem 14 Neruda views himself as being so difficult and odd: 'Cuánto te habrá dolido acostumbrarte a mí' [How you must have suffered getting accustomed to me], and picks out 'a mi alma sola y salvaje, a mi nombre que todos ahuyentan' [to my solitary and savage soul, to my name that everybody flees] (PN1 190). Just his poet's name and reputation is sufficient to scare off the *bien-pensants*.

Yet another version of 'poet' comes from the practice of writing poems, the verbal machine. Neruda imitated earlier poets that he had read and learnt by heart. *Imitatio* is normal poet's practice. You can follow his awareness of writing in his similes and metaphors and key words. Neruda's craft became intuitive, second-nature. Craft is the clue, the skill that he reveals from early on in modulating his words to the meanings. Although most of *Veinte poemas* is writen in fourteen-syllabic alexandrines and free verse, the metrical deft-

---

88 Michael Wood, 'The Poetry of Neruda', p. 8.

89 Neruda, *Confieso*, pp. 43, 48–49: 'provisto de un baúl de hojalata, con el indispensable traje negro del poeta, delgadísimo...' and 'ritualmente vestido de negro desde muy jovencito, como se vestían los verdaderos poetas del siglo pasado'.

ness stands out, as Dominic Moran noted: 'Besides being passionate love poems, they are also painstakingly wrought exercises in style and form.'[90] One last area of skill comes from translating poems and learning them by heart.

A last version of 'poet', already touched on, is the poet as great lover; the poet and his muse. Biographically, we now know many of his muses's actual names, but once these women enter his poems they lose this lived specificity and are internalised as images, white goddesses, equivalents to Dante's Beatrice, to Petrarch's Laura, to Garcilaso's Isabel, to Swift's Celia and up to Breton's Nadja, all dark ladies of the mind. Neruda chose not to cite them as specific women; first, in his memoirs, he gave them nicknames (Marisol and Marisombra), then biographers located their real names and histories. Albertina Rosa Azócar, a fellow student in Santiago, was Marisombra (Neruda gave her countless further nicknames in his letters, especially 'mocosa') and Teresa Vásquez León from Temuco was Marisol or Terusa. Poem 19 was written for a María Parodi.[91] Biography, however, does not help us read them in the poems for these 'women' melt into a generic muse, offering deeper instinctual knowledges.

In 1926, aged 22, Neruda, in the prologue to his sole novel, defined himself within this loose tradition of rebel-poets: 'As a citizen, I am a peaceful man, enemy of laws, governments and established institutions. I am disgusted by the bourgeois and I like the life of restless and dissatisfied people, be they artists or criminals.'[92] The meaning is clear and strong; he identified with the Romantic outsider, like his hero Rimbaud. In 'Mauvais sang' [Bad blood], Rimbaud proudly proclaimed his allegiances with criminals, with an even stronger 'repulsion': 'Maintenant je suis maudit, j'ai horreur de la patrie … Encore tout enfant, j'admirais le forçat intraitable sur qui se referme toujours le bagne …' [Now I am damned, I loathe the fatherland … When I was still a child, I used to admire the stuborn convict on whom the prison gates always close again].[93] We know that Albertina had to hide Neruda's letters to her from her family because he was a rebel 'poet'.

The self is the centre of Neruda's poetic world, but it is a muddled, contradictory self. Just as there are differing 'poets', so there are antagonistic selves. Again, Neruda learnt from Rimbaud, especially his extraordinary letter known as the 'Lettre du Voyant' to his school teacher Paul Demeny, written when 17 years old in 1871. The letter became a manifesto for radical

---

90 Moran, *Veinte poemas*, p. 4.
91 Neruda, *Para nacer he nacido*, p. 265.
92 PN1 217: 'Como ciudadano, soy hombre tranquilo, enemigo de leyes, gobiernos e instituciones establecidas. Tengo repulsión por el burgués, y me gusta la vida de la gente intranquila e insatisfecha, sean éstos artistas o criminales.'
93 Rimbaud, *Oeuvres complètes*, p. 96.

French poets, culminating with the surrealists. He tells Demeny, 'car JE est un autre' [for I is another], that famous ungrammatical abyss between the 'ego' and the other selves. Yves Bonnefoy rephrased this brilliantly in terms of Rimbaud's own life: 'that one is, without knowing it, the receptacle for understanding [connaissance], that one can be, without knowing it, at the moment of revealing it [...] that one's misery is a necessary suffering and that one's very despair is that rupture of the person'.[94] It was a question of breaking through inside. Wallace Fowlie interpreted this same phrase more mundanely as seeming 'to mean that, in addition to the everyday familiar self we believe we know because we are constantly seeing it act and react, breathe, and eat, there is another self, which is the real self'.[95] Rimbaud then outlined his method for exploring this split-self, or anti-self: 'Le premier étude de l'homme qui veut être poéte est sa propre connaissance, entière; il cherche son âme, il l'inspecte ...' [The first study of a man who wants to become a poet is his own understanding, complete; he seeks his soul, he inspects it] and thus deliberately makes himself a *voyant* by a 'long, immense et raisonné dérèglement de tous les sens. Toutes les formes d'amour, de souf- france, de folie; il cherche lui-même ... Car il arrive à l'*inconnu*' [By a long, immense and reasoned disordering of all the senses. Every form of love, of suffering, of madness, he searches himself ... For he arrives at the *unknown*]. Rimbaud, here, cites Baudelaire, his own god-like mentor.[96] This letter is crucial in grasping Neruda's inner strivings to become a poet for it allowed him to become himself and see what he shared and rejected from Rimbaud (women, love, sexuality). The result of this self-analysis is his poetry itself.

One further qualifier about this early poetry must be made. I have called Neruda a great nature poet, but it is the *loss* of this direct contact with nature, of his roots, implicit in wanting to become a poet, that is crucial. This loss of contact with nature surfaces as anguish and alienation in the city Santiago. Once again, Neruda is very clear about this internalised city: 'I felt humili- ated and lost in the city [...] I took refuge in my poetry with the ferocity of a shy man.'[97] Culture shock after that long train journey from Temuco to Santiago, alone, forced him to recreate in his mind the women and life that he had lost, by travelling and by growing up. Santiago, capital of Chile, a boom town with grand nineteenth-century public buildings, based on nitrate and copper wealth, remained beyond his reach as a student called Neftalí Reyes. The country was stratified into almost caste-like classes, yet he was

[94] Yves Bonnefoy, *Rimbaud*, p. 50.

[95] Wallace Fowlie, 1963, p. 49.

[96] Rimbaud, *Oeuvres complètes*, pp. 250–1. He also wrote to Georges Izambard, repeating that 'Je est un autre', p. 249.

[97] Neruda, *Confieso*, p. 67: 'Me sentí humillado y perdido en la ciudad [...] Me refugié en mi poesía con ferocidad de tímido.'

not a *roto* [down and out], not a Mapuche. Santiago and the 'Mediterra-
nean' area around it account for 90 per cent of Chile's population. Isabel
Allende called Santiago a 'pulpo demente' [demented octopus]. She evoked
a country with a terrible sense of public ridicule, always comparing itself to
Europe and valuing what comes from abroad as better than what is local,
where everybody conforms and everything arrives there late. Allende blamed
a bureaucracy gone mad, a maze-like legality where nothing can be done
without contacts; that 'Kafka was Chilean'. Geography, as she and many
others have noted, in the shape of the barrier of the Andes and the Pacific
Ocean, determines national character.[98] Neruda would naturally hate all this,
as Rimbaud had done when he walked to Paris from his provincial farmyard
for he also 'turned his back on the city', as Fowlie put it.[99]

So when Neruda travelled to Santiago to become a poet, he was just one
of millions moving to the overcrowded cities of Latin America. Neruda's
poems narrate this 'urban migration' as bleak emotions, the alien objective
city internalised as his own subjectivity. There is a city-induced melancholia
in his poetry close to the 'blues' or to tango. The Mexican writer Elena
Garro (Octavio Paz's first wife) linked Neruda's *Veinte poemas* with Gardel's
tangos.[100] By the 1920s Gardel's tangos had spread out from the immigrant
slums of Buenos Aires to Paris and back to Latin America. Neruda recalled:
'It was the period when tango reached Chile...'[101] In 1971 he confirmed
that 'tango was in fashion' (PN5 1195). The music is melancholic, deals
with loss of home, of neighbourhood, with urban migration and immigration
anguish. It narrates the macho's betrayal by women who cannot be trusted.
Revenge on these whores was constantly sung in the *lunfardo* slang of tango
lyrics. The tone of Neruda's poems fuses with tango (melancholia, the male,
betrayal, revenge). Later, his greatest love poem was titled 'Tango del viudo'
[Widower's tango]. A coda to this interpretation comes from the Argentine
writer Ricardo Piglia who noted that 'the loss of the woman (named Solveig,
la Maga, Elsa or La Eterna or maybe Beatriz Viterbo) is the condition for the
metaphysical experience. The hero begins to see reality as it is and perceives
its secrets [...] I mean in fact the tradition of tango.' One could substitute
Neruda for that fictional hero and 'knowledge' for 'metaphysics'.[102]

Now we come to the actual *Veinte poemas*. Hernán Loyola makes a crucial

98   Isabel Allende, *Mi país inventado*, pp. 29, 61, 91, 115.
99   Fowlie, p. 62.
100   Elena Poniatowska, *Octavio Paz*, p. 39.
101   Neruda, *Confieso*, p. 47.
102   Ricardo Piglia, *Formas breves*, p. 25: 'la pérdida de la mujer (se llama Solveig, La Maga,
Elsa, o la Eterna, o se llame Beatriz Viterbo) es la condición de la experiencia metafísica. El
héroe comienza a ver la realidad tal cual es y percibe sus secretos [...] Se trata en realidad de la
tradición del tango.' The women cited are from Leopoldo Marechal, Cortázar, Arlt, Macedonio
Fernández and Borges.

point about their order, which is not chronological. He notes a 'late structuring of the book like a *narrative* parable of a love experience'.[103] That is, the book should be read as a diary of an affair and all that crosses the mind of the poet; it tells a story. Neruda had written that his earlier *Crepusculario* was a 'diary of everything that happened to me, inside and outside, of all that reached my sensibility' (PN4 1201). One could stretch this insight about his poetry as a diary to cover all his poetry up to the mid-1930s. Knut Hamsun's novel *Pan*, 1894 (Hamsun won the Nobel Prize in 1920), was, according to Tomás Lago, passionately read by Neruda.[104] Hamsun was also recommended by Gabriela Mistral, and Neruda recommended him to Laura Arrué. A similar case could be made for Pío Baroja, for Neruda was always a great reader of novels.[105] In Hamsun's fiction, then, we have a proper *narrative* version of the jilted man's lament. Narrated by an outcast living in a hut alone in northern Norway, you can easily imagine Neruda identifying with the northern forests, the harbour, the wind, rowing boats, hunting, the life of nature so similar to his Temucan landscape and the lonely rebellious poet / outcast that he was too. The Norwegian, like the Chilean, was tormented by an unattainable woman who teases him. You can read Neruda into Hamsun's character: 'Here you are, burning out your life for the sake of a little schoolgirl, and your nights are full of desolate dreams.'[106] Neruda and Hamsun's Pan share being impulsive, with an 'animal' look in their eyes, self-sufficient, and awkward and rough in polite society. He was also alone, like Neruda. The title, *Pan*, links the man with earth: 'I gazed in the clear sea and it was as if I lay face to face with the depths of the earth, and as if my beating heart went out to those depths and was at home there.'[107] This rooting in 'earth' is Romantic and Nerudan. There is more to this Hamsun / Neruda identification. Hamsun's protagonist broods in silence, is proud and shy and cannot confess 'the secret of my heart'. He also longs to travel, like Neruda, 'to go away, I know not where, but far away, perhaps to Africa or to India, for I belong to the forests and solitude'. The novel explores despair and ends with the hero's suicide in India. *Pan* was early translated into Spanish in 1900.[108] Hamsun's first novel *Hunger*, 1890, was cited by André Breton in his first surrealist manifesto in 1924 so that one can see his protagonist as a proto-surrealist with his irrational acts, living poetry. By the turn of the twentieth century, Hamsun 'literally stunned

[103] Hernán Loyola, 'Notas', in Pablo Neruda, *Obras completas 1*, p. 1146.

[104] Tomás Lago on <www.neruda.uchile/critica/tlago.html> and cited in Rodríguez Monegal, *El viajero inmóvil*, p. 42.

[105] See Loyola, *Neruda*, 2006, pp. 77, 220.

[106] Knut Hamsun, *Pan*, p. 86.

[107] Hamsun, *Pan*, p. 15.

[108] In Madrid by A. Hernández-Cata listed online in the Biblioteca Nacional in Santiago.

Europe', wrote Isaac Bashevis Singer, who added that 'the whole school
of fiction in the twentieth century stems from Hamsun'.[109] Once again, we
learn how Neruda read, with that close analogy about a shared isolation and
shyness, where reading is a dialogue with the author, almost a guru–disciple
relationship, where Neruda 'learns' about himself through Hamsun's autobiographical fictions. Hamsun's earlier 1892 novel *Mysteries* could equally have
stimulated Neruda into defining himself as the misfit, the outsider, like Nagel,
who lies, boasts, seduces and plots, who can play the violin, but despises
this talent and rants philosophically against the conformists, ending with
his protagonist's suicide. As Vivekananda wrote, 'no knowledge can come
without a teacher' and Neruda's teacher was his reading.[110]

Within this narrative of twenty-one love poems, then, the first word of the
collection is 'Cuerpo' [body] and the last word 'abandonado' [abandoned].
Between the presence of her body and the poet's accepting that love has died
out lie twenty-one marvellous poems. If each poem is like a chapter in this
love story, it is also important to mention that Neruda did not put titles to the
poems, just numerals, like Bécquer's *Rimas*. There is less guidance for the
reader, who has to plunge into the poems.

Poem 1

Cuerpo de mujer, blancas colinas, muslos blancos,
te pareces al mundo en tu actitud de entrega.
Mi cuerpo de labriego salvaje te socava
y hace saltar el hijo del fondo de la tierra.

Fui solo como un túnel. De mi huían los pájaros.
Y en mí entraba la noche su invasión poderosa.
Para sobrevivirme te forjé como un arma,
como una flecha en mi arco, como una piedra en mi honda.

Pero cae la hora de la venganza y te amo.
Cuerpo de piel, de musgo, de leche ávida y firme.
Ah los vasos del pecho! Ah los ojos de ausencia!
Ah las rosas del pubis! Ah tu voz lenta y triste!

Cuerpo de mujer mía, persistiré en tu gracia.
Mi sed, mi ansia sin límite, mi camino indeciso!
Oscuros cauces donde la sed eterna sigue,
y la fatiga, y el dolor infinito. (PN1 179)

[Body of a woman, white hills, white thighs, / you look like the
world in your attitude of surrender./ My wild peasant's body digs
into you / and makes the son leap from the depth of the earth. /

---

109 Isaac Bashevis Singer, 'Knut Hamsun, Artist of Skepticism', p. ix.
110 Swami Vivekananda, *Raja-Yogas or Conquering the Internal Nature* (Calcutta: Advaita
Ashrama, 1966), p. 150.

I was alone like a tunnel. The birds fled from me, / and night entered me with its powerful invasion. / To survive myself I forged you like a weapon, / like an arrow in my bow, like a stone in my sling. / But the hour of vengeance falls, and I love you. / Body of skin, of moss, of avid and firm milk. / Oh the glasses of the breast! Oh the eyes of absence! / Oh the roses of the pubis! Oh your voice, slow and sad! / Body of my woman, I will persist in your grace. / My thirst, my limitless desire, my shifting path! / Dark riverbeds where eternal thirst follows / and weariness follows and the infinite ache]

The first line of the first poem: 'Cuerpo de mujer, blancas colinas, muslos blancos' (PN1 179), an alexandrine, establishes the metaphoric associations. The first noun is 'body', not soul; the second noun is 'woman', the generic in her body that she shares with all women, and then the twice-repeated adjective 'white', perhaps combining European desirability and the white page (later Neruda writes on her body). Chris Perriam invoked a 1918 poem by Alfonsina Storni – 'Tú me quieres blanca' [you want me white] – as part of Neruda's male idealisation of women, a feminist critique.[111] But poem 13 complicates this use of 'white' and opens with: 'He ido marcando con cruces de fuego / el atlas blanco de tu cuerpo' [I have been marking with crosses of fire the white atlas of your body] where the crosses are his kisses and the white body, the white unexplored areas on the erotic map, is also the white page. Back to poem 1, we have the visual link hill and thigh, 'natural' woman and that taboo-breaking word 'muslo' epitomising her sprawled 'en tu actitud de entrega'. 'Moss' is suggestive of pubic hair and moisture, an enticing analogy. Loyola cites a prose text where Neruda is seduced by a woman in a hay barn: 'y hundí los dedos en un pubis como musgo de las montañas' [and I sunk my fingers in pubic hair like mountain moss].[112] That key term 'entrega' (an euphemism) suggests that the nameless 'woman' passively surrendered herself to the poet sexually, lost her virginity. So far in the poem, the woman is the passive object of male lust. Moran takes into account a possible critique – 'while we may be embarrassed by Neruda's *machismo*', but moves on.[113]

The second couplet brings in the poet, but disguised as 'mi cuerpo de labriego salvaje' [My body of a wild farm-worker]. Now we have two bodies, hers and the 'wild' farm labourer's. The first association of 'labriego' is with Rimbaud's own self-image of the 'paysan' [peasant], too uncouth and brutally honest for sophisticated Paris salons and cafés ('Paysan!').[114] W.

---

[111] Chris Perriam, 'Re-reading Neruda's *Veinte poemas de amor y una canción desesperada*', p. 100.

[112] Loyola, *Neruda*, 2006, p. 90.

[113] Moran, *Veinte poemas*, p. 40.

[114] Rimbaud, *Oeuvres complètes*, p. 116.

S. Merwin evoked Rimbaud in his translation 'rough peasant'. Neruda was never a farmer / peasant; it is his desired self, his imitation of Rimbaud. The 'wildman', noble savage, digs into 'her' and 'makes the son leap from the depth of the earth' (in W. S. Merwin's translation). Here Tagore enters, the poet as gardener, planting his seeds in the woman's furrow.

The second stanza continues to explore the poet's subjectivity and aloneness. We come to the first simile: 'Fui solo como un tunnel.' Nothing elaborate or literary; just the darkness of the lost self (and allusion perhaps to his train-guard father's life). But, in the same line, Neruda swerves into Romantic rhetoric; the cursed poet, the scarecrow, with 'night' invading him. We then move from this literary comparison, but still accurate, to how he first conceived of 'love'. 'Para sobrevivirme, te forjé …' That is, the thought of her – erotic images of thigh and surrender – allowed him to survive the night and loneliness. Neruda comes up with three similes of what he had turned her into; his weapon, an arrow (a Cupid / Red Indian image), a stone in his sling (a biblical David image). The arrow image recalls Rimbaud's *Une Saison en enfer*, and Neruda re-employs it in poem 3: 'Y soltaré en delirio mi bandada de flechas' [And I will loosen deliriously my flight of arrows], obvious erotic metaphor for the joy of release of words and ejaculation. 'Delirio' meshes with Rimbaud's 'Délires', two sections from his *Une Saison en enfer*.

Then the third stanza opens with the most crucial line in the collection: 'Pero cae la hora de la venganza y te amo.' The whole collection is a series of revenges. The shift to the present tense suggests that at the moment of writing, of thinking about her, he realises that he now 'loves her'. What is this revenge? It is hers. She has induced him to 'love' and now he is in thrall to love, its prisoner. In his mind, he repeats the first line as a musical variation: 'Cuerpo de piel, de musgo, de leche ávida y firme': that skin, that 'moss' (natural woman's pubic or armpit hair), that breast of milk (a mother's breast). The associations are muddling, but intense. Then we reach the orgasmic point with four verbless phrases beginning with 'ah', a release of air (the 'h' is not aspirated in Spanish). If a poem is also a musical score, telling us how to read it aloud, Neruda's idiosyncratic use of exclamation marks (in Spanish there should be an inverted one at the start) states clearly, read loud:

> Ah los vasos del pecho! Ah los ojos de ausencia!
> Ah las rosas del pubis! Ah tu voz lenta y triste!

Here we get all the contradictions. The imagined woman is both present with her breasts and pubis (a daring touch for Chile in 1924, though not all critics agree about this) and 'absent'.[115] That last 'triste' could be his view of her

---

[115] See Perriam, 'Re-reading', p. 95: 'Neruda's *Veinte poemas*, although they name pubis, breasts, neck, lips, are also misty and evasive at times (it would, for example, be extremely

post-coital voice, but post-coital blues affects both lovers as Darío chanted in his sonnet 'Mía': 'Yo triste, tú triste' (more on this poem in the next paragraph). It re-enacts the last line of one of Darío's most commented-on sonnets, 'Venus', from *Azul*, 1886, where the woman pities the man: 'y me miraba con triste mirar' [and she looked at me with a sad look]. This litany of erotic statements opening with the 'ah' is repeated as 'oh's in the 'Canción desesperada': 'Oh la boca mordida, oh los besados miembros, / oh los hambrientos dientes, oh los cuerpos trenzados' [Oh the bitten mouth, oh the kissed limbs, / oh the hungry teeth, oh the entwined bodies] (PN1 198), but this later poem is positively erotic. The breast as a 'goblet' (Merwin's translation) and 'milk' lead Moran to speculate that the associations of 'fertility and child-bearing [...] perhaps suggesting, if rather shockingly in this "poetic" context, that her lover is sucking them'.[116] There is a hint, at least, of pregnancy too.

The poem ends with the poet starting a line with the word for her 'body' for the third time, the sheer music of the word 'cuerpo': 'Cuerpo de mujer mía...', but that possessive pronoun rings hollow for she is no longer there and is *not* his. We return to Darío, master poet of frustrated erotic desire. His sonnet 'Mía' confounds the name 'Mia' with the possessive 'mía' (Mine / Mia). The second stanza also boasts an orgasmic union ('¡oh Mía! ¡Oh Mía!'), with the poet's 'sexo fuerte' [strong sex] fusing with her 'sexo', the lovers melted into Rodin-like bronze, but ends in a post-coital sadness: 'Yo triste, tú triste ... / ¿No has de ser entonces / mía hasta la muerte?' [Me sad, you sad ... / will you not then be mine unto death?], parodying the marriage vow, 'til death do us part / 'hasta que la muerte nos separe'.[117] Jaime Concha called Darío's poem the 'cogito poético modernista' [the poetic thinking of *modernismo*].[118] It is safe to assume that Neruda knew it by heart. After announcing her 'body', the defeated poet – 'venganza' – returns to his unrequited love (that the poet was jilted is part of the unfolding drama), his 'sed', his 'ansia sin fin' and still feeling lost in life. The alienating city of Santiago and his aloneness close the poem, with Romantic exaggeration: 'Y la fatiga sigue, y el dolor infinito.' He sounds like a doomed Romantic hero, close in actual words to Spanish Romantic José de Espronceda's self-pitying 'Soledad del alma' [Soul loneliness]: 'lejos de mí, burlando mi *fatiga*, / huyen y aumentan mi fatal tormento / falaces presentándose a mi vista. / ¡*Triste de mí!*' (my italics [far from me, mocking my weariness, they flee and increase my fatal torment / fallaciously presenting themselves to my sight / Sad me!]), or to the final stanza of his 'A una estrella' [To a star]: 'Yo indiferente sigo

---

difficult to concentrate with any precision on a specific sex act in the undoubtedly sensual Poema 3).'

116 Moran, *Veinte poemas*, p. 43.
117 Darío, 1964, p. 55.
118 Concha, p. 193.

mi camino / A merced de los vientos y la mar, / Y entregando en los brazos del destino, / No me importa salvarme o zozobrar' [I indifferently continue my path / At the mercy of winds and sea, / and surrendering to the arms of destiny, / I don't care if I save myself or sink], clearly the same issues and language as Neruda's,[119] but in any way Romantic clichés about being cursed and unloved. The notion of being cursed reappears in poem 11, with its last three lines: 'Ay seguir el camino que se aleja de todo / donde no esté atajando la angustia, la muerte, el invierno, / con sus ojos abiertos entre el rocío' [Ay, to follow the road that leads away from everything / where anguish, death and winter are not lying in wait / with open eyes in the dew] (PN1 187), and in the anguish of feeling 'abandonado' that criss-crosses the collection.

The first poem, then, condenses the poet's inner drama. Language and memory can almost bring 'her' back to him as body, as breasts and pubis but then her absence reminds him all the more of his misery. The perpetual oscillation between her absence and her presence is the 'pain'. Neruda, in Rimbaud's instructions on how to be a poet, is honestly exploring his soul, its poisons, its desires. Bécquer also hides in this memory pain. Neruda's poem 8 addresses 'her' as 'abeja blanca zumbas – ebria de miel – en mi alma' [White bee, you buzz in my soul drunk with honey]. This bee-analogy returns to close the poem: 'Abeja blanca, ausente, aún zumbas en mi alma. / Revives en el tiempo, delgada y silenciosa. / Ah silenciosa' [White bee, absent, you still buzz in my soul. / You revive in time, thin and silent. / Ah silent woman] (PN1 184–5). That his girl-muse is like a bee drunk with honey stretches the realism of analogy as bees also sting. In his memoirs, Neruda associated the 'abeja' with how poems reverberate in his head, that is, with memory again.[120] The poet once wondered in a letter whether he should not become a bee-keeper.[121] The most poignant link between bee, memory and pain is Bécquer's 'rima' LXIII, which opens with this simile:

> Como enjambre de abejas irritadas,
> De un oscuro rincón de la memoria
> Salen a perseguirme los recuerdos
>   De las pasadas horas.
> Yo los quiero ahuyentar. ¡Esfuerzo inútil!
> Y unos tras otros a clavarme viene
> El agudo aguijón que el alma encona.[122]

119 Espronceda, *Obras poéticas 1*, pp. 163, 115.
120 Neruda, *Confieso*, p. 43.
121 Loyola, *Neruda*, 2006, p. 230.
122 Bécquer, *Rimas*, p. 78.

[Like a swarm of irritated bees / in an obscure corner of memory, / memories of past hours / fly out and chase me./ I want to flee them. Useless effort! / And one after another they come to nail with me their sharp sting that inflames my soul]

The woman's revenge on the poet is to make him suffer, to sting him with the memories of herself nailed ('clavar') inside him. He suffers because she is only a mental image, however real (as in dream imagery). She also makes him suffer because most references to her in the poems are of her not talking back. Either she refuses to communicate, or cannot because of distance or is simply impenetrable, but whatever, she causes the pain. In poem 2, she is 'absorta' [absorbed] and 'muda' [mute]. In poem 3, with its evocative opening, she is a 'caracola' [shell] that he literally puts his ear to and hears the earth and rivers sing, but 'tu silencio acosa mis horas perseguidas' [your silence hunts down my pursued hours]. Poem 5 is another lyrical elegy on 'her' not 'listening'. His words get thin 'como las huellas de las gaviotas en las playas' [like the traces of gulls on beaches], an accurate visual metaphor for the transience of his unheard poem. For his words are really 'hers', his poem a 'collar' [necklace], a 'cascabel ebrio' [drunken bell] for her. For she started the war of love: 'Eres tú la culpable de este juego sangriento' [You are guilty of this bloody game]. Poem 7 reiterates her absence with another accurate metaphor of Neruda the frustrated fisherman, unable to trap water in a net: 'Inclinado en las tardes tiro mis tristes redes / a tus ojos oceánicos' [Leaning into the afternoons, I cast my sad nets into your oceanic eyes]. He repeats this image of frustration (a net cannot catch water) in poem 13). He is the shipwrecked man, making red signals to her 'ojos ausentes' [absent eyes] (PN1 183). Poem 8 calls her again 'silenciosa' (three times), and he, the poet, the 'desesperado' who lost everything (her revenge). In poem 13, another lovely poem, he asks her, without reply, for the poem is not a letter, what are you doing now? In poem 15, she is still silent and absent. Federico Schopf brilliantly summarises this 'woman':

The female lover *is* not but *appears* in diverse ways. She is the object of the male lover's sexual pleasure, is represented as a refuge for the poet, is a guide to his longings, a woman in a poet's arms, but more than anything, is unattainable.[123]

---

[123] Schopf, 2000, p. 82: 'La amada no *es*, sino que *aparece* de diversas maneras. Ella es objecto del placer sexual del amante, es representada como refugio para el poeta, es guía de sus anhelos, instrumento de sus propósitos, dominante, dominada, fuerza cósmica y telúrica, mujer entre los brazos del poeta, pero más bien es inalcanzable.'

Most readers would agree with this version, for it counters the biographic reading. 'She' remains, in Keith Ellis's words, 'abstract and nebulous'.[124]

Poem 5

Para que tú me oigas
mis palabras
se adelgazan a veces
como las huellas de las gaviotas en las playas.

Collar, cascabel ebrio
para tus manos suaves como las uvas.

Y las miro lejanas mis palabras.
Más que mías son tuyas.
Van trepando en mi viejo dolor como las yedras.

Ellas trepan así por las paredes húmedas.
Eres tú la culpable de este juego sangriento.

Ellas están huyendo de mi guarida oscura.
Todo lo llenas tú, todo lo llenas.

Antes que tú poblaron la soledad que ocupas,
y están acostumbradas más que tú a mi tristeza.

Ahora quiero que digan lo que quiero decirte
para que tú las oigas como quiero que me oigas.

El viento de la angustia aún las suele arrastrar.
Huracanes de sueños aún a veces las tumban.
Escuchas otras voces en mi voz dolorida.
Llanto de viejas bocas, sangre de viejas súplicas.
Ámame, compañera. No me abandones. Sígueme.
Sígueme, compañera, en esa ola de angustia.

Pero se van tiñendo de amor mis palabras.
Todo lo ocupas tú, todo lo ocupas.

Voy haciendo de todas un collar infinito
para tus blancas manos, suaves como las uvas. (PN1 181–2)

[So that you will hear me / my words / sometimes grow thin / like the tracks of seagulls on the beaches. / Necklace, drunken bell / for your hands soft as grapes. / And I watch my words far off, / more than mine they're yours. / They climb on my old suffering like ivy. / They climb thus up damp walls. / You are to blame for this bloody game. / They flee my dark lair. / You fill everything, you fill everything. / Before you, they peopled the solitude you occupy, / and they're used more than you to my sadness. / Now I

124   Keith Ellis, 'La búsqueda infructuosa en *Veinte poemas de amor y una canción desesperada*', p. 55.

want them to say what I want to say to you / so that you hear me as
I want you to hear. / The wind of anguish still drags them. / Hurri-
canes of dreams still knock them over. / You hear other voices in
my painful voice. / Weeping of old mouths, blood of old suppli-
cations. / Love me, companion. Do not forsake me. Follow me. /
Follow me, companion, in that wave of anguish. / But my words
become dyed with your love. / You occupy everything, you occupy
everything. / I am making of them an infinite necklace / for your
white hands, soft as grapes]

This lovely poem deals with the way words work in a poem when the reader
is the absent lover. Can the poet's lover hear his words when he is distant?
Separation is the lover's curse. There's a deep frustration about how written
words reach her. The poem's opening formally mimics that 'thinning', while
the simile introduces a cluster of rich associations – the long, empty beaches
near Temuco, with their gulls and how fragile writing is, so easily washed
away. Neruda is the gull, writing in the sand with its feet (sea birds haunt the
West Coast Latin Americans; Vallejo was an 'alcatraz' [gannet] in the first
poem of his *Trilce*).

The second stanza offers us the central image of the 'collar' made up of
words that the poet writes for her to wear around her neck. She can then touch
his words as if stroking him, with 'tus manos suaves como las uvas'. That
sound 'suave-uva' and its association with a lover brushing the poet's skin,
where the shape of the finger's pad is compared to a grape, is a perfect visual
correlative as well as being the metonymic fruit of Chile, with Biblical echoes
from the Song of Songs that reveals the poet's craft. That second stanza is
repeated, slightly modified, as the last stanza: 'Voy haciendo de todas un
collar infinito / Para tus blancas manos, sauves como las uvas.'

The rest of the poem reflects on the poet-lover's words as 'lejanas' and
more hers than his. His pointless words climb up his pain like ivy (another
Romantic term). He accuses his lover: 'Eres tú la culpable de este juego
sangriento' (already cited), where the game is as much his poetry as it is
love (as Dominic Moran noted).[125] The poet's words flee from him, words
that used to accompany him. Words, still the subject of the poem, are no
compensation for her absence, words that 'están acostumbradas más que tú a
mi tristeza'. The poet is forcing abstract words to say 'lo que quiero decirte'
so that she can *hear* them. We will be returning to the stress on 'hearing'
rather than 'reading'. But his actual state, as he is writing alone, is anguish
(that word 'angustia', one of Darío's key words, is repeated throughout the
collection), and dreams (another crucial noun). As a poet, Neruda shows he
is aware that he writes out of a tradition of earlier poets, which he has read

---

[125] Moran, *Veinte poemas*, pp. 70–1.

intensely in his isolation, in two poignant lines that summarise his debts
without naming one poet:

> Escuchas otras voces en mi voz dolorida.
> Llanto de viejas bocas, sangre de viejas súplicas.

The poet then begs his absent muse in two lines that summarise the whole
collection as love song:

> Amame, compañera. No me abandones. Sígueme.
> Sígueme, compañera, en esa ola de angustia.

Here is the myth of the courtly-lover seeking impossible love, and left alone
with his creative anguish, the source of his writing as an 'ola', the cold waves
and wind of the Temucan beaches.

Poem 17

> Pensando, enredando sombras en la profunda soledad.
> Tú también estás lejos, ah más lejos que nadie.
> Pensando, soltando pájaros, desvaneciendo imágenes,
> enterrando lámparas.
> Campanario de brumas, qué lejos, allá arriba!
> Ahogando lamentos, moliendo esperanzas sombrías,
> molinero taciturno,
> se te viene de bruces la noche, lejos de la ciudad.
>
> Tu presencia es ajena, extraña a mí como una cosa.
> Pienso, camino largamente, mi vida antes de ti.
> Mi vida antes de nadie, mi áspera vida.
> El grito frente al mar, entre las piedras,
> corriendo libre, loco, en el vaho del mar.
> La furia triste, el grito, la soledad del mar.
> Desbocado, violento, estirado hacia el cielo.
>
> Tú, mujer, qué eras allí, qué raya, qué varilla
> de esa abanico inmenso? Estabas lejos como ahora.
> Incendio en el bosque! Arde en cruces azules.
> Arde, arde, llamea, chispea en árboles de luz.
> Se derrumba, crepita. Incendio. Incendio.
>
> Y mi alma baila herida de virutas de fuego.
> Quién llama? Qué silencio poblado de ecos?
> Hora de la nostalgia, hora de la alegría, hora de la soledad,
> hora mía entre todas!
>
> Bocina en que el viento pasa cantando.
> Tanta pasión de llanto anudada a mi cuerpo.
> Sacudida de todas las raíces,
> asalto de todas las olas!

Rodaba alegre, triste, interminable, mi alma.
Pensando, enterrrando lámparas en la profunda soledad.
Quíen eres tú, quién eres? (PN1 192–3)

[Thinking, tangling shadows in the deep solitude. / You are far away,
ah further than anybody. / Thinking, releasing birds, dissolving
images, / burying lamps. / Belfry of mists, how far, how high! /
Stifling laments, milling shadowy hopes, / taciturn miller, / night
falls flat on you, far from the city. / Your presence is alien, strange
to me as a thing. / I think, I walk for ages, my life before you.
My life before anybody, my harsh life. / The shout facing the
sea, among the stones, / running free, mad in the sea mist. / Sad
fury, the shout, the solitude of the sea. / Bolted, violent, stretched
towards the sky. / You, woman, what were you there, what ray,
what vane of that immense fan? You were far away like now. /
Fire in the wood! It burns in blue crosses. // It burns, burns, spar-
kles in trees of light. / It collapses, crackles. Fire. Fire. / And my
soul dances wounded with curls of fire. Who calls? What silence
peopled with echoes? / Hour of nostalgia, hour of happiness, hour
of solitude, / my hour among all of them! / Hooter in which the
wind passes singing / So much passion of weeping knotted to my
body. / Shaken of all roots, / Attack of all the waves! / My soul
rolled, happy, sad, interminablel. / Thinking, burying lamps in the
profound solitude. / Who are you, who are you?]

Emir Rodríguez Monegal, Neruda's first biographer, rightly called poem 17
the 'ars poetica' of the collection. It is a turbulent, reflective poem about how
the mind works. The gerund that opens the poem, 'pensando', suggests a
mental activity that never ends. Neruda often linked 'thinking' with 'poetry',
as did André Breton in his definition of surrealism in his first manifesto,
when he underlined '… le fonctionnement réel de la pensée. Dictée de la
pensée …' [the real functioning of thought. Dictated by thought].[126] Immediately, though, Neruda decodes this complex process called 'thinking' (rather
than thought) as 'enredando sombras en la profunda soledad' (PN1 192).
Thinking is a metaphor of your trapped self, that inner life that nobody can
see, that metaphor of your essential alone-ness. The first poem collected in
the posthumous 'Los cuadernos [notebooks] de Neftalí Reyes' is a Chopin- /
Darío-derived 'Nocturno' and its first line is 'Es de noche: medito triste y
solo' [It is night. I meditate, sad and alone] (PN4 53); the verb 'pienso' [I
think] occurs twice. So the source of Neruda's thinking is the adolescent's
bitter self-questioning. Perriam aptly sees this poem casting a 'network of
shadowy, self-reflexive, existential doubt across the book'.[127]

126 Breton, *Manifestes du surréalisme*, p. 40.
127 Perriam, 'Re-reading', p. 99.

The third line picks up on the same gerund 'pensando' and again decodes it as 'soltando pájaros, desvaneciendo imágenes, enterrando lámparas'; again that dark inner life of poetic thought (birds), images that fade and lights that are buried in the dark. Thinking cannot solve lovesickness. Take 'lámparas', a metaphor for 'reason' and light, and surely the poet's sense that he has to dig deeper into the dark. Neruda piles on the analogies to thinking; a 'campanario de brumas', where the poet, now a 'molinero taciturno', mills dark hopes. The verb changes to the present tense in the second stanza, 'pienso', as the poet walks along the seashore surveying his bitter life.

Seeded through the poem are also lines evoking the woman, but she is distant, alien and foreign now to him, like a 'thing'. She was always distant. In the coastal twilight Neruda summarises his affair at the moment of writing: 'Hora de la nostalgia, hora de la alegría, hora de la soledad, hora mía entre todas!'(PN1 193). That chain of associations: nostalgia, joy, loneliness are the key features of love as suffering. He exclaims: 'Tanta pasión de llanto anudada a mi cuerpo': passion as suffering, as tears, knotted into his body, his gut emotions. Love has shaken his roots from him 'sacudida de todas las raíces'; the waves now assault him, endlessly. The poem closes with the third reference to 'pensando' (better not to think) as burying lights in the deep solitude. The poet then asks the identity question that could be about her and about himself. Lovesickness has shaken his inner certainty, and his 'Je' is now 'autre': 'Quién eres tú, quién eres?' – perhaps gender uncertainty, as Perriam notes from earlier critics.[128]

Poem 20

This celebrated poem articulates the relationship between craft and integrity. A poet can, has the verbal skills to, write about anything. The real poet writes about what he has to, for a deeper necessity controls his rhetoric. So Neruda opens this famous poem: 'Puedo escribir los versos más tristes esta noche' [I can write the saddest lines this night] (PN1 195). That he 'can' is the issue; he could pretend to a great passion, or not admit that she took revenge on him in her absence. You could argue, with de Costa, that the 'real subject of this composition is not the speaker's stated sadness but the disparity between the sentiment and the words he can summon to express what he feels'.[129] That 'esta' is also crucial, being the 'now' of writing, and 'night' is the propitious time when the work world sleeps. He asserts: 'Escribir, por ejemplo' [To write, for example] and then gives a lyrical example about stars twinkling blue in the distance, perhaps echoing Poe's 'While the stars that oversprinkle

128   Perriam, 'Re-reading', p. 103.
129   De Costa, 1979, p. 29.

/ All the heavens, seem to twinkle' from 'The Bells'.[130] But the emotional truth is that 'el viento de la noche gira en el cielo y canta' [the wind spins in the sky and sings]. 'Wind' is another crucial word in Neruda's poetics. This natural invisible force, almost the lovers' inspiration, appears in poem 4, which is a poem about the wind, as a wind 'latiendo sobre nuestro silencio enamorado' [beating on our enamoured silence]. The sound of the wind is 'como una lengua llena de guerras y cantos' [like a tongue full of wars and songs] so that the cold Patagonian wind enacts the lovers' bickering. Wind reappears again in poem 14 in a line without verbs: 'El viento. El viento' [The wind. The wind.]. Poem 18 confirms that emotional link between the lovers and nature: 'Y como yo te amo, los pinos en el viento' [And as I love you, wind in the pines]. In June 1923 Neruda outlined his life in a letter: 'I was born and lived in a village full of rain and immense winds' (PN5 933).[131]

At this point, poem 20 then summarises the affair: 'Yo la quise, y a veces ella también me quiso' [I loved her, and she at times also loved me], in the past, and employing the verb 'querer' rather than 'amar'. Nothing falsely poetic in asserting that he once held her in his arms and kissed her. He repeats, as a musical variation, that she once loved him and he, sometimes, loved her. Honesty, then, drives the poet: 'Pensar que no la tengo. Sentir que la he perdido' [To think I have her. To feel I have lost her]. He concludes brusquely: 'Eso es todo' [That's all]. But the pain still hurts: 'Mi alma no se contenta con haberla perdido' [My soul is not happy with losing her]; here 'soul' is that deeper irrational part of the self that still seeks her and she is not there. He repeats the refrain: 'Ya no la quiero' [I now longer love her], aware that they have both changed: 'ya no somos los mismos' [we are no longer the same]. And, in another turn of the screw, 'De otro. Será de otro' [Another's. She will be another's]. He repeats, so that repetition drives the poem, that 'yo no la quiero' and that his 'alma' [soul] does not accept her loss. And the poem closes with the thought that she might not cause more pain and this 'poem' we have just read or recited, 'sean los últimos versos que yo le escribo' [be the last lines that I write her]. It is obvious now that the addressee of the poem is 'her' and that each poem in the collection is a letter to her, as well as a monologue, a confession of the revenge she has wreaked.

The everyday, colloquial tone of the poem make it very modern, but also echoes two of Paul Verlaine's poems, also in couplets and equally direct. Note the Nerudan repetition in 'O, triste, triste' from *Romances sans paroles*:

---

[130] Poe, *The Portable Edgar Allan Poe*, p. 634.

[131] See Keith Ellis on the wind as ubiquitous in the collection, both an actual wind and 'la materialización invisible, inesperada e incontrolable de la inquietud causada por el amor', p. 56.

O triste, triste était mon âme
A cause, à cause d'une femme.

Je ne me suis pas consolé
Bien que mon coeur s'en soit allé,

Bien que mon coeur, bien que mon âme
Eussent fui loin de cette femme ...[132]

[Oh sad, sad was my soul / because, because of a woman. / I did
not console myself / although my heart has gone, / Although my
heart, although my soul, have flown far from that woman]

Verlaine's 'Colloque sentimental' [Sentimental chat], the closing poem of
Fêtes galantes, also moves forward in couplets and analyses an affair between
two lovers strolling in a park as they chat:

Dans le vieux parc solitaire et glacé,
Deux spectres ont evoqués le passé.

–Te souvient-il de notre extase ancienne?
–Porquoi voulez-vous donc qu'il m'en souvienne?

–Ton coeur bat-il toujours á mon seul nom?
Toujours vois-tu mon âme en rêve? – Non.

–Ah! Les beaux jours de bonheur indicible
Où nous joignons nos bouches! – C'est possible. ...[133]

[In the old park, frozen and alone, Two ghosts have evoked the
past. / 'Do you recall our old ecstasy?' / 'Why should I want to
think of that?' / 'Does your heart still beat to my name alone?
When you dream, is it me you dream about?' 'No.' / Oh the sweet
days of our happiness beyond words / where we joined our lips!'
'It's possible.']

Neruda first read this poem in Enrique Díez-Canedo's 1913 anthology of
French poetry where 'Coloquio sentimental' was translated by the Mexican
poet Enrique González Martínez.[134]

---

[132] Paul Verlaine, *Oeuvres poétiques complètes*, p. 195. See also Verlaine, *Selected Poems*,
pp. 72–4.

[133] Verlaine, *Oeuvres poétiques complètes*, p. 121.

[134] Díez-Canedo, *La poesía francesa*, pp. 224–5. Díez-Canedo's 'Advertencia preliminar'
states that it is the 1913 edition updated (p. 5).

'La canción desesperada'

The poet writes in poem 8 that 'Soy el desesperado, la palabra sin ecos, / el que lo perdió todo, y el que todo lo tuvo' [I'm the desperate one, the word without echoes, he who lost it all and had it all], with its rythmical imitation of Nerval's sonnet 'El desdichado' : 'Je suis le ténébreux, – le veuf, – l'inconsolé' [I am the sombre man, the widower, the unconsoled]. The key term 'desesperado' is reflected in the final poem, which rounds up the love story: 'Emerge tu recuerdo de la noche en que estoy' [Your memory emerges from the night where I am] (PN1 197). At night, the poet continues to be tortured by her 'image', but makes the crucial decision to move on in the second stanza (and repeated at the end of the poem): 'Abandonado como los muelles en el alba. / Es la hora de partir, oh abandonado!' [Abandonded like the wharves at dawn. It's the hour of departure, Oh abandoned one!]. Neruda has identified these 'muelles' as real, in Carahue and Bajo Imperial on the river mouth. Dawn arrives and he now knows that love is suffering and despair, the title of the last poem. He has been woken up to his actual state: an orphan of love, left abandoned. He addresses himself as the 'abandoned one'. And it is time to move on. I think it is clear that to be abandoned by love includes the death of his birth-mother when he was two months old, but essentially it concerns actual women. This is another 'farewell' poem, like Rimbaud's 'Adieu' in his *Une Saison en enfer*. The poem ends, 29 stanzas on, by repeating these terms, but inverted: 'Es la hora de partir. Oh abandonado!' But this is not self-pity. The poet has been abandoned as a lover in order to move on and become a real poet. There is an echo of Christ's despair on the cross for 'why hast thou forsaken me?' is translated in Spanish as 'Por qué me has abandonado'. He offers further versions of himself: six rhythmical times as 'naufragio', a sea-image alluding back to *Paul et Virginie* and the shipwreck on the coral reef. He also calls himself a 'hondero', alluding perhaps to young poet David's sling (as in Michelangelo's famous sculpture) or to the Mapuche who used slings in war and several other poems and a 'faro', alluding to Victor Hugo and Baudelaire and twice, a 'buzo ciego' [blind diver], hinting at going deep into water (and associating himself with a futurist / avant-garde version of the poet). In a wonderful image he also recalls the torture of love as still hurting him: 'Cementerio de besos, aún hay fuego en tus tumbas' [Cemetery of kisses, there's still fire in your tombs], itself a reworking of Quevedo's heterodoxic sonnet 'Amor constante más allá de la muerte' [Constant love beyond death], where the lover's body 'serán ceniza, mas tendrán sentido / Polvo serán, mas polvo enamorado' [will become ash, but still retain meaning / Dust they'll be, but dust in love].[135] Three lines repeat the orgasmic physicality of this love, and echo poem 1: 'Oh carne, carne mía, mujer que amé y perdí' [Oh flesh, my

---

[135] Quevedo, *Antología poética*, p. 24.

flesh, woman that I loved and lost], followed, seven stanzas later, by another apostrophe: 'Oh la boca mordida' [oh the bitten mouth] and 'Oh la cópula loca' [oh the crazy copulation]. All he has left are painful memories: 'Sólo la sombra trémula se retuerce en mis manos' [Only the tremulous shadow twists in my hands]. He has finally become the 'desventurado hondero' [luckless slinger], a link also with his delayed collection *El hondero entusiasta*. She is now a shadow in his mind and writhes in his poet's hand (Neruda wrote with a fountain pen in green ink). Marine comparisons are natural given Chile's coastline, referred to in this poem as 'el cinturón ruidoso del mar [que] ciña la costa' [The rustling belt of sea girdles the coast].

Neruda must travel abroad to become himself: 'Ah más allá de todo. Ah más allá' [Ah beyond everything, ah beyond]. Real life is elsewhere, over the horizon, 'là-bas', wrote Baudelaire several times. The collection ends with Neruda's gloss on 'Le voyage'. Baudelaire wrote: 'mais les vrais voyageurs sont ceux-là qui partent / pour partir; coeurs légers' [but the true travellers are those who leave / for leaving, light-hearted]. Neruda saw himself in his poem as a 'descubridor', one of the voyagers of old who were driven to leave home, wife and domesticity, like Ulysses, for a woman and love tie you down: 'la femme, esclave vile …' [woman, vile slave]. Baudelaire closed his complex poem: 'O Mort, vieux capitaine, il est temps! Levons l'ancre. / Ce pays nous ennuie, o Mort! Appareillons!' [O death, old captain. It's time. Let's raise the anchor. / This country annoys us, Oh Death. Let's set sail].[136] Neruda lifts anchor, now a poet 'de pie como un marino en la proa de un barco' [standing like a sailor on the prow of a boat]. This buried allusion to classic discoverers will bear fruit when he finally leaves for Rangoon, Burma in 1927. But he sees himself as heroic, on the front-line, an avant-gardist on his 'proa'. 'Proa' was the name chosen by Jorge Luis Borges in 1921 for his avant-garde magazine in neighbouring Buenos Aires. Neruda has freed himself of his love for being in love, and being 'abandoned' really means becoming a traveller, a nomad, another Rimbaud who, aged 19, travelled East, settling in the Aden and Harar district of the Red Sea. But he had reached as far as Batavia, Java in 1876 on a Scottish ship named, appropriately, *The Wandering Chief.* The coincidence is that Neruda himself would end up in Batavia (today Jakarta) in 1929.

Another much-cited poem, Mallarmé's 'Brise marine', itself a reworking of Baudelaire, articulates, as already noted, a surfeit of books and a need to escape: 'Fuir! Là-bas fuir!' [To flee. To flee over there] to be with the ocean foam, away from blank paper and a woman with a baby:

---

    136 Baudelaire, *Les Fleurs*, p. 158.

Je partirai! Steamer balançant ta mâture,
Léve l'ancre pour une exotique nature!

[I will leave. Steamer balancing its masts, / raise the anchor for
exotic nature]

To leave, in this wonderful poem, even if the storms break the masts and
there are 'naufrages' [shipwrecks], and the word crosses over to Neruda,
to end: 'mais, ô mon coeur, entends le chant des matelots!' [but, oh my
heart, listen to the song of the sailors].[137] That is the siren song in the shell
that beckons Neruda. Neruda knew this poem by heart, and first read it in
Alfonso Reyes's translation in Díez-Canedo's 1913 anthology, where the
word 'naufragio' appears, as does the final call '¡He de partir al fin!' so that
Mallarmé now sounds like Neruda.[138] And once more, there is Rimbaud who
ends his extraordinary poem 'Les poètes de sept ans' [Poets aged seven]
with the poet lying on the floor day-dreaming on some linen 'et pressentant
violemment la voile' [divining violently the sail]. That adverb, and that transformation of linen into sail, re-enacts the transformative power of poetry.[139]

Learning French to read French poetry fed his secret ambitions. It was also
an erotic urge. Neruda once boasted that at the old docks of Carahue he read
the entire novel sequence of *Juan Cristóbal*, without naming the author. This
experience is one of the few times that Neruda linked reading and writing
with a specific place. I cite:

In a slim, long, abandoned boat, from which sunken ship I do not know,
I read the whole of *Juan Cristóbal* and wrote the 'canción desesperada'.
Above my head, the blue was so violent like I've never seen it again. I
wrote in the boat, hidden on land. I believe that I have never again felt so
tall and so deep as in those days. Above, the blue, impenetrable sky. In my
hands *Juan Cristóbal* or the lines born in my poem. Near me all that existed
and continued to exist for ever in my poetry: the distant sound of the sea,
the cry of the wild birds, and the burning love that did not consume itself
like the immortal bush.[140]

---

137 Mallarmé, *Oeuvres complètes*, p. 38.
138 Díez-Canedo, *La poesía francesa*, p. 241.
139 Rimbaud, *Oeuvres complètes*, p. 45.
140 Neruda, *Confieso*, p. 71: 'En un esbelto y largo bote abandonado, de no sé qué barco
náufrago, leí entero el *Juan Cristóbal* y escribí la "Canción desesperada". Encima de mi cabeza
tenía un azul tan violento como jamás he visto otro. Yo escribía en el bote, escondido en la
tierra. Creo que no he vuelto a ser tan alto y tan profundo como en aquellos días. Arriba el
cielo azul impenetrable. En mis manos el *Juan Cristóbal* o los versos nacientes de mi poema.
Cerca de mí todo lo que existió y siguió existiendo para siempre en mi poesía: el ruido lejano
del mar, el grito de los pájaros salvajes, y el amor ardiendo sin consumirse como una zarza
inmortal.'

Crucial to grasping Neruda's poetic formation is this link between sounds of the sea, a wrecked boat, reading a novel and writing the 'Canción desesperada', all as one interlocked continuum. Concerning Romain Rolland's (1866–1944) novel sequence, Neruda must have gone down to the river and sat in the boat for days on end as the novel extended to ten volumes (it won Rolland the Nobel Prize in 1915), opening with *L'Aube* [dawn] in 1904 and closing in 1912. This novel sequence follows the birth and development of a solitary young man, son of a drunkard of a musician, in Germany. It appears that Neruda read it in Spanish. Later, he would insist in a letter that Albertina read this novel, as if it narrated his own *bildungsroman*.[141] No critic has followed up this conjunction of the last poem and this novel sequence.

Tagore, Neruda and poem 16

An early scandal emerged in 1934 in the literary magazine *Pro* (of Buenos Aires) when Neruda was anonymously (actually it was Volodia Teitelboim) accused of plagiarising a poem written by the Bengali poet Rabindranath Tagore. The two poems were simply placed opposite each other: Neruda's poem 16 against Tagore's poem 30 from *The Gardener*, translated from the English by New York-born Zenobia Camprubí de Jiménez, that is, the great Juan Ramón Jiménez's wife (another Neruda antagonist). The method is conclusive: Neruda's prose poem's second paragraph: 'Eres mía, eres mía de labios dulces y viven en tu vida mis infinitos sueños' [You are mine, you are mine of sweet lips and my infinite dreams live in your life] meshes with 'Eres mía, eres mía, y vives en mis sueños solitarios' [You are mine, you are mine and live in my solitary dreams] and more. This plagiarism led to attacks on Neruda's integrity by enemies like Pablo de Rokha and Vicente Huidobro. Rokha still censured Neruda in 1967: 'All his work is pure plagiarism, even the titles ... he copies Tagore and Carlos Sabat Ercasty, Baudelaire, Rimbaud and Chennevière and steals factory, pre-factory and counter-factory from me, the nuptial feast of his poetics of pale rhetoric ...,' though he ridiculously overstated his case.[142] Huidobro simply reprinted the *Pro* comparison in his magazine *Vital* in January 1935. This was repeated a third time in Chile in a surrealist magazine edited by Braulio Arenas, and backed by Huidobro, in *Mandrágora* 4, out in July 1940. And this despite Neruda in 1937 having added a note into the latest edition of his *Veinte poemas* that it was public

---

141 *Cartas de amor*, p. 307.
142 Pablo de Rokha, cited in *Estudios Públicos*, p. 400: 'Toda su obra es plagio total, hasta los títulos [...], copia a Tagore y a Carlos Sabat Ercasty, a Baudelaire, Rimbaud, Chenneviere y saqueándome fábrica, pre-fábrica, contra-fábrica el ágape nupcial de su poética en retórica pálida ...'

knowledge that he had simply 'paraphrased' Tagore's poem.[143] We have a
literary war between two terms 'paraphrase' and 'plagiarism'. This must be
seen in two contexts. The first is T. S. Eliot's famous quip that 'immature
poets imitate; mature poets steal'.[144] That is, all poetry emerges from reading
poetry. In Neruda's case, this is complicated because he rarely included other
poets explicitly in his verse, except as people (poems about his friends García
Lorca, Miguel Hernández etc.). An irony is that Neruda carried over Camprubi's translation 'howler'. Tagore translated himself: 'With the shadow of my
passion have I darkened your eyes, Haunter of the depth of my gaze.'[145] But
Camprubi misread 'haunter' for 'hunter' ['cazadora'], and so did Neruda.

The great Neruda myth is that his poetry comes from life, not other poems.
The second point is more striking and is that we can learn how Neruda read
from this incident. Because one of his real-life female muses loved Tagore's
poem, his love poem to her was to share this reading as his own. The differences between Tagore and Neruda are thus more interesting; what he adds.
The Tagore poem is gently despairing while Neruda's passion has him
shouting: '... voy gritando en la brisa / de la tarde, y el viento arrastra mi
voz viuda' [I go shouting in the breeze / of the evening and the wind drags
my widowed voice]. Equally, the wonderful closing line is his: 'En tus ojos de
luto comienza el país del sueño' [In your eyes of mourning begins the country
of dream]. Note how the distant woman is in mourning, leaving the poet's
voice 'a widower'. The word 'viudo' again echoes Nerval's 'veuf' in 'El
desdichado'. Her eyes announce the death of love and leave Neruda dreaming.
Rewriting Tagore is his attempt to stop being the 'veuf'. W. B. Yeats recognised this 'sharing' a poem syndrome: 'Lovers, while they wait one another,
shall find, in murmuring them (Tagore's poems) [...] a magic gulf wherein
their own more bitter passion may bathe and renew its youth.'[146]

Tagore had just won the Nobel Prize in literature in 1913, mainly based
on his *Gitanjali*, 1910; he had been translated into Spanish by the wife of
the leading Spanish poet of his times and in English was promoted by W. B.
Yeats and in French by André Gide. Neruda from farflung Chile was not far
behind in absorbing the 'new', the fashionable, if not avant-garde. Years later
in an article of 1940 Neruda recognised how he stirred up hatred in others
('Amistades y enemistades literarias'): 'Maybe nobody in these regions has

---

143   See René de Costa's account in *En pos de Huidobro*, pp. 95–107 and Leonardo Sanhueza's compilation, *El Bacalao. Diatribas antinerudianas y otros textos*, pp. 19–31.

144   T. S. Eliot, 'Philip Massinger', in *Selected Essays* (London: Faber, 1934), p. 206.

145   Tagore, *The Gardener*, p. 58. Noted also by Moran, *Veinte poemas*, p. 145.

146   W. B. Yeats, 'Introduction', in *Gitanjali*, p. xv.

had the bad luck to release so much envy as my literary persona. There are people who live from this profession of envying me.'[147]

Dostoyevsky and Neruda

Another fascinating insight into Neruda's mental life emerges from his claim that 'in truth I am scarce with words, my true intimacy is bestowed in my poems', that is, his real self emerges in his identification with what he read and wrote.[148] In an interview in 1983, Albertina Azócar, alias Marisol, confessed that her favourite nickname was 'Netocha'.[149] In a letter to her, Neruda promised to send her the novel. We know that Gabriela Mistral initiated the young Neruda into the thrill of reading Russian fiction; Tomás Lago recalled that Russian literature was read avidly by all his generation.[150] Neruda read Dostoyevsky's first and unfinished novel of 1849 with such passion that he was Netocha. There were two translations into Spanish published in 1921.[151] In the novel, she narrates her desperate growing up with a drunkard of a musician step-father and poor mother, whom she despised. How she observed that her step-father preferred his boast about being a great musician to actually playing his sacred violin; he got drunk and begged in order not to test his boasting. So Netocha, herself a singer, is witness to how creativity and fantasy overlap. Neruda was also growing up as a poet, with censorious parents, forced to conceal his 'poems'. The novel is also about secret passions and failed love affairs, with a lover's farewell letter found folded into a novel. Netocha had also fallen in love with a young girl. So the artistic life and passionate love as the core of experience became a mirror for taciturn Neruda in Temuco.

Netocha overhears two men talking about her step-father:

> He's a dreamer, he imagines that all of a sudden, at the wave of a wand, he'll become the most famous person in the world ... But if such a feeling becomes the main source of an artist's activity then he ceases to be an

---

[147] Neruda, 'Amistades y enemistades literarias', p. 1050: 'Tal vez a nadie por estas tierras le haya tocado en suerte desencadenar tantas envidias como a mi persona literaria. Hay gente que vive de esta profesión, de envidiarme ...' See also Edmundo Olivares, *Pablo Neruda: los caminos del mundo*, pp. 177–81 for another survey of this squabble.

[148] Letter to Carlos Morla, 19 March 1931, in Pablo Neruda, *Epistolario viajero (1927–1973)*, p. 63.

[149] Mónica Guzmán, entrevista con Albertina Azócar, *ABC*, 23 de septiembre de 1983, p. 53.

[150] Cited by Rodríguez Monegal, *El viajero inmóvil*, p. 42.

[151] Listed in George O. Schanzer, *Russian Literature in the Hispanic World: a Bibliography* (Toronto: University of Toronto Press, 1972). Thanks to Dr David Henn for this information.

artist, for he has lost the artist's chief instinct. Which must be to love art simply because it is art, and not for its rewards.[152]

Here is the clue to Neruda's ambitions. Sincerity, love for art itself, is greater than day-dreaming or social prestige. But also, paradoxically, one dreams of being an artist as a dream of freedom. Netochka, on her way to her singing classes, revelled in her happiness: 'I loved music with passionate though diffident hope; I built castles in the air, pictured the most marvellous future and often, as I returned home, was quite transported by my own happiness.'[153] The novel also suggests how Neruda read. Netochka steals a key and takes forbidden books from a library:

> The bookcase was full of novels. I took one of them, shut the bookcase, and took the book off to my room with such a strange sensation and with such throbbing and fluttering of the heart that it was as if I foresaw that a great transformation was going to take place in my life.[154]

Reading novels, then, is a rite of passage, a transgression of the social order. Books promised a fuller, more exciting life. Netochka again: 'I was destined to live through that future by getting to know it first in books, experiencing it in dreams ...' This novel reveals why early reading is so much more formative, for it expresses the shy, rebellious inner self.

Proust and Neruda

Neruda's passion for reading and rereading Proust is not strange. He revealed this love in his memoirs as related to reliving his first adolescent love affairs, but it could also be tied in with the long sensuous sentences, with that analytic vein, exploring memory, love, habit, desire and writing, and with dedicating a life to writing one continuous work. A Proustian reading of Neruda would focus on how, within his writing, like Proust, he offers his readers 'analysis'. Philosophy is embedded in sensations and experiences, not in disembodied ideas. While marooned in Wellawata, Ceylon as consul, Neruda confessed that 'I never read with such pleasure and such abundance as in that suburb of Colombo where I lived alone.'[155] One particular incident stirred him concerning Proust's invented composer Vinteuil's piece of music.

---

152 Fyodor Dostoyevsky, *Netochka Nezvanova*, translated by Jane Kentish (London: Penguin Books, 1985), p. 51.

153 Dostoyevsky, *Netochka Nezvanova*, p. 150.

154 Dostoevsky, *Netochka Nezvanova*, p. 129.

155 Neruda, *Confieso*, p. 133: 'nunca leí con tanto placer y tanta abundancia como en aquel suburbio de Colombo en que viví solitario'.

Neruda guessed (wrongly) that it was based on César Franck's Sonata for violin and piano, got hold of the record and played it endlessly. What Neruda took from Proust was related to his own past: 'His words led me to relive my own life, my distant lost feelings in my self.'[156] The key word is 'revivir' [relive] and it was the 'torments, loves and jealousies of my adolescence'. Jealousy is the Proustian emotion. Neruda pursued a woman who rejected him for a poet friend, and her name was Albertina. He was still trying to lure her back in 1932, after both had married other people. Proust named Albertine more than any other character – 2360 times, according to Edmund White. This biographic overlap between the Albertinas and unrequited love underlines how we read through subjective allusions. Neruda could never possess his Albertina; just reading her name in Proust woke up his anxiety of loss. Samuel Beckett read Proust about the same time (in 1931). He quoted Proust's: 'One only loves that which is not possessed, one only loves that in which one pursues the inaccessible' and added: 'that desert of loneliness and recrimination that men call love'.[157] A perfect description of why Neruda read Proust and what love – its effect on himself, his suffering – had become for him.

Can we trust Neruda when he says he read *all* Proust several times? Only by 1927 (the last volume published) were Proust's 4300 pages available in French (he had died in 1922). I hazard that Neruda only reread the first volume, *Du côté de chez Swann*, which deals with young-love, a love 'never reciprocated', and defined by 'wild attacks of jealousy'; he was rereading his own life.[158]

---

[156] Neruda, *Confieso*, p. 134: 'Sus palabras me condujeron a revivir mi propia vida, mis lejanos sentimientos perdidos en mí mismo.'

[157] Samuel Beckett, *Proust*, pp. 50–4.

[158] Edmund White, *Proust* (London: Weidenfeld & Nicolson, 1999), p. 96.

2

The 1920s: from *El hondero entusiasta* to *El habitante y su esperanza*

El hondero entusiasta (1923–24), 1933

Hernán Loyola, in his notes to Neruda's complete poems, establishes the genealogy of this aborted collection, as an ambitious project begun in the early 1920s, concurrently with the *Veinte poemas de amor*.[1] Neruda tucked them away until he returned to Chile from the Far East in 1931 and published a selection of these poems. He prefaced them with an 'advertencia del autor' [foreword] and blamed their defect on too close an imitation of the Uruguayan poet Carlos Sabat Ercasty (1887–1982), whose work he had reviewed.[2] They exchanged letters (four extant, PN5, 932–5), and Sabat Ercasty agreed that he had been imitated. Amado Alonso was the earliest critic to follow up this explicit but crushing influence. Neruda confessed that he lost many of the original poems and, ten years later, saw them as a 'document of an excessive, ardent youth' (PN1 159). They are the consequence of having read Sabat Ercasty and other poets too passionately, and not having been able to differentiate his own from their voice. Recently, Dominic Moran has studied this debt and the change it forced on Neruda's style, consolidating Neruda's and Loyola's insights. He concluded that the 'similarities of subject matter, style and language which border on plagiarism, making it difficult to believe that Neruda was blissfully unaware of just how derivative his poem was'.[3] In his critical edition, he convincingly argues that the *Veinte poemas* make more sense when read in the light of this imitation and crisis. I would add that Sabat Ercasty reads to me like Whitman, and Neruda had also read Whitman. In a survey of Whitman's influence, Guillermo de Torre called Ercasty one of the 'prole whitmaniana' [Whitman's offspring].[4]

---

1   Loyola, *Neruda*, 2006, pp. 1138–41.
2   Neruda, *Confieso que he vivido*, pp. 69–70.
3   Moran, *Veinte poemas*, p. 11.
4   Guillermo de Torre, 'La estela de Walt Whitman', in *La aventura y el orden* (Buenos Aires: Losada, 1948), p. 146.

A working title had been 'flechero entusiasta' [enthusiastic archer]. The poet as 'archer' suggests both Eros and his arrows and Rimbaud and his Red Indians, and occurs as a self-image in poem 1 of *Veinte poemas*. As does 'hondero' [sling], another weapon, this time associated with David and all boys. The 'entusiasta' indicates Neruda's faith in what poetry stirs up: the prophetic frenzy, being possessed by a god. Later, in his memoirs, Neruda recalled undergoing an 'embriaguez de estrellas' [drunkenness of stars], and that writing these poems meant rushing to his desk 'de manera delirante, como si recibiera un dictado' [in a delirious way, as if receiving a dictation].[5] His later description of inspiration – a dictation – glosses surrealist orthodoxy, for André Breton in 1924 had defined surrealism as 'dictated by thought, in the absence of any control exercised by reason, beyond all aesthetic or moral preoccupations' (William Blake also saw his work as being 'dictated' to him).[6] No wonder that Neruda in 1933 found these poems dictated by his unconscious still 'authentic'.

The collection is divided into twelve sections, without titles, which could be one long poem or twelve different ones. The first word is a verb in the present tense introducing the poet: 'Hago girar mis brazos como dos aspas locas / en la noche toda ella de metales azules' [I spin my arms like two mad blades / in the night all of blue metals] (PN1 161). 'Aspa' is both X-shaped figure and windmill sails. The simile suggests that Neruda is a poet / windmill, and night is his working time. He could be calling for help, or just calling attention to himself, driven by the wind of inspiration. The same line closes the first section. The whole is about a desire to go beyond limits: 'Pero quiero pisar más allá de esa huella' [I want to step beyond this footprint], beyond where stones do not reach.

> Quiero abrir en los muros una puerta. Eso quiero.
> Eso deseo. Clamo. Grito. Lloro. Deseo. (PN1 162)

> [I want to open a door in the walls. That's what I want. That I desire. I call. I shout. I cry. I desire]

These verbs are repeated in alternating orders ('Sufro, sufro y deseo. Deseo, sufro y canto'); three times he repeats 'Grito. Lloro. Deseo'. The rhythm of the poem derives from line openings, anaphora, that repeat the next one ('hacia donde / hacia donde / pero quiero / pero quiero / solo / solo/ todo / todo' etc.), which make it sound like a litany and quite public and loud-voiced. He sees himself shouting. The 'sling' and the stone stand for his poet's skill, aiming his missiles at 'este país negro' [that black country]

5   Neruda, *Confieso que he vivido*, p. 69.
6   Breton, *Manifestes du surréalisme*, p. 40.

that is his 'heart' and his 'dreams'. But the poet fails and his sling's stones drop down.

The rest of the sections develop a set of self-images that articulate the flow of thinking and writing, the 'marea' [tide], the 'agua' [water], the 'espumas' [foam]. There is also some vague woman in the dark night, equally unattainable. He encapsulates 'her', with language carried over into his *Veinte poemas* and *tentativa del hombre infinito*:

> Siento que se me suben los musgos de tu pena
> Y me crecen a tientas en el alma infinita. (PN1 166)
>
> [I feel that the mosses of your pain climb up me / and grow haphazardly in my infinite soul]

She is natural and her 'moss' is the natural metaphor of her pubic hair, while the infinite lies inside the poet, the infinite man. But the image is neither as erotic nor as effective as his use of 'musgo' in poem 1 of *Veinte poemas*.

Entrapment and loneliness stifle the poet, who wants to be free; 'quiero salir de mi alma' [I want to get out of my soul] (PN1 172). He wants to break down the 'puerta', a conventional symbol of the 'way-out'. The avant-garde search for 'freedom' from the conventional self is also Neruda's: 'correr fuera de mí mismo, perdidamente, / libre de mí, furiosamente libre' [to run out of myself, completely / free of myself, furiously free] (PN1 173). As in the closing of his *Veinte poemas de amor*, the poet yearns to travel: 'Irme / Dios mío, / Irme' (and reiterate Baudelaire's and Mallarmé's sea-call).

The poem is also erotic ('Canción del macho y de la hembra!'), repeats the Tagore imagery of 'surco' and 'tierra' and clearly establishes how Neruda deals with love as an inner *agon*:

> Porque tú eres mi ruta. Te forjé en lucha viva.
> De mi pelea oscura contra mí mismo, fuiste (PN1 172)
>
> [Because you are my route. I forged you in living fight. / Of my dark fight with myself, you were]

Here 'she' is both woman and poem; the verb 'forjar' reappears in poem 1 of *Veinte poemas* as does the inner 'pelea' with himself, an acute definition of the poems themselves, in line with W. B. Yeats's well-known adage that 'we make out of the quarrel with others, rhetoric, but out of the quarrel with ourselves, poetry'.[7] The most surprising in a 1920s avant-garde and daring sense are the closing lines of section 7:

---

7   W. B. Yeats, 'Anima Hominis', *The Major Works* (Oxford: Oxford University Press, 2001), p. 411.

> Todo tu cuerpo ardido de blancura en el veintre.
> Las piernas perezosas. Las rodillas. Los hombros.
> La cabellera de alas negras que van volando.
> Las arañas oscuras del pubis en reposo (PN1 171)

> [All your body burning in white on your belly. Your lazy legs.
> Your knees. Your shoulders. / Your hair of black wings that fly. /
> The dark spider of your pubis at rest]

The last line is a visual description of pubic hair where the knots strangely become spiders. In the later *Veinte poemas*, Neruda, as we have already noted, becomes a spider himself: 'Mi boca era una araña que cruzaba escondiéndose' [My mouth was a spider that crossed hiding itself] (PN1 188). Spiders can represent patience and even art with their cobwebs, but as a lover / poet, it is clear that Neruda wants to trap his muse, his lover.

tentativa del hombre infinito, 1926

This experimental poem, one of Neruda's own favourites ('nucleus of my poetry', PN4 1204), appeared in 1926. He suppressed all punctuation, all capitals. However, most critics cite it with an initial capital, even Loyola, except for in his index (PN1 1253), but in the first edition consulted in the British Library the title remains lower-case. It was divided into fifteen sections, without headings and ran to 46 unnumbered pages. The cover is green and inside there is a phrase in red, 'poema de Pablo Neruda', suggesting by its singular that it is *one* long poem. The title heralds its 'tentative' status, what Saúl Yurkievich called its 'indetermination', though 'tentativa' in Spanish has an interesting secondary meaning of 'about to commit a crime that is not carried out', an illicit sense, the poet as criminal.[8] But why 'hombre infinito' [infinite man]? Was this Neruda's version of the depth of the inner unconscious world? Tagore asked in poem 32 of *The Gardener*: 'Is it then true that the mystery of the Infinite is written on this little forehead of mine? Tell me, my lover, if this be true.'[9] Neruda was beginning his long introspective search, based on Rimbaud's boast in his 'Alchimie du verbe' [Alchemy of the word] where the poet contains 'tous les paysages possibles' [all possible landscapes]. Rimbaud wrote: 'Ce fut d'abord une étude. J'écrivais des silences, des nuits, je notais l'inexprimable. Je fixais des vertiges' [At first this was a study. I wrote of silences and of nights, I expressed the inexpressible. I fixed vertigos].[10] Neruda endorsed this 'study', this 'carnet de damné' [notebook of

---

8   Yurkievich, *Fundadores*, p. 188.
9   Tagore, *The Gardener*, p. 62.
10   Rimbaud, *Oeuvres complètes*, p. 106.

a damned soul].[11] This journey inside his mind led Rimbaud to conclude: 'Je finis par trouver sacré le désordre de mon esprit' [I ended by regarding my mental disorder as sacred].[12] This is no other than the journey taken in verse in his 'Le bateau ivre' [The drunken boat]. Rimbaud had also noted in his early long poem 'Soleil et chair' [Sun and flesh] that 'Notre pâle raison nous cache l'infini' [our pale reason hides infinity from us].[13] So Neruda's poem must be seen as a journey, beyond rationality, into the dark endless self, what De Costa labelled as the 'modern voyage poem'.[14] In this sense of a journey, it follows directly from the last poem of his *Veinte poemas*. Neruda's 'self' has become Rimbaud's 'moi, bateau perdu' [me, lost boat] where the poet's identity sails into the unknown, the infinite within, 'ces nuits sans fond' [these bottomless nights].[15] Both poets are in reality children, 'plein de tristesse' [full of sadness]. Robert Pring-Mill once exhibited a pencilled self-portrait that Neruda drew in 1925 of himself as 'el hombre infinito' [the infinite man], graphically synonymous with 'poet'.[16] Loyola claimed that Neruda had read Papini's *Un uomo finito*. Though the Italian means 'finished off', maybe it sparked off its opposite, 'hombre infinito'?[17]

The form of the poem, though, moves from Rimbaud to his disciples, Apollinaire and Mallarmé, as Neruda confessed in 1961. The poem is also a homage to fellow Chilean Vicente Huidobro, the poet who brought the Parisian avant-garde to Spain in 1918 and then Chile. However, it is pertinent here to return to Neruda's debt to French literature for in 1962, in a public lecture at the University of Chile, Neruda played down this deep French influence. He called the poet's work a great 'taller' [workshop] where everybody contributes. He continued:

> … we have been helped by the work of those that preceded us and we now know that there's no Rubén Darío without Góngora, no Apollinaire without Rimbaud, no Baudelaire without Lamartine and no Pablo Neruda without all of them together.

All poets participated in his workshop, not just the French. Neruda did recognise, though, the importance of reading: 'what would become of me without my long readings …?'[18] He also once wrote: 'I didn't sleep or eat reading …';

---

11 Rimbaud, *Oeuvres complètes*, p. 93.
12 Rimbaud, *Oeuvres complètes*, p. 108.
13 Rimbaud, *Oeuvres complètes*, p. 9.
14 De Costa, 1979, p. 51.
15 Rimbaud, *Oeuvres complètes*, p. 69.
16 Robert Pring-Mill, *A Poet for All Seasons*, Exhibition of Nerudiana at the Taylor Institution, Oxford, 1993, p. 61.
17 Loyola, *Neruda*, 2006, p. 147.
18 Neruda and Parra, *Discursos*, p. 77.

he was clearly an unsystematic, omnivorous reader.[19] Later, he would mock his earlier avidity for European novelties as filling his head 'with the latest that arrived with the steamships'.[20]

This absorption by the poet of French literature (and translations into French like Rilke) has two consequences. The first is on a line-by-line debt, influence or intertextuality. To recreate all Neruda's readings as echoes in lines in his poetry would be an endless task and I have only scratched the surface; further, it is what he does with these borrowings that matters. The second level is more general and deals with the idea of the poet and poetry that generated the individual poems, a framing poetics. Behind the individual resonances is an 'ars poetica' that clearly comes from the French. Here we return to Mallarmé and Apollinaire, as these two poets offered Neruda a poetic home. Why we can shrink down so much reading to key texts is that Neruda also learnt beloved poems by heart. The clearest exposition of Mallarmé's ideas and his role for Neruda comes from an interview with Jules Huret in 1891. First, Mallarmé stated that the young and modern poet finds poems in the rhythms of spoken language itself, in prose and not in official verse. A more fluid, mobile poetry has emerged. He also argued for not naming directly, but suggesting. The real symbol is allusive, individual. He is then contested by Huret for promoting 'obscurity'. Mallarmé answers: 'Il doit y avoir toujours énigme en poésie, et c'est le but de la littérature' [there must always be enigma in poetry and it's the aim of literature].[21] A poet can only 'evoke' objects and emotions, and that creates enigma. Neruda's poems of the 1920 follow this guideline, not to worry about difficulty, or meter, but to find rhythms in spoken language itself. Curiously, for Mallarmé, Verlaine was the master. One last Mallarmean point from an 1865 letter: 'Devant le papier, l'artiste se fait' [In front of paper, the artist makes himself].[22] That is, the true self of the poet emerges in the act of writing and then reading what has been written down.

Equally crucial as a master of the idea of the poem and poet is Guillaume Apollinaire and his futurist manifesto 'L'esprit nouveau et les poètes' [The new spirit and poets], 1918. He promoted 'free verse', research into artistic forms and imitation of the freedom of imagery in the newest art form, the cinema. Imagination must grasp what is new in social life. Apollinaire picks on 'surprise' as the key aesthetic concept. For him, and for Neruda,

---

19   Cited in Darío Oses, 'Prólogo', Pablo Neruda, *A éstos yo canto y yo nombro* (Santiago: Fondo de Cultura Económica, 2004), p. 12.

20   Neruda, *Para nacer he nacido*, p. 172: 'estamos ayudados por el trabajo de los que precedieron y ya se sabe que no hay Rubén Darío sin Góngora, ni Apollinaire sin Rimbaud, ni Baudelaire sin Lamartine, ni Pablo Neruda sin todos ellos juntos'.

21   Mallarmé, 'Réponses à des Enquêtes', *Oeuvres complètes*, p. 869.

22   Robert Gibson, *Modern French Poets on Poetry*, p. 79.

the imagination is infinite ('Le domaine le plus riche, le moins connu, celui dont l'étendue es infinie, étant l'imagination' [The richest domain, the least known, the one whose reach is infinite, being the imagination]), for a poet is whoever seeks 'les joies nouvelles qui jalonnent les énormes espaces imaginatifs' [the new joys which mark out the enormous imaginative spaces].[23] Neruda's 'hombre infinito' is Apollinairean. The poet is an explorer, voyaging into the unknown, alone, daring, a prophet, into the dark and into dreams, beyond aesthetic formulae or snobism (meaning fashions / social reputation). The new poet will open new vistas on inner and outer universes. Apollinaire's poem 'La jolie rousse' [The pretty redhead] invokes the same quest as the clash of Order and Adventure, in the quarrel between tradition and invention, for the new poets are on the frontiers of 'l'illimité et de l'avenir' [the limitlessness and of the future]: 'Nous voulons explorer la bonté contrée énorme où tout se tait' [We want to explore good enormous region where everything is silent]. Neruda would have identified with that lovely line where the poet enters the inner silence. In his memoirs, Neruda confirmed that he knew Apollinaire by heart: 'I quote by heart,' he wrote, and copied a line from 'La jolie rousse': 'Piedad para nosotros los que exploramos las fronteras de lo irreal' [pity for us who explore the frontiers of the unreal], which wrongly condenses two lines from Apollinaire's French: 'Pitié pour nous qui combattons toujours aux frontières / De l'illimité et de l'avenir' [Pity for us who fight always at the frontier / of limitlessness and the future].[24] At a formal level, Apollinaire's elimination of punctuation in his long poem 'Zone' was copied by Neruda (and earlier by Huidobro in 1918 in his long Cubist poem *Ecuatorial*). In fact, 'Zone' opens with a famous confession of weariness with the West: 'A la fin tu es las de ce monde ancien' [In the end you are weary with this old world] and ends, like Neruda's *tentativa*, with the arrival of dawn (and a startling image), 'soleil cou coupé' [sun neck cut].[25] What Mallarmé and Apollinaire offered Neruda was a purpose, a method and a deep identity.[26] Neruda was equally aware by 1921 of Dadaism; he even penned a one-liner with the title 'Dada' (PN4 266). Such a debt to French poetry was his secret identity as a poet in a working-class world hostile to poetry, as he said in 1962: 'My poetry had to keep itself secret, separated in an iron-like way from its own origins.'[27]

It is clear that *tentativa del hombre infinito* is one long poem, not fifteen

---

23 Jacques Charpier and Pierre Seghers, *L'Art poétique*, p. 427.

24 Neruda, *Confieso*, p. 63.

25 Guillaume Apollinaire, *Alcools*, pp. 7, 14.

26 See Luis F. Gonález-Cruz on the influence of Apollinaire and Rimbaud in his formalist and line-by-line reading of *tentativa* in *Neruda*, 1979.

27 Neruda and Parra, *Discursos*, p. 54: 'Mi poesía debía mantenerse secreta, separada en forma férrea de sus propios orígenes.'

sections, as there are countless overlapping phrases and words. It is also clear that it continues to project the melancholic persona of the *Veinte poemas* with the repeated phrase 'mi corazón está triste' [my heart is sad] (PN1 203) and countless variants like 'mi corazón desventurado' (PN1 204) / 'mi alma hambrienta' / 'mi alma en desesperanza' [my ill-fated heart / my hungry soul / my despairing soul]. The first simile of the poem, 'como una lancha al muelle lista para zarpar lo creo / antes del alba' [like a launch on the wharf ready to go I hope before dawn] (PN1 203), carries on from the 'Canción desesperada', but again the actual journey has not yet started. Apart from Neruda's admired French poets, the shadow of Vicente Huidobro, almost a French poet himself, falls over this poem.

There has been some critical debate about the influence of surrealism, codified into a poetics in the 1924 manifesto, on this poem. In 1966, Rodríguez Monegal vaguely decided that 'there it seems to follow the foot steps of surrealist poetry'.[28] But his 'seems' betrays him. Gordon Brotherston was more specific when he noted 'something of the uninhibitedness of the surrealists' automatic writing'.[29] Jaime Alazraki was adamant that this poem was the first collection 'of surrealist making written in the Spanish language'.[30] But we will see that this poem is organised musically, Proustianly, and is not dictated by the unconscious, beyond aesthetic and poetic criteria. However, De Costa argued that Neruda was close to automatic writing, adopted 'chance associations' and did not reject anything that occurred to him while writing.[31] But the sequence is opaque, in the Mallarmé sense, not offering any concessions to the reader. Neruda famously complained to Cardoña Peña that it was the 'least read and least studied of my poetry', and Rodríguez Monegal concurred by saying that critically it passed unnoticed.[32] So much so that there is still no translation into English. However, when Neruda passed through Madrid in 1927, he showed Borges's brother-in-law Guillermo de Torre his *tentativa del hombre infinito*. De Torre was becoming his generation's spokesperson for the avant-garde, and he praised Neruda as 'at the head of the actual lyrical promotion', defining this work as 'an abstract and naked lyricism, proscribing all corrective norms and extending the disassociative syntax of Dada to its furthest consequences'.[33]

There is a buried narrative. If we trace the appearances of the word 'sueño'

[28]   Emir Rodríguez Monegal, *El viajero inmóvil*, p. 54.
[29]   Brotherston, *Latin American Poetry. Origins and Presence* (Cambridge: Cambridge University Press, 1975), p. 114.
[30]   Jaime Alazraki, *Poètica y poesía de Pablo Neruda*, pp. 42–3.
[31]   De Costa, 1979, pp. 43–4.
[32]   Rodríguez Monegal, *El viajero inmóvil*, p. 54.
[33]   Cited by Edmundo B. Olivares, *Pablo Neruda: los caminos de Oriente*, p. 61: 'un lirismo abstracto y desnudo, proscribiendo toda norma correctiva y prolongado hasta sus últimas consecuencias, la sintaxis disociadora de "Dadá"'.

[dream], with that of its close association 'noche' [night] and add 'ciudad' [city], all of which appear on the first page, then we can draft this story. A young 20-year-old man ('un hombre de veinte años ...' [PN1 204]), lies in his windowless room ('estoy solo en una pieza sin ventanas' [PN1 211]), alone and desperate ('mi alma en desesperanza') at night in the city, writing ('y vuelto a la pared escribí' [back at the wall I wrote]) and sailing into his dreams at night. He struggles with his sexual vitality, with his lack of a lover, with the stagnant temporal experience of nothing happening and with his lack of inspiration ('Querías cantar sentado en tu habitación ese día / pero el aire frío en tu corazón ...' [You wanted to sing sitting in your room that day but the cold air in your heart]).

The key word, developed through the poem, is 'noche', both a literal night, to be followed by dawn, and the dark inner self. Neruda, like Rimbaud before, is 'embarcado en ese viaje nocturno' [embarked on this night journey] (PN1 204); he is pulled 'entre los brazos del sueño' [among the arms of sleep] (PN1 203). There are repeated invocations to night, with Neruda as the 'centinela' [sentry], the 'sonámbulo' [sleep-walker], with night invading him ('y la noche como vino invade el túnel' [and night like wine invades the tunnel], which repeats the nocturnal 'invasion' of poem 1 of the *Veinte poemas*). This topic of the dream and night links Neruda with the German Romantics, and with Nerval's *Aurélia*, brilliantly studied by Albert Béguin in his *L'âme romantique et les rêves* [The romantic soul and dreams] of 1939, where he established a journey of revelations, descending into the real self. Neruda's image for this inner descent is 'allí trucé mi corazón como el espejo para andar a través de mí mismo' [there I fixed my heart like a mirror to walk through myself] (PN1 208), through a glass darkly or, like Lewis Carroll's Alice, 'through a looking glass'.

A new language emerges from the dream and night, a 'pasión delirante' [delirious passion] (note Rimbaud's 'Délires' from *Une Saison en enfer*), where reason and will-power have no controlling role: 'sin querer suelto el canto la alabanza de las noches' [without meaning to I let loose the praise of nights] (PN1 205). Here is the process of the poet thinking ('estoy pensando'), a verbal process that takes place in the poem and is the poem we read. He discovers a new voice: 'comencé a hablarme en voz baja decidido a no salir / arrastrado por la respiración de mis raíces' [I began to talk to myself in a low voice, determined no to leave, dragged by the breathing of my roots] (PN1 209). This new language has been 'fished' out of him by his 'nets'. The poet is a 'panadero' [baker], he is 'un equilibrista enamorado' [acrobat in love] (PN1 212), positive images of the self, the new poet who has plunged into the self and emerged with a new fruit: 'a tu árbol noche querida sube un niño / a robarse las frutas' [a child climbs up your tree dear night to rob fruit] (PN1 213). The poet is the 'barcarolero', his song the boatman's song that he will continue in later collections. Static time, the time where nothing happens, has been transformed by the poet into living time, *la durée*, the Heraclitean flux 'temblando como una gota / un caudrado de tiempo completamente inmóvil' [trembling like a drop, a square of living time completely still], a lovely image of bliss. He has learnt to celebrate these discoveries; he is the 'yegua' [mare] who gallops, 'como los poetas los filósofos las parejas que se aman' [like the poets, philosophers and couples who love each other], his poetry is a 'campana' [bell], one of the great symbols of his work. Identifying with poets, lovers and philosophers tells us how passion in all its associations has created the persona Neruda in the poems. Through writing and despite his loneliness and isolation, he has benefited from night: 'mi alegre canto de hombre chupa tus duras mamas' [my happy song of man sucks your hard breasts] and the poem has been generated:

> Algo que no te pertenece desciende de tu cabeza
> y se te llena de oro la mano levantada. (PN1 206)

> [Something that doesn't belong to you comes down from your
> head and fills you with gold hand raised]

The symbolism is apt; that 'algo' is the unclassifiable poem that defies culture and reason ('cabeza') and that is the new 'oro' in his hand, almost a masturbatory image, except that it is the hand that writes.

Juan Larrea came across this poem by an unknown Chilean and published a fragment (number 11) in the second number of the magazine *Favorables París Poema* he edited with César Vallejo in Paris in October 1926 (not noted in Neruda's new complete works). So Neruda reached Paris and was published alongside Huidobro, Reverdy, Ribemont-Dessaignes and Vallejo himself.[34] In an essay 'Contra el secreto profesional' of 1927, César Vallejo famously derided his fellow generation of Latin American poets as being 'rhetorical' and lacking in 'spiritual honesty'; they are 'impotent', empty of a sane and authentic human inspiration. They have simply borrowed trendy European literature. He names names: 'A line from Neruda, from Borges or from Maples Arce, are no different at all from one by Tzara, by Ribemont or by Reverdy.'[35] The Latin Americans are cosmopolitan plagiarists. It is interesting that Vallejo does not cite Huidobro, who had had a famous literary feud with Reverdy over plagiarism. But Neruda stands accused. Obviously, he read Neruda in his own magazine. But he had also figured in fellow Peruvian Alberto Hidalgo's 1926 anthology, co-edited with Borges and Huidobro, where Vallejo joined Neruda (poems from *Veinte poemas* and sequences from

---

[34] 'Anexo' in César Vallejo, *Artículos y crónicas completas* II (Lima: Pontificia Universidad Católica del Perú, 2002).

[35] César Vallejo, *Literatura y arte* (Buenos Aires: Ediciones del Mediodía, 1966), pp. 33–9.

tentativa), Borges, Macedonio Fernández, Pablo de Rokha and Maples Arce, a Mexican futurist, with his own poems from *Trilce*.[36]

The key figure concerning *tentativa del hombre infinito* is Vicente Huidobro, with whom Neruda had a long bitter relationship that began as a grateful discipleship. At this stage in his life, Neruda read Huidobro with awe, but not the Huidobro of *Altazor*, 1931, even if fragments had been written as early as 1919 and published in 1924. The Huidobro that moved him was the creator of *Poemas árticos*, 1918, a series of short poems without punctuation and with free-floating lines, saturated with marine and explorer analogies, as we will see. In 1924 Neruda had penned a 'Defensa de Vicente Huidobro' ('qué fresca sensación' [what a fresh sensation] – PN4 322). He had also admitted that he 'deeply admired Vicente Huidobro, and to say deeply is to say little' (PN4 1204). He had probably first read him in 1917 in an anthology *Selva lírica. Estudios sobre los poetas chilenos* from which he had transcribed many poems.[37] But then they squabbled. By 1931, in a letter to Carlos Morla, Neruda stated simply: 'I do not like Huidobro. He seems histrionic and impure in all he does.'[38] René de Costa has outlined their later quarrel, especially Neruda's libellous poem 'Aquí estoy' [Here I am], possibly published in Paris in 1938. Neruda's scurrilous references to Huidobro (and De Rokha) are obvious: 'y me cago en la puta que os malparió, / Derokas, patíbulos, / Vidobras, / y aunque escribáis en francés con el retrato / de Picasso en las verijas ...' [and I shit on the whore who ill-bore you. Derokas, gallows. Vidobras, and although you write in French with a portrait of Picasso near your balls]. Huidobro wrote in French, knew Picasso who sketched a portrait of him and though a Communist, Neruda lampooned him as 'un comunista de culo dorado' [communist with a golden arse], alluding to his vineyard wealth.[39] The relationship had both private and public phases, and chronology is crucial. In 1964, long after Huidobro's death, Neruda generously recalled his love for early Huidobro, but noted that through absorbing his work, he discovered his differences with Huidobro's more intellectual poetry.[40] There are countless Huidobran echoes, beginning with 'ahí sofoco al lado de las noches antárticas' [there I suffocate by the Antarctic nights] (PN1 211), recalling Huidobro's *Poemas árticos*, published in Spain in 1918 and dedicated to the artists Juan Gris and Jacques Lipchitz. The poets could not be more different socially. Huidobro was from the upper-

36 Alberto Hidalgo, Vicente Huidobro and Jorge Luis Borges (eds), *Indice de la nueva poesía americana*. The Neruda poems are on pp. 189–96.
37 Loyola, *Neruda*, 2006, p. 96.
38 Neruda, *Epistolario viajero*, p. 69.
39 René de Costa, 'El Neruda de Huidobro', in Angel Flores (ed.), *Nuevas aproximaciones a Pablo Neruda*, pp. 275–7.
40 Cited in Rodríguez Monegal, *El viajero inmóvil*, p. 188.

class, wine-growing families that ran Chile, was a millionaire who spoke French so naturally that he wrote in French, changing his name to Vincent Huidobro. He was recklessly ambitious, bought and charmed his way into Parisian Cubism, publishing in Reverdy's magazine *Nord-Sud*, befriending every artist who counted, from Picasso to Cocteau to Stravinsky and Satie (all dedicatees of his poems). Neruda knew nobody, his friends were anarchists and poor provincials; his road to Paris was on his way to Rangoon, Burma as an honorary consul, without a penny. The main debt to Huidobro comes from a cluster of sea-travel terms: 'proa' / 'partir' / 'mástil' / 'viaje' [prow, to leave, mast, journey] and a need to sing that is frustrated ('no sé hacer el canto de los días ...' [I don't know how to sing the days]), with the poet as voyager: 'estoy de pie en la luz como el medio día en la tierra' [I am on foot in the light like the half day on earth], repeated throughout the poem.[41] It is an image of the poet that is carried forward into *Altazor*, 1931: 'Yo estoy aquí de pie ante vosotros' (373).

Huidobro evoked his persona in his poems as a 'marinero huérfano' [orphan sailor], as a 'viejo marino' [old sailor] (319) and 'barco' [ship], 'mástil' [mast] and 'levantar ancla' [raise anchor] are leitmotifs of the collection. In an earlier collection, *El espejo de agua*, 1916, the title poem closes:

> De pie en la popa siempre me veréis cantando
> Una rosa secreta se hincha en mi pecho
> Y un ruiseñor ebrio aletea en mi dedo. (256)

> [Standing in the poop you will always see me singing A secret rose swells on my chest And a drunk nightingale flutters on my finger]

That 'de pie' becomes an emblem of Neruda as imaginary ship captain (biographically, his sailor's hat), evoked in titles like *Los versos del capitán*, a natural Chilean motif, no doubt, but also a borrowing from Huidobro.

At one moment in *tentativa*, the poet notices a bee: 'Veo una abeja rondando no existe esa abeja ahora / pequeña mosca con patas lacres mientras golpeas cada vez tu vuelo / inclino la cabeza desvalidamente' [I see a bee flying about that bee doesn't exist now little fly with bright red legs while you knock every time your flight I bow my head helplessly] (PN1 210). How cryptic are these lines? The key term suggesting some change in awareness is the 'ahora'. Something in the 'now' of writing has made the poet alter his perceptions. 'Abeja' figures in *Veinte poemas* as emblem of his muse; a bee may sting, but it has a waist, produces honey, has Virgilian echoes. A bee could be poetry itself, with a Proustian ring (the hive is memory). But now, the poet sees a

---

41   Vicente Huidobro, *Obras completas*, p. 213. Henceforth, page numbers in text.

'mosca' with bright red legs, banging against a window pane, while the poet feels helpless, abandoned. So we can trace a brief narrative from the lines in this poem about the poet no longer attaining traditional beauty. The shift of a bee to a fly, though, occurs in Rubén Darío's poem 'Augurios' [Auguries]. After a litany of the great birds of myth and literature (eagles, falcons, owls, nightingales) that simply fly past, the poet has to cope with far more mundane realities, namely a bat, a bee and a fly: 'Pasa un murciélago, / Pasa una mosca. Un moscardón. / Una abeja en el crespúsculo. / No pasa nada. La muerte llegó' [A bat passes by. A fly passes by. A horsefly. A bee in the twilight. Nothing passes by. Death arrived]. However, while Darío's poem deals with resignation, Neruda's *tentativa* is about breaking through.

A sign of Neruda's daring, of his exploring the sounds and ranges of words from deep in his infinite self, emerges in an anecdote about discovering many errata in this poem, but not altering them.[42] I discovered one of them in the passage from the poem that Larrea and Vallejo published in *Favorables París Poema*, number 2, of October 1926, where we read the line 'inmóvil navío ávido de esas leguas azules' [immobile avid boat of these blue leagues], which in his later complete works becomes 'inmóvil navío ávido de esas lenguas azules' [immobile avid boat of these blue *tongues*]. 'Legua' or 'lengua' ... Neruda did not care.[43] However, the first edition in the British Library has 'leguas', so the later *Obras completas* are wrong. De Costa showed how Neruda increased the mystery of his lines by suppressing too precise a reference to 'Sirio' in the line 'sólo una estrella ['Sirio'] inmóvil su fósforo azul'.[44]

We come to the ending of *tentativa del hombre infinito*. The poet addresses himself on his imaginary boat, the 'centinela' [sentry], the 'pescador intran-quilo' [restless fisherman] (PN1 213), with food, songs and the ocean awaiting:

> oh espérate
> sentado en esa última sombra o todavía después
> todavía
>
> [Oh wait, sitting in that last shadow or still after still]

That closing temporal adverb 'todavía' joins the act of writing with that of imaginary waiting; it suggests alert temporality, alive in the now, a sign of Neruda's vitality. It also echoes Sabat Ercasty's closing of *El infinito océano* (where infinity, the title and ocean merge in Neruda's mind): 'Todavía es la

---

[42] Neruda, *Para nacer he nacido*, p. 246.

[43] Pablo Neruda, 'De "Tentativa del hombre infinito"', in Vallejo, *Artículos y crónicas completos*, II.

[44] De Costa, 1979, p. 43.

noche, / todavía los mundos flotan en la música' [It is still night, still the worlds float in the music].[45]

El habitante y su esperanza, 1926

In a modest prologue to his sole and laconically short novel Neruda confessed that he wrote it because his publisher asked him to and that he respected literature too much to just write 'bailables o diversiones' [dance music or entertainment]. As a poet, rather than as a novelist, Neruda prefers that 'alegría de bastarse a sí mismo' [the joy of being self-sufficient]. I guess that he meant not inventing character and plot for a novel-reading public, but drawing on his own inner drama and dreams. He snipes also at 'los equilibrados imbéciles que forman parte de nuestra vida literaria' [those balanced imbeciles who form part of our literary life] (PN1 217). He clearly has written an extremist or experimental novel, and not much critical attention has been paid to it.[46] In 1974 Enrique Anderson-Imbert claimed it as 'of the first Spanish American experiments that break established norms'.[47]

It is hard to outline what happens in the story. The setting is Cantalao, a fictitious port at the mouth of the Imperial river (in fact, Puerto Saavedra). A narrator who works in a shop is also a horse thief. He fancies Irene, the wife of his fellow horse thief. He has been in prison. He wants to kill his friend. She is killed, or dies. But darkness and night are also protagonists, as if the whole is a dream, with fragmentary events and images. Lucía Guerra Cunninham has broken down this 'novel' into two parts. The first runs from sections I to VII and reveals the outer reality of southern Chile, the two horse thieves etc. This shifts to interior reality, becoming more and more dream-like and ends with the narrator's 'impotence'. Her main point is that 'the narrator does not appear to feel the necessity of explaining logically his evocations to his fictitious reader'.[48]

If the story-line is blurred, the language and similes are odd from the opening paragraphs where, for example, winter 'surges suddenly from the sea like a net of sinister fish' (PN1 219). To compare winter to a net full of

45   Cited in R. Bula Piriz, Sabat Ercasty (Persona y creación) (Montevideo: A. Monteverde, 1979), p. 36.
46   It was translated by G. S. Fraser into English in 1948 as 'The Inhabitant and his Hope', Adam, March / April, pp. 19–27.
47   Enrique Anderson Imbert, 'La prosa vanguardista de Neruda', in Simposio Pablo Neruda, p. 298.
48   Lucía Guerra Cunningham, 'El habitante ...', p. 85. She does not deal with literary models, and refers critically back to Carlos Cortínez's 'Interpretación de El habitante y su esperanza de Pablo Neruda', Revista iberoamericana, 82–3 (enero–junio 1973), pp. 159–74. Loyola, in his Neruda, 2006, also breaks down this novel into a story-line, pp. 222–5.

fish is typical of the 1920s avant-garde. The narrator is wild, an outlaw, loves galloping his horse. The title 'habitante' refers to him, and also to Neruda's later 'Residencia en la tierra', as Loyola has pointed out, and 'la esperanza' [hope] seems to contradict his earlier 'canción desesperada' [song of despair]. There are erotic moments. The narrator kisses his woman, then suddenly bites her white arm. The 'hope' of the title is to do with love: 'a man with a vocation for solitude can wait every afternoon for the same woman' (PN1 227); a good self-portrait of the poet. For the novel reflects his own 'destierro' [inner exile] before leaving for Burma in 1927. At the same time, the whole novel comes out of his head as he sits out another night waiting for dawn. There is a quality of 'unknowability' about life that torments the narrator. He addressed this novel to those who try to make sense of the secrets of night, the 'desinteresados vigilantes que tenéis los ojos abiertos en la puerta de los túneles' [disinterested guards who keep your eyes open at the door of tunnels] (PN1 233), a phrase that applies to the isolated persona of his later *Residencia en la tierra*. The narrator, clearly Neruda himself, identifies with 'los pescadores, poetas, panaderos, guardianes de faro' [fishermen, poets, bakers, lighthouse guards] who 'know the risk of having been even once faced with what cannot be deciphered' (PN1 233). That is the 'risk' of art, the wager behind all his early poems. The novel closes with the 'wall' still there and his solitude filling up with monsters as the 'alba saca llorando los ojos del agua' [dawn takes its eyes out of the water weeping] (PN1 235). This is the third time that Neruda closes a work with 'alba'. Four lines from the end of his 'Canción desesperada' we have 'Abandonado como los muelles en el alba', and *tentativa*, as noted, ends on dawn. All three works, then, can be seen as explorations of a night journey into the sources of creativity, ending with the diurnal, work world.

The tone and ferocity of this dream novel derive from Rimbaud's *Une Saison en enfer*, with similar rhythms and similar narrators outside the law and the same staccato lists. Wallace Fowlie characterised Rimbaud's violence as syntactical: 'The violence of the work is not in the ideas, and facts, but rather in the rhythms, in the movements of the phrases ...'[49] Take the following from Neruda:

> Yo escogí la huida, y a través de pueblos lluviosos incendiados, solitarios, caseríos madereros en que indefectiblemente uno se espera con los inmensos castillos de leña, con el rostro de los ferroviarios desconocidos y preocupados, con los hoteleros y las hoteleras, y en en el fondo del cuarto donde la vieja litografía hamburguesa, la colcha azul [...] (PN1 226).

[49] Wallace Fowlie, *Rimbaud and Jim Morrison*, p. 54.

[I choose to flee and across rainy, burning villages, wooden huts in which infallibly one waits with the immense castles of wood with the face of unknown and worried railwaymen, with hotel owners, and in the depths of a room where the old lithograph of Hamburg, the blue bedcover]

I detect the same flow in Rimbaud's prose. For example, 'Délire II':

Je dus voyager, distraire les enchantements assemblés sur mon cerveau. Sur la mer, que j'aimais comme si elle eût dût me laver d'une souillure, je voyais se lever la croix consolatrice. J'avais été damné par l'arc-enciel.[50]

[I was forced to travel, to distract the enchantments crowding in my brain. On the sea, which I loved as if it was sure to cleanse me of filth, I saw the cross of comfort rising. I had been damned by the rainbow]

However, Neruda adapts Rimbaud to his own experiences in Ancud, on Chiloé island in provincial Chile, without imitating him. What counts is not the content, but the way the prose is organised. His editor Hernán Loyola notes the influence of Rilke's *Sketches of Malte Laurids Brigge* (which Neruda had partially translated from the French) and Pierre Loti's *Mon frère Yves* (an epigraph in Neruda's novel). Loyola showed how both Rilke and Neruda open with 'Ahora bien' [Now then], both texts are written in the present tense and both offer 'imprevistas conexiones' [unexpected connections].[51] But neither match Rimbaud's jerkiness as model.

50   Rimbaud, *Oeuvres complètes*, p. 111.
51   Loyola, *Neruda*, 2006, p. 227.

3

The 1920s and 1930s: *Residencia en la tierra 1*

Residencia en la tierra 1, 1933

Between the publication of his *Veinte poemas* in 1924 and *Residencia en la tierra* in 1933, Neruda lived what I will call his years of loneliness in the desert, or his season in hell. A brief chronology begins in Chile in 1925, then finds him in Rangoon in October 1927, then Calcutta in November–December 1928, Ceylon (Sri Lanka) in 1928, Batavia (Jakarta) in 1930 and back in Chile in 1931 (with further trips to Japan and China). But place names do not figure in the poems, such is the intensity of introspection. There is something uncanny in his awareness that to become a great poet, to be different and find his own voice, he must suffer isolation and travel as he explores his relationship with himself and with the outer world. The consequence of this alchemical laboratory is *Residencia en la tierra 1*, his single most radical book, according to Saúl Yurkievich 'that insuperable pinnacle in Pablo Neruda's work'.[1] This view is gaining currency. Jorge Edwards, although a Chilean himself, goes further so that *Residencia en la tierra 1* becomes 'one of the greatest books of poetry of the twentieth century, perhaps the peak of poetry in the Spanish language'.[2] However, it baffled and divided critics, and Neruda himself would later dismiss it as too pessimistic for Soviet youth when he refused permission for it to be translated into Russian, because a young man had committed suicide with that book in his hand.[3] Neruda told Alfredo Cardona Peña that these poems were soaked in pessimism: 'they do not help you to live, they help you to die'.[4] Yet despite this increasing prestige, it is significant that the first edition ran to just 100 copies.

Neruda was driven, as already noted, to travel by the siren voices of Baudelaire's 'Le Voyage' and Mallarmé's sequel 'Brise marine'. He travelled south in Chile for a year and then accepted a poorly paid, honorary consul's post in Rangoon, Burma, which meant travelling to Buenos Aires, then Paris

---

[1]   Saúl Yurkievich, *Fundadores*, p. 188.
[2]   Jorge Edwards, 'Un adiós a muchas cosas', in Fontaine, *Estudios Públicos*, p. 293.
[3]   Rita Guibert, 'The Art of Poetry XIV', *Paris Review*, 1971, p. 174.
[4]   Emir Rodríguez Monegal, *El viajero inmóvil*, p. 12.

and finally out to Burma, a far-flung outpost of the British Empire. He was accompanied some of the time by an eccentric Chilean amateur writer and follower of Eastern religions called Alvaro Hinojosa. Neruda had many affairs, loathed the British and finally married a Dutch woman in Java in 1930. All the poems emerge from this self-exile. The nine poems he wrote while still in Chile were written in Ancud, accompanying a poet friend with a teaching job, while the rest came from five long years abroad. In a prolific writing life, these five years abroad led to just nineteen poems. He hardly ever spoke Spanish, but was constantly aware that he needed this foreign experience to become a real poet. He wrote in a letter to his Argentine pen pal Héctor Eandi: 'Yes, that depressing moment, disastrous for many, is noble matter for me,' meaning that he was conscious that living in the 'horror of those colonies of abandonment' was good for his poetry.[5] While in the Far East (Rangoon, Wellawata, Delhi and Batavia), he read voraciously and broke away from his working-class roots, from his birth origins: 'I come from an obscure province.'[6] So the second half of the collection's title 'en la tierra' [on earth], a cosmopolitan boast, assures his readers that he has travelled around the earth. However, not to Paris like Vicente Huidobro or César Vallejo, or even Madrid like Rubén Darío, but to other obscure provincial backwaters (for Chileans). He once summarised the gestation behind these poems as 'this knowing myself and recognizing myself, this long self-absorption, with wind, fruit and sea, is contained in my little book *Residencia en la tierra*, tormented dictionary of my personal investigations'.[7] If we peel away some self-mythification (the torments), we touch that 'exploration of the self' at the source of all great poetry, and of the Delphic Oracle. In a prose poem, Neruda assured his reader that 'me miro' [I look at myself], a self-inspection or, in Antonio Melis's words, a 'profound self-awareness'.[8]

Thanks to painstaking work, the Chilean critic Hernán Loyola has established when and where most of the poems in this collection might have been written.[9] Neruda has not preserved their chronology for he traces out a greater pattern that re-enacts an inner journey into hell along Rimbaud's lines. Enrique Molina was aware of this mythic paradigm and of Neruda's daring: 'it would seem impossible to go further'.[10] The working title had

---

5   Margarita Aguirre, *Pablo Neruda / Héctor Eandi*, pp. 34, 42: 'Sí, ese momento depresivo, funesto para muchos, es una noble materia para mí' / 'horror de estas colonias de abandono.'

6   Pablo Neruda, *Para nacer he nacido*, p. 430.

7   Neruda, *Para nacer he nacido*, p. 228: 'este conocerme y reconocerme, este largo ensimismamiento, con viento, frutos y mar, está contenido en mi pequeño libro *Residencia en la tierra*, diccionario atormentado de mis indagaciones personales'.

8   Antonio Melis, 'Neruda y la poesía', p. 22.

9   Hernán Loyola, 'Introducción' to Pablo Neruda, *Residencia en la tierra*, pp. 13–16.

10 Enrique Molina, 'Neruda de siempre', p. 8.

been *Colección nocturna* [Nocturnal collection] (and became the title of one of the poems), which prolongs Neruda's fascination with dreams, with inner night, the self, the pulse of life.[11] It suggests a deeper structure than chronology, some epiphany that can be reached only through suffering, patience and sexual pleasure. To explore this stunning book I will rely on the extraordinary letters that Neruda wrote to his Argentine friend Héctor Eandi, especially when they deal with his intentions and his reading. We also learn about his voracious reading from his own memoirs.

Neruda always knew his own worth as a poet. He sent poems and even a whole manuscript to magazines. Already, he had published in the Buenos Aires magazine *Martín Fierro* in 1924,[12] had appeared in the Alberto Hidalgo, Jorge Luis Borges and Vicente Huidobro's anthology *Indice de la nueva poesía americana* in 1926, and, the same year, had reached Paris in César Vallejo and Juan Larrea's magazine *Favorables. París. Poema*. He created a sense of expectation from his outposts in the Far East. For example, he sent three poems ('Arte poética', 'Diurno doliente' [Daily mourner] and 'Colección nocturna') to the crucial Mexican avant-garde magazine *Contemporáneos* where they were published in April 1931 and September–October 1931.[13] A 17-year-old reader of that magazine, Octavio Paz, claimed that he had discovered modern poetry through reading translations of Blake, T. S. Eliot and Saint-John Perse; he never mentioned Neruda, but Paz knew 'Arte poética' by heart, exactly the poem that appeared there in Mexico. Neruda published the opening poem 'Galope muerto' (written in 1925 in Chile) in Ortega y Gasset's prestigious *Revista de Occidente* in March 1930 (with 'Serenata' and 'Caballo de los sueños'). He sent the whole manuscript to a wealthy Argentine patron, Elvira de Alvear, in Paris for whom Alejo Carpentier worked as secretary in the sole number of her magazine *Imán*. But she lost it. Alejo Carpentier denied this version of events and said that he had asked for the manuscript from Paris, could not publish it as the magazine had gone bust thanks to the great Wall Street Crash and then sent it to José Bergamín in Madrid who published it. Thus Carpentier claimed that it was thanks to him that Neruda arrived in Spain and fame.[14] Above all, it was the Spanish poet Rafael Alberti who passed the manuscript around his friends in Madrid and whose reactions are most eloquent about Neruda's originality: 'From first reading them those poems surprised me and left me in admira-

---

[11] Pablo Neruda, *Epistolario viajero*, p. 50.
[12] See *Revista Martín Fierro. 1924–1927*, edición facsimilar (Buenos Aires: Fondo Nacional de las Artes, 1995), mayo 15 de 1924.
[13] Cited in Merlin Forster, *An Index to Mexican Literary Periodicals*.
[14] Alejo Carpentier, 'Presencia de Pablo Neruda', in Fontaine, *Estudios Públicos*, p. 441.

tion, so far from the accent and climate of our poetry.'[15] Alberti had published his marvellous, quasi-surrealist *Sobre los ángeles* in 1929 and yet could not account for the originality of Neruda's work. That 'tan lejos [...] de nuestra poesía' defined Neruda's difference with the Hispanic tradition.

In his geographical isolation, Neruda was able to survey the European and Latin American avant-gardes and absorb whatever he wanted. This freedom from a school or movement is crucial in determining Neruda's aesthetic position. As a student of French literature, there is no way that he could have ignored Parisian surrealism in the late 1920s. Yet Neruda's confessed knowledge of surrealism is superficial and barely enters his poems. In 1962 he wrote:

> Then surrealism came from France. It's true that it didn't yield any complete poet, but it did reveal Lautréamont's howling in the hostile streets of Paris. Surrealism is fecund and worthy of the most solicitous reverences for the way, with catastrophic values, it changed statues around, put holes in bad paintings and a moustache on the Mona Lisa, which as everyone knows, needed one.[16]

He agreed that surrealism freed Latin American poetry from 'numbness' and that it was a fertile provocation, but Neruda does not mention its exploration of erotic power, nor its research into creativity, automatic writing, dreams and the Freudian metaphors describing the inner self. Surrealism was just cheeky gestures, the 1920s version, spitting at priests, upsetting the bourgeois reader. Years later, André Breton, in an interview and without having read *Residencia en la tierra*, but knowing about Neruda's Stalinist stance, denied Neruda any surrealist affiliation.[17] Nevertheless, it could be argued that Neruda is the greatest surrealist of them all, free from having to belong or sign manifestos. An early book-length critic, Amado Alonso, in 1940, picked out the following lines as the kernel of Neruda's surrealistic poetics: 'O sueños que salen de mi corazón a borbotones' [Oh dreams that bubble out of my heart] (PN1 319), a phrase that defies physiology (the brain) to assert metaphor (the heart) as the affective source of poetry. The phrase 'a borbotones' implies spontaneity and

---

15 Rafael Alberti, *La arboleda perdida. Libros I y II de memorias*, p. 293:'Desde su primera lectura me sorprendieron y admiraron aquellos poemas, tan lejos del acento y el clima de nuestra poesía.'

16 Pablo Neruda y Nicanor Parra, *Discursos*, pp. 58–9: 'Luego viene el surrealismo desde Francia. Es verdad que éste no nos entrega ningún poeta completo, pero nos revela el aullido de Lautréamont en las calles hostiles de París. El surrealismo es fecundo y digno de las más solícitas reverencias por cuanto con un valor catastrofal cambia de sitio las estatuas, hace agujeros en los malos cuadros y le pone bigotes a Mona Lisa que, como todo el mundo sabe, los necesitaba.'

17 André Breton, *Entretiens*, p. 285.

is an onomatopoeia, like bubbles bursting from a bottle underwater. If surrealism was 'a systematic illumination of the hidden places' and 'a perpetual promenade right in the forbidden zone', as Norman O. Brown argued, then Neruda was decidedly surrealist.[18]

When Neruda was discovered in the 1950s in the United States through Robert Bly's translations, it was as a natural, exuberant, even telluric surrealist. Bly called Neruda's poems 'the greatest surrealist poems yet written in a Western language' and that 'French surrealist poems appear drab and squeaky besides them'.[19] Hugo Williams reacted in his English way to Bly's terms:

> ... South American 'hot' surrealism, as Bly called it, as opposed to the 'cold' French surrealism of André Breton and Marcel Duchamp [...] personally I could do without either. Surrealism is [...] the epitome of self-licensing artiness...[20]

However, in the North American poetic tradition, John Felstiner pinpointed the reasons for Neruda's presence as antidote to the 'sterile and effete symbolism of T. S. Eliot and the Wastelanders'.[21] Neruda's influence on later Spanish American poet was equally crucial. In 1974 Octavio Paz noted that *Residencia en la tierra* was an 'essential book'. He added that 'Neruda's influence was like a flood which spread and covered miles and miles – confused, powerful, sonambulistic, shapeless waters.'[22] A good example is the Argentine surrealist poet Enrique Molina. His first book *Las cosas y el delirio* [Things and delirium], 1941, branched from Neruda's sensual materialism, as did his later *Pasiones terrestres* [Terrestrial passions], 1946 and *Costumbres errantes o la redondez de la tierra* [Errant customs or the roundness of the Earth] 1951 (note his insistence on 'tierra' in both collections in the wake of *Residencia en la tierra*). In 1973 Molina wrote his obituary in the newspaper *La Nación* under the heading 'Neruda de siempre' [Neruda everlasting], picking on *Residencia en la tierra* as a 'profound adventure of being in its blood and time' (using Nerudan metaphoric language to epitomise the book).[23] A hostile critic to Neruda, Mario Benedetti, found Neruda's influ-

---

[18] Norman. O Brown, *Love's Body*, p. 241.

[19] Robert Bly, 'Refusing to be Theocritus', *Neruda and Vallejo: Selected Poems*, p. 3. First appeared in 'On Pablo Neruda', *London Magazine*, 4, July 1968, pp. 24–35.

[20] Hugo Williams, 'Freelance', p. 16.

[21] John Felstiner, *Translating Neruda*, p. 16.

[22] Octavio Paz, *Obra completa 1*, p. 460: 'la influencia de Neruda fue como una inundación que se extiende y cubre millas y millas – aguas confusas, poderosas, sonámbulas, informes'.

[23] Molina, 'Neruda de siempre', p. 1. See also my 'Spanish American Surrealist Poetry', in Robert Havard (ed.), *A Companion to Spanish Surrealism* (Woodbridge: Tamesis, 2004), pp. 253–76.

ence 'paralysing'. He amplified: 'Neruda's way of using metaphors has such power, that through countless acolytes or followers or epigones, it reappears as an indelible, inextinguisable gene.'[24] That is, Neruda marked a generation of 1940s poets in Latin America. Benedetti was writing while Neruda still lived and from a Cuban-biased political irritation. The Chilean critic Federico Schopf, examining the reception of Neruda's work in Chile, declared that Neruda's language in his *Residencia* poems had become a 'new rhetoric' called 'nerudismo'.[25] The Chilean poet Enrique Lihn, arbiter of taste for his politicised 1960s generation, defined himself against the later Neruda, but it 'was in *Residencias* that Neruda gave us the unique and untransferable tone of his poetry'.[26] Another generational leader, the Argentine critic and fiction writer Ricardo Piglia, said recently in an interview in *La Nación* that 'we all admire *Residencia en la tierra* without reservations. That book justifies everything.'[27]

In a wonderful passage in a letter to Eandi of 17 February 1933, Neruda reiterated his anarchist beliefs and distaste for proletarian art, odes to Moscow and 'trenes blindados' [bullet-proof trains] to say, in his own surrealist way: 'yo sigo escribiendo sobre sueños' [I continue to write about dreams].[28] This theme of dream-work binds Neruda to surrealism. Neruda, then, was a surrealist in spirit who explored his dreams and his psyche through poetry, in Nerval's wake as already argued. He developed his own theories about writing and especially how sound controls meaning. Neruda became, famously, a popular reader of his own work. Like Federico García Lorca, he believed that poetry must be read aloud, that its sound-sensuousness is crucial in separating it from 'prose'. Albertina Rosa Azócar, the great unrequited love of the 1920s, told an interviewer in 1983 that he 'declamaba poesías con un sonsonete monótono' [declaimed his poetry in a monotonous singsong].[29] Another friend, the Chilean diplomat Carlos Morla Lynch, heard Neruda read in Madrid in 1934 'with his slow, lazy and sad voice'.[30] In 1934 Neruda told his Argentine friend La Rubia, nickname for Sara Tornú, in a letter that his then latest poem 'Alberto Rojas Giménez viene volando' [Alberto Rojas Giménez comes flying] had to be read 'con voz acongojada, porque de otra

---

24 Mario Benedetti, 'Vallejo y Neruda: dos modos de influir', in *Letras del continente mestizo*, p. 63: 'El modo metaforizador de Neruda tiene tanto poder, que a través de incontables acólitos o seguidores o epígonos, reaparece como un genes imborrable, inextinguible.'

25 Federico Schopf, 'Recepción y contexto de la poesía de Pablo Neruda', in *Del vanguardismo a la antipoesía en Chile*, p. 88.

26 Enrique Lihn, 'Momentos esenciales de la poesía chilena', in *Panorama actual de la literatura latinoamerican*, p. 252.

27 Ricardo Piglia, *La Nación*, abril 2006.

28 Aguirre, *Neruda / Eandi*, p. 119.

29 Mónica Guzmán, *ABC*, 23 de septiembre 1983, p. 52.

30 Olivares, *Pablo Neruda II*, p. 171.

manera no estaría bien' [in a distressed voice, otherwise it wouldn't be right] (PN5 1031).[31] He insisted on the elegiastic nature of the poem about his close bohemian friend who had died in 1934. In his recordings, he read aloud in this litany-way, as if poetry required a special and monotonous voice that came from grieving. His early friend and biographer Voloida Teitelboim once heard him read from the *Residencia* poems where he 'mumbled almost without inflections, in a monochord, moaning, like spreading a sleeping drug around'.[32] Neruda told Eandi that *Residencia en la tierra* was 'a heap of lines of great monotony, almost ritualistic, with mystery and sadness as the old poets wrote. It's something very uniform, with one single thing begun and begun again,' like rain or waves on a Chilean shore (Jaime Concha praised this 'intense monotony' across Neruda's work). The monotone is part of the message, and this message ties Neruda back to the western lyrical tradition ('los viejos poetas').[33]

Neruda's poems embody what T. S. Eliot, in 1933, articulated as the 'auditory imagination', in terms of how a poet penetrates far below the 'conscious levels of thought and feeling' and sinks to the 'most primitive and forgotten, returning to the origin and bringing something back'.[34] This primitive auditory imagination as a journey inwards does not invoke melody, the sound of verse, that sound-meaning fusion that describes all lyric poetry. The word 'sonnet' etymologically comes from the word sound, but involves the traditional music / poetry analogy that is lyric poetry. There are countless references in Neruda's *Residencias* to music just in his titles: sonata, barcarola, madrigal, serenata, tango, cantares, odes. He deliberately wanted his poems to mimic popular songs (like tango); 'my old desire to make a poetry of the heart, that consoles afflictions like popular songs and tunes, like the music of cities'.[35] The auditory imagination does not suggest French *symboliste* aesthetics, Baudelaire's sonnet 'Correspondances', that secret and dark harmonic ideal, though Neruda grew up as a poet out of *modernismo*

---

[31]   Alberto Rojas Giménez was a student friend, poet, editor of *Claridad*, and a dandy without a penny. This poem mourning his death was the first Neruda wrote in Spain. According to Feinstein, Rojas Giménez was 'decisive in persuading him [Neruda] to give up any intention of becoming a French teacher and to dedicate himself to literature' (p. 26).

[32]   Volodia Teitelboim, *Neruda*, p. 140: 'musitaba casi sin inflexiones, monocorde, gemebundo, como esparciendo una droga soñolienta'.

[33]   Aguirre, *Neruda / Eandi,* p. 48: 'un montón de versos de gran monotonía, casi rituales, con misterio y dolores como los hacían los viejos poetas. Es algo muy uniforme, como una sola cosa comenzada y recomenzada'. Jaime Concha, 'Neruda, desde 1952', in Angel Flores (ed.), *Nuevas aproximaciones a Pablo Neruda*, p. 217.

[34]   T. S. Eliot, *The Use of Poetry and the Use of Criticism*, pp. 118–19.

[35]   Cited by Olivares, *Pablo Neruda II*, p. 305: 'mi viejo deseo de hacer una poesía del corazón, que consuele aflicciones como las canciones y tonadas populares, como la música de las ciudades'.

and Verlaine's rich rhymes. Neruda is far from Rubén Darío's ideal music ('Como cada palabra tiene un alma ...' [As each word has a soul]).[36] The auditory imagination begins in the amniotic waters of the womb as heart-beat and voice vibration, it suggests that language is first of all meaningless sound, phoneme, pure vowels, mother's voice, as Annie Karpf has recently summarised.[37] Steven Pinker has surveyed this developmental process in infants, from babble (sounds or phonemes), to one word (or morphemes), to two words, phrases and sentences by three years old.[38] These early non-linguistic modes of vocal communication, according to Terence Deacon, have co-evolved with language. There seem to be two kinds of sounds in unison: the very ancient non-linguistic vocal or vowel calls (common to humans, whales, monkeys, birds etc.) and language as a fusion of vowels and conso-nants, that is, words, sentences, syntax etc., which is dependent on specific human anatomy.[39] T. S. Eliot's concept reverses this developmental process: 'Poetry begins, I dare say, with a savage beating a drum in a jungle, and it retains that essential of percussion and rhythm.'[40] However, he did not connect that savage with the foetus in a womb, though he did link the source of poetry with black culture, jazz, African masks, pre-European origins that excited early twentieth-century avant-garde thinking. Neruda did not need to read Eliot's criticism, though he read *The Waste Land* in Wellawata. He did not need to read Eliot the critic, because he tapped into this source through sexual initiation, breaking through his Catholic guilt with different Burmese lovers, especially Josie Bliss, as we will illustrate shortly. What Eliot talked about, Neruda experienced. George Steiner has best explored this thinking by starting with the dilemma of how to inquire into the sources of language with language itself, a circular or mirror process. His solution is 'metaphor', relating unrelated areas of experience. Citing Wittgenstein and Benjamin, he privileges poetry as going to 'the roots of language'.[41] But Steiner does not envisage this as an erotic journey. 'Pensando', as we noted, was a key verb in Neruda's *Veinte poemas*. 'Pienso' appears in 'Unidad' (PN1 100) and later the phrase 'yo examino sin arrogancia' [I examine without arrogance] (PN1 119) and later still the gerunds '... absorbiendo y pensando ...' (PN1 220): these are verbal signs of his awareness of meditation. We will now turn to how Neruda's self-conscious thinking works.

36   From the 'Palabras liminares' in Rubén Darío's *Prosas profanas*, p. 11.
37   Annie Karpf, *The Human Voice. The Story of a Remarkable Talent*, especially chapter 6, 'Mothertalk: the Melody of Intimacy', pp. 83–93.
38   Steven Pinker, *The Language Instinct*, esp. chapter 9.
39   Terence Deacon, *The Symbolic Species. The Co-evolution of Language and the Human Brain*, p. 54.
40   Eliot, *The Use of Poetry*, p. 155.
41   George Steiner, *Extraterritorial*, pp. 65–8, 94.

Neruda convinced his reader that he became a poet before he could write poems; that he was a natural poet. This organic, Romantic notion of the birth of a poet could derive from Neruda's isolation in Temuco; it clearly ties in with the omnipresence of nature, the wind, rain, drips from leaking roofs, the waves and forests of this frontier region. But, more crucially, it evokes the 'auditory imagination'. The sound of rain on a corrugated metal roof is more than the sweet music of rain in Verlaine's: 'O bruit doux de la pluie / Par terre et sur les toits' [Oh sweet din of rain / on earth and on roofs]. It is more John Cage territory, sound, noise. Cage once defined a composer as an organiser of sounds; he explored noises and percussion and told of the din his body made in the anechoic chamber at Harvard (his nervous system, his blood circulating); probably as close as you can get to the womb sounds. Neruda, in comparison with Cage's focusing on sound and randomness, is a bizarre mixture of traditional bard in love with melody and song with a modern, dissonant, percussive sound register.[42] Neruda's 'defamiliarising abruptness' (Seamus Heaney's phrase) emerges from this clash between melody and noise.[43] Neruda was aware of this divergence of melody from noise; it anguished him as a poet that the world didn't rhyme with the word. In the poem 'Débil del alba' [Weak from dawn], from 1926, the poet reveals his awareness of sounds deeper than melody: 'Yo lloro en medio de lo invadido, entre lo confuso, / entre el sabor creciendo, poniendo el oído / en la pura circulación' [I cry amid invasion, among confusion, among the swelling taste, placing my ear to the pure circulation] (PN1 261). To listen to the 'pure circulation' is to hear the world's noise. In the elegy 'Ausencia de Joaquín' [Joaquín's absence], he overhears 'un ruido / un determinado sordo ruido siento producirse' [a noise, a determined deaf noise I feel producing itself] (PN1 263).[44] Inside his heart, he says in 'Barcarola', you can hear a 'ruido oscuro, con sonido de ruedas de tren con sueño' [an obscure noise, with sound of train wheels with sleep] (PN1 303). So much for anguishing noise. The powerful word 'campana' that cuts across all Neruda's writing, associating Catholic rituals with Edgar Allan Poe's poem 'The Bells' and José Asunción Silva's reworking of Poe, became during his exile 'una campana un poco ronca', out-of-tune, avant-garde music. In his poem 'Arte poética', the anguish is evident in the shift from 'todo sonido que acojo temblando' [all sound I gather trembling] to 'un oído que nace'[a hearing that is born].[45] Neruda hears his own scary 'auditory imagination'. Hearing is the sense that

---

[42] John Cage, *Silence*, p. 8.

[43] Seamus Heaney, *The Government of the Tongue*, p. 117.

[44] This poem is another poem mourning a Chilean friend, Joaquín Cifuentes Sepúlveda. Neruda had written a student poem, 'A los poetas de Chile', demanding Cifuentes Sepúlveda's release from jail (Feinstein, *Pablo Neruda*, p. 27).

[45] Pablo Neruda, *Residencia en la tierra*, edición de Hernán Loyola, p. 133.

most stimulates the imagination and the first sense alive in a foetus, from
45 days old so that ears hear some seven and a half months before eyes see;
orality is at the source of all literature, and every child's development; you
hear first. Hernán Loyola picked on the verbs 'oír' [to hear] and 'escuchar'
[to listen] as nodal terms in Neruda's opaque vocabulary.[46] I will link these
verbs with a self-conscious practice. Neruda hears his way inside: 'escucho
en mi interior' [I listen in my inside] (PN1 267), and oddly, hears his dream
('Yo oigo el sueño' [I hear the dream], PN1 267).

Neruda's explorations of sound become the opening poem 'Un día sobresale' [A day stands out] of the second volume of his *Residencia en la tierra*,
possibly written in 1933. Here Neruda coins a term from a unique Spanish
construction of a noun from an adjective, *lo sonoro*. The poem opens 'De lo
sonoro salen números' [From sonorousness come numbers] (PN1 299), and
this phrase shifts to 'en lo sonoro' and 'a lo sonoro', and more traditionally
turns into 'silencio', pre-language. Neruda now knows where poetry is born,
and how to contact it 'en lo sonoro'. Loyola's note to this poem confirms
Neruda's poetico-philosophical understanding: 'Such insistence seeks to
propose in *lo sonoro* the beginning or foundation of life, the cosmic origin of
existence and at the same time its manifestation,' confirming how profoundly
Neruda speculated within his art.[47] What Loyola does not state is the way
Neruda came to this source through sexual initiation, that both sexual ecstasy
and poetic inspiration emerge from the same 'oculto fuego' [hidden fire].

'Lo sonoro', then, is Neruda's term for the poetic unconscious, the Chest
of Language, the sonar string of vowels like the 'o's in 'lo sonoro'. Its closest
analogy in the poem is the word-concept 'ocean', and perhaps Verlaine's
'L'océan sonore / palpite sous l'oeil' [The sonorous ocean / palpitates under
the eye].[48] There is also an echo of Darío's 'Marina' with the 'Mar armo-
nioso, / mar maravilloso, / tu salada fragancia, / tus colores y músicas sonoras
/ me dan la sensación divina de mi infancia' [Harmonious sea, marvellous
sea, your salty fragrance, your colours and sonorous musics, give me the
divine sensation of my childhood].[49] In his later lament for the death of his
close friend 'Alberto Rojas Giménez viene volando', the poet makes this link
explicit: 'te oigo / venir volando bajo el mar sin nadie, / bajo el mar que me
habita, oscurecido' [I hear you / come flying under the sea with nobody, /
under the sea that inhabits me, darkening] (PN1 286). 'Oscuro' and 'oculto'
merge in this inner sea. Out of 'lo sonoro', then, come dying numbers, codes
of dung, humid lightning bolts, the night itself like a widow, even day and

---

    [46] Loyola, *Residencia*, p. 357.

    [47] Loyola, *Residencia*, p. 193.

    [48] From Paul Verlaine's 'Marine', in *Selected Poems*, p. 18.

    [49] Darío, *Cantos de vida y esperanza*, p. 63. First published in *Caras y caretas*, 18 de abril
1903.

light. Out of this inner bag of sound comes 'un viento de sonido como una ola retumba' [a wind of sound like a wave crashes]; out of this ocean of sonority emerge sharks and 'salmones azulados de congelados ojos' [blueish salmon with frozen eyes]. It's like a flea-market or a junk-shop, with tools, carts of vegetables, 'rumores de racimos aplastados' [rumours of squashed bunches], violins full of water, submerged motors, factories, kisses, and surprisingly, 'botellas palpitantes' [palpitating bottles] (PN1 299). Neruda extracts from 'lo sonoro' a random, heterogeneous list, a literal chaotic enumeration that echoes surrealism, and all of it as sounds:

> en torno a mí la noche suena,
> el día, el mes, el tiempo,
> sonando como sacos de campanas mojadas (PN1 299)

> [Around me sounds the night, the day, the month, time, sounding like sacks of wet bells]

All this and more wakes up in this inner sea. The poem suggests that the dream is analogous to the ocean, to inner silence and to *lo sonoro* (a chain of synonyms). This surrealist poetics invokes sleeping machines and 'trenes de jazmín desalentado y cera' [trains of dejected jasmine and wax]. Neruda offers his version of Lautréamont's new beauty, the chance meeting of an umbrella and a sewing machine on an operating table where meaning has to be found; it is a process, not a given, and that became one of the key definitions of surrealism.[50] Here it is train, jasmine and wax. Even the soul emerges from this inner silence.

At a more mundane level, the poem records the birth of a day. The poet hears day-time activities begin, with 'zapatos bruscos, bestias, utensilios / olas de gallos duros derramándose, / relojes trabajando como estómagos secos .../ y water-closets blancos despertando' [brusque shoes, beasts, utensils, waves of tough cocks overflowing, watches working like dry stomachs and ... white water closets awakening] (PN1 300). This last, Neruda's version of Duchamp's urinal, the W. C. with its wooden eye (the lid), its twisted pigeons (pipes), and drowned throat (bowl), sounding suddenly like waterfalls (pulling the chain). Neruda's ears make sense of a waking world.

The following poem in the second *Residencia*, 'Sólo la muerte' [Only death], explores this sonorous unconscious in terms of death, that 'oscuro, oscuro, oscuro' [dark, dark, dark] that Neruda locates 'hacia adentro' [towards inside]. For death too is a 'sonido puro' [pure sound]. The poet repeats his crucial phrase, 'A lo sonoro llega la muerte / ... / llega a gritar sin boca,

---

50 'comme la rencontre fortuite sur une table de dissection d'une machine à coudre et d'un parapluie', in Isidore Ducasse, Comte de Lautréamont, *Oeuvres complètes*, p. 234.

sin lengua, sin garganta' [To sonorousness comes death, it arrives shouting without mouth, without tongue, without throat], too deep down for language and poetry (the next poem in the collection 'Barcarola' also employs 'de lo sonoro'). The last stanza couples death with the 'catre' [folding cot], with blankets and 'sopla un sonido oscuro que hincha sábanas' [a dark sound blows that swells sheets] (PN1 302).

The way back and down into this 'oculto fuego' is sexual, and this is Neruda's greatest insight. The prose poem 'Material nupcial' [Nuptial matter] has the poet staring at a girl 'temblando y respirando y blanca' [trembling, breathing and white] (PN1 320). He enumerates her nipples and her 'rosal reunión' where 'su sexo de pestañas nocturnas parpadea' [her sex of nocturnal eyelashes blinks]. As the poet stares at this image, he feels words sinking in his mouth and drown in the ocean, en *lo sonoro*. He will open this girl's legs until death, will make her retreat with her eyes closed into a thick river of green semen ('espeso río de semen verde'). Making love will drown her with *amapolas, rodillas, labios, crimen* and *pelos empapados* [poppies, knees, lips, crime, soaked hairs] dragging her down into the speechless inner world, 'hacia nunca, hacia nada' [towards never, towards nothing] (PN1 321). Neruda knows, as an introspective and experimental poet, that *lo sonoro* means nothing, it is just pure sound, and is nowhere, outside time, the inner senselessness of sound without referents, without words. There is no transcendence, just sensation (and Neruda's vast difference from 'transcendalists' like D. H. Lawrence or Octavio Paz). The poet fights his way down there through 'her', and the poem closes:

> y con gotas de negra materia resbalando
> como pescados ciegos o balas de agua gruesa. (PN1 321)
>
> [with drops of black matter slipping like blind fish or bullets of thick water]

What is this slippery black matter in drops but ink and sperm fused? The poet, like the lover, is immersed in his unconscious like a blind fish; his weapons are his sound-words, the bullets. The last phrase in the poem. 'agua gruesa' (it has to be voiced). again opens out through vowels. There is also meaning, despite the unpredictable adjective 'gruesa', and it suggests the prime life element 'water', inspiration in the inner desert.

The poem that follows 'Material nupcial' in section three of *Residencia II* is a coda on this notion of water and sex, even in its title 'Agua sexual' [Sexual water]. The sexual drops (perhaps sweat) fall biting, smash the axis of symmetry, 'pegando en las costuras del alma' [sticking to the seams of the soul], breaking abandoned things 'empapando lo oscuro' [soaking the darkness] (PN1 322). We arrive in Neruda's thinking at another adjectival noun, *lo oscuro*. Inner darkness is given attributes of liquid, sweat and movement, the deliquescent release of fluids during copulation and inspiration. This inner darkness is where the poet actually can see, like a visionary. Neruda sees in this dark, thanks to his kind of cognitive sexual witnessing. The poem moves forward on this visionary wave of the verb 'veo' [I see], where he sees ships, the summer, cellars, rooms, girls, blood, stockings, man's hair, beds, blankets, hotels (there is a coded story there). The poet also sees back into time 'y también los orígenes' [and also the origins], those origins that Eliot referred to in his 'auditory imagination'. For Neruda sees what should not be seen, with that dramatic, prophet's simile 'como un párpado atrozmente levantado a la fuerza / estoy mirando' [like an eyelid atrociously lifted by force, I stare] (PN1 322) that Emir Rodríguez Monegal saw as the core lines of his poetics.[51] When you are able to stare with your eyelids forcibly kept open, you don't *see*, but *hear*. The succeeding stanza opens:

> Y entonces hay este sonido:
> un ruido rojo de huesos,
> un pegarse de carne,
> y piernas amarillas como espigas juntándose.
> Yo escucho entre el disparo de los besos,
> escucho, sacudido entre respiraciones y sollozos. (PN1 323)

> [And then there's this sound, a red noise of bones, a beating of flesh and yellow legs like ears of wheat joining. I listen among the shots of kisses, I listen, shaken between breathing and sobs]

The poet, to borrow a famous 1912 title by Walter de la Mare, is a listener.[52] The poet sees with his ears, the red noise of bones, the pistol shots of kisses.

Neruda has tried to think the unthinkable, to find a language to evoke experiences that an Eliot or a Paz can only ironise about (there is never irony in Neruda). He comes up with a series of linked expressions that must be read aloud, *lo sonoro*, *lo oscuro*, *oculto fuego*, *agua gruesa* [sonorousness, darkness, hidden fire, heavy water] and that can be poorly translated conceptually as silence, the unconscious, the inner ocean, inspiration, the origin of language. To get there, you don't think, you listen, eyes shut but seeing and hearing. Sexual initiation in Rangoon with Josie Bliss, and many others,

---

[51] There is a coincidence with Eliot's 'Pressing lidless eyes and waiting for a knock upon the door' from section II, 'A Game of Chess', in *The Waste Land*, p. 68.

[52] Walter de la Mare published his poem 'The Listeners' in *The Listeners and other Poems* (London: Constable, 1912). The poem opens: '"Is there anybody there?" said the Traveller, / Knocking on the moonlit door; / And his horse in the silence champed the grasses', to close 'And how the silence surged softly backward, / When the plunging hoofs were gone' (pp. 69–70). The poem is a treatise on 'silence'.

knotted sexual knowledge with writing poetry.[53] The poem is clearly more than 'sordid' (John Felstiner). Neruda's 1934 poem 'Las furias y las penas' [Furies and sorrows] confirms this quest; the poet is guided by his lover's legs and kisses and led down into a 'húmeda sombra' [humid shadows] and rebirth into a deeper self that is mindless: 'Nada sino esa pulpa de los seres / Nada sino esa copa de raíces' [Nothing but this pulp of beings, nothing but this glass of roots] (PN1 361). In this poem, Neruda coins a term for his thinking: 'una sorda ciencia con cabello y cavernas' [a deaf science with hair and caverns] as his new knowledge found in 'las grandes coronas geni-tales' [the great genital crowns]. It is an experiential 'nada' [nothing] that was the 'pulpa de los seres', the origins. It is worthwhile linking Neruda's thinking with N. O. Brown's aphoristic defence of symbolic-consciousness in his manifesto against literal-mindedness: 'Knowledge is carnal knowledge. A subterranean passage between mind and body underlies all analogy, no word is metaphyiscal without being first physical; and the body that is the measure of all things is sexual.'[54]

In a much-commented-on poem 'Entrada a la madera' [Entrance to wood] the poet falls into inner darkness, in his sensualist, materialist way, 'Con mi razón apenas, con mis dedos' [with my reason scaarcely, with my fingers], discarding reason and feeling his way in, as if caressing his lover, into this eroticised matter to reach his true self: 'Es que soy yo ...' (PN1 324) and 'Soy yo ...' (PN1 325), he repeats confidently, answering the opening of André Breton's *Nadja*'s 'Qui suis-je?' [Who am I?].[55] Deep inside, he sees and hears: 'Oigo tus vegetales oceánicos' [I hear your oceanic vegetations] (PN1 325). The poem repeats the verb 'caer' [to fall] and ends with the 'nosotros' [we] of two lovers:

> y hagamos fuego, y silencio, y sonido,
> y ardamos, y callemos, y campanas. (PN1 325)

> [and let's make fire and silence and sound and let's burn and be silent and bells]

To burn in passion is to experience silence and sound simultaneously, which is poetry, that ecstatic 'campanas' [bells] that ring out in our ears. We expect a third verb following 'arder' and 'callar', and unpredictably it is a noun that is almost a verb, 'campanemos / campanas'. Loyola's note points out that Neru-da's critic Amado Alonso interpreted this use of 'campanas' as synonym for

---

[53] See my *Darío, Borges, Neruda: the Ancient Quarrel between Poets and Philosophers*, for more on Josie Bliss.

[54] Brown, *Love's Body*, p. 249.

[55] André Breton, *Nadja*, p. 9.

sin antecedentes, una absorción física del mundo, a pesar y en contra de nosotros. La historia, los problemas 'del conocimiento', como los llaman, me parcen despojados de dimensión [...] Cada vez veo menos ideas en torno mío, y más cuerpos, sol y sudor. [67]

[Borges who you mention seems to me more worried about cultural and societal problems that do not seduce me, that aren't human. I like the great wines, love, suffering and books as consolation to inevitable loneliness. I have even a kind of scorn for culture as an interpretation of things, it seems to me that a knowledge without antecedents, a physical absorption in the world, despite and against us. History, problems of 'knowledge' as they're called, seem stripped of dimension. More and more I see less ideas around me than bodies, sun and sweat]

In 1930 Borges was becoming a cultural leader in booming Buenos Aires, with three books of poems, his own magazine, three books of essays and an eccentric biography already behind him. He was clearly bookish, but also an adventurer (Neruda met and was impressed by his friend the painter and metaphysician Xul Solar). And he had not started on the 'fictions' that would make him famous in the 1940s.[68] Neruda was measuring himself against the best mind of his times. Contrary to Borges, his own brand of knowledge was a total immersion in matter, whatever the result. You can see how Neruda's painful exposure in the Far East had placed 'books' and the library in question. He called Borges and Xul Solar 'ghosts of old libraries'.[69] Yet, he continued to read. Borges and Neruda met once in Buenos Aires in 1927, and Neruda dedicated a copy of his *tentativa del hombre infinita* to 'Jorge Luis Borges, su compañero, Pablo Neruda' after they had both admitted admiring Whitman.[70]

As suggested, Neruda's exploration of 'lo sonoro' merged with his discovery of a liberating sexuality. In a letter of 1928 he described Rangoon as an oven, a hell, a terrible exile; he could neither write nor read, he felt like a ghost, dressed in his white suit and white cork hat. He was not English, was not even European, but was white, despite his miserable, irregular salary. The 'horror of these abandoned colonies' drove most Europeans to drink, the *chota pegg*, the 'terrible tropical whisky'. Neruda's bizarre social position ensured that he was not fascinated by eastern glamour and did not become a spiritual tourist; he mingled with the dispossessed crowds, 'the street was

67 Aguirre, *Neruda / Eandi*, p. 46.

68 See my *Jorge Luis Borges*, pp. 53–82.

69 Aguirre, *Neruda / Eandi*, p. 61.

70 Donald Yates, 'Neruda and Borges', in Juan Loveluck and Isaac Jack Lévy (eds), *Simposio Pablo Neruda. Actas*, p. 240. Bioy Casares recorded Borges lamenting that Neruda's poetry was so bad that it could not be memorised by heart. See Adolfo Bioy Casares, *Borges*, edición al cuidado de Daniel Martino (Buenos Aires: Destino, 2006), p. 894.

my religion'.[71] Louis MacNeice recalled an Indian novelist who confirmed Neruda's anti-western views about India: 'It was all a mistake, Mulk said, India was not spiritual, no Indian had even thought so until fifty years ago. India was earthy, matter-of-fact; it was Anglo-Indians who had loud-pedalled her alleged mysticism.'[72] What Neruda did find were 'girls with young eyes and hips' with flowers in their hair and rings on their toes and ankles, and one of these girls became his lover. Her name was Josie Bliss, though that was not her Burmese name, which Neruda never revealed, if he remembered it at all, or could spell it. They communicated in English, and she lived out her name bliss to the full; it could even have been his nickname for her, for over those years of exile from Chile Neruda devoured D. H. Lawrence. Bliss in his English meant sexual, not religious bliss. It was also, as Loyola discerned, the first time that Neruda had lived with a woman.[73]

That Josie Bliss was crucial to his poetry as a real-life muse simply confirmed Neruda's romantic view that experience, the more intense the better, informed his poetry. The last culminating poem of his *Residencia en la tierra I y II*, 1935, is titled 'Josie Bliss' as recognition of her muse-like status, but the gently nostalgic poem conceals her reality; however, she surfaced, namelessly, in six earlier poems in the collection, according to Edmundo Olivares.[74] She haunted Neruda's memory for the rest of his life, although they were probably together only for a few months. All we know of Josie Bliss is what Neruda tells us. In his memoirs Neruda recreated this affair in this British colony run along caste lines, the Burma George Orwell hated where 'you see the dirty work of Europe at close quarters' and where Orwell learnt that 'imperialism was an evil thing'.[75] Neruda was boycotted by the English and their Strand Hotel club life because he lived with a native. Jan Morris saw concubinage as typical of colonial life. She wrote: 'Most Englishmen took mistresses, and thus got close to the life and feelings of Indian people,' but perhaps not so blatantly as Neruda.[76] Josie Bliss was forced to dress like an Englishwoman, but in his house threw off her shoes, put on a sarong and used her Burmese name, though they spoke English to each other. As their free relationship flourished she became intensely jealous, would stalk Neruda's mosquito-netted bed with a long knife, threatening to kill him until Neruda could take this passionate jealousy no more and escaped to Ceylon without telling her, leaving everything behind, his clothes, his shoes, his books. Neruda mythified this incident; in fact he was transferred

---

[71] Pablo Neruda, *Confieso que he vivido*, p. 119.

[72] Louis MacNeice, *The Strings are False. An Unfinished Autobiography*, p. 209.

[73] Loyola, PNI 351.

[74] Olivares, 2000, p. 121.

[75] George Orwell, *Inside the Whale and Other Essays*, p. 91.

[76] Jan Morris, *Pax Britannica*, p. 134.

to another diplomatic post. Later, she followed him out to Ceylon, moved in next door and played the Paul Robeson records they both loved, insulting the women who visited him, until she was persuaded to leave. At the port in Colombo Neruda fixes Josie Bliss, 'amorous terrorist' in an unforgettable image; she had bent down and kissed his chalked shoes, then stood up with tears running down her chalk-smudged face. He confessed that after she left that 'mi corazón adquirió allí una cicatriz que no se ha borrado' [my heart acquired a scar that has not healed].[77] It is for reasons like these that Rodríguez Monegal corrected the earlier critic Amado Alonso about whether Neruda's poetry is hermetic by stating that it was 'más desgarradamente confesional que hermético' [more heart-breakingly confessional than hermetic].[78]

Reading Neruda's poems as 'scars' reveals another story. This secondary story does not focus on the kitchen knife or the coconut palm, on castration fears and jealousy, but on a sexual relationship where Neruda contacted a mystery, a powerful energy that panicked him and literally forced him to run away. Neruda boasted that his path to knowledge, both of the self and the world, was not through bookish culture. In a 1928 letter to Eandi he evoked his poetic credo: 'la poesía debe cargarse de sustancia universal, de pasiones y cosas' [poetry should be charged with universal substance, with passion and things].[79] This sensual and material position was tested to the full by Josie Bliss, his Burmese muse.

The poem 'Tango del viudo' [Widower's tango], written in 1928 after fleeing Josie Bliss, recreates the dramatic mosquito-net and knife incident in Dalhousie Street, Rangoon and is one of Neruda's greatest poems. The Spanish poet and critic Guillermo de Torre recognised it as 'profound' in 1934, while John Felstiner called it a 'superb poem'.[80] More recently, in 2004, Mario Vargas Llosa averred that it still sent 'a shiver down my spine' and gave him 'that sense of wonderful unease and shock that only the best literature can produce'.[81] The fertile title: first I will deal with tangos. From being brothel music without words in Buenos Aires, the tango added lyrics around 1916–17, with Gardel voicing them. Tango was then taken up in fashionable Paris when Gardel travelled there in 1928, spread around Latin America and became respectable, but not without complaints about its brothel origins. This subversive element to early tango was to Neruda's liking. The writer Enrique Larreta, then Argentine ambassador in Paris, complained that 'tango

---

77 Neruda, *Confieso que he vivido*, p. 133.

78 Rodríguez Monegal, *El viajero inmóvil*, p. 16.

79 Aguirre, *Neruda / Eandi*, p. 61.

80 Torre cited by Olivares, *Pablo Neruda II*, p. 147; Felstiner, *Translating Neruda*, p. 88.

81 Mario Vargas Llosa, *Touchstones* (London: Faber, 2007), p. 127. Note that there is a novel by Cristián Barros called *Tango del viudo* (Santiago: Seix Barral-Editorial Planeta, 2003) based on the affair.

in Buenos Aires is a dance of ill repute from cellars of the worst kind. It is
not danced in the drawing rooms of decent people...'[82] Its words tended to
be a man's lament at being betrayed by his woman, often taking his revenge,
with a knife. The brothel origins of immigrant men waiting for whores, whom
they could never trust or love, are implicit in the very melodies of the music;
it is metonymically South American. Tango melody contaminated the way
Neruda read his poetry. I have already quoted Volodia Teitelboim, who once
heard Neruda reading from these *Residencia* poems without inflections, in a
monochord, moaning manner, without making the obvious association with
tango.

The 'Viudo' of the title is equally rich in echoes; Neruda was not married
to Josie Bliss, but was tempted to settle with her. According to Norman
Lewis, sexual mores were extremely lax in Burma ('marriage is considered
to exist, without further ceremony, when a couple are seen to eat together [...]
an extraordinary sexual freedom').[83] Confirming this sexual laxity, Neruda, in
a short prose poem 'El joven monarca' [The young monarch], wrote:

> Sí, quiero casarme con la más bella de Mandalay, quiero encomendar mi
> evoltura terrestre a ese ruido de la mujer cocinando, a ese aleteo de falda y
> pie desnudo que se mueven y mezclan como viento y hojas. (PNI 282)

> [Yes, I want to marry the most beautiful woman in Mandalay, I want to
> entrust my earthly wrapping to that noise of woman cooking, to that flut-
> tering of skirt and naked foot that move and mix like wind and leaf]

Note the link of sounds and woman. Now, Neruda wrote this prose poem
after abandoning his 'wife' Josie Bliss, for it closes with the poet crying her
absence. Thus, the title 'Tango del viudo' asserts that Josie Bliss left Neruda
a widower, she 'died'; the poem deceitfully reverses the biographical situation for in fact he 'killed' her, to extend the death metaphors, by running off.
The reference to 'Mandalay' (which Neruda visited) evokes Kipling's cock-
nified poem of that name where a Burmese girl under a palm-tree summons
her fugitive lover, 'come you back to Mandalay'.[84] But Neruda ignored this
plea, pretended to be a 'Viudo'. More, *le veuf* [widower], recalls, as already
sugggested, Gérard de Nerval's sonnet 'El desdichado', with its Spanish title
meaning he who lost his *dicha* or happiness, an elegy to loss and melancholy,
with already noted references to Mélusine and Orpheus. Nerval's sonnet
opens: 'Je suis le ténébreux, – le veuf – l'inconsolé, / Le prince d'Aquitaine
à la tour abolie.'[85] If we read this sonnet as read by Neruda, that he was 'le

---

82 Cited in Horacio Salas, *El tango*, p. 118.

83 Norman Lewis, *Golden Earth. Travels in Burma*, pp. 52–3.

84 Rudyard Kipling, *Selected Poems*, p. 182.

85 Gérard de Nerval, *Les Chimères*, p. 28. In section 12 of his *Canto general*, Neruda writes
a letter-poem to an Argentine friend called González Carbalho and reminds him: 'Recordáis

veuf', then we have both a confession of his active rejection of Josie, and his subsequent bleakness and melancholy. Thirty years later in his collection *Estravagario*, 1958, Neruda changed the gender of Nerval's sonnet to 'La desdichada'. It opens laconically: 'La dejé en la puerta esperando / y me fui para no volver' [I left her in the door waiting and left not to return]. Passing time and the Second World War have blotted out his presence on his verandah, with his hammock, his plants, and 'aquella mujer esperando' [that woman waiting] (PN2 665). Neruda still suffered guiltily for having abandoned Josie Bliss; in fact, he is the one still waiting, he is the 'desdichado'. In 1964, in a poem called 'Amores: Josie Bliss II' we read: 'Quise decir que yo también / sufrí: / no es bastante: / el que hiere es herido hasta morir' [I wanted to tell her that I too / suffered: / it's not enough: / he who wounds is wounded himself until death] (PN2 1235). Now we move beyond psychology, for Neruda wanted to abandon his muse in order to write, and his consolation would be his poems. Neruda's real predicament was that in order to write poems he, like Nerval, had to reject his muse and become a *viudo*; a poet cannot write and live the poem. In Yeats's terms, he must choose: either perfect the work or the life, not both.[86] The real decision was that Neruda preferred to *write about* Josie Bliss than live intensely with her. That is, he chose to be a poet, not live poetically. He confessed as much in a letter of 1928 after bolting from her. That depressing moment, disastrous for many, was 'noble materia para mí' [noble matter for me].[87] Melancholy, widower's grief, is the real muse.

The 1928 poem 'Tango del viudo' opens as a verse-letter written to Josie, though she is not named, in the intimate *tú* address from on board the ship as the poet escapes, and vividly evokes their domestic life together in one long sentence:

> Oh *Maligna, ya habrás hallado la carta, ya habrás llorado de*
>   *furia,*
> *y habrás insultado el recuerdo de mi madre*
> *llamándola perra podrida y madre de perros,*
> *ya habrás bebido sola, solitaria el té del atardecer*
> *mirando mis viejos zapatos vacíos para siempre,*
> *y ya no podrás recordar mis enfermedades, mis sueños*
>   *nocturnos, mis comidas*
> *sin maldecirme en voz alta como si estuviera allí aún,*

otro? Príncipe de Aquitania: a su torre / abolida...' (PN1 742), confirming that he still retained his memory of Nerval.

86 From W. B. Yeats, 'The Choice': 'The intellect of man is forced to choose / Perfection of the life, or of the Work, / And if it take the second must refuse / A heavenly mansion, raging in the dark,' in *Collected Poems*, p. 278.

87 Aguirre, *Neruda / Eandi*, p. 112.

> *quejándome del trópico, de los 'coolies coringhis',*
> *de las venenosas fiebres que me hicieron tanto daño*
> *y de los espantosos ingleses que odio todavía.* (PN1 291)

[Oh evil one, you must by now have found the letter, you must
have wept with fury, and you must have insulted my mother's
memory, called her rotten bitch and mother of dogs, you must
have drunk alone, all by yourself, your afternoon tea, looking at
my old shoes forever empty, and you won't be able any longer to
recall my illnesses, my night dreams, my meals, without cursing
me aloud as if I was still there, complaining about the tropics,
about the *corringhis* coolies, about the poisonous fevers that did
me so much harm, and about the awful English that I still hate][88]

The syncopation of the temporal adverb 'ya' sharpens painfully in memory
the explicit references, especially hating English colonial arrogance, as much
as Orwell had. He even cites the dockside 'coolies' from the aboriginal tribe
called the Coringhi in English. The key word of his hate for the British is
that 'todavía'. Why does Neruda call her 'Maligna'? Is she the real 'maldita',
not him? Rimbaud has a sonnet about a waitress from the kitchen titled 'La
maline' [Evil-minded woman], and 'kitchen' appears in Neruda's poem.[89]
Verlaine's 'Poèmes saturniens' are about sages who live 'd'une influence
maligne' [under an evil influence], equivalents to his subversive heroes, the
'poetas malditos' (by calling the woman 'maligna', he hints that she is the
real poet, not him).[90] The famous tango 'Mi noche triste' [My sad night],
sung by Carlos Gardel in 1917 (music by Samuel Castriota and lyrics by
Pascual Contursi), replays Neruda's poem as the man's lament at being 'todo
triste, abandonado' [all sad and abandoned]. It opened:

> Percanta que me amuraste
> en lo mejor de mi vida
> dejándome el alma herida
> y splín en el corazón,
> sabiendo que te quería
> que vos eras mi alegría
> y mi sueño abrasador.
> Para mí ya no hay consuelo
> y por eso me encurdelo
> pa' olvidarme de tu amor

---

[88] Slightly modified version of Donald D. Walsh's translation in his *Residence on Earth*,
1976, pp. 85–7.

[89] Rimbaud, *Oeuvres complètes*, p. 33.

[90] Verlaine, *Oeuvres poétiques completes*, p. 37.

[Lover, you cheated on me in the best of my life, leaving my soul wounded and spleen in my heart, knowing I loved you and you were my happiness and my burning dream. For me there's no consolation and for that reason I get drunk to forget your love].

The opening word 'Percanta' (meaning 'lover' in Lunfardo, underworld slang in Buenos Aires) matches Neruda's 'Maligna' as an explosive vocal opening, as does the accusation of betrayal. It also allows one to read 'maligna' as an endearment and not an insult.[91] When W. S. Merwin translated the poem, he kept Maligna in English, as if a name.[92] Thus, the tango 'Mi noche triste' summarised Neruda's tango poem. Jean-Philippe Barnabé cited that opening and defined all tango as a lament at being abandoned, a form of loss, even 'duelo' (grief), a tradition that only began in 1917 (roughly thirteen years before Neruda wrote his poem).[93]

The poem's second stanza evokes Neruda's return to what he loathes most but has cunningly chosen – loneliness, the absence of his lover; he is back to eating cold food alone in restaurants, living without coat-hangers or portraits on the wall. He misses Josie: 'Cuánta sombra de la que hay en mi alma daría por recobrarte' [How much of the darkness in my soul I would give to recover you] (PN1 291). But it was too late. The third stanza returns to Josie in Rangoon and the famous knife that Neruda feared would kill him, which he buried under a coconut tree; but memory transformed this metal knife into a mental fetish:

> *y ahora repentinamente quisiera oler su acero de cocina*
> *acostumbrado al peso de tu mano y al brillo de tu pie:*
> *bajo la humedad de la tierra, entre las sordas raíces,*
> *de los lenguajes humanos el pobre sólo sabría tu nombre*
> *y la espesa tierra no comprende tu nombre*
> *hecho de impenetrables substancias divinas* (PN1 291)

[And now suddenly I would like to smell its kitchen steel, accustomed to the weight of your hand and the shine of your foot: under the moisture of the earth, among the deaf roots, of all human languages the poor thing would only know your name made of impenetrable and divine substances]

Knife then, like *cadera*, is synedoche for Josie, her touch, her smell; she is danger; her real Burmese name never explicitly mentioned by Neruda is the

91 Salas, *El tango*, p. 348. See José Gobello, *Nuevo diccionario lunfardo*, p. 199.

92 W. S. Merwin, in Neruda, *Selected Poems*, 1970, p. 81.

93 Jean-Philippe Barnabé, 'Homero Manzi: entre las letras y los hombres', in Daniel Attala, Sergio Delgado and Rémi Le March'hadour, *L'Écrivain argentin et la tradition* (Rennes: Mondes Hispanophones 28, Presses Universitaires de Rennes, 2004), pp. 238–9.

only word worth repeating, hoarded by him as a talisman. That Josie Bliss is
knife is repeated metaphorically in all the later poems alluding to her; she is
often the 'enemy', the 'wide-hipped enemy', the 'pursuer', the 'panther' and
'tiger' with claw-knives out to hunt him like a harpy. In the poem 'El abandonado' where Neruda continued to invert the facts as if he had been abandoned
by her, she is the oracle, the enigma: 'no sé quién eres pero tanto te debo /
que la tierra está llena de mi tesoro amargo' [I don't know who you are but I
owe you so much that the earth is full of my bitter treasure] (PN1 354). Josie
Bliss is the hostile muse who provoked the poet to be himself and choose
what kind of poet to be, who spoke a forgotten language, 'the sweetest sighs'
(perhaps her Burmese name), buried deep inside her.

In the third stanza of 'Tango del viudo' Neruda recreates Josie Bliss in
his memory in cosmic and telluric metaphors; her legs 'detenidas y duras
aguas solares' [still and hard solar waters] (PN1 292), her eyes 'la golond-
rina' [swallow], her heart 'el perro de furia' [the dog of fury]. Josie Bliss as
dog of fury awakens a mythical resonance, and alludes to another of Neruda's great Josie-love-poems, 'Las furias y las penas' [Furies and heartaches],
1934 (but not published until 1947). For Josie Bliss, the enemy, literally
reincarnated the Erinnyes or Furies, the angry ones who, according to Robert
Graves, 'avenge crimes of parricide and perjury', induce remorse and bad
faith, 'punish such crimes by hounding the culprits relentlessly from city to
city and from country to country', with their snake-hair, coal-black bodies
and blood-shot eyes.[94] Neruda's melancholia is Josie Bliss, the dog of fury,
hounding him in his heart, dictating poems to her fearful power, her 'rencor
de puñal' [rancour of dagger] (PN2 1238). The last phrase of this stanza is
deeply Romantic: he is alone again, repeating 'para siempre' (PN1 292), that
emotional exaggeration the test of his sincerity. Another way of phrasing the
emotion behind the poem would be to say that the poet will never forget her.
The last poem of the second *Residencia*, 'Josie Bliss' ends in the present
tense, 'Ahí están, ahí están / los besos' [there they are, there they are, the
kisses] and the smiles and suits, and death's mouth will not bite them, 'ahí
están' (a third time) fixed in memory 'con su azul material vagamente invencible' [with their vaguely invincible blue matter] (PN1 345). The last word is
'invincible', a term that ensures that nothing will dim Josie's memory.

The last stanza of 'Tango del viudo' suggests a Faustian exchange. Neruda
would give everything to hear 'tu brusca respiración' [brusque breathing],
that *brusca* making Josie so suddenly there in his mind, suggesting lover's
panting. But more extraordinarily, for Neruda witholds this detail to the
poem's end, he would give everything in his soul:

[94] Robert Graves, *The Greek Myths*, p. 122.

Y por oírte orinar, en la oscuridad, en el fondo de la casa,
como vertiendo una miel delgada, trémula, argentina, obstinada
(PN1 292)

[and to hear you pee in the dark at the back of the house like
spilling a thin, tremulous, silvery, obstinant honey]

Neruda condensed the thrill of Josie Bliss in his memory into this aural image
of a woman 'peeing', pure sound, at night in the silent house. Neruda has
accepted everything in Josie Bliss as divine and poetic, down to her excretory
functions. He has put into poetic practice what Whitman claimed about the
body: 'If anything is sacred the human body is sacred.'[95] His lover's acceptance turns ordinary *orina* into *miel* and four incantatory adjectives; that is,
her 'urine' triggered off his poetic fancy, made him a poet. Josie Bliss freed
Neruda's unconscious, vividly depicted by him as 'lo sonoro' (explored, as
noted, in the poem 'Un día sobresale'), a silent house at night, where poetry
emerges freely, truthfully, as 'sounds'. Neruda located the Dionysiac source
of poetry in incantatory sound, thanks to Josie Bliss. In this 'lo sonoro' *les
mots font l'amour*, in André Breton's phrase, for only when the poet Neruda
breaks the sexual taboos can his inner poetic language break linguistic taboos
– a clear link between experience and creativity that Neruda learned from
Josie Bliss ('pues ella era el sonido que me hería' [for she is the sound that
wounds me]).[96] In a 1936 manifesto Neruda advocated a poetry that excluded
nothing, that accepted everything, without moral discriminations, a penetra-
tion into matter in an act of 'arrebatado amor' [ecstatic love] that was Josie
Bliss's lesson.[97] In 1964 in the poem 'Rangoon 1927' Neruda evoked this
'arrebatado' [furious] love as 'desmedido' [excessive], submerging the lovers
in the 'placer amargo de los desesperados' [bitter pleasure of the desperate]
(PN2 1199). It is telling that Amado Alonso, in his 1940 study, did not
dare quote or comment on this erotic simile, instead claimimg that Neruda
conjured up 'strange associations, substances practically heterogeneous and
poetically identical' to add in brackets '(¡una explicación del modo de sus
imágenes!)' [an explanation of the ways of his metaphors].[98]

Urine transformed erotically into honey brings us back to the 'Song of
Songs', as if written by Neruda: 'Thy lips, o My Spouse, drop as the honey
comb: honey and milk are under thy tongue: and the smell of thy garments
is like the smell of Lebanon,' echoed in his line 'ay, your huge thighs coated
with green honey'. The transformation of urine to honey, mimicking the
transformatory power of poetry itself (a kind of mental honey), leads us

95　Whitman, *Leaves of Grass*, p. 102.
96　André Breton, 'Les mots sans rides', in *Les pas perdus*, p. 171.
97　Cited in Rodríguez Monegal, *El viajero inmóvil*, p. 89.
98　Alonso, *Poesía y estilo*, p. 238.

to why Neruda backed away, and cowardly wrote about his encounter with Josie Bliss. The Josie Bliss experience, within the poems, suggests Neruda's unwillingness to forget, an act that generates countless rewritings of the same Nervalian poem of loss. As Freud noted: 'In the unconscious, nothing can be brought to an end, nothing is past or forgotten,' only here the unconscious is the body of poems. Adam Phillips linked this to love itself, where there are 'no experts on love. And love, whatever else it is, is terror.'[99]

Las furias y las penas (1934), 1947

Neruda's long, 1934 love-lament 'Las furias y las penas' refers, as already hinted, to the woman / muse, possibly Josie Bliss (or Josie Bliss in another woman), as a dog of fury and to his own 'penas de amor'. The poem's title, as the epigraph reveals, evokes a sonnet by the Spanish Golden Age poet Francisco de Quevedo (1580–1645). Neruda came to Quevedo quite late, but wrote an admiring essay 'Viaje al corazón de Quevedo' [Journey to the heart of Quevedo] in 1942, calling him the greatest poet of them all (PN4 452). He wrote: 'porque Quevedo ha sido para mí no una lectura, sino una experiencia viva, con toda la rumorosa materia de la vida' [because Quevedo has been for me not a reading but a living experience, with all the rumorous matter of life] (PN4 457), an apt example of how Neruda read. Quevedo's mocking sonnet has a long title that, if read as Neruda's own, becomes a bizarre confession: 'Finge dentro de sí un infierno, cuyas penas procura mitigar, como Orfeo, con la música de su canto, pero sin provecho' [He fakes in himself a hell, whose pains he tries to mitigate like Orpheus, with the music of his song, but without success].[100] This ironic title suggests the question: did Neruda pretend passion or is his poetry the failure to quench it? In Quevedo's case, given church censorship, you could argue that he pretends to pretend, and is sincere by lying. In Neruda's case sincerity underscores his Romantic poetics, so this Quevedo sonnet consciously confesses his duplicity. What Quevedo / Neruda assert is that art is no compensation for the kind of love Josie Bliss offered him. Quevedo / Neruda see themselves as threatened by the 'burning flame' of love, so they pretend to be Orpheus ('pruebo a ser Orfeo') but cannot really become Orpheus as trapped in their heart are 'furias y penas'; love remains an inner tyrant. The sonnet ends:

> Y yo padezco en mí la culpa mía,
> oh dueño sin piedad, que tal ordenas!

---

[99]   Adam Phillips, *Terrors and Experts*, pp. 1, xi.

[100] Francisco de Quevedo, *Antología poética*, p. 39. There is some debate as to whether Quevedo put his own title to this sonnet.

Pues del castigo de enemiga mano
no es preciso, ni rescate la armonía

[And I suffer in myself my own guilt, oh pitiless master, who
has ordered this. For with this punishment from enemy's hand,
harmony is impossible, cannot rescue me]

We can now read, through Neruda / Quevedo, that he accepts the blame, that
even if he were a poet like Orpheus he could never compensate his abandonment of Josie / Eurydice, for writing verse is no 'rescate'. In 1942 Neruda
confessed that his favourite line in poetry was Quevedo's heretical ending
about love overpowering everything: 'polvo serán, mas polvo enamorado'
[dust they will be but dust in love] (PN4 467).

Now we can explore why Neruda could not abandon his enemy-muse. Josie
embodied an asocial, inner knowledge imparted by Dionysus, as freedom
from rules and law and bourgeois life that Neruda wanted but could not actually handle. The poem 'Las furias y las penas' narrates this infernal journey
into her inner depths, into a 'cañaveral', with tigers and dangers where the
lovers 'con la boca olfateando sudor y venas verdes / nos encontramos en la
húmeda sombra que deja caer besos' [with our mouths scenting sweat and
green veins / we meet in the damp shade that lets kisses fall] (PN1 357).
Neruda insinuates this vertiginous inner experience through metaphor and
image, the dissolving zone explored by Georges Bataille: 'Ce qui est en jeu
dans l'érotisme est toujours une dissolution...' [What's at play in eroticism is
always a dissolution] who links this dissolution with the effects of poetry: 'La
poésie mène au même point que chaque forme de l'érotisme, à l'indistinction,
à la confusion ...' [Poetry leads to the same point as every kind of eroticism, to
indistinction, to confusion].[101]

Josie Bliss is the 'enemiga de grandes caderas que mi pelo han tocado /
con un ronco rocío, con una lengua de agua' [enemy with huge hips that
touched my hair / with guttural dew, with a tongue of water] (PN1 357), who
granted Neruda rebirth into an asocial, alternative self, baptised with the
waters of his lover, in a new bodily configuration. Note the 'agua' / 'lengua'
rhyme. She helps him pass through a wall to find himself at 'el centro de unos
dulces miembros' [the centre of some sweet limbs] (PN1 358) where he (and
she) can 'muerde cada hoja de un bosque dando gritos' [bite every leaf of the
forest, letting out screams] (PN1 358). This is the same convulsive love that
André Breton evoked in his narrative of male cowardice, his abandoning of
his Mélusine, or *Nadja*, published in 1928. Gut-knowledge of self is tested
and proved as intense sensations, as intense metaphors. Josie Bliss taught the
poet 'divination', a new way of being, through her legs 'que te guían' [that

---

[101] Georges Bataille, *L'érotisme*, pp. 23, 30.

guide you] (PN1 359); for she, guided by her body, initiated Neruda into the sexual enigma.

In this 1934 poem, Neruda's evocation of Josie's ritual skills is extraordinary; she throws off her clothes, her keys, her coins, and is naked; she rolls on the floor where 'el viejo olor de semen como una enredadera / de cenicienta harina se desliza a tu boca' [the old smell of semen like a creeper of ash-like flour glides to your mouth] (PN1 359). The poet touched raw life that 'palpitas desde el dulce ombligo hasta las rosas' [throbs from the sweet navel to the roses] (PN1 360) This is mindless brute life (already cited):

> nada sino esa pulpa de los seres,
> nada sino esa copa de raíces. (PN1 361)

Neruda characterised this erotic descent into woman's 'great genital crowns' (PN1 362) as poetic wisdom, a 'sorda ciencia' [deaf science]. This extraordinary liberational poem of 1934 echoed the poem 'Material nupcial' of the same year, which, as noted, posits knowledge through her 'sexo de pestañas nocturnas parpadea' [sex of nocturnal eyelashes that blink] (PN1 320). The knowledge gained is a death-like sensation; the poet would drown her in 'un espeso río de semen verde' [a thick river of green semen].

For in his grief, hounded by his dog of fury, his enemy-muse, Neruda read D. H. Lawrence in English, lent to him by an English poet called Andrew Boyd (a 'true friend') after he had abandoned Josie Bliss, while living alone in exile in Wellawata, Ceylon. He does not state which books, but Lawrence's *Collected Poems* had just appeared in 1928 and *Pansies* in 1929. Andrew Boyd (1905–62) translated Neruda's already English-titled 'Walking around', from *Residencia en la tierra,* in Geoffrey Grigson's *New Verse* in 1936 (more on this later). Reading Lawrence allowed Neruda to pen frank and free-flowing poems evoking his discovery of self through passion-suffering for Josie Bliss, a materialist metaphysics, for, as Coleridge put it, 'sensation itself is but vision nascent',[102] that intense sensation is philosophically the sole starting point. Neruda chanced to read the 1927 privately printed Florence edition of Lawrence's banned *Lady Chatterley's Lover*, and read the book as if he were Mellors and Josie were Connie. Only the roles are reversed, and Connie / Josie teaches Neruda. When Mellors explains in his dialect that 'if tha shits an' if tha pisses I'm glad. I don't want a woman as couldna shit nor piss,'[103] Neruda hears Josie 'pee' in the silent house of primal sounds and knows that nothing in her is taboo, and later, when Connie feels reborn, that 'she had come to the real bed-rock of her nature, and was essentially shameless. She was her sensual self, naked and unashamed ... That was life!' (258)

---

102   Samuel Taylor Coleridge, *Biographia Literaria*, p. 148.
103   D. H. Lawrence, *Lady Chatterley's Lover*, p. 232.

we can hear Neruda's relief that he too had found his own bed-rock, his life, liberated from his Catholic and Chilean shame and taboos (his national formation). Josie Bliss taught Neruda freedom. There is no doubt that Neruda nick-named Josie 'Bliss' in honour of D. H. Lawrence, whose *Women in Love* has bliss as the code-word for this new knowledge of self: 'In the new, superfine bliss, a peace superceding knowledge, there was no I and you ... a new, paradisal unit'; and again: 'she was such bliss of release, that he would have suffered a whole eternity of torture rather than forego one second of this pang of unsurpassable bliss'.[104] However, one further literary source is Katherine Mansfield's short stories *Bliss and Other Stories*, out in 1920. The title story has a 30-year-old Bertha Young catching her husband in adulterous whispers. She explains her strange feeling of 'bliss' as: 'How idiotic civilisation is! Why be given a body if you have to keep it shut up in a case like a rare, rare fiddle!', so that bliss is being 'ardent', being 'modern', with trembling lips.[105]

We are dealing with a poet's way of writing new kinds of poems where Neruda could 'relate directly, with a kind of virility and scorn for formal concerns' that liberated him from his Hispanic worries about the primacy of poetic *form*,[106] where craft and formal skills override real meaning. Neruda has pierced into a zone beyond ethics and aesthetics. A parallel poetic source concerning breaking free of shame could be Walt Whitman's poem 'A Woman waits for me'. Whitman includes everything: 'Sex contains all, bodies, souls, / Meanings, proofs, purities, pride, the maternal mystery, the seminal milk ...' and summarises in the following stanza: 'Without shame the man I like knows and avows the deliciousness of his sex, / Without shame the woman I like knows and avows hers.'[107]

Neruda had written to Eandi to confess that 'la cuestión sexual es otro asunto trágico' [the sexual question is another tragic matter].[108] It is not clear what he meant, except that intense love and sex created an existential dilemma about being a poet. Josie Bliss forced Neruda to flee from the dangerous knowledge that she offered him; his writing a vain exorcism. Rodríguez Monegal reckoned that 'a deep horror and sexual fascination cross' Neruda's *Residencia* poems, without exploring the poetic knowledge and dilemmas implied.[109] In a short prose poem already cited, 'El joven

---

[104] D. H. Lawrence, *Women in Love*, pp. 309, 330. Loyola, in his *Neruda*, 2006, pp. 410–13, links 'bliss' to a religious bliss in Buddhism and yoga, but is not convincing.

[105] Katherine Mansfield, *Bliss and Other Stories* (London: Century Hutchinson [1920], 1988), pp. 93–103.

[106] Aguirre, *Neruda / Eandi*, p. 118.

[107] Whitman, *Leaves of Grass*, p. 105.

[108] Aguirre, *Neruda / Eandi*, pp. 77–8.

[109] Rodríguez Monegal, *El viajero inmóvil*, p. 226.

monarca', Neruda described his affair with Josie Bliss alone in their 'terri-
torio amoroso' [amorous territory] as a 'patria' [fatherland] limited by two
long, warm arms, by a long parallel passion; implying that his love affair
had created an alternative 'patria' bounded by mutual physical passion, his
identity no longer that of a Chilean poet in exile in Rangoon, but that of a
lover with a real woman who taught him elemental freedom from all social
taboos, but he fled. Loyola noted that this affair was 'the only true temptation
to put roots down that the poet lived in the East'.[110] It is striking to compare
this sexual 'patria' with D. H. Lawrence's 'Song of a Man who is Loved', which
opens with 'Between her breasts is my home, between her breasts', that is then
repeated, to close with 'So I hope I shall spend eternity / With my face down
buried between her breasts; / And my still heart full of security, / And my still
hands full of her breasts.'[111] Unlike Lawrence, Neruda did not find 'security',
though both articulate home as 'her' body.

In this nodal drama, I discern mythic parallels. As a traveller in the Far
East and far from home, but without a wife waiting and weaving, I can read
Neruda as the wandering Ulysses (Neruda had read Joyce's *Ulysses*) who in
book 10 of Homer's *The Odyssey* reaches Circe's island. With a little help
from Hermes, Ulysses avoided being turned into a tame animal, and lived
as Circe's lover for a year until he yearned to return home, to his *patria*.
Now, Circe's drug, according to Homer, made men *lose all memory of their
native land*; Hermes had warned Ulysses that he would 'never see your home
again'.[112] This incident illustrates Neruda's rejection of Josie Bliss's love, for
such love offered an alternative home, deeper roots, a private, asocial space
living in the present tense of sensations, without future civic projects. Chal-
lenged by Josie Bliss Neruda opted for a less intoxicated, ecstatic version of
home; rather than Josie he wanted a socially acceptable and public position,
and so left Circe / Josie. I can read Neruda's story into one last wandering
literary hero's plight to make his inner decision to reject Josie Bliss quite
clear, and to insinuate Josie's response to Neruda's cowardice. In Virgil's
Aeneid Queen Dido of Carthage, a widow, succumbs to Aeneas, and hopes
to live with him, but the gods oblige him to leave her bed and found Italy.
She caught him trying to escape. He, 'duty-bound', like Neruda, stood mute
'held fast his eyes, / And fought down the emotion in his heart', but still left
her. Queen Dido cursed Aeneas, now her 'enemy': 'I shall be everywhere / A
shade to haunt you! You will pay for this, unconscionable!', but she refused to
follow him 'like a slave', and having lost her integrity, 'in bitter mourning',
killed herself. Queen Dido was the one woman who stirred him to 'simple

110 Loyola, 'Introducción', Pablo Neruda, *Residencia en la tierra*, p. 319.

111 D. H. Lawrence, *Love Poems*, pp. 46–7. Loyola, 'Introducción', Pablo Neruda, *Residencia en la tierra*, p. 319.

112 Homer, *The Odyssey*, p. 163.

human emotion'. How tempting to read Josie Bliss into Queen Dido's fate, for the silent, excluded Burmese Josie Bliss never left Neruda alone, and their agon endured in his tantalic memory. The sole critic who sought out some mythic pattern behind the Josie Bliss poems was Enrico Mario Santí, who noted both that 'Josie Bliss is the woman most often thought of in connection with Neruda' and that 'no overt mythological overtones ... [but] Josie Bliss is a kind of Medusa is – obvious'.[113] Hernán Loyola also suggested an 'unconscious development in a terrible way about his own truthfully glimpsed sexuality';[114] however, he denies Neruda the understanding I have discerned in him.[115]

To put in perspective my reading about 'Las furias y las penas' as a replay of his affair with Josie Bliss I refer to a good close-reading of 'Las furias y las penas' by Florence Yudin. Starting from Amado Alonso's pertinent claim that Neruda had faced 'sin rodeos ni derivaciones con el impulso erótico mismo' [the erotic impulse itself directly, without derivations], Yudin then categorised the poem's journey as 'emotionally savage', with 'wild contradictions' that go nowhere, based on 'alienated sex', even 'brutalization' that denies man's 'freedom'. Yudin's conclusion is the opposite of my own. Such is the metaphorical density of the poetry that any interpretation sounds weak.[116]

So we turn back to *Residencia en la tierra I* as gut-thinking poems that embody a language and rhythm that is the process of thinking-in-poetry itself. This first *Residencia* also outlines a story that centres on the 'yo' [I, ego], the persona called Neruda, working out his feelings and sensations. The vague plot situates this 'yo' in the world of impenetrable matter and undermining passing-time; the 'yo' is alone, vulnerable and loveless. The outer world impinges on his psyche as torrents of language, waves of words, dark rhythms as he struggles to make sense of things, a kind of passive hero of the dream-world (all dreamers are passive). The book is structured as a journey into consciousness (Neruda calls himself the 'traveller' [PN1 276]), which we as readers follow, in the dark like Neruda himself. Julio Cortázar called it 'that descent into hell', locating it within Rimbaud's domain.[117] Nothing is made easy so that we share a similar sense of invasion, of not being able to transform sensations into the comfort of reason and meaning; that is, it is akin to dreaming.

In a 1930 prose poem, 'El deshabitado' [The uninhabited one] (almost 'El desdichado'), possibly written in Jakarta, the poet explores his isolation ('aislado' / 'rodeado' [isolated / surrounded]) and closes with what I call his introspective manifesto:

---

[113] Enrico Mario Santí, *Pablo Neruda. The Poetics of Prophecy*, pp. 90, 96.

[114] Loyola, 1987, p. 32.

[115] The previous sections were first explored by me in Wilson, *Darío, Borges, Neruda*.

[116] Florence L. Yudin, 'Dialectical Failure', pp. 56–61.

[117] Eulogio Suárez, *Neruda total*, p. 64.

A menudo, de atardecer acaecido, arrimo la luz a la ventana, y me miro, sostenido por maderas miserables, tendido en la humedad como un ataúd envejecido, entre paredes bruscamente débiles. Sueño, de una ausencia a otra, y a otra distancia, recibido y amargo. (PN1 282)

[Often, when night has fallen, I bring the light to the window and I look at myself, supported by miserable planks, stretched out in the damp like an aged coffin, between walls brusquely weak. I dream, from one absence to another, and at another distance, welcomed and bitter]

What is that absence and distance? Is it the loss of Josie Bliss, or even Albertina in Chile? More telling are the expressions 'sueño' [dream / sleep] and that already cited 'me miro' [I look at myself]. Self-scrutiny brings Neruda close to Buddhist doctrine about the self as in this Pali text: 'If a man holds himself dear, let him diligently watch himself.'[118] But what Neruda sees in his self-discovery is 'her' absence. Introspection, through poems, was painful; there is no detachment. Neruda is going in the opposite direction to a Buddhist.

Section 1 of the four sections in the book contains twenty poems. It opens with the magnificent 'Galope muerto' [Dead gallop], which has received many close-readings by critics (Yurkievich, Felstiner, Loyola, De Costa, Alonso and Alcides Jofré are some of them) and closes with 'Sonata y destrucciones' [Sonata and destructions].[119] Both titles suggest movement and stasis, or vitality and death, or art and suffering. 'Destruction' is a key term for it implies clearing the way to the source of words ('La destruction fut ma Beatriz' [Destruction was my Beatrice], wrote Mallarmé; Baudelaire wrote a sonnet titled 'La destruction'), the dream as the inner voice of inspiration and truth. The first section of the closing poem ends with one long sentence, which when read aloud forces the reader to run out of breath, of voice:

> Acecho, pues, lo inanimado y lo doliente,
> y el testimonio extraño que sostengo
> con eficiencia cruel y escrito en cenizas,
> es la forma de olvido que prefiero,
> el nombre que doy a la tierra, el valor de mis sueños,
> la cantidad interminable que divido
> con mis ojos de invierno, durante cada día de este mundo
>
> (PN1 277)

---

118 S. Radhakkrishnan (ed.), *The Dhammapada*, p. 112.

119 De Costa, 1979, pp. 61–5; Yurkievich, *Fundadones*, pp. 181–91; Amado Alonso, *Poesía y estilo*, pp. 216–23; Manuel Alcides Jofré in Angel Flores (ed.), *Nuevas aproximaciones a Pablo Neruda*, pp. 93–100 and most recently, Loyola, *Neruda*, 2006, pp. 232–36, 238–45. A comparative study of these close-readings should be made.

[I spy, then, on the inanimate and painful, and the strange testimony that I affirm, with cruel efficiency and written in ashes, is the form of oblivion that I prefer, the name that I give to the earth, the value of my dreams, the interminable quantity that I divide with my winter eyes, during each day of this world]

These lines tell us that the poet is aware of his novelty, his 'testimonio extraño', that he also knows that this poem concludes a section, that 'pues' of an argument. He tells us that he exploits his dreams, that he suffers lovelessness ('invierno', 'cenizas') and that key words 'cantidad interminable' is a musical analogy for a dream reality and language that never end (perhaps that psycho-babble). The title of the collection appears – 'tierra' – as does his self-defence of naming, being a poet. A poet is his own best psychoanalyst, as Freud had insinuated.

The opening poem, 'Galope muerto', is fundamental and there for a purpose. The title is a paradox and the two clashing terms suggest paralysis. Throughout his work the noun 'caballo' [horse] conveys its archetypal force of animality. Neruda's vitality, his animal energy, his sexuality are stuck in a vicious circle. The poem asks two questions: 'Es que de dónde, por dónde, en qué orilla?' [But from where, through where, on what shore?] (PN1 257) and 'Ahora bien, de que está hecho ese surgir de palomas / que hay entre la noche y el tiempo, como una baranca húmeda?' [Well now, what is it made of, that upsurge of doves that exists between night and time, like a moist ravine?] (PN1 258). Neither question is clear or rational, but the poem will answer them in the same tone. The difficulty of answering these questions is made clear in the line releasing the poet's anguished emotion, starting with the convention of 'ay': 'ay, lo que mi corazón pálido no puede abarcar' [ah, what my pale heart cannot embrace] (PN1 257). His heart is pale because it lacks blood, life and love. His heart, not his brain, cannot 'abarcar' or capture anything. 'Abarcar' is Neruda's term for 'pensar' [to think] and 'entender' [to understand]. We have questions from an impotent questioner. Thus if the poet is unclear, so will be the reader.

Amado Alonso pointed out that the poem's opening simile does not state what is to be compared to what.[120] It forces the reader to repeat the 'como' three times as pure sound (no word play in Neruda with 'como' as 'I eat'). The reader must hold this silenced point of comparison until she comes up with possibilities: life, reality, a dream, the world, matter, time. But the main point is that the poet does not know. So the reader must read out aloud 'Como cenizas, como mares poblándose' [Like ashes, like seas people themselves] as if sound directs meaning; sound comes first. The opening line is a wave of sound breaking in the mind. The second simile focuses on this sound – 'o

---

[120] Amado Alonso, *Poesía y estilo*, p. 163,

como se oyen' [or as is heard] – of bells whose ringing is 'ya aparte del metal,
confuso, pesando' [now sundered from the metal, confused, weighing], one
of Neruda's key words, but here alienated. The poem itself is not joyous
or mellifluous, the music of its bell is atonal, avant-garde. The adjective
'confuso' joins us to the poet.

The closing metaphor of the first stanza is vivid: 'y el perfume de las
ciruelas que rodando a tierra / se pudren en el tiempo, infinitamente verdes'
[and the perfume of the plums that rolling to the ground rot in time, infinitely green] (PN1 257). These fruit should be eaten, are sensuous, but never
mature and rot in time. The 'ciruela' is the poet's youthfulness, without love
to guide him to maturity. His situation appears eternal and the fruit remains
acid. But as with all metaphor, there can be no certainty about its interpretation. Neruda does not employ similes: 'I am like a plum etc.'. Hofmannsthal's
ballad, cited by the poet-critic Alvaro García, says the same as Neruda's:
'y los ásperos frutos dulces vuélvense / y caen en la noche, como pájaros
muertos / y yacen unos días para luego pudrirse' [and the bitter sweet fruit
return and fall in the night like dead birds and lie for days to then rot].[121] It
confirms a paralysis of the future (no ripe fruit).

The second stanza enlarges on the topic of time being so fast and yet stuck
so that the next simile is obvious: 'como la polea loca en sí misma' [like
the pulley wild within itself]. The poet is running on the spot, spinning in
a pointless circle. And language cannot help; it is 'callado' and 'mudo'. The
noun 'el rodeo', repeated throughout the collection with its verbal equivalent
'rodear', suggests the lone individual surrounded by this stuff of matter and
time like a prisoner. The second stanza ends with two startling similes. This
silent, constant, mute reality is 'como las lilas alrededor del convento' [like
lilacs around the convent]. Lilacs do not speak and a convent is where the
vow of chastity rules. Is loveless Neruda the convent? Again, we cannot be
sure. The next simile is long: 'o la llegada de la muerte a la lengua del buey
/ que cae a tumbos, guardabajo, y cuyos cuernos quieren sonar' [or death's
reaching the tongue of the ox that stumbles to the ground, guard down, with
horns that struggle to blow] (PN1 257). The ox's horns want to make a sound,
to make music, but it falls to the ground dead. The poet is the frustrated ox
and, like Roland in the *Chanson de Roland*, he falls dead as he blows his
horn. His knight companion Oliver had wanted him to blow his horn (named
Olifant) to alert the king, but he deemed it cowardly, preferring to drop dead
fighting the Saracens. This complex self-image integrates Neruda's view of
himself as an animal, his not being heard as a poet (horn) and his anguish.[122]

121 Alvaro García, *Poesía sin estatua. Ser y no ser en poética*, p. 38.
122 *The Song of Roland*: 'Count Roland's mouth with running blood was red; / He's burst
asunder the temples of his head; / He sounds his horn in anguish and distress,' Anon., tr.
Dorothy L. Sayers, p. 120.

Tellingly, this comparison was sparked off by Neruda's reading in French of a crucial moment from an early twelfth-century epic poem.

The third stanza implies that some narrative sequence is over 'Por eso ...' and links the sounds as those of an 'aleteo' of bees, numbers etc. For Neruda, Romantic poet, the fourth stanza opens with yet another narrative or logical device 'Ahora bien' [Now then] as if an argument has been won. He returns us to 'ese sonido ya tan largo' [that sound so prolonged now] so that we are now almost forced to concede that it is the sound of reality, its vibrational percussion, that extends 'sin tregua' [without truce]. The final stanza has the verb 'escuchan' [they listen], and hints that we must listen to this sound and capture it for it is the music of being. The poet is like the great 'zapallos' [gourds] becoming 'obscuros de pesadas gotas' [dark with heavy drops] (PN1 258), a strange metaphor for the poet's mute self, filling with inspiration (and 'zapallo' links with 'caballo' as rhyme). But rather than being a poem about despair, I see the whole poem as being about the dream state, where the dreamer becomes paralysed by the dreaming experience (lying still, all the senses closed up etc.). It relates to the opening of Nerval's *Aurélia*: 'Le rêve est une seconde vie. [...] Les premiers instants du sommeil sont l'image de la mort' [The dream is a second life ... The first moments of sleep are the image of death], where the word 'immobile ' characterises the state.[123] This is very similar to J. Alan Hobson's description of being asleep with the sensory input blocked, as is the motor system, so we become immobile, paralysed.[124]

The third poem of this section, 'Caballo de los sueños' [The horse of dreams], offers another variant on the poet's frustration that life is not allowing him to be the poet he yearns to be. In Amado Alonso's words, 'the theme is the poet's struggle to accommodate his individuality to communality'.[125] 'Caballo de los sueños' suggests the dream compensation, the horse-self that office and urban life do not allow to gallop free. Neruda rewrites Baudelaire's 'Le vin des amants' [Lovers' wine], which suggests escape through wine into dream freedom, with horse and swimming analogies: 'Partons à cheval sur le vin / Pour un ciel féerique et divin!' [Let's leave by horse on wine / for a fairy-like, divine sky].[126] Neruda feels unnecessary, looks in the mirror and tastes of weeks, cinemas and papers, urban spleen. Work, always the antagonist of the idle poet, leads to a gesture of despair: 'arranco de mi corazón al capitán del infierno' [I rip out from my heart the captain of hell] (PN1 259). He proceeds to establish clauses, work on documents etc. Who is this captain but Rimbaud and his heroic journey into hell? The poet is obliged to talk to 'sastres' [tailors], Neruda's short-hand term for putting a suit on, cutting

---

123 Nerval, *Aurélia*, p. 2.
124 J. Allan Hobson, *Dreaming. An Introduction to the Science of Sleep*, pp. 39–67.
125 Amado Alonso, *Poesía y estilo*, p. 235.
126 Baudelaire, *Les Fleurs*, p. 124.

you down to size, making you an anonymous wage-slave etc. His detestation
for 'tailors' could come from poverty: to his sister Laura, he moaned that 'it
happens that the very stupid tailors need a letter that effectively guarantees
payment'; to poetic sources like his master Quevedo's rants against 'sastres'
in 'Sueño de la muerte' [Dream of death] in his *Sueños* [Dreams], 1627.[127]
Quevedo's antipathy came from 'sastres' being able to put on a false front,
fake being 'hidalgos', being 'red-haired' like Judas, thus liars and hypo-
crites (he puns 'sastre' with 'desastre'). They are also thieves.[128] These urban
dwellers chase away poetry ('hacen huir los maleficios'). The poet cries out
that there is more to life than office work and going to the cinema: 'Hay un
país extenso en el cielo' (viz. Baudelaire's 'Pour un ciel féerique et divin')
and he dreams among its 'legumbre confusa' [tangled vegetation]. Work has
left a depressing taste in his soul. Suddenly, in the third stanza, the poet
wakes up to his reality:

> He oído relinchar su rojo caballo
> desnudo, sin herraduras y radiante.
> Atravieso con él sobre las iglesias,
> galopo los cuarteles desiertos de soldados
> y un ejército impuro me persigue.
> Sus ojos de eucaliptus roban sombra,
> su cuerpo de campana galopa y golpea (PN1 260)

> [I have heard its red horse neigh naked, shoeless and radiant. I
> cross with it over churches, I gallop through barracks deserted by
> soldiers and a foul army pursues me. Its eucalyptus eyes steal the
> shadows, its bell body gallops and strikes]

The syntax at the start of the quotation suggests a dawn sun that the poet
transforms into a naked, red horse (the 'su' refers back to 'Qué día ha sobre-
venido'). This imagistic leap reveals how Neruda works. No explanation as he
bypasses the simile and turns the metaphor (horse) into a noun, referring not
only to the sun but to his imagination. Red sun becomes red horse becomes
Neruda's inner imaginative power. There is a clear animal self-identification.
The poet is as wild and primitive as a naked red horse, without shoes. He
rides over churches and barracks and is chased by the mob (alone against the
crowd as in Munch's Expressionist painting 'The Scream'). Neruda's image
of his 'eucalyptus eyes' is odd (referring to leaf-shape, colour or scent?). That
his body is a bell that gallops and knocks (almost a pun in Spanish) shows

---

[127] Neruda, *Cartas a Laura*, p. 31: 'resulta que los muy imbéciles sastres necesitan una
carta que garantice efectivamente el pago'.

[128] See 'Sueño de la muerte' on <www.ensayistas.org/antología/xvii/quevedo> and
Maryrica Ortiz Lottman in Cervantes on <www.h-net.org/~cervantes/csa/artics96>.

how Neruda refuses to be logical in defining himself as both a horse and a bell (that is, a wild poet). A bell that 'golpea' even hints at a Rimbaudian aggressiveness.

The fourth poem, 'Débil del alba', explores the poet's lack of hope for love (no proper dawn). It develops two terms, 'crying' and 'rain' and their inter-penetration. The third stanza could be another attempt at defining himself and his poetics. Note the affirmative and repeated 'yo':

> Yo lloro en medio de lo invadido, entre lo confuso,
> entre el sabor creciente, poniendo el oído
> en la pura circulación, en el aumento,
> ...
> yo sueño, sobrellevando mis vestigios morales (PN1 261)

> [I weep amid invasion, among confusion, among the swelling taste, lending an ear to the pure circulation, to the increase ... I dream, carrying my moral remains][129]

The poet weeps, is sad, listens to what few can hear in his inner confu-sion, letting whatever arrives, arrive, as in a dream. All is there in that chain of associations. The poem ends with a clear self-image of orphanhood and pain:

> Estoy solo entre materias desvencijadas,
> la lluvia cae sobre mí, y se me parece,
> se me parece con su desvarío, solitaria en el mundo muerto,
> rechazada al caer, y sin forma obstinada. (PN1 261)

> [I am alone among rickety substances, the rain falls on me and it seems like me, like me with its ravings, alone in the dead world, rejected as it falls, and without persistent shape]

The poet is alone like the rain, and is rejected and lacking consistency, like the rain.

The 'unity' of time surrounds him in the poem 'Unidad', closing around him like a wall (PN1 262). The final stanza offers another comparison: 'Trabajo sordamente, girando sobre mi mismo, / como el cuervo sobre la muerte, el cuervo de luto' [I work deafly, spinning above myself, like the crow above death, the mourning crow] (PN1 262). Neruda, dressed in black, was loveless like Nerval's 'veuf' and a harbinger of death, like Poe's 'The Raven'

---

[129] Donald D. Walsh has 'mis vestigios mortales' and translated it as 'my mortal remains', while Loyola's text has 'morales'. I follow Loyola, but think that Walsh's text is more Nerudan.

and its cry of Nevermore. In this poem we find the crucial verb 'Pienso' that confirms these poems as dream-thinking.

This opening section of *Residencia* also contains several love poems similar in tone of rejection and heartbreak to the *Veinte poemas* where the lovesick poet 'moans', longing for the 'refuge' of love ('ay, refúgiame' [O shelter me] [PN1 264]). The poet inhabits 'la noche del corazón' [the heart's night], listening to what it says to him (PN1 265–6). These love poems also reveal a deeper insecurity. The 'dama sin corazón' (lady without a heart, his muse, his erstwhile lovers) bites into 'el centro de mi seguridad' [the centre of my security] (PN1 270) and makes him realise that his enemy is within: 'hay algo enemigo temblando en mi certidumbre' [there is some enemy trembling in my uncertainty] (PN1 271), but without analysing what that 'algo' is. Remember that Neruda translated Baudelaire's sonnet 'L'ennemi', which outlines how youth lived through a storm, with thunder and rain destroying all the fruit of his garden. It ends with a lament about pain, time and absence of love:

> O douleur! O douleur! Le temps mange la vie,
> Et l'obscur Ennemi qui nous ronge le coeur
> Du sang que nous perdons croît et se fortifie!
>
> [Oh pain! Oh pain! Time eats life / And the obscure ennemy who gnaws our heart / grows strong with the blood we lost]

The 'enemy' is time passing and the lack of love.[130]

The most moving of these love poem is 'Angela Adónica', one of Octavio Paz's favourite love poems, where the poet lies down next to a green-eyed young woman with breasts like two flames and a climate of gold around her body. The poem closes with pure sound of sexual bliss 'y oculto fuego' [and hidden fire] (PN1 276). But most of these love songs are about 'duelo' [mourning] (PN1 273).

The poem 'Colección nocturna', once title to the whole book, has been called 'oscurísimo' [very difficult] by Loyola, and so it is when a critic tries to explain it word by word.[131] I think that Amado Alonso's summary remains the best attempt: 'the theme is first the invasion of the dream and then the frenzy of dreams'.[132] However, as sound and meaning and as attempt to interpret the primal sounds of the cosmos and 'being' through sleep and dreaming, it is not so remote. That is, Neruda's confusion is mirrored in his language, *on purpose*. The key term is the poet's quest for 'un opaco sonido de sombra'

---

130 Baudelaire, *Les Fleurs*, p. 17.
131 Loyola, *Residencia en la tierra*, p. 117.
132 Amado Alonso, *Poesía y estilo*, p. 235.

[opaque sound of darkness] where Neruda hints that 'sonido' and 'sueño' ('soñar' / 'sonar') come from the same root-sound. We see how listening to dreams is the theme: 'y escucho en mi interior temblar su instrumento' and 'Yo oigo el sueño de viejos compañeros y mujeres amadas, / sueños cuyos latidos me quebrantan' [I listen to its instrument tremble inside me ... I hear my dream of old friends and loved women, dreams whose pulsings shatter me] (PN1 267). To listen to a dream is to hear the muse singing. The poem has the poet as a seeker and examiner as the last lines state: 'Yo busco desde antaño, yo examino sin arrogancia, / conquistando, sin duda, por lo vespertino' [I seek since long ago, I examine without arrogance, conquering, doubtless, by twilight] (PN1 268). That 'yo examino' and another reference to the 'captain' recalls Rimbaud, in the hell of the self like a cellar with grapes like 'odres' [wineskins] and a general foul sense of death and humid birth. The title helps, for, alone at night, the poet can only look inside and examine himself, a very Rimbaudian task, with the verb 'examinar' carrying over from one poet to the other ('le poete s'examine' etc.).

That Neruda was conscious of his craft is obvious when we look at his 'Arte poética', another of his great poems, though, as De Costa noted, it does not deal with the art of composition, but presents 'an image of the artist at work'.[133] The poet is again the 'viudo' (biographically a post-Josie Bliss poem), who cannot make sense of his inner experiences, that 'angustia indirecta' [indirect anguish] (PN1 274). This poet is trapped between people and institutions, not belonging anywhere, the outsider. His version of himself is still the Romantic poet 'dotado de corazón singular y sueños funestos' [endowed with a singular heart and sorrowful dreams], an acute self-image, who is pale and exhausted like any Romantic hero. For each sound that he welcomes there is still the 'sed ausente' [absent thirst] and 'fiebre fría' [cold fever]; that is, the music he is hearing is not harmonious, adjectives contradict nouns. He then uses five similes to define himself. This technique of 'approximations', versus the 'mot juste' approach, typifies Neruda's baroque stance, what Rodríguez Monegal called his 'essential baroquism'.[134] The first defines his self as invaded by thieves and ghosts. The second is that he feels 'como un camarero humillado' [like a humiliated waiter]. The third simile is that of a 'campana un poco ronca' [slightly raucous bell]. The fourth is that of an old mirror. So far, Neruda tries out approximations. No one simile is apt, but the waiter and bell ones expand previous self-images. The fifth is longer and closer to what has undermined his sense of ontological security, namely, not having a woman around the house: '... como un olor de casa sola / en la que los huéspedes entran de noche perdidamente ebrios, / y hay un olor

---

133 De Costa, *The Poetry of Pablo Neruda*, p. 68.
134 Rodríguez Monegal, *El viajero inmóvil*, p. 13.

de ropa tirada al suelo, y una ausencia de flores' [like the smell of a solitary house where the guests come in at night wildly drunk and there is a smell of clothes thrown on the floor, and an absence of flowers]. Neruda has used words to define what he felt like in that very moment of writing; invaded, alone, longing for a woman to pick up his laundry and put flowers in the empty house. Then we realise that Neruda is aware that there is another way of saying everything: 'posiblemente de otro modo aún menos melancólico' [possibly in another even less melancholy way]. Absence of a lover reveals a deeper pain: 'pero, la verdad, de pronto' [but the truth is that suddenly], and he lists the wind whipping his chest, the long nights, the din of a day that demands that he be 'prophetic', that he see beyond appearances, be a visionary as Rimbaud insisted in his letter to his schoolteacher Demeny, or like Verlaine in his 'Art poétique' where he asks that 'tu canto sea la profecía' [your song be prophecy].[135] The closing lines are weirdly perfect:

> y un golpe de objetos que llaman sin ser respondidos
> hay, y un movimiento sin tregua, y un nombre confuso
>
> (PN1 274)

> [and a knocking of objects that call without being answered, there
> is, and a movement without truce, and a bewildered name][136]

The outer world calls him, but has no inner meaning and only a vague or confused name (the name is never the thing). There is just time passing, that 'sin tregua' taken from earlier poems, with that 'hay', repeated through this poem as both 'hay' and 'ay' and pronounced the same way, but with a grammatical break – after 'hay' should come the noun, but we get 'y', which means 'and' and 'both' (y / y). The stuttering quality, the grammatical hiatus convey the poet's inner anguish, without similes or images. Manuel Durán well summarised this ending: 'It is the perception of a visionary who does not believe in trancsendence, different to Blake, but close to Rimbaud.'[137] This poem is also Neruda's rewriting of Verlaine's 'Art poétique', which famously separated literature from 'poetry'. It was translated by Alfonso Reyes in Díez-Canedo's anthology in 1913 (which Neruda had studied). Two words cross over from the Reyes translation into Neruda's poem: 'tu canto sea *la profecía* / que va exteniendo *la brisa* húmeda / por la manaña sobre los campos' (my italics). Neruda continues with his task 'piden lo *profético* en mí', but now

---

135 I quote the translation from Díez-Canedo, *La poesía francesa*, p. 231.

136 Donald D. Walsh ends the poem with a 'bewildered man', translating 'hombre confuso' rather than Loyola's 'nombre' (name, noun), pp. 46–7. Both endings are equally plausible and Nerudan, though the 1935 edition has 'nombre'.

137 Manuel Durán, 'Sobre la poesía de Neruda, la tradición y la desintegración del yo', *Simposio Pablo Neruda*, p. 135.

the 'brisa' has become a '*viento*' (my italics) and the 'campos' simply chaotic objects. Verlaine had also written in the final stanza: 'Que ton vers soit la bonne aventure / Eparse au vent crispé du matin' [May your verse be the good adventure / scattered in the nervy morning wind] (where 'matin' carries over into Neruda's 'mañana').[138] He has updated Verlaine for the twentieth century, but hangs on to the latter's role as seeing into reality.[139]

Section 2 of *Residencia en la tierra 1* is again purposefully articulated, with five prose poems and one lyrical poem. Neruda's mixture of prose poems and lyrical poem emerges from Baudelaire and Rimbaud's examples and also hints at the surrealist genre (the prose poem), embodying novelty and the new beauty. I propose to glance at how Neruda recreates himself in these texts. The opening piece is titled 'La noche del soldado' [The night of the soldier]. The poet identifies himself from the first line: 'Yo hago la noche del soldado ... del tipo tirado lejos por el océano y una ola y que no sabe que el agua amarga lo ha separado ...' [I make the night of the soldier ... of the type cast far by the ocean and a wave and doesn't know that bitter water has separated him] (PN1 278). So the poet is a soldier, alone in bitter exile, but defined by being a warrior. According to Baudelaire, the warrior, the priest and the poet represent the origins.[140] Neruda once evoked Baudelaire's 'soldado negativo' [negative soldier], and there is a further sense of the poet as Roman soldier consigned to a far-off province, as well as the soldier as the arrogant, lonely male, the avant-gardist in the military sense.[141] So we have a complex of associations. This poet / soldier is 'sinceramente oscuro' [sincerely dark], a wonderful self-definition that invokes a poetics of direct feelings and inner darkness. The poet / soldier is an outsider, a nobody: 'y paso entre mercaderes mahometanos, entre gentes que adoran la vaca y la cobra, paso yo, inadorable y común de rostro' [And I pass among Muslim merchants, among people who worship the cow and the cobra, I pass, unadorable and common-faced] (PN1 278). The poet evokes the tropical heat, sweat, malaria, ostracism and monsoons. This soldier then asks what has happened to the previous poet he was with, his 'conciencia resplandeciente' and dressed in blue (Darío's 'azul', the poet of hope and love). To combat isolation and identity crisis, the soldier / poet visits 'muchachas' [girls]. He takes off their rings and jewels because he wants to 'sorprenderme ante un cuerpo ininterrumpido y compacto' [surprise myself before an uninterrupted and compact body]. Already, uninhibited sexual encounters with female bodies compensate his being a soldier with his 'sed masculina y en silencio' [masculine

138   Verlaine, 1962, p. 327.

139   See Stephen Roberts, *The Self-adjusting Sonnet: Pablo Neruda's 'Arte poética'*, Queen Mary and Westfield College, London, 2002, for an excellent reading of this key poem.

140   Baudelaire, *Mon coeur mis à nu*, p. 64.

141   Neruda, *Confieso*, p. 396.

thirst and in silence]. The soldier needs several lines to describe these female 'bodies', without individual names. These nightly encounters cover him with a 'polvo temporal' and 'y el dios de la substitución vela a veces a mi lado, respirando tenazmente, levantando la espada' [temporal dust ... and the god of subsitution keeps watch at times by my side, breathing tenaciously, raising his sword] (PN1 279). 'Espada' is a key personal symbol in Neruda's work; it is the pen transformed into phallic weapon, even penis (hence, poet as soldier). But what is the 'substitution' that sometimes takes place? Is this a becoming another, a doubling of his self along Rimbaud's 'Je est un autre' lines? Does the poet prefer being the soldier? Does this new, strange sexual love as battle between bodies seduce him more than writing? His affair with Josie Bliss almost convinced Neruda that sexual pleasure was greater than the thrill of writing. So in this poem, we have a cameo of the whole collection. Who is freer, the soldier or the poet? Equally clear is that the poet's earlier 'angustia indirecta' has now become a conflict about how to live an intense life, as a soldier or as a poet. The sexual problem, the soldier with his brothel but starved of love and what Cesare Pavese called his 'sexual loneliness', start to define the poems. Loyola summarised this crucial poem as an 'oblique representation of Pablo's falling in love in the frame of a poetic chronicle about his situation of loneliness and creative paralysis'.[142]

The second prose poem, 'Comunicaciones desmentidas' [Contradicted communications], with its reek of official correspondence, continues the military version of the self: 'aguardo el tiempo militarmente' [I await time militarily] (PN1 280) as how he evokes life without a lover. The prose poem mentions his 'larga residencia marina' [long marine residence] (biograph- ically surely Wellawata, after jilting Josie Bliss), as well as his sensuous attachment to the material world, 'un gusto ensimismado por la tierra' [a meditative taste for the earth]. Here we have the two words of the collec- tion's title 'Residencia' and 'tierra' in the same poem, so that residence is literally where he lived and earth is what he was discovering in himself. The prose poem develops his changing self, his losing of his 'sentido profético' [prophetic sense], his lover's 'duelo' [mourning], his feeling of being aban- doned and with his 'novelesco' heart. In one strange image he summarises his new, uncertain self: 'y la carta de amor, pálida de papel y temor, sustrajo su araña trémula que apenas teje y sin cesar desteje y teje' [and the love letter, pale with paper and fear, subtracted its tremulous spider that barely weaves and ceaselessly unweaves and weaves] (PN1 280). Is this new self at last free from the chains of love? The sentence has the love letter as subject of 'sustraer' (remove) and the spider is the visual image for handwriting, but also for hope, almost a Penelope symbol of weaving and unweaving. The

---

[142] Loyola, *Neruda*, 2006, p. 342.

spider, as we have already noted, is also a poet, creator of a web of words to trap his female reader. Is this then what writing a love poem is, a continuous writing and unwriting? Neruda lets the image speak to him and to us, and we cannot quite translate it into common sense, except as a doing and undoing that once more suggests paralysis.

By the third section of this collection, Neruda, the poet within his poems, has located his anguish as sexual isolation. This insight might correspond to his biography, but in this sequence suggests a journey towards some revelation. The title 'Caballero solo' [Gentleman alone] places the lone male at the core of the poem, but ironically. The anguish is no longer hidden inside the poet's dreams, but is corporeal. This 'caballero' has no 'dama'. Neruda employs the same litany of lists to create a rhythm:

> Los jóvenes homosexuales y las muchachas amorosas,
> y las largas viudas que sufren el delirante insomnio,
> y las jóvenes señoras preñadas hace treinta horas,
> y los roncos gatos que cruzan mi jardín en tinieblas (PN1 285)

> [The young homosexuals and the amorous girls, and the long widows who suffer from delirious insomnia and the young wives thirty hours pregnant and the raucous cats that cross my garden in the dark]

Everybody, it seems, but Neruda is fornicating. These four opening lines lead to an extraordinary simile (and close with two more):

> Como un collar de palpitantes ostras sexuales
> rodean mi residencia solitaria,
> como enemigos establecidos contra mi alma,
> como conspiradores en traje de dormitorio (PN1 285)

> [like a necklace of throbbing sexual oysters, they surround my solitary residence, like enemies established against my soul, like conspirators in night clothes]

The noun 'collar' emerges from his *Veinte poemas* as something the poet hands to his muse (poem 5 – 'Voy haciendo de todas un collar infinito / para tus blancas manos, suaves como las uvas' [PN1 182]); here he wears it. Neruda is shockingly explicit. 'Ostra / oyster' is an ancient symbol of the female vagina, modernised by D. H. Lawrence, and the oyster is often swallowed as an aphrodisiac. Neruda makes his point obvious with the adjective 'sexuales' and makes the oysters 'palpitate' with a life of their own (they are usually eaten raw). What is absent from his life, the female sexual organ, hangs around his neck. He is a Tantalus. This is not a surrealist simile, however, for a necklace is usually made of pearls, which are secreted in oysters. So 'ostra' implies some kind of beauty buried in sexual pleasure. Years later, in 1962, Octavio Paz wrote a poem celebrating his friendship with surrealists André Breton and Benjamin Péret titled 'Noche en claro' [Sleepless night] and how their version of love moved him. He noticed a couple of lovers in the London underground: 'las cuatro letras de la palabra Amor / en cada dedo ardiendo como *astros* / [a drawing of the fingers] / Tatuaje escolar tinta china y pasión / anillos *palpitantes* / Oh mano *collar* al cuello ávido de la vida' [The four letters of the word love, in each finger burning as stars/ school tattoo in China ink and passion, palpitating rings, oh hand necklace on life's avid neck].[143] Neruda's simile (Ostra / collar / palpitante) secretly resurfaces in Paz (in my italics). Despite later political differences, then, Paz knew this Neruda poem by heart.

This copulating rabble 'hecho de gordas y flacas y alegres y tristes parejas' [made of fat and skinny and happy and sad couples] surround the solitary poet and torment him. We have another image relating to the overall title 'residencia solitaria' (*Residencia en la tierra*) and again that key verb 'rodear' [to surround] that suggests the poet's isolation, alone in his own body. The poet *hears* this sexual activity: 'un rumor de medias de seda acariciadas' [a rumour of silk stockings caressed]. The stanza ends with 'y senos femeninos que brillan como ojos' [and feminine breasts glinting like eyes], echoing the famous passage that prompted Mary Shelley to write *Frankenstein*, 1818. In 1816, according to Dr John Polidori's diary, Byron 'was looking at Mrs S. and suddenly thought of a woman he had heard of who had eyes instead of nipples, which, taking hold of his mind, horrified him'.

Neruda is not done with incorporating his readings into his poem (D. H. Lawrence / Mary Shelley) for the third stanza plagiarises a passage from T. S. Eliot's *The Waste Land*, 1922 (though Yurkievich wondered, incorrectly, if this was not a coincidence).[144] As critics have pointed out as early as 1948, Neruda rewrites lines from 'The Fire Sermon'.[145] One verb – to caress – is actually carried over: Eliot's 'young man carbuncular' seduces the typist and 'endeavours to engage her in caresses' while Neruda's 'pequeño empleado' [little employee] achieves it: 'y acaricia sus piernas llenas de dulce vello' [and caresses her legs covered with soft hairs] (PN1 285). In Eliot we have degrading sex; in Neruda the clerk's hands stroke the 'dulce vello' [soft hairs] and they are 'ardientes y húmedas' [burning and moist].[146] The hand that writes is the hand that caresses a woman's leg. The little clerk is as much Neruda himself after his week's boring work, and much reading of novels

---

[143]   Octavio Paz, *Poemas (1935–1975)*, p. 351.

[144]   Saúl Yurkievich, 'Pablo Neruda: persona, palabra y mundo', p. 37.

[145]   Betsy Scone, 'Comparison of Pablo Neruda and T. S. Eliot' (MA thesis), cited in Loyola, 1987, p. 79.

[146]   T. S. Eliot, *Collected Poems, 1909–1962*, p. 72.

at night and absorbing stock heroes in the cinema, who finally seduces his 'vecina' [neighbour]. Octavio Paz noted this Eliotic echo and commented that 'Eliot's eroticism is very little erotic and the image he gives us of physical love is sordid. Neruda is truly and powerfully sexual. It's one of the positive poles of his poetry: energy, erotic irradiation.'[147] Much more could be written about what differentiates Eliot from Neruda, starting with Eliot's constant citation of erudite and popular texts across cultures and languages, his deep cosmopolitanism, his polyglottal asides, for this Eliot is close to the over-cultured Darío that Neruda had rejected. Yet, Eliot also cites the first line in French from Nerval's 'El desdichado', identified in a note.[148] No one line of poetry is more important to Neruda. Years later, in 1949, Neruda would abominate Eliot as a capitalist reactionary, as perverse, as degrading life, and agreed with Faedéiv that if hyenas could write, they would write like Eliot (PN4 765). Neruda's reactions to Eliot concord with his denial of his own earlier *Residencia* verse. One further linguistic tick is borrowed from Eliot and the English langauge in general and that is Neruda's rhythmical use of the gerund. Amado Alonso noted this; another critic, Armando Roa, has it derive from Whitman. But it is from Eliot that he found this music of time.[149] The opening of *The Waste Land*: 'April is the cruellest month, breeding' closes with that gerund and then followed by five further gerunds in the next six lines, ending each phrase.[150]

The long closing stanza, held by many lines starting with 'y' [and], lists every kind of sexual encounter. Neruda is no moralist and sexual pleasure, as he has learnt from Josie Bliss, knows no censoring (teenage sex, masturbation, incest, adultery, envy). A second simile has all this activity 'como dos sábanas sepultándome' [like two sheets burying me] (PN1 286); the bed linen of the lonely man turned into a shroud. The list has to be read aloud as one long sentence, running out of breath:

> y las horas después del almuerzo en que los jóvenes estudiantes,
> y las jóvenes estudiantes, y los sacerdotes se masturban,
> y los animales fornican directamente,
> y las abejas huelen a sangre, y las moscas zumban coléricas,
> y los primos juegan extrañamente con sus primas,
> y los médicos miran con furia al marido de la joven paciente,
> y las horas de la mañana en que el profesor, como por descuido,

---

147 Paz in conversation with Emir Rodríguez Monegal and Roberto González Echeverría, *Convergencias / divergencias / incidencias*, p. 177: 'el erotismo de Eliot es muy poco erótico y la imagen que nos da del amor físico es sórdida. Neruda es verdadera y poderosamente sexual. Es uno de los polos positivos de su poesía: la energía, la irradiación erotica.'

148 Eliot, *Collected Poems*, pp. 78, 86.

149 Armando Roa, 'Reincidencia en la tierra', *Estudios Públicos*, p. 210.

150 Eliot, *Collected Poems*, p. 63.

cumple con su deber conyugal, y desayuna,
y más aún, los adúlteros, que se aman con verdadero amor.

(PN1 286)

[and the hours after lunch when the young men students and the
young women students and the priests masturbate, and the animals
fornicate directly, and the bees smell of blood, and the flies buzz
angrily, and the boy cousins play strangely with their girl cousins,
and the doctors look furiously at the husband of the young patient
and the morning hours when the teacher absentmindedly fulfils
his conjugal duty and has breakfast, and still more, the adulterers,
who love each other with true love]

Two lines stand out. The first ackowledges Baudelaire about animals fornicating directly: 'La brute seule bande bien, et la fouterie est le lyrisme du
peuple' [Only the brute screws well and fucking is the people's lyricism],
though Neruda does not agree that art stops the artists fornicating.[151] What we
could read into this Neruda / Baudelaire conjunction is that the consequence
of *not* fornicating like the animals is this poem (a theory of constrained libido
and creativity). The second is Neruda's definition of true love as adultery,
breaking the moral law, his Romantic outsider's values. All these figures,
then, 'seguramente, eternamente me rodea' [surely, eternally surround me],
like a breathing forest of mouths, false teeth, finger nails and shoes (the last
word).

A final framing of this poem could be its differences with Whitman's
enumeration in section 15 of 'Song of Myself'. His list jumps from squaw
to one-year wife to canal boy to peddler to opium-eater to prostitute, rather
like Neruda's, generating a rhythm, but he ends with a celebration of such
diversity for he, Whitman, was them: 'And of these one and all I weave the
song of myself.'[152] Neruda too could be all of the people he lists and his poem
is his song, but he asserts being the outsider.

The second poem 'Ritual de mis piernas' [Ritual of my legs] continues
with the new tone of the collection, that shift from anguish to mockery, from
an inner dream vagueness to a visible, tactile world. It is a long, baroque
description of the lonely man's own legs as if they were the legs of 'una mujer
divina' [divine woman] (PN1 286). It is what happens when his woman is
absent: 'y pasa, el tiempo pasa, y en mi lecho no siento de noche que / una
mujer está respirando, durmiendo, desnuda y a mi lado' [and it passes, time
passes and in my bed I do not feel at night that a woman is breathing sleeping
naked and at my side]. From this perception of Josie Bliss's absence, Neruda
develops another D. H. Lawrence insight, that our bodies have been ignored:

---

[151]   Baudelaire, *Mon coeur mis à nu*, p. 122.
[152]   Whitman, *Leaves of Grass*, pp. 60–1.

'las gentes cruzan el mundo en la actualidad / sin apenas recordar que poseen un cuerpo y en él la vida, / y hay miedo, hay miedo en el mundo de las palabras que designan el cuerpo, / y se habla favorablemente de la ropa ...' [People cross through the world nowadays scarcely remembering that they possess a body and life within it and there is fear, in the world there is fear of the words that designate the body and one talks favourably of clothes] (PN1 287). The stanza ends with a common avant-garde image: streets with empty suits wandering about (César Vallejo penned a similar kind of poem in *Trilce* lxxv). Neruda's concluding insight is that the hostile world begins where his tickly feet end. That is, the body is his sole defence; his vulnerability is his naked body. That is his definition of 'soledad' [loneliness], reality as 'abiertamente invencible y enemigo' [openly invincible and an enemy] that cannot be wished away. A source might be Lawrence's poem 'She Said as Well to Me' where the woman mocks the man for being ashamed of his body: ' "Why shouldn't your legs and your good strong thighs / be rough and hairy?" [...]'. That spurs the poet 'so that I began to wonder over myself, and what I was'.[153] Neruda's poem springs from that last line. I also hear section 2 of Whitman's 'I Sing the Body Electric' where the poet sings the love of man and woman's bodies in a litany: 'it is in his limbs and joints also, it is curiously in the joints of his hips and wrists, / It is in his walk, the carriage of his neck, the flex of his waist and knees, dress does not hide him.'[154]

The section continues with Neruda's poem 'El fantasma del buque de carga' [The ghost of the cargo ship], alluding to the poet's long return journey to Chile on the English tramp steamer *Forafric*, married, where the poet is the 'fantasma' in the 'desolado espacio', the last lines. As a teenager, Neruda had tried to translate a Conrad novel with an anarchist friend Romeo Murga, and his ship is one of those tramp-steamers. The section closes with the narrative poem 'Tango del viudo', already analysed as central to Neruda's explorations of himself and his readers. By placing this poem outside his chronology, after the poem about coming home ('El fantasma ...'), we can read that he still carries his guilt about Josie with him back to Chile.

Section 4 opens with a sad 'Cantares' [Songs], an allusion to Gallician 'fado', where the poet continues to travel over the oceans as a 'perro infinito' [infinite dog], a mocking of his earlier 'hombre infinito', whose song comes from his guitar and 'la sal de mi ser' [salt of my being], a lovely self-image of the source of many of these poems. And 'perro del infinito' springs from Lautréamont's Maldoror: 'Moi, comme les chiens, j'éprouve le besoin de l'infini' [I am like the dogs, I suffer the need for infinity].[155] This is the passage translated by Julio Gómez de la Serna (Ramón's brother) in the Díez-Canedo

---

153 D. H. Lawrence, *Complete Poems*, pp. 198–9.
154 Whitman, *Leaves of Grass*, p. 99.
155 Isidore Ducasse, Comte de Lautréamont, *Oeuvres complètes*, p. 29.

anthology of 1913 that Neruda perused so avidly.[156] The last stanza evokes a wounded lover who has survived. This key verb 'sobrevivo' [I survive] (PN1 294) suggests that the poet Neruda has emerged from the hell of his years abroad 'solo y locamente herido' [alone and madly wounded], but persisting and abandoned. There is a curious parallel with Rafael Alberti's last poem in *Sobre los ángeles*, which is titled 'El ángel superviviente' [The surviving angel] – cf. Neruda's 'sobrevivo' – and the last line 'Menos uno, herido, alicortado' [Less one, wounded, single-winged], that last one-winged angel who remains as the poet's muse, where the adjective 'herido' unites both poets. Alberti had published this book in 1929 and Neruda could have read it. Alberti too based his book on Rimbaud's journey into hell. He was also the promoter to Neruda in Spain. This overlap is more than coincidence.[157] The last word of the poem 'Cantares', 'abandonado', links Neruda back to his *Veinte poemas*. The closing poem of *Residencia 1*, 'Significa sombras' [Signifies shadows], ends with a stanza we have already cited: Neruda as the 'ardiente testigo' aware of his 'deber original', of the poems that he has rescued from his trip through hell.

[156] Díez-Canedo, *La poesía francesa*, p. 186.
[157] Rafael Alberti, *Sobre los ángeles*, p. 105.

4

The 1930s: *Residencia en la tierra II* and *Tercera residencia*

Poem 9 from *Veinte poemas de amor ...*, 1932

Poem 9 from Neruda's 1924 collection of love poems was substituted by the following poem in 1932:

> Ebrio de trementina y largos besos,
> estival, el velero de las rosas dirijo,
> torcido hacia la muerte del delgado día,
> cimentado en el sólido frenesí marino.
>
> Pálido y amarrado a mi agua devorante
> cruzo en el agrio olor del clima descubierto,
> aún vestido de gris y sonidos amargos,
> y una cimera triste de abandonada espuma.
>
> Voy, duro de pasiones, montado en mi ola única,
> lunar, solar, ardiente y frío, repentino,
> dormido en la garganta de las afortunadas
> islas blancas y dulces como caderas frescas.
>
> Tiembla en la noche húmeda mi vestido de besos
> locamente cargado de eléctricas gestiones,
> de modo heroico dividido en sueños
> y embriagadoras rosas practicándose en mí.
> Aguas arriba, en medio de las olas externas,
> tu paralelo cuerpo se sujeta en mis brazos
> como un pez infinitamente pegado a mi alma
> rápido y lento en la energía subceleste (PN1 185–6)

[Drunk with turpentine and long kisses, summery I steer the sail of the roses, twisted towards the death of the thin day, cemented in the solid marine frenzy. Pale and lashed to my devouring water, I cruise in the sour smell of the naked climate, still dressed in grey and bitter sounds and a sad crest of abandoned spray. I go, hard with passions, mounted on my unique wave, lunar, solar, burning and cold, all at once, asleep in the throat of the fortunate islands, white and sweet as fresh hips. My suit of kisses trembles in the moist night, madly charged with electric actions, in a heroic

way divided into dreams and intoxicating roses practising on me.
Upstream, in the middle of external waves, your parallel body
submits to my arms like a fish infinitely stuck to my soul, quick
and slow in the sub-celestial energy]

This opaque poem, if judged chronologically, jars with the twenty other
poems of 1924. It belongs to the *Residencia en la tierra 1* love poems, yet
Neruda backdated it. A biographic, not poetic, explanation might be that the
poet still hoped that Albertina would return his love (though both he and
she were married), so as a poem about love-longing it belonged to the 1924
collection. But what is this dark poem about?

The poet is at sea in a love yacht, drunk on 'turpentine' and 'long kisses'.
That noun 'trementina' is the first problem: is it pure sound? Is it an alluring
smell? Is it a reference to cheap wine or a secret rhyme with 'Albertina', as
Loyola guessed (PN1 1153)? Does 'trementina' echo with 'tremante', that
daring Dantean kiss? Donald Shaw suggested more plausibly that 'turpentine'
is linked to 'pine', one of Neruda's totemic trees and thus 'to be full of the
sap of life'.[1] Perhaps the mystery and sensuality remain at the word's surface
sound. But clearly, poem 9 is a love poem, and the lovers are underwater
'en el sólido frenesí marino', Neruda's protracted metaphor for the blissful
experience of love-making (swimming underwater, the salivary, sweaty sea
etc.). Robert Pring-Mill aptly called it 'one of the most intensely erotic
poems Neruda ever wrote'.[2] But the poet is now alone ('mi única ola'). Is
this another post-Josie Bliss poem written from Chile? The poet still projects
himself as 'pálido', as he did in his 'Arte poética', as bitter, dressed in the
bureaucrat's grey suit. Sexual desire makes 'duro de pasiones', phallically
alive underwater, where making love, dreaming and writing a poem, diving
into the inner sea of the unconscious, merge into one complex metaphor, a
chaos of sensations, lunar, solar, hot and cold and sudden. That 'repentino'
could be the release of orgasm. The key noun 'cadera', associated with Josie
Bliss, crops up again. Yet her absence links this poem to his earlier lover's
absence in 1924 (Albertina etc.). So his life is divided 'heroically' between
dreams (of her) and 'drunk roses practising themselves in him'. This bizarre
line blends 'rosa' with 'art' and 'woman's sexual organ', but inside him (that
is, he is alone). Could this be a masturbation poem? The lover lying down
with him exists in his mind only. That final simile 'como un pez infinitamente
pegado a mi alma' could be the lost Josie Bliss, forever glued to his very
deep self, his soul. The 'net' image now functions as his trapping mind; he
has trapped her and that image creates his sense of being in 'pure energy'.
The secret narrative chain might be: making love with Josie Bliss woke up

---

[1] Donald Shaw, ' "Ebrio de trementina" ', p. 236.
[2] Robert Pring-Mill, 'Introduction', *A Basic Anthology*, p. xviii.

a poetic energy that only dreaming and memory can restore in the poet's actual despair. Juan Loveluck summarised this poem as written 'from an oneiric perspective', with the ship as sexual climax, a 'nave de eros' [ship of Eros], while Shaw agreed and added that 'the poet is always conscious of his divided self', turning it into a psychological poem.[3]

However, one further way of grasping this 'enigmatic' poem is as a rewrite of the original poem 9. Neruda reread the 1924 poem in 1932 and wrote the replacement in the light of his later sexual experience. Images of the 'barco' and the 'sea' cross over from the old poem 9 to the new one. In 1924 the poet had written:

> Líbrame de tu amor mujer lejana y bella
> que por bella y lejana me duelas cada día.
> Rompe las claras cuerdas, suelta las blancas velas
> del barco que aprisionan tus manos todavía
> [...]
> Mi alma errante y nostálgica a toda sed se enreda.
> ¡El mar inmenso y libre para nadie es más triste
> que para un barco atado por anclas de oro y seda![4]

> [Beautiful, distant woman, free me of your love, for being beautiful and distant you hurt me every day. Break the clear ropes, free the white sails of the boat which your hands still imprison. My immense and nostalgic soul to thirst tangles itself. The immense sea, free for nobody, is sadder than for a boat tied with gold and silk anchors]

The poet no longer wants to be tied with *modernistas* phrases like 'gold' and 'silk' for he has tasted freedom by substituting romantic yearning for sexual bliss.

However, as Loyola's careful notes in the complete works and Moran's detailed commentaries have shown, Neruda modified several further poems in his 1924 *Veinte poemas* from this 1932 perspective. Poem 2 'underwent wholesale revision', as Moran shows in his critical edition, including the suppression of the French word 'carousel'; the whole poem is more 'dense and oblique', in keeping with *Residencia I*. Poem 4 also was modified.[5] What we read today as a collection published in 1924 and often biographically interpreted, has to be revised in the light of these 1932 additions that include Neruda's years abroad in the Far East.

---

3   Loveluck, 1975, p. 231, and Shaw, ' "Ebrio de trementina" ', p. 239.

4   Loyola prints this poem in PN1 1154, but does not include the inverted exclamation mark of Neruda's first edition.

5   Dominic Moran, *Veinte poemas*, pp. 48–9.

Residencia en la tierra II, 1935

In Madrid in 1935, the poet republished the first *Residencia* poems that had appeared in Chile in an edition of 100 copies, and added *Residencia en la tierra II* to them in two volumes (they were combined into one volume in 1944), without pagination. The publishing house was the prestigious Cruz y Raya, run by José Bergamín, with whom later Neruda would squabble. This double 1935 volume is the book that, in Octavio Paz's term, 'nos estremeció' [it thrilled us].[6] The new poems of *Residencia II* were written between 1931 and 1935 and track Neruda's geographical displacements, from when he returned to Santiago de Chile in 1931, to Buenos Aires in 1933, then briefly Barcelona and finally Madrid from 1934 (he was back in Chile in September 1937). Like the first *Residencia*, the poems are essentially chronological, but also convey a secondary story by their ordering. For example, as already mentioned, the final poem is titled 'Josie Bliss', the first time her name appeared in print, but it is a nostalgic, not passionate poem. Only Neruda knew the real story, and why he inserted the poem as the concluding one. Neruda was married over these years 1931 to 1935 to his Dutch wife Maruca Hagenaar, had a sick child and began a passionate relationship with the Argentine Delia del Carril, sister-in-law to the writer Ricardo Güiraldes and twenty years older than the poet. His extraordinary erotic poems *Las furias y las penas*, written in 1934 and which could have been included in *Residencia II*, were kept apart and not published until 1939 and republished in 1947 in *Tercera Residencia en la tierra*.

What is evident at the narrative level is that the poet remains lonely in the early poems exploring sound and sex, but grows in confidence as he moves from Buenos Aires to Madrid, to become the leader of a group of extraordinarily talented poets, the so-called 'generación del 27' in Spain. By this period he had in fact turned into a public figure, assuming the public name of Pablo Neruda. The poems relate more and more to the material world, away from inner dreams and confusions. His long 'journey through hell' was well over by 1935. From this date onwards, Neruda was a group poet, belonging to collectives, no longer the solitary outsider, and this group confidence would culminate when he joined the Communist Party in 1945.

Residencia II is also subdivided into sections. The four poems of section 1 –'Un día sobresale', 'Sólo la muerte', 'Barcarola' and 'El sur del océano' – have been commented on as Neruda's making sense of what a poem is and how it works and who the poet is (see above pp. 102–103). They locate his identity at profound levels of sensation and natural sound, so that the wind, waves breaking on a shore, silence etc. become the sounds of his deeper self. For example, in the opening 'Un día sobresale' [A day stands out] the poet

6 Octavio Paz, *Obra completa 1*, p. 460.

avoids the 'yo' completely, as if it is superficial, irrelevant. In 'Sólo la muerte' [Only death], the poet appears as barely in touch with this inner dark world – '*oscuro, oscuro, oscuro*' [dark, dark, dark] (PN1 310) – and his persona is vulnerable to the death of the self: '*Yo no sé, yo conozco poco, yo apenas veo*' [I do not know, I know little, I hardly see] (PN1 302), but in reality he asserts another kind of knowledge, deeper than rationality, beyond the retina and daylight. The closing lines of the fourth poem 'El sur del océano' [South of the ocean] evoke the lack of substance of the ego faced with annihilation by the world or the id or simply just the non-human immensities and infinite: '*es una región sola, ya he hablado / ... / y no hay nadie sino unas huellas de caballo / no hay nadie sino el viento, no hay nadie / sino la lluvia que cae sobre las aguas del mar, / nadie sino la lluvia que crece sobre el mar*' [It is a solitary region, I have already spoken ... and there is no one but the wind, there is no one but the rain that falls on the waters of the sea, no one but the rain that grows on the sea] (PN1 307). With such a repetitive rhythm of 'nadie', no wonder Neruda turned to the human world of animal warmth, love in cafés and lovers' beds and busy cultural and later political activity.

The second section of this collection opens with another of his great poems, titled in English (which he spoke well) as 'Walking around', according to Loyola, a wink to James Joyce (PN1 1184). As noted, he read *Ulysses* in Ceylon (Sri Lanka), and translated Joyce's poems *Chamber Music* for a poetry review in Buenos Aires in 1933. Leopold Bloom 'walks' past shops and signs in Dublin free-associating, just as Neruda walked past shops in Buenos Aires.[7] The verb 'walk' punctuates Joyce's novel so that it slips into 'travel' and Bloom into Ulysses. Neruda lived some eight months in Buenos Aires with his home on the twentieth floor at the head of Avenida Corrientes. In this poem his persona is confident, aggressive and surrealist, faced with urban life and work. Amado Alonso put it that the poet 'da rienda suelta a su repugnancia por la vida organizada de los hombres' [frees his repugnance for man's organised life].[8] The first line is famous: 'Sucede que me canso de ser hombre' [It happens that I am tired of being man] (PN1 308).[9] There is a latent philosophy in that verb 'sucede'. It happens, a chance circumstance, no patterns, no deeper meaning, no destiny, a godless world etc. What he means by 'hombre' is more confused, but by the end of the poem we see that he means 'urban man', even 'Western' man as in D. H. Lawrence's 'Give us Gods': 'Give us Gods. / We are so tired of men / and motor-power,' which

---

7   For example: 'By lorries along Sir John Rogerson's Quay Mr Bloom walked soberly, past Windmill lane, Leask's the linseed crusher's, the postal telegraph office,' James Joyce, *Ulysses* (London: The Bodley Head, 1967), p. 85.

8   Amado Alonso, *Poesía y estilo*, p. 335.

9   Walsh's translation is not quite exact: 'I happen to be tired of being a man', by emphasising the 'yo' and changing 'hombre' to 'un hombre', p. 119.

mirrors Neruda's 'me canso de ser hombre'.[10] There is also an echo of Quevedo's famous sonnet '¡Ah de la vida!' [Ah, about life] with the line 'soy un
fue y un será y un es cansado' [I am a was and a will be and an am tired].[11]
If this poem describes Buenos Aires as a very urban, grey city, with few
green spaces, suffering under a corrupt, right-wing, nationalistic government,
bending democracy to suit itself, then the place would depress anybody (it
was the *década infame* of fraudulent elections). However, Neruda is still the
Romantic outsider, shocking the bourgeoisie. 'Hombre', then, could be the
opposite of 'poeta'.

   The poet is tired of entering urban spaces; Neruda is a nature poet and
freedom is his quest. So the 'sastrerías' [tailors], 'cines' [cinemas], 'pelu-
querías' [hairdressers], 'mercadería' [merchandise], 'anteojos' [glasses] and
'ascensores' [lifts] (a wonderful list) stand for urban claustrophobia. The poet
feels 'marchito, impenetrable, como un cisne de fieltro' [withered, impenetrable, like a felt swan] by these places (in an earlier poem – 'Arte póetica'
– his heart was 'marchito'). Feeling like a felt swan (a hat?) has Neruda
mocking Rubén Darío's fascination with 'swans' in his *Prosas profanas* as the
epitome of beauty. Then the poem changes tack with a sudden 'sin embargo'
[nevertheless] and the poet asserts his imagination as verbal gestures:

>   Sin embargo sería delicioso
>   asustar a un notario con un lirio cortado
>   o dar muerte a una monja con un golpe de oreja.
>   Sería bello
>   ir por las calles con un cuchillo verde
>   y dando gritos hasta morir de frío (PN1 308)

>   [Nevertheless it would be delightful to scare a notary with a cut
>   lily or kill a nun by hitting her with an ear. It would be beautiful
>   to go through the streets with a green knife and shouting until
>   dropping dead with cold]

The urban enemies are 'notarios' (the law) and nuns (church law); the poet
brandishes flowers, an ear, a green knife and shouts aloud. He is free, a threat.
This is the new beauty. It is close to surrealism's provocation, that famous
photo of Benjamin Péret insulting a priest from the cover of *La Revolution
surréaliste* in 1924. The green knife alludes to Lorca, as Loyola noted.[12]
According to Adam Feinstein, Neruda altered the line about killing a nun
with a blow on the ear from 'matar a una monja con un irrigador' (sprin-

---

[10] D. H. Lawrence, 2002, p. 354.
[11] Francisco de Quevedo, *Antología poética*, p. 36.
[12] Loyola, *Residencia*, p. 220.

kler) because the Chilean writer María Luisa Bombal objected.[13] The lines are outward-directed, no longer explore inner darkness. The poet is fed up with being 'raíz en las tinieblas' [root in the darkness], enough of 'tiritando de sueño' [shivering with dream], of excavating the inner self 'hacia abajo, en las tripas mojadas de la tierra' [down inside into the moist guts of the earth] (PN1 308). He has had enough of his task of 'absorbiendo y pensando' [absorbing and thinking]. This is the crux, and foreshadows a move away from the poem as site for thinking the unthinkable. The poet feels that he has become a 'tumba' [tomb], a 'bodega' [cellar], and that he is dying of 'pena' [grief]. He has a 'cara de cárcel' [prison face] on Mondays, the day the work-week begins. That prison face implies being trapped indoors, in 'ciertas casas húmedas' [certain humid houses], for the River Plate climate is extremely humid, and, a lovely line, in 'hospitales donde los huesos salen por la ventana' [hospitals where the bones stick out of windows] (PN1 309). He is trapped in 'zapaterías' [shoe shops], forced to conform, to wear tight shoes, a final allusion to Buenos Aires and the strict urban dress-conformity of the 1930s.

The penultimate stanza is generated by Neruda's rhythmical repetition of 'hay', suggesting that the external world just *is*, no two ways about it. 'Hay' also introduces an arbitrary, surrealist list representing ugly urban reality:

> Hay pájaros de color de azufre y horribles intestinos
> colgando de las puertas de las casa que odio,
> hay dentaduras olvidadas en una cafetera,
> hay espejos
> que debieran haber llorado de vergüenza y espanto,
> hay paraguas en todas partes, y venenos, y ombligos.
>
> (PN1 309)

> [There are sulphur-coloured birds and horrible intestines hanging from the doors of the houses I hate, there are dentures forgotten in a coffee pot, there are mirrors that should have wept with shame and fright, there are umbrellas everywhere, and poisons, and navels]

The verb 'hate' introduces a note of aggression that Neruda will later cultivate as vituperation. The umbrellas hint at that surrealist beauty, derived from Lautréamont's chance meeting of an umbrella and a sewing machine on an operating table that Breton made the credo of surrealist metaphor. Note also how some of the nouns like 'venenos' are generic. What poisons does Neruda mean? He likes the sound of the word and likes the arbitrariness, but does not care for particularity or realism.

---

13   Adam Feinstein, *Pablo Neruda*, p. 98.

The poem closes with the poet walking around the unnamed city, 'yo paseo' (and the poem's title, a Baudelairian *flâneur*), in shoes, past offices and 'tiendas de ortopedia' [orthopaedic shoe shops]. He spots a patio with clothes hanging on a line, which he then enumerates:

> calzoncillos, toallas, camisas que lloran
> lentas lágrimas sucias (PN1 309)

> [underpants, towels and shirts that weep slow dirty tears]

This closure is visual and moral. The water dripping from these clothes becomes tears, and the dirt is not only urban but inner contamination, perhaps lovelessness again. You have to read these closing lines aloud, the endings '-as', to get their full force of sound-suggestion.[14] Manuel Durán raised an interesting point about how this poem reveals the 'dissolution of the critical and aesthetic ego' in an anti-poetic song, but the alliteration of the last lines brings back a 'survival of traditional poetic language', without stressing how this mixture of the very modern and traditional is the key to Neruda's poetry.[15] American poet James Wright found that H. R. Hays' 'version of *Walking Around* remains, to me, one of the greatest poems in the modern American language', that is, as a poem in English.[16] Clayton Eshleman's list of poems that have taught him about life and poetry and that still haunt him includes Neruda's 'Walking around'.[17] This single poem, then, stands for all his *Residencia* cycle. It is curious that biographically Neruda might have appeared contented in Buenos Aires. My point is that when he sat down to write this poem deeper anxieties surfaced, but as a poem not a confession.

The following poem, 'Desespediente', rewrites his earlier hate-for-office-work poem 'Caballo de los sueños'. The title is a neologism, combing 'desesperanza' [despair] and 'expediente' [dossier], a condensation of the experience of office tedium. The 'paloma' [dove] is stained with glue, weeks and blotting paper. 'Paloma' is an obvious symbol for himself, a natural bird, not born for work. Biographically, Neruda had to earn his bread as a diplomat, and loathed this dead time and the 'interminables trajes' [interminable suits] (PN1 310) and 'serious' socks he had to wear. This intense hate-work poem closes: 'Venid conmigo al día blanco que se muere / dando gritos de novia asesinada' [Come with me to the white day that dies screaming like an assassinated bride] (PN1 311), echoing Duchamp's mocking glass panel, 'The Bride stripped bare by her bachelors, even', where the poet now leads

---

[14] For another close-reading, see Enrico Mario Santí, 1982, pp. 70–5.
[15] Manuel Durán. in *Simposio Pablo Neruda*, pp. 135–36.
[16] James Wright, *Review*, p. 29.
[17] Clayton Eshleman, *Companion Spider*, p. 75.

the reader ('venid'), no longer a solitary soul in his aloneness. The poem is the 'grito' [shout], the poet the 'asesinado'. Neruda endorses Rimbaud's 'J'ai horreur de tous les métiers' [I have a horror of all jobs] and his cry 'Voici le temps des *Assassins*' [now is the time of assassins] (the title of Henry Miller's study of Rimbaud).[18]

There are further poems dealing with urban angst. 'La calle destruida' ends with exclamations: 'Nadie circule! Nadie abra los brazos / dentro del agua ciega!' [Let nobody wander about! Let nobody open their arms / within the blind water!] (PN1 312). Life's wound in which 'las guitarras azules' [blue guitars] fall and die. Blue guitar stands for the poet, for music and for Darío's 'azul' (I do not think that Neruda had read Wallace Stevens's 'The Man with a Blue Guitar', though his poems, like Stevens's, assert art over everything else: 'Poetry / Exceeding music must take the place / Of empty heaven and its hymns ...').[19]

However, the poet is still the centre of the world, his melancholic Romantic 'yo' the summa of experience. 'Melancolía en las familias' [Melancholy in the families] closes with the repetition: 'porque estoy triste y viajo, / y conozco la tierra, y estoy triste' [because I am sad and travel and know the earth and am sad] (PN1 314). The collection's title resurfaces – I know the earth – and so does the underlying sadness linked to not yet finding his place in life and love in his travels. The last stanza of 'Enfermedades en mi casa' reiterates this suffering 'yo': 'Estoy cansado ... / estoy herido ... / y me ahogo ...' [I am tired, I am wounded, I drown] to end with the sole rhythmical act that justifies his pain: 'escribo este poema que sólo es un lamento, / solamente un lamento' [I write this poem which is only a lament, only a lament] (PN1 318).

Section III includes sexual and love poems – 'Material nupcial', 'Agua sexual' – which we have already commented on, and leads on to section IV – 'Tres cantos materiales' – which was published separately in 1935 in Madrid. This 16-paged pamphlet, titled *Homenaje a Pablo Neruda de los poetas españoles. Tres cantos materiales*, was signed by sixteen of his new friends, including Rafael Alberti, Vicente Aleixandre, Manuel Altolaguirre, Luis Cernuda, Gerardo Diego (later an enemy), León Felipe, Federico García Lorca, Jorge Guillén, Pedro Salinas, Miguel Hernández, José A. Muñoz Rojas, Luis Rosales and others – that is, by the poets of Spain's fabled 1927 generation (only Muñoz Rojas still lives). These signatures confirm Neruda's arrival as poet, accepted in the *madre patria* and for a short while to become even their leader as editor of the magazine *Caballo verde para la poesía* in 1935. The little prologue praised him as a great poet ('insigne'), with 'obras personalísimas' [very personal works], reiterating 'su extraordinaria person-

---

18   Rimbaud, *Oeuvres complètes*, p. 94.
19   Wallace Stevens, 'The Man with the Blue Guitar', in *Collected Poems* (London: Faber, 1984), p. 167.

alidad' [his extraordinary personality], stressing his persona and his work being 'without dispute one of the most authentic realisations of poetry in the Spanish tongue'. In a letter, Neruda mentioned another underlying reason for this pamphlet as it would alert Huidobro, on his arrival in Madrid, about who Neruda's poet friends were: 'todos ellos indefectibles amigos míos' [all were unfailingly friends of mine].[20] Much has been made of these three poems about material objects – wood, celery, wine – as prefiguring Neruda's turning away from the inner to the outer world, leading in time to his famous odes, his espousal of Marxism as a materialist philosophy, and his interest in food, company and eating. Jaime Concha echoed many critics in claiming that these poems are the 'obra maestra' [masterpieces] of the *Residencias* (but are the least typical, and most adaptable to Marxist theory).[21] René de Costa noted Neruda's new 'poetic realism', based on the poet's own confession in 'Estatuto del vino' [Ordinance of wine]:[22]

> Hablo de cosas que existen, Dios me libre
> de inventar cosas cuando estoy cantando!
> Hablo de la saliva derramada en los muros,
> hablo de lentas medias de ramera,
> hablo del coro de los hombres del vino
> golpeando el ataúd con un hueso de pájaro. (PN1 329)

> [I talk of things that exist, God free me from inventing things when I'm singing! I talk of spit spilt on walls, I talk of slow socks of a whore, I talk of a chorus of men of wine knocking the coffin with a bird bone]

However, these 'things' that exist are not easy to interpret. What is the saliva spilt on walls? Why the whore's slow stockings (is she slowly taking them off)? What the poet means is more to do with his poetry finding its symbolism, its objective correlatives, in words that single out objects. The chorus of men drinking wine, banging the coffin with bird bones, is based on nouns, but whose meaning still defies immediate comprehension. In fact, 'Entrada a la madera' (already discussed on p. 106) opens with this warning: 'Con mi razón apenas, con mis dedos' [Scarcely with my reason, with my fingers] (PN1 324). It suggests understanding through the senses (especially tactility and maybe holding a pen), but beyond reason as if the materiality of the world – its nouns – was enough to generate sense. In the poem 'Vuelve el otoño' [Autumn returns], Neruda is well aware of this lack of 'reason', of not being understood rationally: 'No sé si me entiende: cuando desde lo alto

[20] Julio Neira, 'De Pablo Neruda a José María Souvirón, una carta inédita', p. 19.
[21] Jaime Concha, 'Interpretación de *Residencia en la tierra* de Pablo Neruda', p. 59.
[22] René de Costa, *The Poetry of Pablo Neruda*, p. 79.

/ se avecina la noche, cuando el solitario poeta / a la ventana oye correr el corcel del otoño' [I don't know if I make myself clear: when from above night approaches, when the solitary poet at the window hears autumn's steed run] (PN1 342). He remains the Romantic outsider, alone at his window, *hearing* what we do not hear.

Lorca and Neruda

The opening poem of section V is an 'Oda a Federico García Lorca', written in Madrid in 1935, according to Loyola, that is, a year before Lorca's murder in Granada in August 1936. The title mimics Lorca's own 'Oda a Salvador Dalí' of 1926 as a celebration of close friendship between two artists ('Pero ante todo canto un común pensamiento que nos une ... / Es primero el amor, la amistad o la esgrima' [But first of all I sing a common thought that unites us. It's first love, friendship or fencing]).[23] Biographically, the two similar kinds of poet met in Buenos Aires in 1933: Neruda was 29 years old, Lorca was 33.[24] There is much gossip about their antics. According to Neruda, Lorca stood guard while Neruda seduced an Argentine female admirer, then fell and hurt his leg. The two poets dressed as sailors for Norah Lange's book launch and gave a radio broadcast 'al alimón' (a bullfighter's term for two *toreros* sharing one cape), during a PEN conference held in the grand Plaza Hotel in 1933, complaining that Buenos Aires had no statues celebrating Rubén Darío.[25]

The two poets also collaborated in a small 'book' with the long title *Paloma por dentro o sea la mano de vidrio* [Inner dove or else glass hand], with the sole copy dedicated to their Argentine hostess Sara Tornú, where Lorca illustrated several of Neruda's poems from *Residencia en la tierra*, including 'Walking around', 'Material nupcial', 'Sólo la muerte' and 'Agua sexual'. For the latter poem, Lorca has a lined drawing (in *tinta china*) of a naked woman, splashing water from her vagina.[26] The last drawing by Lorca portrays both poets as severed heads. It is notable that Lorca illustrated Neruda. Indeed, Lorca famously once asked Neruda to stop reading a poem as he might be influenced by him. That Neruda vied – and won as it were – with Spain's greatest poet, whose *Romancero gitano* was republished by Sur in Buenos

---

[23]   Federico García Lorca, *Obra completa*, pp. 621–2.

[24]   For more on the biographic relationships, see Feinstein, *Pablo Neruda*, pp. 98–100.

[25]   'Charla Federico García Lorca y Pablo Neruda y su discurso al alimón sobre Rubén Darío (toreo al alimón)', in García Lorca, *Obras completas*, pp. 145–7. There is now a statue to Darío outside the Bibliotecta Nacional.

[26]   All the drawings are collected in the catalogue, Federico García Lorca, *Dibujos*, ed. Mario Hernández (Madrid: Ministerio de Asuntos Exteriores de España, 1987).

Aires in 1933, is an important moment in Neruda's confidence, and heralds his change to the later contented, sociable poet exploring the empirical world. Margarita Aguirre copied down Lorca's dedication of his *Romancero gitano* to Neruda: 'Para mi queridísimo Pablo, uno de los grandes poetas que he tenido la suerte de amar y conocer' [For my very dear Pablo, one of the great poets that I've had the luck to love and know].[27] Poetically, both poets shared crucial attitudes towards poetry. Lorca's then unpublished *Poeta en Nueva York* built its sense through the same kind of rhythmic repetitions as Neruda's. Lorca had jettisoned meter as the musical container and replaced it with anaphora and worked on images that remained strangely archaic, as did some of Neruda's. Both were rural poets, sickened by urban life (New York / Buenos Aires). Both mixed 'roses' with contemporary images like 'melting pianos' and muddled abstract nouns with concrete ones. Though some of Lorca's New York poems had appeared in Ortega y Gasset's *Revista de Occidente*, as did some of Neruda's, I doubt that either poet influenced the other. The point is that their friendship had direct poetic equivalents – they were similar, quasi-surrealist poets who 'thought' at subliminal and imagistic levels, both reluctant to rationalise their gifts. Indeed, Lorca astutely said of Neruda, and of himself, that he was 'un poeta lleno de voces misteriosas que afortunadamente él mismo no sabe descifrar' [a poet full of mysterious voices that luckily he himself doesn't know how to decipher].[28]

Neruda's 'Oda a Federico García Lorca' is long (127 lines) and clearly reveals Neruda's admiration for his fellow poet. The poem can also be read as a poet's literary criticism. If he could ('Si pudiera' structures the poem), the first stanza opens, Neruda 'would' cry in an empty house and 'sacarme los ojos y comérmelos' [rip out my eyes and eat them] (PN1 331) because of Lorca's 'voz de naranjo enlutado' [voice of widowed orange tree] and because his poetry 'sale dando gritos' [leave shouting]. The orange tree that gives its juicy fruits in winter is metonymically Andalusian. Lorca's obsession with his own death is notorious. That Lorca was a fabulous 'reader' of his poems is also well attested. Neruda was never interested in a purely literary form; poetry had to do with life. Nobody better than Lorca illustrated this, where words become shouts of vitality. Lorca had felt the same about Neruda, whom he astutely defined in 1934 as 'un poeta más cerca de la muerte que de la filosofía, más cerca del dolor que de la inteligencia, más cerca de la sangre que de la tinta' [a poet closer to death than philosophy, closer to pain than intelligence, closer to blood than to ink], a description that unites Lorca and Neruda. Neither was bookish; they had blood in their fountain pens, not

---

27 Aguirre, 1967, p. 87.
28 García Lorca, *Obra completa*, p. 147.

ink; they both repudiated 'el odioso monóculo de la pedantería libresca' [the odious monocle of bookish pedantry] (perhaps thinking of Borges).[29]

The second stanza is structured on opening repetitions 'por ti' and 'y', and shows the startling *effect* of Lorca's poems: hospitals are painted blue, wounded angels gain wings (perhaps a wink to Rafael Alberti's *Sobre los ángeles*) and hedgehogs (or sea urchins) fly. The most developed of these effects is to do with 'sastrerías' [tailors' shops], Neruda's private term for urban imprisonment. Lorca's poetry makes them fill up with spoons and blood, makes them swallow broken ribbons: 'y se matan a besos, / y se visten de blanco' [kill themselves with kisses and dress in white] (PN1 331). Lorca's poetry transforms the grim, urban world into an erotic and innocent feast.

The third stanza continues the repetitive rhythms ('cuando' and 'me moriría') where Neruda reveals that he would 'die' for his friend (repeated four times). When Lorca sings cities smelling of wet onions await him and 'silenciosos barcos de esperma te persiguen, / y golondrinas verdes hacen nido en tu pelo' [silent ships of sperm chase you / green swallows nest in your hair] (PN1 332). These direct surrealist images defy explanation, though they do signal Lorca's exceptional status as green is his colour from the popular opening of his 'Romance sonámbulo': 'Verde que te quiero verde ...' Neruda then invokes Lorca's house, to which arrive ('llegar' opens 14 lines) many odd images ('arados muertos y amapolas' [dead ploughs and poppies]) as well as Neruda himself and a list of first-named friends from South America (Oliverio Girondo / Norah Lange / Ricardo Molinari / María Luisa Bombal) and from Spain (Aleixandre / Alberti / Altolaguirre / Rosales etc.), as well as his own wife and baby daughter (PN1 333). He then invites Lorca to be 'crowned' as the Poet on Parnassus, and gives his reasons. Because Lorca is 'puro', is young with health and 'mariposa' [butterfly] (a favourite Lorca self-image) and because Lorca is 'free' and 'lively': 'como un negro relámpago perpetuamente libre' [like black lightning perpetually free]. We then arrive at the heart of the poem as self-definition and literary criticism.

What Neruda relishes is their 'conversando entre nosotros' [conversing between themselves] (PN1 333), a poet-to-poet relationship. He develops this desired chatting: 'hablemos sencillamente como eres tú y soy yo' [we talk simply as you and I are] and even asks if poetry should not be defined as this kind of intimacy, that is, real poetry *is* sharing confidences. His poetry up to 1935 cannot be termed 'sencillo' [simple], nor can Lorca's, but there is a seed and a sign that deeper inner explorations of the solitary self are almost over (Lorca was not an introspective poet either). Lorca, addressed with the intimate 'tú', has seen reality ('tú ves el mundo, las calles, / el vinagre ... [you see the world, the streets, the vinegar]), as Neruda has too. Both are poets who

---

[29] García Lorca, *Obra completa*, p. 147.

ask questions. The poem closes with Neruda offering his 'amistad' [friend-ship] and identifying himself as a 'meláncolico varón varonil' [melancholic manly man], stressing his heterosexuality, perhaps sensitive to Lorca's same-sexuality. The poem closes with the key verb 'saber' [to know]; for Lorca *knows* and will continue to know what counts, as in the last line: 'y otras irás sabiendo lentamente' [and other things you will slowly get to know]. That adverb 'lentamente' suggests deep absorption and knowledge of reality.

When Lorca was murdered, Neruda did not write a poem, as many others did, the best being by Antonio Machado 'El crimen fue en Granada' [The crime was in Granada]. Instead he contributed in prose in 1937 to a *Home-naje al poeta García Lorca contra su muerte*, which was also an anthology, prepared by the poet Emilio Prados. His piece is directed to a 'vosotros', probably a public speech, and categorised Lorca as an 'antiesteta, en este sentido de llenar su poesía y su teatro de dramas humanos y tempestades del corazón' [anti-aesthetic in that sense of filling his poetry and theatre with human dramas and heart storms].[30] The term 'antiesteta' is crucial for Neruda as well, for poetry never stops within the poem, but moves into life (and the reader's imagination) as passion and pain. A 'louable mépris de ce qui pour-rait s'ensuivre littérairement' [a praiseworthy scorn for what might follow in a literary way] (André Breton) is also a surrealist principle and part of the 1924 definition of surrealist art, 'en dehors de toute préocupation esthétique ou morale' [outside all aesthetic or moral preoccupations].[31] It is also close to Nicanor Parra's anti-poetry of the 1950s. For Neruda, Lorca 'buscaba con avidez dentro y fuera de sí' [searched with avidity inside and outside himself], like himself, and was the sole poet of that 1927 group (celebrating Góngora's tricentenary) not dominated by the latter's 'dominio de hielo' [dominion of ice]. Neruda contrasted Lorca with Alberti, and defined his own position in 1937, in the middle of the violent Spanish Civil War, as that of a 'latinoa-mericano', an important confession in terms of his late work. His swearing revenge for Lorca's murder is not political. He admits still in 1937 that 'no soy político ni he tomado nunca parte en la contienda política, y mis palabras, que muchos habrían deseado neutrales, han estado teñidas de pasión' [I am not political nor have I ever taken part in the political fight and my words, that many wanted neutral, have been stained with passion].[32]

The final section of *Residencia II* contains four poems, ending, as noted with 'Josie Bliss'. The penultimate poem 'No hay olvido (sonata)' could equally have been the concluding one for it summarises Neruda's *saison en*

[30] Emilio Prados, *Homenaje al poeta García Lorca contra su muerte. Selección de sus obras*, p. 45.

[31] André Breton, *Manifestes*, pp. 37, 40.

[32] Prados, *Homenaje*, p. 49.

enfer. He has survived, has changed, and offers advice to his reader (who has not gone through hell). 'No hay olvido (sonata)' [There is no forgetting, sonata] invokes the reader: 'Si me preguntáis en dónde he estado / debo decir "sucede"' [If you ask me where I have been, I must say 'It happens'] (PN1 343). He has slowly evolved from a private poet, with poems essentially aimed at his lovers as the prime readers, to a public poet with a public persona. All he can offer this new reader is a philosophy without explanations. Things happen – 'sucede' – that is all (and Neruda associates himself with this verb from an earlier poem 'Walking around'). The river of life destroys itself, leaving shadows of stones. The knowledge that the poet has acquired is one of loss, of grieving (the poet as 'viudo'): 'no sé sino las cosas que los pájaros pierden, / el mar dejado atrás, o mi hermana llorando' [I only know the things that birds lose, the sea left behind or my sister crying] (PN1 343). The poet also asks four questions about time, loss and death that cannot be answered: 'Por qué muertos? [why the dead?]' His new poetry is a 'conversar con cosas rotas' [to converse with broken things], with bitter utensils, rotting beasts, and with his 'acongojado corazón' [anguished heart]. Neruda's crucial metaphor for the self remains 'heart', source of passion and pain. What he has seen over the nine years of writing *Residencia en la tierra I* and *II* is 'caras con lágrimas, / dedos en la garganta' and 'nuestra triste sangre' [faces with tears, fingers in the throat, our sad blood]. For some, life might be violets, swallows, anything sweet, but he has seen beyond that rosy version. He warns the readers: 'Pero no penetremos más allá de esos dientes' [but let's not penetrate beyond those teeth] (PN1 344), for he has no answers – 'porque no sé qué contestar'. The poem ends with Neruda employing his device of 'hay', with the litany of repetitions:

> hay tantos muertos,
> y tantos malecones que el sol rojo partía,
> y tantas cabezas que golpean los buques,
> y tantas manos que han encerrado besos,
> y tantas cosas que quiero olvidar (PN1 344)

> [there are so many dead and so many sea walls that the red sun splits, and so many heads that beat against the ships, and so many hands that have locked kisses in and so many things that I want to forget]

The title of this poem suggests that there is no forgetting, while the last line states that the poet wants to forget. What does he yearn to forget but cannot? He lists the pains of life, but we suggest it was Josie Bliss, and that is why her name titles the last poem. Perhaps also the sonata in the title hints that music – here verbal rhythms – transforms pain into the consolations of art.

'Severidad'

Edmundo Olivares printed one poem that Neruda eliminated from *Residencia en la tierra II* titled 'Severidad', collected posthumously in *Fin de viaje* in 1982, though it was included in the book Lorca and Neruda created together in Buenos Aires in 1933. His friend Eandi had recommended this excision.[33] It is another 'hate' poem for sedentary, urban life in Buenos Aires, and the city's conformist poets. Structured on a curse – 'Os condeno a cagar' [I condemn you to shit] – it provocatively lists what nauseates the poet: 'periódicos atrasados', 'novelas amargas', 'casas llenas de bicicletas y canarios', 'posaderas azules y calientes', 'embajadores gordos', 'cines averiados' [dated newspapers, bitter novels, houses filled with bicycles and canaries, blue and hot buttocks, fat ambassadors, broken-down cinemas], and more. The reason for this vituperation is that he is a different kind of poet and astutely defines himself with metaphors: 'porque yo tengo llamas en los dedos / y lágrimas de desventura en el corazón, / y amapolas moribundas anidan en mi boca ...' [because I have flames in my fingers and tears of misfortune in my heart and moribund poppies nest in my mouth]. This self-defining dark poet hates the local poets surrounding him: 'odio vuestras comidas y vuestros sueños, / y vuestros poetas que escriben sobre "la dulce esposa", / y "las felicidades de la aldea" [I hate your meals and your dreams and your poets who write, 'sweet wife' and 'village happinesses']. He asks to be left alone – 'dejadme' opens three lines. The last line is: 'Dejadme un buque verde y un espejo' [leave me a green boat and a mirror]. So the poem defines Neruda against Argentine poets. But who were they? One guess is Baldomero Fernández Moreno, a hugely popular poet and doctor who had lived in Spain and wrote about Buenos Aires. His book *Aldea española*, 1925, won the Primer Premio Municipal de Poesía with its simple and direct lyrics.[34] Another guess is Ezequiel Martínez Estrada, famous for caged birds ('canaries') in his home and an uxorious poet with five books of poems in the 1920s. However, Neruda may also have been caricaturing any poet who worships his wife and village and is a traditionalist, for the phrases also evoke the Song of Songs and Lope de Vega.

The reception of Neruda's two-volumed *Residencia* involved generous reviews and presentations by key figures in Spain like Guillermo de Torre, Rafael Alberti and Federico García Lorca, who predisposed the reading public to identify with the persona Neruda in his poems. A good example of this kind of criticism is from the shepherd poet Miguel Hernández (who died in Alicante prison in 1942), who reviewed Neruda in 1936 in Madrid's

33 Aguirre, 1980, p. 138.
34 Edmundo B. Olivares, *Pablo Neruda: los caminos del mundo*, 2001, pp. 85–6. See Emilio Carilla, *Genio y figura de Baldomero Fernández Moreno* (Buenos Aires: Eudeba, 1973).

daily *El sol*. He placed Neruda above all other poets writing in Spanish at the time: 'Estamos escuchando la voz virgen del hombre que arrastra por la tierra sus instintos de león; es un rugido' [we listen to the virgin voice of the man who drags his lion instincts along the ground; it's a roar] and compares him both to a book and nature: 'En él se dan las cosas como en la Biblia y el mar; libre y grandiosamente' [in him things are as they are in the Bible and the sea, free and grandiose]. Neruda's presence 'belittles' all that Hernández had considered great.[35]

Caballo verde para la poesía

Neruda edited four numbers of this poetry magazine, with a fifth one ready and dedicated to the Uruguayan poet Julio Herrera y Reissig (although number 4 included an anthology of that poet's sonnets), but the fifth number was never published owing to the outbreak of the Spanish Civil War. In the first number, for example, of October 1935, Neruda included poems by his Spanish friends Vicente Aleixandre, Miguel Hernández, Arturo Serrano Plaja, Leopoldo Panero and Federico García Lorca, and two Argentine poet friends, Ricardo Molinari and Raúl González Tuñón, plus something from the dissident surrealist Robert Desnos in French (not a minor or forgotten poet there). Later numbers included poems by Luis Cernuda, Jorge Guillén, Moreno Villa, Altolaguirre, Rosa Chacel, Prados etc. Neruda assumed a leader's role, penning manifestos on the opening page of each number in the magazine that tried to define poetry for poets in the 1930s, in the same way that André Breton drafted the surrealist manifestos, but with the difference that Breton coerced many others to agree and sign. Neruda was aware of his new role: 'Few poets have been treated as I was in Spain. I found a brilliant brotherhood of talents and a full knowledge of my work.'[36] Neruda's thinking-about-poetry remained avant-garde, at odds with the massive influence in Spain both of Juan Ramón Jiménez and of Góngora on his fellow Spanish poets. He remained subjective, self-involved and outside politics. He was still the poet as the centre of his subjective world, as he wrote to a politicised Rafael Alberti at the time: 'Yo no entiendo nada de política, soy un poco anarcoide, quiero hacer lo que me plazca' [I understand nothing of politics, I'm slightly anarchistic, I want to do what pleases me].[37]

---

[35] Cited in Olivares, *Pablo Neruda II*, p. 278.

[36] Cited in Emir Rodríguez Monegal, *El viajero inmóvil*, p. 80: 'Pocos poetas han sido tratados como yo en España. Encontré una brillante fraternidad de talentos y un conocimiento pleno de mi obra.'

[37] Cited in Volodia Teitelboim, *Neruda*, p. 148.

As Neruda wrote little criticism and despised intellectualising his gifts, his manifestos are often cited by critics when isolating his poetic intentions. The key one from the first number has a battle cry as title: 'Sobre una poesía sin pureza' [On a poetry without purity], which alludes obviously to Juan Ramón Jiménez's trumpeted 'poesía pura' [pure poetry], essentialist poems that eliminate all prose, all references to politics, history and even the gross, sensual self in a quest for beauty. Neruda sought the opposite, a new kind of beauty. He lists what he thought poetry should deal with as 'los deberes de la mano, penetrada por sudor y el humo, oliente a orina y a azucena' [duties of the hand, penetrated by sweat and smoke, smelling of urine and lily] (that last echoes his 'Tango del viudo' and Josie Bliss urinating in the dark). This new poetry should be like a suit or body with food stains and 'arrugas, observaciones, sueños, vigilia, profecías, declaraciones de amor y de odio, bestias ...' [wrinkles, observations, dreams, wakefulness, prophecies, declarations of love and hate, beasts] (PN4 381–2). It should be open to all life: 'sin excluir deliberadamente nada, sin aceptar deliberadamente nada, la entrada en la profundidad de las cosas en un acto de arrebatado amor' [without deliberately excluding anything, without deliberately accepting anything, entering into the depth of things in an act of rapt love] (PN4 382). This ambition is Whitmanian, in D. H. Lawrence's words: '*Reject nothing*, sings Walt Whitman.'[38] Succinctly, it should be a poetry of 'mal gusto' [bad taste], beyond aesthetics. The second manifesto was titled 'Los temas' [The themes] (November 1935) and located the source of poetry in the 'heart', for real poetry should 'mete las manos en el miedo, en las angustias, en las enfermedades del corazón' [put its hands in fear, in anguish, in the heart's diseases] (PN4 383) and closed with a Nervalian self-definition: 'El poeta vestido de luto escribe temblorosamente muy solitario' [The poet dressed in mourning writes tremblingly very alone] (PN4 383). This is the kind of poet he has become. The third manifesto, 'Conducta y poesía' [Behaviour and poetry] (December 1935), recalls Lorca's earlier definition of Neruda's metaphorically writing in blood, not ink: 'en la casa de la poesía no permanece nada sino lo que fue escrito con sangre para ser escuchado por la sangre' [in the house of poetry nothing remains that's not written with blood to be listened by blood] (PN4 384). Neruda should have written 'passion', for, obviously, 'blood' cannot hear, but it does reveal Neruda's system of tactile, metaphorical substitutions. 'Sangre', then, is a metaphor that is close to how Lawrence shrinks a philosophy into that one word 'blood' in a poem like 'Climb Down, O Lordly Mind': 'The blood knows in darkness, and forever dark, / in touch, by intuition, instinctively. / The blood also knows religiously, / and of this, the mind is incapable [...] / Only that exists which exists dynam-

---

38   D. H. Lawrence, *Complete Poems*, p. 328.

ically and unmentalised, in my blood. / Non cogito, ergo sum. / I am, I do not think I am.'[39] The message is obvious for 'sangre' is the non-rational, inner, instinctual knowledge that poets discover.

From innuendos in these manifestos, and further slights in Madrid's social life, Juan Ramón Jiménez reacted to Neruda's towering presence. As Rodríguez Monegal and Ricardo Gullón have outlined, in 1939, he attacked Neruda as being a great, bad poet, who could not use or understand his own gifts. Famously, his sharp tongue came up with a brilliant insight: 'Neruda parece un torpe traductor de sí mismo y de los otros' [Neruda seems like an awkward translator of himself and of others]. Unlike Joyce, Eliot and Saint-John Perse, he is not 'un consciente profundo de lo subconsciente' [deeply consciously of the subconscious], that is, he lacks critical self-aware-ness.[40] But he was only half-right, for Neruda was accurate about the limits of 'pure poetry' in a period like 1930s Europe. He also saw through the playful avant-garde adopted by another antagonist, Vicente Huidobro, and in general the Spanish version called *ultraísmo* that the philosopher Ortega y Gasset had singled out in his 1924 essay *La deshumanización del arte*, for Neruda sought a deeper humanity, governed by fear, blood and heart. As for his squabble with the Nobel laureate Juan Ramón, Gullón found a letter in the archives from Neruda in 1942 asking him to contribute to a homage to Miguel Hernández, expressing his 'honda emoción' [deep emotion] in reading about his rectification over Neruda.[41] The last point to make about this magazine is that Neruda did not publish his own poetry, just that of his friends (in a letter to Souvirón, he asked the Chilean poets Juvencio Valle and Rosamel del Valle to collaborate).[42]

Tercera residencia en la tierra (1935–45)

As Loyola has pointed out, the dates for this third collection with the same title are not exact, for the poems included start with the 1934 love poem 'Las furias y las penas'. The publication date of 1947 also overlaps with the writing and publishing of sections of Neruda's Latin Americanist *Canto general* as if he deliberately separated his European poems from them. The collection was also the first published by the Spanish Republican exile Gonzalo Losada in Buenos Aires, who would remain Neruda's publisher until the latter's death. Keeping the same title for his ongoing poems associates Neruda with Luis

[39] Lawrence, *Complete Poems,* p. 389.
[40] Cited in Emir Rodríguez Monegal, *El viajero inmóvil,* pp. 86–7 and Ricardo Gullón, 'Relaciones Pablo Neruda–Juan Ramón Jiménez', pp. 141–66.
[41] Gullón, 'Relaciones Pablo Neruda–Juan Ramón Jiménez', p. 164.
[42] Neira, 'De Pablo Neruda a José María Souvirón', p. 19.

Cernuda's *La realidad y el deseo* and Jorge Guillén's *Cántico*, who both inserted new work into an ongoing title (both were published in *Caballo verde para la poesía*).

The collection is divided into five sections, with two of them published separately. I have already scrutinised 'Las furias y las penas' as an intense, cognitive love poem where the poet relives his Josie Bliss days, perhaps through another lover (biographically it might correspond with Delia del Carril). The title, from a Quevedo sonnet, hints that Neruda's poem is more a remorse poem: 'Hay en mi corazón furias y penas, / en él es el amor fuego, y tirano, / y yo padezco en mí la culpa mía' [There are furies and grief in my heart, in it love is fire and a tyrant and I suffer in my self my guilt].[43] What 'culpa' [guilt] is the poet suffering in his heart? An illicit affair? The relived abandonment of Josie Bliss? The poems do not reveal this biographical secret, though the mixture of guilt and eroticism is potent.

Neruda delayed publishing these poems for private reasons until 1939, republishing them in *Tercera residencia* in 1947. Part of this delay could be the way social and political life speeded up and imploded with Lorca's murder, the Spanish Civil War and then the Second World War forcing Neruda to return to Chile. In 1939 and back home in Chile, Neruda published *Las furias y las penas* as a 29-paged book. He included an oft-cited preface that he would slightly change in its 1947 version. Neruda stated plainly that 'el mundo ha cambiado y mi poesía ha cambiado' [the world has changed and my poetry has changed], but not these actual poems; that is, only after 1939 did his poems change. Private poems about inner sensations and sexual knowledge seemed self-indulgent by 1939. His preface closed with his passionate promise: 'Juro defender hasta mi muerte lo que han asesinado en España: el derecho a la felicidad' [I swear to defend to my death what they have assassinated in Spain: the right to happiness].[44] However, Neruda clearly referred to Lorca's death, converted by circumstances into a symbolic killing of innocence and joy. The murder of a poet who was also a close friend figured mightily in Neruda's mind. In 1947 he changed his last sentence to 'Una gota de sangre caída en estas líneas quedará viviendo sobre ellas, indeleble como el amor' [a drop of blood fallen in these lines will remain alive above them, indelible like love] (PN1 357). By the fall of Republican Spain in 1939, lyrical poetry could not 'aplacar la ira del mundo' [placate the world's anger], only 'la lucha y el corazón resuelto' [the struggle and a determined heart] can. Here then is the clue to a change in the poet and his poems for 'lucha' is a code-word for Communist Party discipline, and the 'heart', so crucial to Neruda's making sense of life through pain and sex and

---

[43] Quevedo, *Antología poética*, p. 39.

[44] It was Loyola who noted this difference: see his Pablo Neruda, *Obras completas 1*, p. 1195.

love, is now 'resuelto'. Neruda is no longer a solitary individual, but part of a fighting collective. But before publishing this poem in 1939, Neruda had written another poem about his 'change of heart'.

España en el corazón, 1937

Neruda's anger and fighter's poems about Spain, *España en el corazón. Himno a las glorias del pueblo en la guerra (1936–1937)* were published while there was still hope that Franco and his side would be vanquished. The first edition appeared in Chile in 1937, with 16 photographs by Pedro Olmos, and was written on board ship on his way home. Here the book would have been Neruda's report from Spain, the mother-country, to readers in an ex-colony, Chile. The second edition was printed on handmade paper on the battle-front in Spain by Manuel Altolaguirre in November 1938 by the Ejército del Este, with obvious propaganda and hortatory intentions, to be handed around and read by all the fighters. Neruda's public had shifted dramatically from his lovers to his poet-friends to fellow Chileans to anybody militating on the left. From now on, Neruda would write 'for the world, for an international audience'.[45] His 'heart' had been taken over by 'mother Spain' and everybody who supported the cause.

The axial poem, all critics agree, is 'Explico algunas cosas' [I explain some things], first published as 'Así es' [So it is].[46] The poem is personal and political, and presumes that Neruda is already well-known to his reading public. It opens with the 'vosotros': 'Preguntaréis' [You will ask], hinting that readers may expect more of the dark, turbulent Neruda, but, no, he has changed. These readers will ask three questions: 'Y dónde están las lilas? / Y la metafísica cubierta de amapolas? Y la lluvia que a menudo golpeaba / sus palabras llenándolas / de agujeros y pájaros?' [And where are the lilacs? And metaphysics covered in poppies/ And the rain that often struck his words filling them with holes and birds?] (PN1 369). What we have first is self-analysis. 'Lilacs' and 'rain', especially the cold, relentless rain of southern Chile, identify Neruda, as does that link between metaphysics and poppies, that is, he knew that his poems explored beyond the surfaces of life into roots, pain, pleasure, beauty and sadness.

The poet inserted a personal anecdote into his Civil War poems; he lived in the 'barrio' of Argüelles in Madrid in Castile 'como un océano de cuero' (a lovely simile for the landscape). His house was named 'la casa de las flores' because of its geraniums. He addressed three of his close poet-friends, Raúl

45 Schopf, 2000, p. 91.
46 See De Costa, 1979, pp. 93–98 and Mike Gonzalez, pp. 138–41.

(González Túñón), an Argentine poet and journalist who published *La muerte en Madrid*, his Civil War poems, with its opening poem 'Madrid' dedicated to Neruda. He had married a Chilean, Amparo Mom, and in 1939 returned in the same boat as Neruda to Chile. Neruda does not give his surname, but there is an inner group; the second name is Rafael (Alberti), the third Federico (García Lorca, murdered, but vividly there in spirit). All came to his house, suddenly engulfed in bombs and war and blood. These 'bandidos' with airplanes, moors, rings and priests killed children. Here Neruda deals with simile, refusing its poetic potential, emphasising the literal:

> Y por las calles la sangre de los niños
> Corría simplemente, como sangre de niños. (PN1 370)

> [And through the streets the blood of the children ran simply, like the blood of children]

He repeats this 'blood in the streets' as the closing of the poem. Immediate understanding is the aim, with buzz-words that trigger instant political emotions ('Chacales', 'víboras', 'traidores' etc.). From each dead child arises a rifle with eyes, from every crime (like Lorca's), bullets. Poetry takes second place, can only encourage the fight. The penultimate stanza recalls the opening 'preguntaréis' and refers to Neruda's already massive reputation: 'por qué su poesía / no nos habla del sueño, de las hojas, / de los grandes volcanes de su país natal' [why does your poetry not speak to us of dream, of leaves, of the great volcanoes of your native land] (PN1 371), because, he insisted, that was not the time to explore the selfish self. Mike Gonzalez well summarised the power of this poem: 'It has the same feeling of personal pain as Picasso's "Guernica". Neither work is in any direct sense an explanation of events; rather it is a cry of disbelief, of solidarity and of impotent anguish.'[47] The extent to which Neruda shared a generational Civil War poetics has been debated by Stephen Hart. Unlike his Spanish contemporaries, Neruda did not turn to the ballad ('romance') form for propaganda, but he did incorporate colloquial language and 'raw political propaganda' that, though not composed on the battlefield, clearly sacrificed his earlier voice.[48] That Neruda's Spanish Civil War poems became so well-known could be linked to how long Franco survived in power, so that Republican opposition could recite Neruda's propagandist poems to keep their hopes alive over three decades.

Against this clinging to his own experience as important to others (that is, a public poet who owed this kind of poem to his readers), Neruda published

---

[47] Mike Gonzalez and David Treece, *The Gathering of Voices. The Twentieth-century Poetry of Latin America*, p. 138.

[48] Stephen Hart, 'War within a War: Poetry of the Spanish Civil War'. in Hart (ed.), *¡No pasarán! ...*, pp. 109–11.

a poem without referring to his 'yo', such as the long 'Cómo era España?'
[How was Spain?]. This poem is a litany of place names without verbs, like
the later section IX of his 'Alturas de Macchu Picchu'. Just to cite a town
or village was sufficient to resurrect Spain for his readers. It must have been
wonderful to hear Neruda reciting these towns. The poem expands Miguel de
Unamuno's untitled poem 'Avila, Málaga, Cáceres / Játiva, Mérida, Córdoba
...', which ends with an explanation that Neruda, in his poem, does not give:
'sois nombres de cuerpo entero, / libres, propios, los de nómina, / el tuétano
intraducible / de nuestra lengua española' [you are names/nouns of full body,
free, yourselves, roll call, the untranslatable marrow of our Spanish tongue].[49]
Neruda's place names had no emotional significance for him as a Chilean,
but for Unamuno his place names are the 'marrow' of Spanishness. You must
read Neruda and Unamuno together to catch this; perhaps Neruda knew this
poem as Unamuno was a figurehead in 1936, who resigned as rector of Salamanca University after the war broke out. De Costa argued, oddly, that the
poem was meant to tax the reader's patience, and thus 'overwhelm him with
the extent of the tragedy'.[50] Finally, the Spanish Civil War poems were the
start of Neruda's committed phase, but they were written too close to events.
Even Pring-Mill found them a 'raucous diatribe'.[51]

    The rest of the poems of *Tercera residencia*, covering eleven years, move
from personal anguish – 'yo me detengo y sufro' [I halt cold] in 'La ahogada
del cielo' [The drowned woman from the sky] and 'Vals' [Waltz], where the
poet remains in his 'terreno herido' [wounded territory] (PN1 352). The poem
'Bruselas' [Brussels] ends 'aquí estoy con aquello que pierde estrellas, / vege-
talmente, solo' [Here I am with what loses stars, vegetably alone] (PN1 353).
Even the title 'Al abandonado' recalls poems going back to 1924. Underneath
the imagery and despair, there is a simmering melancholy about love. All
this changed with Spain. In his later 'Nuevo canto de amor a Stalingrado'
[New love song to Stalingrad], the opening stanza reveals his public change
of mood: 'Yo escribí sobre el tiempo y sobre el agua, / describí el luto y su
metal morado, / yo escribí sobre el cielo y la manzana, / ahora escribo sobre
Stalingrado' [I wrote about weather and about water, I described mourning
and its purple quality, I wrote about sky and apple, now I write about Stalin-
grad] (PN1 396). It is the first of many *mea culpas* for the self-indulgence of
his past poetry. However, there is something tired about his self-description;
it does not capture the thrill of self-exploration and summarises the themes
in a rhetorical way. For example, what does he mean by 'luto y su metal
morado'?

49 Miguel de Unamuno, *Antología poética*, p. 122.
50 De Costa, *The Poetry of Pablo Neruda*, pp. 96–7.
51 Pring-Mill, *A Basic Anthology*, p. xxvii.

Despite aesthetic quibbles, there is no doubt that with *España en el corazón* Neruda found a new, far wider public than a literary group of fellow poets. His language is simplified to be understood by people who would never dream of buying a book of poems, even by illiterates, who can listen and do not have to read. He had also created his 'persona' as a public poet, with responsibilities. From the 1940s, he would attract more and more followers, and haters.

On 15 September 1938, a young Mexican poet, Octavio Paz, published a wordy article tellingly titled 'Pablo Neruda en el corazón' [Pablo Neruda in the heart] (which Paz soon disclaimed and never republished in his lifetime). Neruda was the stimulus for Paz to work out his own aesthetics. For Paz, Neruda wrote more than poetry; he tapped into a 'fluir vivo' [living flow] that was like the 'parto de las mujeres, al fuego de los volcanoes, al esperma del hombre' [women's childbirth, volcano's fire, man's sperm].[52] The poet Neruda dissolved his self into the world 'ya metido en lo humano, a la misma fuente que Marx' [now inside humanity, the same source as Marx]. He had reached 'essence', and, more instructively, his poetry tapped the same awareness as Marx's political doctrine. It made Neruda as crucial as Marx. Neruda then was judge and partisan, had become 'conciencia del mundo, es el mundo' [consciousness of the world, is the world]. Paz had clearly seen in his poetry a critical and ethical awareness close to surrealism, but more vital ('fluir vivo'). However, by 1941, Neruda had become the enemy.

Translating Neruda

One of the earliest translations from Neruda's *Residencia* cycle was by an English friend met in Ceylon called Andrew Boyd. Boyd, with his poet brother A. C. Boyd, published their joint version of the already English-titled 'Walking around' in Geoffrey Grigson's important but slim poetry review *New Verse* in September 1936. It was the opening poem. The translators included an interesting note: 'Neruda is the poet laureate of Chili.' It closed with 'Neruda does not count himself as a surrealist.'[53] The translation was later included in Grigson's anthology of poems from *New Verse* where Neruda follows Auden.[54] This difficult, free poem allowed translators to add their personal flourishes. As usual, it is meaning that gets translated, not sound. For example, Neruda's mocking 'como un cisne de fieltro' where this urban swan is perhaps a man with a hat, becomes with the Boyds 'like a flannel swan'; with Donald Walsh it is literal, 'like a felt swan', with Ben

---

52 Octavio Paz, 'Pablo Neruda en el corazón', p. 27.
53 *New Verse*, 22, September 1936, p. 3 (New York: Kraus Reprint, 1966).
54 Geoffrey Grigson (ed.), *New Verse*, pp. 183–4.

Belitt 'like a big wooly swan' (a poor version). Neruda's surrealist gesture 'O dar muerte a una monja con un golpe de oreja' has the Boyds write 'or do'in an abbess with a box on the ears' (which sounds right), with Walsh 'or kill a nun with a blow to the ear' (literal) and Belitt's 'or finish a nun with a left to the ear' (too free). Neruda's Lorcan 'un cuchillo verde' is literal with Merwin: 'with a green knife'; pumped up by the Boyds: 'with a bright green knife'; Walsh elaborates wildly: 'with a sexy knife', while Belitt has 'with a green switchblade handy'. Neruda's self-mocking 'cara de cárcel' leads to three versions: 'prison face' (Boyds), 'jailbird face' (Walsh) and 'my jail-face' (Merwin). The stanza opening with the chaotic list: 'Hay pájaros de color de azufre y horribles intestinos' has these four versions:

> There are brimstone-colored birds and horrible intestines (Walsh)
> Birds of sulphur-colour, horrible intestines (Boyds)
> There are birds the colour of sulphur and horrible intestines (Merwin)
> There are sulphurous birds, in a horror of tripe (Belitt)

The final line of disgust for this unnamed city is strong with sound in Spanish: 'Lentas lágrimas sucias':

> And where with their slow and dirty tears (Boyds, and not the closing
>   of the poem)
> Slow dirty tears (Walsh)
> Slow dirty tears (Merwin)
> Slowly dribbling a slovenly tear (Belitt)[55]

So what do these variations imply about translating Neruda? The critic Martin Dodsworth reviewed translations of Neruda's *Residence on Earth* in 1975 and chose Robert Bly as the best. He censured Walsh as being too 'faithful' and then decided (rightly) that Neruda 'writes in a tradition of symbolism and surrealism that is alien to us' and which leads to 'outrageous phrases like that "felt swan"' referred to above.[56] John Felstiner alluded to the difficulties of translating Neruda, which I will touch on later. There have even been squabbles between different translators, as noted by Stavans, when Bly attacked Walsh for not feeling 'emotional intensity', while Walsh responded by underlining Bly's errors.[57] The poet and translator Clayton Eshleman also attacked Bly's translations as too casual, too colloquial, as presenting Bly himself (all his translations sound the same) and as too pleasing for an audi-

---

55   I have cited from Donald D. Walsh's translation of *Residence on Earth*, 1976, pp. 118–21; W. S. Merwin in N. Tarn's *Selected Poems*, 1970, pp. 104–7; Ben Belitt from *Selected Poems*, 1961. See my appendix on Neruda in English.
56   Martin Dodsworth 'Words and Music', p. 16.
57   Ilan Stavans, *The Poetry of Pablo Neruda*, p. xxxviii.

ence, to entertain (Bly is a great performer). This sharp critique even taps into the weakness of Neruda's later poetry as being too 'simplistic'.[58]

Nancy Cunard, who met Neruda in Spain in 1936 and worked with him for the Republican cause, and published on her press leaflets titled *Los poetas del mundo defienden al pueblo español* (with Auden's rejected 'Spain' the fifth).[59] She had been Louis Aragon's lover. In his memoirs, Neruda evoked her as 'one of the most quixotic, chronic, brave and pathetic and curious people I have known'.[60] She defended Blacks and attacked her mother who had disinherited her with *Negro Man and White Lady Ship*, which Neruda compared in its venom to Swift. She visited Neruda in Chile in 1940 with a matador lover, and left him for a scruffy, toothless Chilean poet (who Neruda does not name, nor does her biographer).[61] She also edited the *Left Review* questionnaire about supporting Spain, listing 148 signatories, with 126 supporting the Republic and 16 neutral (including T. S. Eliot).[62] She translated some of Neruda's 'España en el corazón' poems from *Tercera Residencia*, including the poem 'Almería'. By now Neruda was easier to translate, writing a more literal, vituperative poetry. However, Cunard tampered with Neruda; it could be because her sense of English could not digest his poem (the usual battle of particulars in English v. the Latinate generalities of Spanish), or that she does not know Spanish, or that she is not a good poet herself.

I will highlight what I mean, with examples. Neruda's rhythm depends on repetition (anaphora). The first stanza repeats 'un plato' four times, and the second, another four times. Cunard keeps seven 'dishes', but changes one into a 'bowl'. She changes a repeated 'mañana' in the third stanza to 'noon' (a poeticism); she changes 'suaves manos' to '*soigne* hands' (Donald Walsh gets it exact with 'soft' hands); she adds an exclamation mark, expands 'cada' to 'each, every'; the 'esposa del Coronel' becomes 'the *frau* of the Colonel' (a second foreign word) and adds a line of her own, 'Aristocrats, landowners, writers labelled *neutrality*'. But she slightly changes even the associations with the title 'Almería', for Neruda repeats 'un plato de sangre de Almería' while Cunard has 'a dishful of blood – Almeria' (again Walsh is closer with 'a bowl of Almería blood').[63] Now, the point of this poem was political and rhetorical as much as poetic, so her licence as a translation is her freedom to

[58] Eshleman, *Review*, pp. 40–3. See also Janice A. Jaffe, 'Speak through My Words: the Poetics and Politics of Translating Neruda', in Longo (ed.), *Pablo Neruda and the U.S. Culture Industry*, pp. 13–22.

[59] Anne Chisholm, *Nancy Cunard*, p. 239.

[60] Neruda, *Confieso*, p. 174.

[61] Chisholm, *Nancy Cunard*, pp. 258–9.

[62] See Rafael Osuna, *Pablo Neruda y Nancy Cunard*, with an anthology of the poets that their press published.

[63] 'Almeria', in Valentine Cunningham (ed.), *The Penguin Book of Spanish Civil War Verse*, pp. 379–80.

make the poem more meaningful in English to her 1930s readers. As hinted in the brackets, Donald Walsh remains literal, word-for-word correct, with one flourish: 'señoras de confortable té' is made more sarcastic: 'ladies with cozy tea parties'.[64]

[64] Donald Walsh, Pablo Neruda, *Residence on Earth*, pp. 278–9.

5

The 1940s: from *Alturas de Macchu Picchu* to *Canto general*

Alturas de Macchu Picchu, 1945

The twelve-part *Alturas de Macchu Picchu* was written in September 1945 at Isla Negra, and first appeared in a magazine *Revista Nacional de Cultura* in Caracas in 1946. It was then published separately in Chile in 1947 as part of a recording, though Robert Pring-Mill claimed it was 1948.[1] It reappeared as the second section of the ambitious but flawed *Canto general*, 1950, which Paz labelled a 'gran olla en donde hay de todo' [a great stew in which there's everything] and lists 'arengas, diatribas, kilómetros de lugares comunes y de pronto, sin aviso, luminosos ... esplendores' [harangues, diatribes, kilometres of commonplaces and suddenly, without warning luminous splendours].[2] As Rodríguez Monegal first mooted, there was a gap of two years between Neruda's ascent in 1943 of the Incan ruins discovered by Hiram Bingham in 1911 and the actual writing of the poem in 1945. Neruda was clearly not writing a tourist's breathless impression of the most iconic ruins in the Americas. In fact, it was reported that his first comment on seeing the ruins was '¡Qué lugar para comer un asado de cordero!' [what a great place to roast lamb], though a biographer deemed this a joke.[3] He also imposed his own spelling of the ruins (the official guide book has Machupicchu) and never corrected himself (did he feel as the poet of the Americas that he had the right to rebaptise it?). Most critics agree that this is a Janus poem, assessing the first twenty years of the poet's career, and announcing his future intentions as the date 1945 coincided with his officially joining the Chilean Communist Party. It has been translated at least six times into English, with John Felstin-

---

[1] Robert Pring-Mill, *A Poet for all Seasons*, p. 21.
[2] Octavio Paz, 'Poesía e historia ("Laurel" y nosotros)', *Sombras de obras*, pp. 84–5.
[3] Rodríguez Monegal, *El viajero inmóvil*, p. 112.

er's version included in one of the finest works of criticism on Neruda.[4] The poem is so crucial that few question its value.

The eleven-year gestation of Neruda's attempt to rewrite Latin American history in verse as his *Canto general* is a complex story that gripped Robert Pring-Mill over many years.[5] The disparate background elements that frame its writing include: the Second World War, the defeat of Nazism at Stalingrad (so crucial to Neruda), the 1940 murder of Trotsky in Mexico City (with Neruda involved through giving a visa to the guilty muralist Siqueiros), the opposition of the Communist Party to US capitalism known as the Cold War, and a long stay in Mexico as a Consul General for Chile. Neruda drew close to some of Mexico's grand muralists like Diego Rivera and David Alfaro Siqueiros.[6] He was now a public personage, and his biography reflected the dramatic times. Much has been made by Neruda and his critics, for example, of his betrayal and persecution by President González Videla in Chile, his clandestine life on the run, crossing the Andes incognito on horseback, graphically portrayed by Adam Feinstein in his biography. Roberto González Echevarría sees 'betrayal' as the basic story of Neruda's Latin America, a 'litany of perfidies committed in the name of promises for justice'.[7] This hectic life as the people's poet was as thrilling as writing the work. Neruda had a massive following and what he said or did had repercussions. He had become his 'persona'.

The issue, then, is not biography, but how to read political poetry, by definition more than an aesthetic undertaking. If, as a Latin American reader, you share Neruda's Cold War Communist Party position, you will admire, even love his poetry. This political partisanship did not attract the same reader as his earlier ontological poetry exploring and defining the murky selves. He himself took sides against his earlier self, as we will see in *Alturas de Macchu Picchu*. Antonio Melis placed this self-critique as a turning point in Neruda's poetics: 'an ever more violent repudiation of his existential problems in the name of a voluntary and often abstract optimism'.[8] Later, in the wake of the 1959 Cuban Revolution and especially Che Guevara's self-sacrificial policies, the left would splinter and Neruda would no longer speak for this bloc. The far-left Salvadorean poet Roque Dalton put it this way to Mario

4   See my Appendix on 'Neruda in English', with versions by Flores, 1950, Tarn, 1966, Felstiner, 1980, Young, 1986, Schmitt, 1991 and Kessler, 2001.

5   See 'La composición del *Canto general* en la clandestinidad', 2000, a typescript given to me by Robert Pring-Mill. See also Hernán Loyola, PN1, 1201–6.

6   See Hugo Méndez-Ramírez, *Neruda's Ekphrasric Experience. Mural Art and* Canto general.

7   Roberto González Echevarría, 'Introduction', Pablo Neruda, *Canto general*, translated by Jack Schmitt, 1991, pp. 9–11.

8   Antonio Melis, 'Neruda y la poesía', p. 31.

Benedetti: 'I wanted to be one of Vallejo's grandsons. I had nothing to do with Neruda's family.'[9] However, if you did not share Neruda's politics, as Breton, Paz and Sucre did not, then his later poetry is that of a party hack. As Enrico Mario Santí put it crudely, Neruda 'remained an obedient Stalinist, a virtual accomplice of the Soviet mass murders, persecution and the Gulag'.[10] The least that could be said in Neruda's favour is that, as historical events and passions fade, what remain are poems that are overtly and overly dependent on historical circumstances.

A defining moment in the debate about political poetry took place in Mexico City in 1941 when Pablo Neruda refused to allow his poems to be included in *Laurel*, a fundamental anthology co-edited by Octavio Paz, Xavier Villaurrutia (the principal organiser) and two Spanish poets in Mexican exile, Emilio Prados and Juan Gil Albert. He was not alone, for León Felipe also refused. The Catholic poet José Bergamín, who had published Neruda's *Residencia en la tierra* in Spain and was in exile in Mexico City, was the bone of contention (as was Juan Larrea). Paz had published his admiring essay 'Pablo Neruda en el corazón' [Pablo Neruda in my heart] in 1938, but in 1941 he came to blows with Neruda after a farewell dinner. Paz wrote about this incident in his 'Respuesta a un cónsul' [Answer to a consul] in *Letras de México* in 1943, accusing Neruda's friends of being lackeys, his poetry of being contaminated by politics and he of being 'titanically' vain. According to Paz, political poetry cannot spark political change; far better a text by Lenin than bad poems by Mayakovsky or Neruda. In 1959, Paz told the French critic Claude Couffon that Neruda was the living example of the poet degraded by politics, and his 1951 prose poem 'A poet' surely envisioned Neruda 'con la lengua hinchada de política' [tongue swollen with politics].[11] Paz returned to this symbolic clash about the function of poetry in 1983 in a long essay on the anthology *Laurel*.[12] He called Neruda the great poet of America, a tyrant, a 'taciturn volcano'. With hindsight, Paz claimed that Neruda 'suffered the disease of Stalinism: I must add that this leprosy took over his spirit because it fed from ego mania and psychic instability', suggesting a subtle blend of totalitarian politics and personal pathology.[13] Paz touched again on the 1941 fracas. Neruda had introduced Paz as having a white shirt cleaner than his conscience and then launched into insults about

9   Mario Benedetti, *Los poetas comunicantes* (Montevideo: Marcha, 1972), 'Yo quisiera ser uno de los nietos de Vallejo. Con la familia Neruda no tengo nada que ver', p. 33.

10   Enrico Mario Santí, 'Politics, Literature and the Intellectual in Latin America', p. 109.

11   See Jason Wilson, *Octavio Paz* (Boston: Twayne, 1986), pp. 22–4; Octavio Paz, *Poemas*, p. 221.

12   Octavio Paz, 'Poesía e historia ("Laurel" y nosotros)', *Sombras de obras*, pp. 47–93.

13   Paz, 'Poesía e historia', p. 53: 'padecía el contagio del estalinismo: hay que agregar que esa lepra se apoderó de su espíritu porque se alimentaba de su egolatría y de su inseguridad psíquica'.

Bergamín and the anthology. Paz was pulled out of the meal, and in 1983 said that he felt 'como un camarero humillado, como una campana un poco ronca, como un espejo viejo' [like a humiliated waiter, like a slightly hoarse bell, like an old mirror], without saying that he was quoting from Pablo Neruda's poem 'Arte poética' from *Residencia en la tierra 1*. Paz admitted that the Neruda on his bookshelves was the author of *Residencia 1* and *2*, and the complete run of the magazine *Caballo verde para la poesía*. Paz, as critic, called these poems of the 1930s 'extraordinary' and 'crossed through by a powerful dream-like passion', both close to and distant from surrealism.[14] Neruda also broached the 1941 Paz incident in Mexico City in his moving poem 'A Miguel Hernández, asesinado en los presidios de España' [To Miguel Hernández, assassinated in the prisons of Spain] in the *Canto general*. Those who killed the goatherder poet will pay: 'Que sepan los malditos que hoy incluyen tu nombre / en sus libros, los Dámasos, los Gerardos, los hijos / de perra, silenciosos cómplices del verdugo' [Let the cursed who today include your name in their books, the Dámasos, the Gerardos, the sons of bitches, silent accomplices of the executioner] (PN1 746). The 'verdugo' is Franco and Dámaso is Dámaso Alonso, poet and literary critic who supported Franco, and Gerardo the equally Catholic and anti-communist Gerardo Diego, poet and author of a crucial anthology in 1932 that excluded Hernández. Neruda insults them for their shameful politics, which has polluted their writing. Then he attacks Octavio Paz as editor of *Laurel*, by then an anti-Stalinist in Paris, in the sentence: 'Y a los que te negaron en su laurel podrido, / en tierra americana' [and to those who denied you in their rotten laurel on American soil] (PN1 746).

Neruda's attack on Bergamín, his erstwhile publisher, probably derived from the latter's championing of Vallejo in 1931 where in a note to the second, Madrid edition of *Trilce* he criticised Neruda's poetry as 'monotonous' and 'less inventive, less flexible, less agile' than Vallejo's. Neruda attacked him in 1931 in a letter to Morla Lynch lambasting Vallejo as 'dry and appalling', with *Trilce* being 'a cruel, literary and sterile book', while his own poetry, in a key admission, 'quiere abrir una puerta de salida al corazón' [wants to open an exit door in the heart]. By the 1940s Neruda's heart / emotional poetry may have changed, but his memory of a literary slight has not.[15]

A ramification of Paz's dismissal of Neruda's later poetry as 'Stalinist' is the way the Venezuelan critic and poet Guillermo Sucre scandalously excluded Neruda from his brilliant survey of twentieth-century Spanish-American poetry, *La máscara, la transparencia*, in 1975. Sucre reviewed an edition of *Canto general* in Paz's magazine *Vuelta* in March 1977. Neruda

14   Paz, 'Poesía e historia', p. 79.
15   Cited in Loyola, *Neruda*, 2006, pp. 506–7.

had summarised the totality of Spanish-American history but confused this with totalitarianism, with exaltation of Stalin, comparing him to Lincoln, that is, 'executioner' with 'a victim'. Sucre censored the poems as embodying 'the worst *partisan* spirit', with an attack on poetry that he cannot approve of politically. Sucre particularly attacked the editor of the edition under review, the Chilean Fernando Alegría, but the point is how Neruda still, after his death, stirred up vituperation.[16] René de Costa highlighted this critical response of 'two camps', which depended on the critic's political persuasion, leaving 'no middle ground'.[17]

The issue of how to read political poetry will not go away. There is no neutral position. Maurice Bowra, an excellent critic on Lorca and Alberti, wrote sensibly on politicised poetry: 'Neruda's production is enormous, and one half of it is very poor stuff indeed, political rhetoric unredeemed by imagination or insight. But the other half is by any standards remarkable.' He then puts his finger on the pulse: 'the division between the bad and the good is not so much within single poems as between one poem and another'. I would add, even within a bad poem, there are wonderful lines or images. Bowra underlined how Neruda employs 'standardised ideas', which in a poem become 'platitudes'. The bad poetry is 'often full of Marxist doctrine stated with a rhetorical emphasis', though his Marxism is not at fault, but how it has been assimilated.[18] An often-made fertile comparison with the way César Vallejo absorbed his Marxism confirms Bowra's point. Vallejo wrote in November 1927 that the artist is, inevitably 'un sujeto político' [political individual] who writes beyond political programmes, beyond propaganda, from the confusions of his organic being, his honesty, his sincerity.[19] Vallejo despised 'los doctores del marxismo' [doctors of Marxism] and abstract, dialectical thinking. Hegel and Marx discovered laws, but he, Vallejo, sought to 'cabrearse contra ella [la ley dialéctica] y llegar a tomar una actitud crítica y revolucionaria delante de este determinismo dialéctico' [to get livid with dialectical law and attain a critical and revolutionary attitude to dialectical determinism].[20] What a contrast Vallejo's attitude is to Neruda's. Efraín Kristal compared Vallejo's and Neruda's Spanish Civil War poems and correctly emphasised Neruda's expression of outrage 'but also his certainty about the ultimate outcome'. Vallejo's poem are 'more anguished and uncertain', more 'emotionally intense'.[21] Both poets, and countless contemporaries, were faced with a searing dilemma about the artist. Which side to take in the Marxist /

---

16   Guillermo Sucre, '*Canto general* de Pablo Neruda', pp. 36–7.
17   De Costa, 1979, p. 106.
18   Maurice Bowra, *Poetry and Politics*, pp. 132–5.
19   Vallejo, *El arte y la revolución*, pp. 29, 35.
20   Vallejo, *Contra el secreto profesional*, p. 99.
21   Kristal, in Vallejo, *The Complete Poetry*, pp. 3–4.

Fascist split in society was complicated by a realisation that, in Michael Hamburger's words, 'all the poets with Romantic-Symbolist attitudes have been non-political, in as much as their values have sprung from the imagination, and the imagination is too radical and utopian to adjust to political issues proper'.[22] Vallejo struggled over the 1930s, scarcely publishing, to bridge his imagination and being 'utterly himself', with a political urge, while Neruda discovered a new, proletarian public and simplified his works to be understood immediately. What Hamburger wrote about Brecht applies equally to Neruda, but not to Vallejo: '[he] was less interested in the quality of his own feelings, in the "oven" of his heart, than in a dilemma that must be resolved by political action'.[23] Communist Party dictates resolved individual problems, working as a kind of inner censor. Neruda's political poetry, and how a reader reacts to it, spins round notions of 'individuality' and 'collectivity'. Vernon Watkins arbitrated in 1981 when he wrote that a poet may write propaganda, and that a reader need not share his beliefs, 'yet even then the quarrel should be his own quarrel; the words may be shaped by his beliefs, but he remains a man caught up in a dialogue which may be overheard by the rest of the world'.[24] Neruda stifled this poetic dialogue with himself and with his readers.

In the fifth section of his *Canto general*, titled 'La arena traicionada' [sand betrayed], a series of poems denouncing the enemies of a free Latin America, Neruda included his poem 'Los poetas celestes' (the title's 'celeste' hints at 'cielo', sky blue and heaven). He asks his fellow poets what they have done for the people, the poor and downtrodden. The tone and taut invective he inherited from his favoured Quevedo. The poem opens:

> Qué hicisteis vosotros gidistas,
> intelectualistas, rilkistas,
> misterizantes, falsos brujos
> existenciales, amapolas
> surrealistas encendidas
> en una tumba europeizados
> cadáveres de la moda,
> pálidas lombrices del queso
> capitalista ... (PN1 586)

> [What did you do, Gidists, intellectualists, Rilkists, mystifiers, fake existentialist wizards, surrealist poppies in a tomb Europeanising burning corpses of fashion, pale cheese worms of capitalism][25]

22 Michael Hamburger, *The Truth of Poetry*, p. 83.
23 Hamburger, *The Truth of Poetry*, p. 230.
24 Vernon Watkins, 'For Whom does a Poet Write?', p. 93.
25 The translator Jack Schmitt confused 'amapola' [poppy] with 'mariposa' [butterfly] in his translation of *Canto general*, p. 167.

Neruda has read European fashions into his fellow poets; they mimic Gide (target of left-wing and Communist Party hate after his *Retour de l'URSS*, his critique of Stalin, in 1936) or Rilke (whom Neruda had translated) or existentialism or surrealism, then Parisian left-bank fashion, all busy with their purely mental and escapist 'art'. Neruda summarised: 'No hicisteis nada sino la fuga' [you did nothing but flee]; they sought 'blue hair' (clever metaphors), pure beauty, magic but are 'pobres asustados' [poor scared things], eating scraps thrown to them by their capitalistic masters. This political critique, an either / or forcing choice on poets, runs through much Latin American cultural life. It could also be a *mea culpa*. De Costa noted how Neruda could have been called 'existentialist' and how he constantly returns to his political 'conversion'.[26] I would add that Neruda employed 'amapolas' [poppies] in his own surrealistic work of the 1930s.

Already in Spain, Neruda had felt himself become Latin American (as later Julio Cortázar would become Latin American in Paris, for being outside their countries enlarged their belonging). However, his first idea when wondering how to write a modern epic was to write a *Canto general de Chile*, which he partially published in Mexico in 1943 and later placed as section VII in the *Canto general*. He aimed to evoke Chile's geography, its people, their work and places. Then he felt that Chileans were no different from Peruvians, that a liberator like O'Higgins was similar to Miranda, Lautaro like Cuautemoc (PN4 931–2). He started seeing his continent in Bolivarian terms, as an exploited, suffering unity. Marxist theory helped, for the working class was one in its struggle against class and imperialism across the many, false national frontiers. My guess is that Neruda's clue to American unity derived from how 'nature' does not respect artificial national frontiers. He wrote: 'Our plants and our flowers must be counted and sung for the first time. Our volcanoes and our rivers ...' for a new America would rise freed from its dependency. He believed the Marxist analysis to be the best one: 'We are the chroniclers of a delayed birth. Delayed by feudalism, by backwardness, by hunger.' Also, the post-war years in Latin America did convey a new sense of freedom from Europe, ruined by the war, and from the United States. Writers as diverse as Alejo Carpentier, with his theory of 'lo real maravilloso' elaborated in the 1940s and equally based on how different Nature is from the tamed European version, and Octavio Paz's *El laberinto de la soledad*, 1950, suggesting that urban alienation and 'soledad' were part of Mexican identity, contribute to this revision of the Latin American experience. Neruda's version might be straight Communist Party doctrine, but is grounded in matter, the earth; it is a materialistic interpretation. When he climbed up to Machupicchu, he claimed that he had a mountain top vision (a Romantic

---

26   De Costa, p. 120.

topos) of all Latin America as one (it was not a vision but an idea). Up there, he felt that he too had helped build the fortress or ploughed the terraces or cut stones. Machupicchu was a resistance symbol for an authentic Latin America that waited out the conquest and Spanish colonisation. Neruda claimed that 'I felt Chilean, Peruvian, American.'[27] He had found a new faith and justification for continuing to be a poet, but no longer a solitary self-explorer. So his new political poetics (he had joined the party in 1945, remember) was to unite his continent Latin America by describing and recovering what made it unique, its rivers, histories, heroes. Julio Cortázar said it was a 'tabula rasa', a 'starting from scratch'.[28] In the poem 'A mi partido' [To my party] each line begins, like a prayer, with 'Me has dado' [you have given me] and the 'partido' is addressed like a lover in the intimate 'tú'. The last line is crucial: 'Me has hecho indestructible porque contigo no termino en mí mismo' [You have made me indestructible because with you I do not end in myself] (PN1 835). In Marxist theory there is no individual, no unique psychology. The self merges with the other suffering selves; the working class is one. The party has replaced the individual, and that is why he feels 'indestructible', one of a crowd. That Neruda adapted to Stalin's thought of his own volition is, in Alice Kelly's words, 'how Soviets induced themselves to conform to Stalin's wishes', an 'inner-directed' urge. She outlined how 'soul-searching' was avoided and how an authentic self-fulfilment 'was realized through collective acts of fulfilling the laws of history'. Neruda was just one of many who surrendered their individuality, was 'hostile to culture' and went through 'a process of self-cleansing through self-criticism'. It was his 'faith' in the 'all-seeing party' that he worked out in his poems.[29] As a poet, he must then write or speak like the crowd, to be understood by people who do not read books. He must be as simple and direct as possible. He knew from experience that his voice carried over its message of anger and hope to listeners like the men and women in the fish market in Santiago in 1938: 'To speak simply was the first of my poetic duties' (PN4 889).

His model for this reaching out beyond books was Walt Whitman, whose daguerrotype he had on his desk in Isla Negra. Whitman was admired by Rubén Darío in 1896, by Jorge Luis Borges in the 1920s, and by Federico García Lorca in *Poeta en Nueva York*, where his long 'Oda a Walt Whitman' defined himself through Whitman's tortured sexuality. Whitman is the only poet named in Vicente Huidobro's *Altazor*, 1931. Neruda first read Whitman in translations in 1923 by Arturo Torres Rioseco (later a don at Harvard); he saw Whitman as an Adam: 'to believe himself the first discoverer of things and their first owner on giving them a name' (PN4 310). Despite this

27 Pablo Neruda, *Confieso que he vivido*, p. 230.
28 Julio Cortázar, 'Neruda', p. 69.
29 Alice Kelly, 'Why they Believed in Stalin', pp. 59–61.

Whitman worship, Neruda created his own Whitman, the strong voice of a 'varón' [man] accepting everything, creating a new democratic America, one of a crowd, outside in the streets and prairies. He told Robert Bly that Whitman 'was open-eyed [...] He taught us to see things.'[30] Walt Whitman entered Neruda's *Canto general* in canto IX, 'Qué despierte el leñador' as 'mi hermano profundo' [my deep brother] with his 'barba de hierba' (Whitman's beard is iconic). Whitman tells Neruda that he sees how factories work in Stalingrad (the new Manhattan); he sees the new tractors, the 'reconstructions' (after the war). Neruda begs Whitman to lend him 'tu voz' [your voice] (PN1 689–90). Whitman reappeared in Neruda's *Nuevas odas elementales*, 1956, where Whitman taught him 'to be American' and take his eyes off books to see 'el tesoro / de los cereales' [the treasure of cereal] (PN2 429) and the 'fraternidad sobre la tierra' [brotherhood on earth] (the last line). Whitman has been politicised, converted into a Communist. Enrico Mario Santí conveyed Whitman's influence on Neruda as a Romantic analogy of the Bible, and that the Bible and its myths inform Neruda's *Canto general*, a 'kind of Latin American bible', with its Genesis, its exile and wandering, but I do not sense that grand pattern in the actual language.[31] Surveying the Hispanic appropriation of Whitman, Harold Bloom decided that they all had failed to read him 'closely enough'. In Neruda's case, he made the telling point that 'Whitman's Emersonian gnosis is very different from Neruda's Manichean Communism.'[32] That is evident from Whitman's role in this canto. To his credit, Neruda admitted this to Rita Guibert in 1974: 'Walt Whitman was a great companion for me. I have hardly been Whitmanian in the way I write, but I am deeply Whitmanian in his vital lesson' (PN5 1154).[33] Whitman's shadow led one critic to complain that Neruda's *Canto general* had a 'tendency to lapse into a kind of Whitmanesque flatulence'.[34] A lucid account by Djelal Kadir confirmed that Neruda's reading of Whitman went beyond themes to 'enumerative style', with a shared focus on the corporal and concrete. The essay concluded that 'their descriptive processes are strikingly similar', as if Neruda inherited a technique, but not a philosophy for he explored 'disembodied individualities', not the loss of ego to a generic self.[35]

---

[30] Harold Bloom, *The Western Canon*, p. 479.

[31] Santí, pp. 182–6, 22.

[32] Bloom, *The Western Canon*, pp. 482, 485.

[33] 'fue un gran compañero para mí. Yo he sido poco whitmaniano en mi manera de escribir, pero soy profundamente whitmaniano en su lección vital.' See Djelal Kadir, 'Neruda and Whitman: Short-circuiting the Body Electric', pp. 16–22 on their 'enumerative' style and differences.

[34] Dudley Fitts, *Review*, p. 25.

[35] Djelal Kadir, 'Neruda and Whitman', pp. 19–22.

However, Neruda's 'yo' made a comeback in this epic account of Cold War Latin America, for it is his personal experience that makes the history alive (as opposed to the official patriotic histories and the cold, archival ones). That is, he strives for his own personal history to become archetypal and representative. He consciously voices oppressed Latin America. Several times in the poems, he announces that 'they' speak through him: 'te habla por boca mía' [it speaks to you through my mouth], he writes in his 'Homenaje a Balboa' (PN1 456) or, more famously, the closing line of his 'Alturas de Macchu Picchu': 'Hablad por mis palabras y mi sangre' [Speak through my words and my blood] (PN1 447). Section XV of the *Canto general* 'Yo soy' [I am] echoes Whitman's 'Song of Myself' where he celebrates life, the dissolution of self, through his senses in a wonderful colloquial free-verse – 'Walt Whitman, a kosmos, of Manhattan the son, / Turbulent, fleshy, sensual, eating, drinking and breeding, / No sentimentalist, no stander above men and women or apart from them ...'[36]

The opening sections of 'Alturas de Macchu Picchu' revise Neruda's own biography, and his new values condition his view of history. This is not political, but personal, a grudge. Thus, famously, González Videla, traitor of Chile in 1947, is given a section all to himself as the worst of Latin America's 'verdugos' [hangmen] because he personally betrayed Neruda and the Chilean Communist Party, even though Julio Cortázar said that in the 1970s you should change his name to Pinochet. Jorge Luis Borges rightly castigated Neruda as biased for not including Juan Domingo Perón in his list of traitors. Ricardo Paseyro explained that Neruda omitted Perón because his publisher, Losada, was in Buenos Aires at the time, though he did attack Victoria Ocampo in *Las uvas y el viento* as friend of spies and Nazis like T. E. Lawrence, Heidegger and 'notre petit Drieu' (a reference to Drieu la Rochelle, one of her lovers and a Nazi sympathiser). Then the Argentine Communist Party forbade collaborating with Peronism, so Neruda published in the anti-Peronist newspaper *La Prensa*. Paseyro called this attitude Nerudaism, serving both Communists and anti-Communists, dealing with both packs and writing a falsely revolutionary poetry.[37] Neruda did publish an open letter to Perón in May 1953 asking him to release Victoria Ocampo from prison.[38] However, Neruda also explained to Rodman that he thought Perón

---

36   Walt Whitman, *Leaves of Grass*, p. 67.

37   Ricardo Paseyro, 'The Dead World of Pablo Neruda', pp. 209–10. Paseyro, born in Montevideo in 1925, and exiled in Paris from 1974, was once Neruda's secretary, but became, in Alone's words, his 'enemigo número uno', <www.neruda.uchile.cl/critica/alone>. His diatribe against Neruda was published in 1969 and in French as *Le mythe Neruda* in 1971. Paseyro was the son-in-law of Jules Supervielle, and wrote on him. Feinstein refers to his 'routine vicious attack' on Neruda, *Pablo Neruda*. p. 333.

38   Neruda, *Yo respondo*, p. 224.

had done some good curbing oligarchs and landowners and for that reason 'Perón disturbs Borges', though he was also a dictator (quite a balanced view, but certainly not Borges's).[39]

Pablo Neruda deemed his *Canto general* as 'my most important book'.[40] It is certainly his most 'ambitious', an adjective that most critics have employed as a way of avoiding being critical. The writing of section II, 'Alturas de Macchu Picchu', can best be seen as his celebration of his joining the Chilean Communist Party, as Loyola noted back in 1971.[41] This was far more than a political decision; in fact, it resolved deep emotional issues of belonging and meaning. Neruda's journey as a poet began with rebellion against state and family by identifying with the 'poète maudit' tradition, and then with intense erotic love as his real 'patria'. Politically, his attitude could be termed anarchistic. With joining the Chilean CP he had found a new 'family' that allowed him to find his roots in the working class and still rebel and express anger against Capitalism. In this sense, then, *Canto general* is a rebirth poem and a poem about a conversion. The closing, dated poem ('5 de febrero, en este año / de 1949') with the title 'Aquí termino (1949) [Here I end] is clear about this poetic rebirth:

> Este libro termina aquí. Ha nacido
> de la ira como una brasa, como los territorios
> de bosques incendiados, y deseo
> que continúe como un árbol rojo
> propagando su clara quemadura.
> Pero no sólo cólera en sus ramas
> encontraste: no sólo sus raíces
> buscaron el dolor sino la fuerza,
> y fuerza soy de piedra pensativa,
> alegría de manos congregadas. (PN1 836)

> [This book ends here. It was born of fury like a live coal, like territories of burned forests, and I hope that it continues like a red tree propagating its clear burning. But you found not only rage in its branches: not only its roots sought pain but also strength, and I am strength of pensive stone, joy of joined hands]

The symbolism is direly obvious and immediate. Neruda is the 'red' tree of propaganda and anger. He has found a new inner strength; he is not a fragile, Pascalian thinking reed, but a 'thinking stone'. He is hard, and can be used to build and attack (the 'hondero' or sling metaphor lurks there still). He has

---

[39] Selden Rodman, *South America of the Poets*, p. 257.

[40] Neruda, *Confieso que he vivido*, p. 239.

[41] Hernán Loyola, in Pablo Neruda, *Antología esencial*, pp. 24–5.

also found a new set of companions, 'manos congregadas', where his writer's hand and the worker's hands join. 'Manos' [hands] is one of the key symbols of Neruda's politicisation, as Jaime Concha pointed out.[42] That 'árbol rojo', those 'manos' are too fixed as symbol, with no sense of having worked it out. Charles Tomlinson coined 'paranoid gusto' for Neruda's political rants and added that 'there is something sinisterly autistic in this black-versus-white ideology which possesses all the unforgiving Manichaeism of the frescos of his friend, the Mexican Diego Rivera'.[43]

As a reborn member of the Communist Party, Neruda surveyed his life and poetry up to 1945 in the first five cantos of 'Alturas de Macchu Picchu'. He is bound to dismiss these pre-Communist years as those of a solitary poet who plunged into deepest matter to return to 'la gastada primavera humana' [worn-out human spring]. The opening lines, 'Del aire al aire, como una red vacía / iba yo entre las calles y la atmósfera, llegando y despidiendo' [from air to air like an empty net I went among the streets and atmosphere, arriving and saying goodbye] (PN1 434), touch on an earlier self-metaphor of the failed poet / lover whose net could not catch 'her', but now he is the empty 'net'. But in dismissing his earlier subjective quests, the poet forgot that he had also created magnificent poems. By separating the poet from his work, and concentrating on the poet's own biography, we see that Neruda the poet and Neruda the person become one, unlike Jorge Luis Borges who separated them in his prose allegory 'Borges y yo' [Borges and I] where the famous writer and the private blind man do not overlap. That Neruda found personal contentment in his conversion to a public persona is clear; but that his poetry lost out is the price paid.

The second stanza summarised in brackets his earlier love life. The new love is the Party, not individual women like Josie Bliss. Neruda had lived 'en la intemperie / de los cuerpos' [in the exposure of bodies], but had got worn out, as if sexual and erotic love simply exhausted him 'hasta la última harina' [to the last flour] ('ground him down' is the metaphor here). He saw himself as 'estambres agredidos de la patria nupcial' [assaulted stamens of the nuptial fatherland] (PN1 434). If I read this correctly, through Neruda's self-images, he is the natural poet – 'stamen' – an assaulted phallic image of that earlier, mistaken notion of 'patria' that was love. He does not use direct language; he disguises himself with mythical symbols. Section I rounds off this hindsight view of his earlier poetic self who had burrowed deep into the earth through sexual encounters 'más abajo, en el oro de la geología' [deeper down into the gold of geology]. The poet confesses: 'hundí la mano turbulenta y dulce / en lo más genital de lo terrestre' [I sunk my turbulent

42 Jaime Concha, *Neruda (1904–1936)*, pp. 49–86.
43 Charles Tomlinson, 'Latin America Betrayed', p. 5.

and sweet hand into earth's most genital matter], where 'mano' means the poet, his writer's hand, his lover's hand, exploring the dark inner self, but kept as a geological metaphor (gold). That this gold is sexual is clear with the adjectives 'dulce' and 'genital', but nothing on the alterity and actuality of his lovers, just his own self. There is a veiled reference to his magnificent love poem 'Angela adónica' from *Residencia 1*, with her gold and 'oculto fuego' (PN1 276). Here, he has become 'ciego' [blind].

Section II develops the poet's quest for some greater solidity and certainty, beyond sexual and erotic love. At first, he had sought this inside himself, in his 'soul', but that 'eterna veta insondable' [eternal fathomless vein] that he had once found in stones and the lightning of love ('en la misma gruta del placer humano' [in the very cave of human pleasure]) was no longer attainable. All he found were 'masks', false selves. He had lost contact with 'life'. This version of his previous self ignores the many and extraordinary love poems that had made contact with exactly that life energy. In fact, in the whole of the *Canto general*, as Juan Larrea first indicated, 'woman does not interest him'.[44] Sections III and IV shift into a critique of death, the pointless little death of urban capitalist societies and selfish, subjective poets, and 'la poderosa muerte' [powerful death], which is where workers are reborn in a utopian socialist future beyond death. Loyola put it thus: 'Neruda opposes death with human solidarity.'[45] Neruda searched everywhere for this certainty but 'rodé muriendo de mi propia muerte' [I rolled dying of my own death] (PN1 437). Enrico Mario Santí found a source for this egotistic little death in Neruda's 1926 translation of a passage from Rilke's *Notebooks of Malte Laurids Brigge* (from the French) with 'death as hyperbole of isolated individuality'.[46] Thus, Neruda reinvented his earlier life as a pessimistic dead-end. No question about his sincerity during these war years, but he described, rather than relived his earlier poems, almost parodying what he had achieved. Perhaps the key term is how he turned the intense pleasures of sexuality, sounds and language, only available to the lonely self, into 'grutas' [grotto], his cold symbol for female sexuality, and thus eliminating the pleasure. I can only guess that he was questioning the role of love in his life behind his turning to that other version of love, the companionship of comrades. It is telling that his next book was in fact a love song, *Los versos del capitán* [The captain's verses], 1952.

The poem proper starts with stanza VI and that emphatic adverb 'Entonces' [then] of logic. We now accompany the poet up through the 'atroz maraña' [atrocious tangle] of jungle to Macchu Picchu and Neruda's new self, discovered as both a Communist and a Latin American. Macchu Picchu is given

---

[44] Juan Larrea, *Del surrealismo a Machupicchu*, p. 181.
[45] Hernán Loyola, *Ser y morir en Pablo Neruda*, p. 168.
[46] Santí, *Pablo Neruda. The Poetics of Prophecy*, pp. 131–2.

epic connotations as a symbol of authentic, suffering America: 'Madre de piedra, espuma de los cóndores. / Alto arrecife de la aurora humana' [Mother of stone, spray of condors, high reef of human dawn] (PN1 438). These verb-less lines sound magnificent when read aloud on his record.[47] But what did he mean by the condors' 'espuma'? Is not 'aurora' an irrelevant term for the ruins, what 'dawn' awaits them – and why not 'amanecer', why that poeticism 'aurora'? Well, for the pure sounds.

Section IX, famously, joins 43 lines without a verb, a Macchu Picchu constructed word by word, where seven lines end with the word 'piedra', as if the poet built the ruins with his 'stony' nouns. Neruda read this section like a litany in what John Felstiner called his 'incantatory tone'. With his voice falling at the end of each phrase, it is hard to question the meaning. But as a reading-act, these lines are muddling. Once or twice, he hits on an enig-matic poetic equivalent like 'Arquitectura de águilas perdidas' [architecture of lost eagles]. More often, you sense his recycling of CP terms like 'pan' or 'paloma'. The section opens:

> Aguila sideral, viña de bruma.
> Bastión perdido, cimitarra ciega.
> Cinturón estrellado, pan solemne.
> Escala torrencial, párpado inmenso.
> Túnica triangular, polen de piedra ... (PN1 443)

> [Sidereal eagle, vineyard of mist, lost bastion, blind scimitar. Starred belt, solemn bread. Torrential ladder, immense eyelid. Triangular tunic, stone pollen]

At the poet's level of finding a new identity, the key line is 'Cúpula del silencio, patria pura' [Cupola of silence, pure fatherland] (PN1 444), implying his Latin American-ness recovered. Felstiner pinpointed how some of his metaphors 'are surprising, but not surprisingly true, and at such times Neruda virtually parodies himself' and his reader becomes 'careless of what they signify'.[48] Earlier, in 1966, Juan Larrea showed how the nouns were 'inter-changeable', like a bad Dada poem. Of the 171 nouns the poet used in this section, only two were South American ('puma', 'andino'). Thus, the whole canto was 'una tras otra [de] banalidades pretenciosas' [one after another of pretentious banalities].[49] Given this kind of critique, Santí decided that Larrea's piece was 'one of the most violent attacks to which Neruda was ever

---

[47] Pablo Neruda por él mismo, *Alturas de Macchu Picchu*, no date.

[48] Felstiner, *Translating Neruda*, p. 178.

[49] Larrea, 'Machupicchu, piedra de toque', in his *Del surrealismo a machupicchu*, pp. 146, 149.

subjected'.[50] Enrique Lihn added his scorn, calling the poem a 'mountain of rhetoric called Macchu-Picchu'.[51] The counter to these critiques is that Neruda was celebrating his own rebirth, not the ruins, as he clearly states in section VIII where he explores the 'piedras' and his new love: 'Besa conmigo las piedras secretas' [kiss with me the secret stones] (PN1 441) and his many questions, turning from the ruins to its humiliated anonymous builders. Neruda asked his new audience: 'Ven a mi propio ser, al alba mía' [Come to my own being, to my dawn] (PN1 442). It is *his* dawn that matters (thus reintroducing his ego or self into the picture). Stanza X movingly explores 'hunger' and 'rags' as the root of his new vision of the world, and his anger and the Incan workers who slaved to build the hill site:

> Macchu Picchu, pusiste
> piedra en la piedra, y en la base, harapo?
> Carbón sobre carbón, y en el fondo la lágrima?
> Fuego en el oro, y en él, temblando el rojo
> goterón de la sangre?
> Devuélveme el esclavo que enterraste! (PN1 445)

> [Macchu Picchu, did you put stone on stone and at the base rags? Coal on coal and at the bottom a tear? Fire in the gold and, in it, trembling the red drop of blood? Give me back the slave you buried!]

Neruda addressed these forgotten workers as fellows in rebirth: 'sube a nacer conmigo, hermano' [Rises to be born with me, brother] (PN1 446), and that 'brother' is related directly from the contemporary Juan Cortapie-dras back to Wiracocha. That same line asking these workers to accompany Neruda in rebirth then opens the final section XII: 'Sube a nacer conmigo, hermano'. The poet then asks his 'brother' to speak through his words: 'Yo vengo a hablar por vuestra boca muerta' [I come to speak through your dead mouth] (PN1 447). William Rowe finds this invocation a sign of Neruda's 'strong tenderness', which 'holds a principle of sociability', but there is also anger.[52]

That emphatic 'yo', unnecessary in Spanish as it is implicit in the verb, touches on both the vision and the inflated self. To speak for mankind was a Romantic topos ennobling the solitary poet, whether Shelley's unacknowl-edged legislator or Victor Hugo's lamp leading the masses. The point is that in terms of a new self-creation in the work, Neruda is now 'anclado'

---

50 Santí, *Pablo Nertpda*, pp. 122–5.

51 Cited in Schopf, p. 100.

52 William Rowe, 'Latin American Poetry', in John King (ed.), *Companion to Modern Latin American Culture*, p. 139.

[anchored] (the ruins were compared to a 'nave enterrada' [buried ship]). But the poem demands more. It incites these American workers to 'sharpen their knives' and 'ponedlos en mi pecho y en mi mano' [put them on / in my chest and in my hand]. The second part is clear: put a knife in his hand for the class war. But on or in his chest? Felstiner translated this as a sacrificial plea (nothing like a translation for a close-reading) and came up with: 'Drive them into my chest and my hand' and justified this choice: 'I make the decision – a risky one – that he wants to suffer the knives, not use them ... Clearly, Neruda desires to take onto himself the pain of those he is addressing.'[53] Jack Schmitt's translation restored the literal verb 'poner': 'Put them in my breast and in my hand', leaving the meaning ambiguous. I sense that Neruda wanted to use the knives and suffer the knives ('Y dejadme llorar ...' [and let me cry]). But he wants 'esperanza' [hope] from these workers. Here is the CP vision of the classless society (the relentless progress of History) of the future finally rid of the owners and exploiters (the poem is unclear if the same class exploitation plagued the Incas who built the fortress). Only concerted, party action, a revolution, will bring about this change: 'Dadme la lucha, el hierro, los volcanes' [Give me the fight, iron, volcanoes]. Neruda is now strong, metallic (Stalin meant 'steel'), so his self-image of the new poet is 'Apegadme los cuerpos como imanes' [Stick your bodies to me like magnets] (PN1 447). The last line of the poem affirms that as a poet he will speak for them – standard Marxist vanguard theory: 'Hablad por mis palabras y mi sangre' [Speak through my words and my blood]. That last word 'sangre' is a muddled metaphor. Neruda wrote with 'blood' not ink, a verbal sign of his passion. He closed his 1936 manifesto 'Sobre una poesía sin pureza' with 'y en la casa de la poesía no permanece nada sino lo que fue escrito con sangre para se escuchado por la sangre' [in the house of poetry nothing remains that isn't written in blood to be heard by blood]. Blood is a primal metaphor of understanding. But there is also pain in his vision of abused workers, the blood of sacrifice, even a Christ-like assumption of suffering.

So the section 'Alturas de Macchu Pichu', which should stand alone as a self-contained poem, became the poet's confession about a new self-identity. Most critics agree that his work is a kind of 'testimonio' [witness] and that it is written in a style 'de difícil comprensión' [of difficult understanding].[54] Raúl Silva Castro saw this testimony as the unifying thread in Neruda's self-awareness: 'Of his works in general it could be affirmed that they usually reflect, like an intimate diary, the state of the poet's soul ...'[55] From the late 1930s, Neruda turned his 'párpado forzosamente abierto' [forcibly opened eyelid] outwards on to social life, to become 'accusing witness who exposes

53 Felstiner, *Translating Neruda*, p. 196.
54 Schopf, p. 97.
55 Raúl Silva Castro, *Pablo Neruda*, p. 106.

facts', in Loyola's summary of his attitude.[56] The 'lucha' that Neruda joined
was his party's and its shared political views. He seemed to have given up
thinking on his own and adopted Marxist slogan-thinking. Silva Castro, like
many critics, saw this as simplistic: 'for Neruda, in the end, there's a very
facile dichotomy to establish and that once launched will divide men into
totally differentiated groups, without any possibility of mixing them'.[57] The
whole of his *Canto general* is constructed on this duality.

Another way of calibrating Neruda's poem about the iconic ruins is to
compare it with Peruvian versions in Jesús Cabel's anthology *Opera de piedra
(poemas a Machu Picchu)*, 1981, in the wake of a Chilean anthology in 1972.
Neruda is here the starting point and the poems respond to his poem as much
to the ruins, with an irreverent version from Alberto Hidalgo, to a self-questioning and religious one from Martín Adán. The most amusing version, by
Juan Gonzalo Rose, implies a critique of Neruda's monumental one as being
in effect about himself: 'Machu Picchu, dos veces / me senté en tu ladera /
para mirar mi vida. / para mirar mi vida / y no por contemplarte, / porque
necesitamos / menos belleza, Padre, / y más sabiduría' [Machu Picchu, twice
I sat on your slope to look at my life, to look at my life and not to contemplate
you because we need less beauty, Father, and more wisdom].[58]

Canto general, 1950

The collection of fifteen books called *Canto general* first appeared in Mexico
City in 1950, illustrated on the fly leaf as you open the huge book by the
muralist Diego Rivera and on the end leaf by David Alfaro Siqueiros, and
was 567 pages long. The paper is brown, like wrapping paper. At the back,
instead of a publisher, there is a long list of subscribers under countries,
which includes Frida Kahlo, Luis Buñuel, Carlos Pellicer, Paul Robeson,
Picasso, Léger, Aragon, Eluard and, from England, just two names: George
Fraser and Nancy Cunard. Robert Pring-Mill described Rivera's fly leaf as
a 'composite image of pre-Columbian America as seen by the most *indi-
genista* of the Mexican muralists', with Aztecs sacrificing somebody on a
pyramid, Mayan craftsmen and farmers and on the right Machu Pichu and the
Incas.[59] The Siqueiros closing image is Blakean, with a giant worker flying

---

56 Loyola, *Ser y morir en Pablo Neruda*, p. 171.

57 Silva Castro, *Pablo Neruda*, p. 208: 'para Neruda, en fin, hay una dicotomía muy fácil
de establecer y que, una vez lanzada, dividirá a los hombres en dos grupos totalmente diferen-
ciados y sin posibilidad alguna de mezcla'.

58 Jesús Cabel (ed.), *Opera de piedra (Poemas a Machu Picchu)* (Arequipa: Dirección
Universitaria de Investigación UNSA, 1981), p. 44.

59 Pring-Mill, *A Poet for all Seasons*, p. 26.

free from the earth. There is no doubt that Neruda shared the Mexican view of the indigenous past of natural, innocent natives ravished by the Spanish invaders, skeletons in suits of armour. The pre-Columbian world resurfaced as the working class, still ravished but now by European and US imperialistic capitalism. To this vision of primal innocence, Neruda added the great telluric or nature myth underlying his poetics and feelings.

The unity of *Canto general* is an interesting debate. On the basis of the self-sufficiency of section II, 'Alturas de Macchu Picchu', I have suggested that there is no narrative unity, no unfolding or progression. Saúl Yurkievich found that it lacked 'rigorous articulation', that it was a mixture of 'cosmogenesis, geography, ritual, chronicle, pamphlet, fabulation, harangue, satire, autobiography, rapture, hallucination, spell, testament'.[60] However, that list (typical of Yurkievich's critical style) is to do with subject matter and might cover any poem. A deeper unity, touched on already, is political and ethical. Most critics sympathetic to Neruda's politics follow this line. All the perceptions, all the genres used, obey his conversion to an unproblematic Marxism in its Stalinist version (Bloom called this a 'wart on the texture of his poems').[61] As early as 1972 Frank Riess attempted a structuralist approach, based on cultural and linguistic binary opposites (culture v. nature, man v. nature etc.) and looked at basic symbols like 'árbol', 'oro', 'ala', 'pueblo' [tree, gold, wing, people] as part of an organic unity. Raúl Silva Castro isolated a special vocabulary in his early essay on the *Canto general* with key words that condense Neruda's thinking, like 'azul', 'campana', 'cereales', 'cintura' to 'metal', 'miel', 'número', 'polen', 'sal' etc. [blue, bell, cereals, waist, metal, honey, number, pollen, salt]. These shorthand terms crop up throughout the poems and do shape the whole.[62] Mike Gonzalez suggests that the novelty and unity of the *Canto general* comes from how the poet 'introduces into Latin American poetry a new language, an idiom of public rhetoric. The poem presumes a relationship with a mass audience, and makes itself accessible to them.'[63] This view is endorsed by Neruda's deliberate poetry of 'sencillez' [simplicity]. The mass audience is crucial in trying to define the work, and is often invoked by Neruda, as in the 'vosotros' [you] of 'Alturas de Macchu Picchu'. However, this question of the work's tone can be nuanced, as Yurkievich suggests, by contrasting two basic styles that clash and are not harmonised into one. He showed that 'the writing alternates between hermetic, very plurivalent poems,

---

[60] Saúl Yurkieviech, 'Mito e historia, dos generadores del *Canto general*', *Fundadores de la nueva poesía latinoamericana*, p. 226: 'cosmogénesis, geografía, rito, crónica, panfleto, fabulación, arenga, sátira, autobiografía, rapto, alucinación, profecía, conjuro, testamento'.

[61] Bloom, *The Western Canon*, p. 479.

[62] Silva Castro, *Pablo Neruda*, pp. 104–5.

[63] Gonzalez and Treece, *The Gathering of Voices*, p. 224.

of great metaphoric density' with others that are close to 'prosaic elocution,
where the language becomes simplified, direct, discursive, truthful, fact-like,
referential'.[64] These contrasting modes imply contrasting themes. Neruda's
'afán naturalizante' [naturalising zeal] suspends rationality and self-reflex-
ivity by exaggerating intuition, while the other mode lends itself to anger,
accusation, invective.[65] One could add that anger clarifies the rhetoric. Lastly,
there is a gripping biographic unity that accounts for the Neruda 'legend'
that reveals that much of the *Canto general* was written while the poet was
on the run, pursued by the Chilean authorities. Neruda hardly alludes to this
personal level, and readers have to supplement the lack of information within
the poem with a biography like Feinstein's.

   Canto general opens with canto I, 'La lámpara en la tierra' [The lamp on
– or in – the earth]. 'Tierra' continues the earlier title, *Residencia en la tierra*,
but with a positive connotation of rootedness. 'Lamp' is a private word that
confuses miner's light with writing table lamp to mean poet and guiding
light (a version of Baudelaire's lighthouses, 'Les Phares', the artists who
lead humankind). The opening poem articulates Neruda's new-found Latin
American-ness as love, 'Amor América (1400)'. J. M. Cohen, in his study
of twentieth-century poetry, claimed that the *Canto general* was Neruda's
greatest achievement, the first book of Spanish-American poetry 'to have
freed itself almost entirely from the European tradition', akin to Whitman.
In the best poems, Cohen located Neruda's desire to 'restore the earth to its
earliest inhabitants and to its primitive simplicity'.[66] Neruda opened: '*Antes
de la peluca y la casaca / fueron los ríos, ríos arteriales: / fueron las cordill-
eras, en cuya onda raída / el cóndor o la nieve parecían inmóviles: / fue la
humedad y la espesura, el trueno / sin nombre todavía ...*' [Before the wig
and the cassock, there were rivers, arterial rivers: there were mountain chains
on whose worn wave the condor or the snow seemed immobile; there was
dampness and dense growth, thunder, without a name yet] (PN1 417). The
wigs and cassocks of rapacious Europeans arrived late. Rivers, mountains,
snow, condors ... this list evoked Neruda's southern Chile, and posited a
world without names, but he meant without European names. His vision of
early American culture was close to his Guatemalan friend Miguel Angel
Asturias's 1949 novel *Hombres de maíz*. Asturias connived with Neruda to
escape Argentine immigration by lending him his passport in 1949 when he
was on the run from González Videla. Asturias was living in Buenos Aires

   [64] Yurkievich, 'Mito e historia', pp. 224–5: 'la escritura alterna entre poemas herméticos,
muy plurivalentes, de gran densidad metafórica' ... 'la elocución prosaria, donde el lenguaje
se simplifica, se vuelve directo, discursivo, verista, fáctico, referencial'.
   [65] Yurkievich, 'Mito e historia', pp. 233–4.
   [66] J. M. Cohen, *Poetry of this Age*, pp. 220–4.

at the time. Later, they would write a book together, *Comiendo en Hungría*, 1956. Asturias also posited a loss of mythical density and authenticity with the coming of European civilisation. Neruda borrowed the Mayan creation myths for his original man of 'tierra fue, vasija, párpado / del barro trémulo' [earth was, vase, tremulous, mud-like eyelid] (PN1 417). As in Asturias's novel, 'nadie pudo / recordar después' [nobody could remember after], except for later writers, like Neruda and Asturias. So he can announce 'Yo estoy aquí para contar la historia' [I am here to tell the story], a phrase that Santí called the most telling in the volume, because 'tu aroma me trepó por las raíces' [your aroma climbed up the roots] (PN1 418).[67] Before, the poet's sensuousness spoke to him through physical love, now that he is rooted in Marxist philosophy, the 'smell' of America informs his vision. The rest of section I is the act of naming as magic. He enumerates plants like jacaranda, araucaria, mahogany, maize, tobacco, then animals, then birds, then rivers, including Chile's most symbolic river. The 'Bío-Bío' divided Mapuche territory, never conquered, from Spanish colonial Chile; it was 'la frontera' [the frontier]. This river speaks through him 'son tus palabras en mi boca, / las que resbalan, tú me diste / el lenguaje, el canto nocturno / mezclado con lluvia y follaje' [are your words in my mouth / the ones that slip, you gave me the language, the nocturnal song, mixed with rain and leaves] (PN1 425). Then we get a list of minerals and, finally, the people. All are gone, have been destroyed. The poet can only listen to stones and trees: 'No hay nadie. Escucha. Escucha el árbol, / escucha el árbol araucano' [There's nobody. Listen. Listen to the tree, listen to the araucarian tree] (PN1 432). This lovely opening canto exemplifies Yurkievich's notion of Neruda's deeper contact with natural forces that only a poet taps.

Canto III, 'Los conquistadores', illustrates Diego Rivera's mural version for the mass of indigenous Latin Americans who live outside bookshops and art galleries. Neruda's anger poetics aimed at stirring up immediate reactions, from the first line: 'Los carniceros desolaron las islas' [the butchers desolated the islands], for the Spanish conquest was a history of 'martirios' [martyrdom] (PN1 448). Neruda followed a rough geographical chronology from Columbus in the Caribbean outwards. The Marxist message is obvious as the massacred indigenous population are merged into 'la innumerable y castigada / familia de los pobres del mundo' [the innumerable and punished family of the poor of the world] (PN1 451). After a poem on Cortés, the poet reveals his identification with these poor: 'hundiendo hasta el codo en la sangre / de mis hermanos sorprendidos' [sinking up to my elbows in the blood of my surprised brothers] (PN1 453). He ranges through Alvarado,

---

[67] Santí, *Pablo Neruda*, p. 190.

Balboa, a foot soldier, Quesada, Almagro, Valdivia, cursing them all as 'mi patria verde y desnuda' [my green and naked land] (PN1 459) is drenched in blood. He brings this raped American past back to his present, as if history constantly repeats itself. In the middle of this historical review, Neruda enters the scene more completely with 'Elegía' and his own sadness; the poet asks Ocllo to 'echa en mis venas tu consejo' [throw in my veins your advice] (PN1 464) for he belongs to this ravaged history – 'Estoy hecho de tus raíces, / pero no entiendo, no me entrega / la tierra su sabiduría' [I am made of your roots, but I do not understand, the earth does not surrender its wisdom to me]. What is this 'wisdom' but the message that the poet wants to share, this American 'desdicha'? This core poem to the collection could have developed into a fascinating personal response, but the poet too often hides behind facile denunciations. Towards the end of the section, he writes about the epic poet Alonso de Ercilla in Chile and reveals his method. Neruda might read books, gather facts, but prefers to use his senses, especially 'hearing': 'Hombre, Ercilla sonoro, oigo el pulso de agua / de tu primer amanecer, un frenesí de pájaros ...' [Man, sonorous Ercilla, I hear the pulse of water of your first dawn, a frenzy of birds] (PN1 471). This quotation suggests that by reading a *poet* ('sonoro'), Neruda is able to understand his land more deeply ('Oigo'). There is information and magic in sound that the poet passes on through reading his poems aloud. Neruda is puzzled ('De dónde soy, me pregunto a veces, de dónde diablos / vengo...' [where am I from, I ask myself at times, where the hell am I going]), and the land speaks to him by asking him to listen 'Oyes / el agua lenta ...' [Do you hear the slow water] (PN1 473). This language that the poet hears is nature's 'idiomas rumorosos, dulces gotas' [rumorous languages, sweet drops] (PN1 476). The last song is 'A pesar de la ira', when light arrived (the progress myth intrinsic to Marxism). I have pointed out some of the poet's responses, from cursing to questioning and especially listening to the silent, empty nature of America.

Canto IV switches to 'Los libertadores', the 'pueblo' linked to nature, trees, leaves, rivers etc. Neruda begins with the Aztec emperor Cuauhtemoc and his personal role – 'recibo el don de tu patria desnuda' [I receive the gift of your naked fatherland] (second time 'desnudo' is used as an adjective for the vulnerable people). He has poems on Bartolomé de la Casa, on the Mapuche (he calls them Arauco), on Lautaro, on Caupolicán. These local heroes are all part of nature: 'Arauco era el rumor del agua errante' [Arauco was the rumour of errant water]. The poet moves towards the 1940s through colonial Latin America and the 'criollos' landowners in power who took everything in the name of a 'santa cultura occidental' [holy western culture] (PN1 500). Again, Neruda sounds far better when insulting his class enemies. He enumerates the 'revolutionaries' from O'Higgins to San Martín, Miranda, Carrera, Sucre, Zapata, Sandino etc. but clearly has not done much historical research and adds little to general knowledge. As a reading act, it can be dull. Charles Tomlinson voiced most readers' reactions: 'Was there ever a major poet so incapable of knowing where to stop?'[68]

However, when the poem is personal, the reader sits up. Neruda suddenly intrudes in a poem on the Mexican Juárez: 'Yo visité los muros de Querétaro, / toqué cada peñasco en la colina / ... / nadie persiste allí, se fue el fantasma' [I visited Querétaro's walls, I touched each crag on the hill, nothing persist there, the ghost has gone] (PN1 532). The sudden arrival of the poet's 'yo' ensures that quite another poem leaps out: the poet touched the actual landscape, like a braille, and found the past has vanished. History is always the present. But in this long poem, he was too much in a rush and too much gushing Marxist propaganda gags his subjectivity.

The canto ends on a high with the Chilean example and songs to Recabarren and Neruda's own conversion, but again not explicitly personal enough. In the mines in the desert north of Chile, he realised his ignorance of the people's suffering: 'Pero yo no sabía nada. / El hierro, el cobre, las sales lo sabían' [But I didn't know anything. Iron, copper, the salts knew] (PN1 544). In that line we find an intriguing poetics and a hint of how to learn about history through things and suffering. In Chuquicamata, the great mine, he was led to his truth, to his conversion. He wrote: 'fui venciéndome: / hasta sumirme en hombre, en agua / de lágrimas' [I was overcoming myself, as far as sinking myself in man, in the water of tears] (PN1 548). The pain of the exploited, illiterate others taught him how to overcome himself, his selfishness. His new version of 'love' is CP patriotism. There at the mine, the poet 'touched' the landscape, a personal gnosis: 'metí la mano entre los piojos, / anduve por los rieles hasta / el amanecer desolado, / dormí sobre las tablas duras' [I placed my hand among the lice, I walked along the rails until desolate dawn, I slept on hard planks] (PN1 550). Again in these words, we catch the seeds of another deeply personal poem instead of the eulogy to the '*Partido comunista*' and a poem-speech in Brazil praising Prestes.

I will close my analysis of *Canto general* with some notes on canto V, 'La arena traicionada', which brings the 'betrayal' narrative to the fore. It opens with the poet justifying his epico-lyrical poem because he must fight oblivion. The poet's function is to review the past and remind the People of what they have suffered, in order for them to be 'invencibles' (PN1 566). An example of not giving into forgetfulness is his poem titled 'El Doctor Francia', a Paraguayan dictator made notorious later by Augusto Roa Bastos in his long novel *Yo el supremo*, 1974. Gaspar Francia attracted the attention of Europe (Carlyle wrote about him) as an erudite madman who closed Paraguay's frontiers to foreigners. He ruled from 1814 to 1840 and created a self-sufficient economy, along the previous Jesuit mission lines. He was an

68 Tomlinson, 'Latin America Betrayed', p. 6.

amateur astronomer, always dressed in black, was a bachelor, forbade people from looking at him as he rode around Asunción, in a fit had all the dogs in town killed and admired Thomas Carlyle. In Neruda's poem we do not get any dates, none of the colourful gossip, just a vivid description of Paraguayan nature with its rivers and water and warm mud. We do learn that he watched the stars, that he was a Platonist and that when he died nobody dared go into see what had happened (an irony that Neruda ignored is that the same happened to Stalin when he died). Francia becomes a type, the solitary man locked up 'en la soledad del palacio' (as García Márquez portrayed his love-less dictator in *El otoño del patriarca* [The Autumn of the Patriarch], 1975). You will not learn much history from Neruda, just who the 'baddies' are, according to his political views. His so-called Manichean view is most clear in 'Promulgación de la ley del embudo' [Promulgation of the funnel law]:

> Para el rico la buena mesa.
> La basura para los pobres.
> El dinero para los ricos.
> Para los pobres el trabajo.
> Para los ricos la casa grande.
> El tugurio para los pobres.
> El fuero para el gran ladrón.
> La cárcel al que roba un pan.
> París, París para los señoritos.
> El pobre a la mina, al desierto (PN1 582)

> [For the rich a good meal. Rubbish for the poor. Money for the rich, work for the poor. For the rich a grand house. The hovel for the poor. Privilege for the great thief, prison for he who steals bread. Paris, Paris for the rich young men and the mine in the desert for the poor]

It is worthwhile comparing this unsubtle but skilled, rhythmical poem where Paris is mentioned twice with César Vallejo's famous 'Un hombre pasa con un pan al hombro', which also has Paris and bread in it. Vallejo is more aware of emotional and political complexities, the suffering of the poor and his own frustrations in his final cry: 'Alguien pasa contando con sus dedos / ¿Cómo hablar del no-yó sin dar un grito?' [Someone passes by counting with his fingers. How to speak of the non-self without screaming?][69]

As I have suggested throughout this section, the poems gain in lyrical intensity when Neruda turns personal. They gain also when he is in his invective vein. A good example, to read aloud, of his Quevedan rhetoric:

---

[69] César Vallejo, *Poesía completa*, p. 657. Eshleman's translation, p. 517.

Escuché más tarde el discurso,
del Senador así elegido:
'Nosotros, patriotas cristianos,
nosotros, defensores del orden,
nosotros, hijos del espíritu'.
Y estremecía su barriga
su voz de vaca aguardentosa
que parecía tropezar
como una trompa de mamuth
en las bóvedas tenebrosas
de la silbante prehistoria.
Or:
Grotescos, falsos aristócratas
de nuestra América, mamíferos,
recién estucados, jóvenes
estériles, pollinos sesudos
hacendados malignos, héroes
de la borrachera en el Club,
salteadores de banca y bolsa,
pijes, granfinos, pitucos,
apuestos tigres de Embajada (PN1 584–5)

[Later I heard the speech of the senator thus elected: 'We, Christian patriots, we, defenders of the order, we children of the spirit.' And his belly trembled, his voice of an alcoholic cow that seemed to stumble like a mammoth's trunk in the tenebrous cellars of whistling prehistory. Grotesque, false aristocrats of our America, recently stuccoed mammals, sterile young, brainy chickens, malignant estate owners, heroes of drunkenness in the club, bank and stock-exchange robbers, snobs, refined fools, upper class dandies, well-dressed embassy tigers]

In 'Las tierras y los hombres' [The earths and the men], we can read about Neruda's personal solution to so much glimpsed suffering. He dated this section 1948 and opened with direct experience: 'Yo entré en las casas profundas, / como cuevas de ratas, húmedas / de salitre' [I entered into the deep houses like caves with rats, humid with nitrate] (PN1 602). He explained his anguish: 'Me atravesaron los dolores / de mi pueblo, se me enredaron / como alambrados en el alma: / me crisparon el corazón: / salí a gritar por los caminos' [My people's suffering pierced me, entangled like wire in my soul, tensed my heart. I left shouting along the roads]. This personal reaction is moving, as is the way he recycles his earlier symbols – corazón, gritar. We reach another 'Entonces', a grammatical term that suggests a summary of what happened: 'Entonces me hice soldado: / número oscuro, regimiento, / orden de puños combatientes' [Then I became a soldier, obscure number, regiment, order of combatant fists] (PN1 603).

To summarise this uneven poem is hard, but it would begin with the impli-
cation that it sounds better read aloud than read quietly to oneself. A close
reading must take this starting-point on board. However, Neruda does not
write in colloquial or street Spanish; he still employs metaphors. The poem
as pure song is how the poet defined his role at the end of canto IX: 'Yo no
vengo a resolver nada. / Yo vine aquí para cantar / y para que cantes conmigo'
[I have not come to resolve anything. I came to sing and that you should sing
with me] (NP1 700). From this summary of the poet's role, you can establish
that the audience as much as the politics defines the language. Secondly, the
poem intensifies when Neruda uses the 'yo', when he deals with personal
experience, or confessions. Thirdly, the poem springs to life when he insults,
employs his verbal sarcasm, imitating Quevedo's knotty, nouny vituperation.
Fourthly, Neruda is a marvellously sensuous nature poet, especially about
his sodden, cold, woody Chile in the 'Canto general de Chile' and in 'El
gran océano' [The great ocean], which Pring-Mill found 'oddly at variance
with the main scene', but also 'included some of his finest poetry'.[70] Lastly,
Neruda never stopped viewing himself as a bard, writing for the people: 'Yo
aquí me despido, vuelvo / a mi casa, en mis sueños ... / soy nada más que
un poeta: os amo a todos' [Here I say goodbye, I return home, in my dreams
I am nothing more than a poet, I love you all] (PN1 700). His self-identity is
contained inside that 'being a poet'. Neruda no longer complied with Keats's
famous description of the creative process, that '*negative capability*' where
the poet is 'capable of being in uncertainties, mysteries, doubts, without any
irritable reaching after fact and reason'.[71]

Translating Neruda 2

One of the most stimulating books on Pablo Neruda's poetry is John Felstiner's *Translating Neruda: The Way to Macchu Picchu*, first published in 1980.
As preparation for translating with students, Felstiner tried to put himself
in Neruda's shoes, learnt Spanish, read all the poetry up to 1945. Part of
the reason for choosing this long poem to translate was the site itself, a
magic talisman of a name and also partially because he was disappointed
with earlier translations (criticising Belitt in particular). As I have noted in
a review, Felstiner had to make choices and render Neruda's Spanish into
adequate English, despite a bilingual text. One example: Neruda's 'Hundí
la mano turbulenta y dulce / en lo más genital de lo terrestre' becomes 'I
plunged my turbulent and gentle hand / into the genital quick of the earth'

---

[70] Pring-Mill, *A Basic Anthology*, p. xlvii.
[71] John Keats, *Letters of John Keats* (Oxford: Oxford University Press, 1965), p. 53.

where the adjectival noun of 'lo genital' is turned into 'the quick'. Felstiner knew he was tuning up Neruda's Spanish 'slightly', but are 'la tierra' and 'lo terrestre' the same and do they differ only through sound? He has worked as much on the sense as the sound, as any translator must.[72] In a review of Nathaniel Tarn's 1967 translation *The Heights of Macchu Picchu*, the anonymous reviewer claimed that it was a 'clumsy rendering' and was 'neither acceptable as English nor particularly accurate', adding Christian associations where 'vaso' became 'chalice' and 'campana' 'church bell'. Tarn equally missed Chilean Spanish; a 'cajón serrano' is not a 'coffer' but a 'mountain ravine'.[73] Alastair Reid in his review of Felstiner's book invoked the 'translation police', those 'dusty figures (dons, we were always sure) who used to patrol the pages of published translation on the lookout for errors to denounce'. But Reid noted a crucial paradox about all translations (even his own): 'translations are the residues of a long and complex process, and it may be true that, in the end, it is the process which is the more interesting'.[74] This crucial insight into the precarious nature of translating poetry, with Frost's warning of poetry getting lost in translation, could as well apply to criticism: more interesting as a temporal process than as any final reckoning. So apart from avoiding errors, the translation must deal with sound in a different language, and that is daunting and subjective.

[72] Jason Wilson, 'In the Translator's Workshop', pp. 30–2.
[73] Anon., 'Tarnished Neruda', p. 220.
[74] Alastair Reid, 'Climbing Macchu Picchu', p. 55.

6

The 1950s: from *Los versos del capitán* to *Cien sonetos de amor*

Los versos del capitán, 1952

This scandalous book came to fill the vacuum that we noted concerning the *Canto general*, that is, the absence of erotic poems addressed to a woman by the poet Neruda. What was happening biographically is clear; Neruda abandoned Delia del Carril for Matilde Urrutia, who became his third wife and then his widow, and wrote about their life together in *Mi vida junto a Pablo Neruda (Memorias)* [My life next to Pablo Neruda, memoirs], 1986. The first 1952 publication in Naples of 44 copies of the love songs, as Neruda stated in successive editions, was anonymous because their affair was secret. There could also be a political self-censoring as if writing love poems was not appropriate in the aftermath of the war, in the year 1950 that Neruda, Picasso and Paul Robeson won the International Peace Prize. That only Matilde knew who the real author was brings Neruda back to his earliest love poems directed at a particular reader, his current muse. It remained 'anonymous' until 1962 and his 'Explicación' [Explanation] (PN1 841). The title claims the poet as 'captain', a self-image that goes back to his teenage poetry and forward to all the marine imagery of his work and life (though his 'Carta-prólogo' [Letter-prologue], written by a pretend woman, suggests the author was a captain from the Spanish Civil War).

These love songs celebrate falling in love again, but the middle-age version and with a happy result, far from the melancholia and sexual excess of his earlier love poems. They are poems of contented lovers. Neruda called them 'tender' as befits his age, but also underlined that some of the poems are 'terribles en su cólera' [terrible in their anger] (PN1 843). The poems are very direct, avoid obvious literary echoes and complex metaphors, and continue to combine the poet's two passions, a woman and politics. They look forward to his odes and enshrine art as immediate understanding. Being read aloud is their inner nature; it is like hearing Neruda talk.

The first section is titled 'El amor' and taps into the poet's erotic vocabulary, by now well-known to his readers – words like 'rosa', 'boca', 'besar' [rose, mouth, to kiss]. There are echoes of his earlier, more famous work – Neruda recycles his imagery – as in 'suben tus hombros como dos colinas' [your shoulders rise like two hills] (cf. poem 1 of the *Veinte poemas*), and she is 'tierra', the natural world. The second poem 'La reina' [the queen] is an allegory of lovers' intimacy and of the kind of reader he can write for. The muse wakes up 'campanas' [bells] in the poet for 'sólo tú y yo, amor mío / lo escuchamos' [only you and I, my love listen to it] (PN1 846). Self-referentiality is part of Neruda's fame, so his sensuous basic symbolic vocabulary, sometimes overlapping with tiresome Communist Party images, is formed of 'paloma', 'copa', 'pan', 'ola', 'espada', 'trigo' etc. [dove, wine-glass, bread, wave, sword, wheat]. Her breasts are like 'palomas gemelas' [twin doves] or later 'dos panes hechos' [two made breads] (PN1 853). In 'El insecto' the poet parodies the odd spider he was in *Veinte poemas*: 'De tus caderas a tus pies / quiero hacer un largo viaje' [from your hips to your feet I want to take a long trip] (PN1 863). A section called 'Las furias' echoes, tepidly, his marvellous 1934 poem *Las furias y las penas*.

The unevenness of his work still allows for the occasional delightful poem, like 'Tus pies': 'Cuando no puedo mirar tu cara / miro tus pies. / Tus pies de hueso arqueado, / tus pequeños pies duros' [When I cannot look at your face I look at your feet. Your feet of arched bones, your little hard feet] (PN1 848) or the poem 'La noche en la isla' where the lovers kiss at dawn: 'y al despertar tu boca / salida de tu sueño / me dio el sabor de tierra, / de agua marina, de algas, / del fondo de tu vida' [and when your mouth wakes up, leaving your dream, it gave me the taste of earth, of salt water, of seaweed from the depths of your life] (PN1 853). The poet's love is less sexual, less cosmic. In fact, it is downright domestic, with little quarrels, little silences, jealousies about the past, but no courtly-love suffering ('No me has hecho sufrir / sino esperar' [You didn't make me suffer but hope] PN1 877), as if the hope supporting his politics has infused his love. The last line of the collection is 'sin ninguna tristeza' [without any sadness]. That last phrase encapsulates the change in the persona in the poems. He has jettisoned the melancholic, loveless poet, *el desdichado*, for the contented, fulfilled, very busy, travelling lover and poet who can write lines like 'Bésame de nuevo, querida / limpia ese fusil, camarada' [kiss me again, dear, clean the rifle, comrade] (PN1 883). He was not an arms-carrying subversive and his weapons were his poems, but he is posing as a soldier in a war. That 'fusil' is his pen (but obviously a pen is not a gun). No wonder, then, that Ricardo Paseyro called these poems a 'notebook of stories and bedroom tales', a 'caricature of love poetry'.[1] I would add, a betrayal of his earlier love poetry.

---

1   Ricardo Paseyro, 'The Dead World of Pablo Neruda', p. 220.

Las uvas y el viento, 1954

These poems were written while the biographical Neruda travelled the world, including his first visits to Moscow, China, Prague, Berlin and Warsaw. Robert Pring-Mill was critical of this long book of poems (422 pages in the first edition) as 'little more than a hasty and rather superficial public diary'.[2] Federico Schopf found it one of his 'most controversial books' and the closest to socialist realism, the work of a civic poet with a strict didactic role.[3] The book narrated Neruda's contact with the Soviet Union. The poet was aware of the poor reception of a book that was a 'poem of geographic and political content' and that its political passions were difficult for many readers to swallow (PN1 1227). The prologue is subtitled 'Tenéis que oírme' [You have to listen to me]. The poem opens with 'Yo', as if Neruda, the persona in his poems, was intrinsically fascinating; his life read like a chronicle. The piling up of the first-person singular underscores the collection, giving ammunition to those, like Octavio Paz, who accused Neruda of a having a titanic ego. In these poems, the poet's 'yo' represents all America ('Yo, americano errante …' [I, errant American]). In Florence, for example, he writes that 'Yo no sé / lo que dicen los cuadros ni los libros / … / pero sé lo que dicen / todos los ríos. / Tienen el mismo idioma que yo tengo' [I don't know what the paintings and books say, but I know what all the rivers say. They have the same language as mine] (PN1 915). This identification of poet with the powerful flow of a river, a natural force, speaking a natural language, is the self myth that generates so much poor poetry. The Argentine poet Enrique Molina was rightly convinced that Neruda's 'political activities contributed as much as his poetry to spread his name' and that this political source was based on a 'ciega resolución' [blind resolution].[4] In these 'flowing' poems, there is no self-awareness, no inner questioning. Neruda slides along on certainties. At the end, in italics, he concludes like Julius Caesar: '*Yo he visto*' [I have seen] (PN1 1126).

Then, suddenly, in 'Los frutos' [the fruit] a vivid description of an olive: 'Dulces olivas verdes de Frascati, / pulidas como puros pezones, / frescas como gotas de océano' [Sweet green olives of Frascati, polished like pure nipples, fresh like drops of ocean] (PN1 919), that lead to his sensuous grasping of the simple things of life in his Odes. There are homages to Picasso, to Ehrenburg, to Miguel Hernández, to Mao Tse-tung, to Paul Eluard, to the Party and above all to Stalin, the 'Capitán', and his death that hit Neruda 'como un golpe de océano' [like a blow from the ocean] (PN1 998). He also published an obituary in the newspaper *El Siglo* on 10 March 1953, referring to Stalin as

2   Robert Pring-Mill, 'Introduction', Pablo Neruda, *A Basic Anthology*, p. xlix.
3   Federico Schopf, 2000, pp. 100–2.
4   Enrique Molina, 'Neruda de siempre', p. 8.

'our master' and 'the great figure of contemporary philosophy', outstanding for his 'clarity' and 'sencillez' (simplicity).[5] The poet is an insider, constantly celebrating his faith in direct, vaguely narrative and short-lined poems. In his poem 'London', a foggy city of shops selling chairs, he spots T. S. Eliot: 'el poeta Eliot / con su viejo frac / leyendo a los gusanos' [the poet Eliot with his old frock coat reading worms] (PN1 1051). This cartoon view of Eliot was not what Neruda thought about him in 1927 when he imitated him out of admiration for his poems. In another poem on England, Neruda praised London for sheltering Lenin, and for Darwin and for W. H. Hudson: 'Más tarde Hudson / en las praderas / se ocupó de los pájaros que habían / sido olvidados por los libros / y con ellos / llenó la geografía / que nos está pariendo poco a poco' [Later Hudson in the fields busied himself with the birds forgotten by books and with them filled the geography that is slowly giving birth to us] (PN1 1056). The section on Neruda's expulsion from France shifts to his invective mode, and makes easy-reading. However, this is the book that gave him his bad name as an unrepentant Stalinist. As a poet, it was as if whatever he wrote was by Neruda, and thus a good poem.

Odas elementales, 1954

Neruda had written odes before ('Oda a Federico García Lorca', for example), but most critics agree that the 1954 publication with Losada in Buenos Aires inaugurated a new cycle of direct poems, clearly identifiable on the page, with many lines of just one word, devouring paper and ordered alphabetically. They are clearly oral, to be understood through the ear. He followed this book with *Nuevas odas elementales*, 1954, then with *Tercer libro de las odas*, 1957, and finally and still principally odes, *Navegaciones y regresos*, 1959. The second volume of his *Obras completas* covers ten years and 1330 pages of text. He wrote every day, was as productive as his comrade Picasso. This abundance, or 'graphomania' in Paseyro's term, has aesthetic consequences.[6] If you do not like a poem, move to the next. Some poems will appeal to you. A negative side effect is sheer facility and superficiality, and a lowering of lyrical intensity. The key point, though, is that Neruda never doubted his status as poet. He had identified with the *pueblo* and the Party and removed inner scruples. Over these years, his work, in Saúl Yurkievich's phrase, 'lays the foundations for how Neftalí Ricardo Reyes Basoalto transforms himself into Pablo Neruda'.[7] At another level, as a Communist, Neruda had taken on

5   Pablo Neruda, *Yo respondo*, p. 222.
6   Paseyro, 'The Dead World of Pablo Neruda', p. 213.
7   Saúl Yurkievich, 'Prólogo', Pablo Neruda, *Obras completas II*, p. 24. Henceforth, PN2 plus page number.

board some aspects of Andrea Zhdanov's 1934 tenets of 'socialist realism', depicting the phenomenal world (a materialistic poetics), and revealing how Marxist-Leninism led to happy souls, the smiling peasants and Neruda's brandishing of 'alegría' [happiness] during the Cold War. Zhdanov spoke of a new literature 'impregnated with enthusiasm', deliberately 'optimistic'. He took up Stalin's infamous aphorism of the writer as engineer of human souls by defining it as meaning 'standing with both feet firmly on the basis of real life'.[8] Neruda saw himself as a leader in terms of Lenin's pamphlet *What is to be done?*, 1902, where revolutionary intellectuals create a new awareness in the illiterate masses. But he himself was no intellectual and probably never read Hegel, Marx, Engels, Lenin or Trotsky.[9]

The term 'Ode' derives from the Greek 'to sing, to chant'. It suggests a public utterance and develops from three great poets – Horace, Pindar and Anacreon – and was adapted through the ages, for example by Verlaine with his *Odes* in 1893.[10] Yurkievich decided that Neruda 'emulates rather Horace', with his mix of hendecasyllables and heptasyllables.[11] Yurkievich also pointed out that the adjective in Neruda's title suggests two kinds of 'elementales': that of 'basic' and that of elementary, the elements. What is absolutely clear from the first poem is Neruda's continuing diatribe against his earlier 'hermetic' poetry, what Yurkievich called his 'pure divorce' with *Residencia en la tierra*.[12] Jaime Alazraki also wrote a lucid introduction to this ode cycle, stressing how Neruda chose to transform the lyric poet into a 'chronicler of his period', insisting that his poems appear on the news page of his friend Miguel Otero Silva's newspaper *El Nacional* (Caracas) in order to catch another kind of reader.[13] He also pointed out that everything including the rain, sea, ocean and stars was drafted into his new politics and forced to take sides; he also noticed a common structure based on thesis, antithesis and synthesis in the form of a moral, a threat, a warning, and decided, contrary to Yurkievich, that this structure was closest to the Pindaric ode.[14] This prosaic intention to inform, as attempted by newspapers, is attacked by the critic Ricardo Paseyro who rewrote the ode to the artichoke as prose and then

[8]   Andrei Zhdanov, 'Speech to the Congress of Writers', in Charles Harrison and Paul Wood (eds), *Art in Theory. 1900–1990. An Anthology of Changing Ideas* (Oxford: Blackwell, 1992), pp. 409–12.

[9]   I refer the reader to Edmund Wilson, *To the Finland Station*, 1940.

[10]   Alex Preminger and T. V. F Brogan (eds), *The New Encyclopedia of Poetry and Poetics* (Princeton: Princeton University Press, 1993), p. 856.

[11]   Yurkievich, PN2 11.

[12]   Yurkievich, PN2 13.

[13]   Jaime Alazraki, 'La estructura de la oda elemental', in Angel Flores (ed.), *Nuevas aproximaciones a Pablo Neruda*, p. 224.

[14]   Alazraki, 'La estructura de la oda elemental', pp. 227–8.

showed that there was no *poetic* reason, apart from capricious typography, as to why Neruda cut them up into single words.[15]

The opening ode is titled 'El hombre invisible' (no link with Ralph Ellison's novel *Invisible Man*, 1952, or H. G. Wells's science-fiction novel of 1897), more a self-reference to the poet he was before in *tentativa del hombre infinito*, only now Neruda lives for the *pueblo*, and thus his 'ego' is invisible. So the opening lines 'Yo me río, / me sonrío / de los viejos poetas / ... / siempre dicen "yo"' [I laugh I smile at the old poets who always say 'I'] (PN2 39). But he too began his poem with 'Yo'. So what he means is that before, he and most poets only explored their own selves, their monstrous 'ego'. Poets are special, what happens to them is all that matters. Nobody else counts, claims Neruda. But real poetry is the 'pueblo' and its suffering. The old poets (Neruda himself) wrote about oceans 'que no conoce' [that he doesn't know], stare at fields of maize but 'él pasa sin saber / desgranarla' [but he walks without knowing how to thresh it] (PN2 40). The old poet does not 'touch' the earth. He calls himself 'maldito' [cursed], thinks he is unique, but, and here we come to the core of Neruda's critique of all poets before his conversion to Marxism:

> Todos los días come pan
> pero no ha visto nunca
> un panadero
> ni ha entrado a un sindicato
> de panificadores,
> y así mi pobre hermano
> se hace oscuro,
> se tuerce y se retuerce
> y se halla
> interesante (PN2 41)
>
> [Every day he eats bread, but he has never seen a baker nor entered a baker's union, and so my poor brother makes himself dark, twists and twist even more and finds himself interesting]

That 'hermano' refers to Baudelaire's famous addressing of his reader as his 'brother' ('– Hypocrite lecteur, – mon semblabe, – mon frère!'), while the 'maldito' writing obscure poetry must be Neruda himself as he was.[16] However, he does not phrase this opening ode as a *mea culpa*. He is the different one now: 'yo soy el único / invisible' [I am the only invisible one] (PN2 41) because the people ask him to sing for them, by telling him their problems. The long ode ends: 'mi canto los reúne: / el canto del hombre

---

15 Paseyro, 'The Dead World of Pablo Neruda', pp. 213–16.
16 Baudelaire, *Les Fleurs du mal*, p. 3.

invisible / que canta con todos los hombres' [my song unites them, the song of the invisible man who sings with all men] (PN2 45). It is an obvious and strangely boasting poem where the 'lucha' [struggle] is conveyed by a new breed of poet. In 'Oda al aire', Neruda defines himself; 'cuando me neces- ites, / yo soy el poeta hijo / de pobres, padre, tío, / primo, hermano carnal / y concuñado / de los pobres' [when you need me I am the poet son of poor, father, uncle, cousin, flesh brother and related to the poor] (PN2 47). That is, he is a poet because he is poor and from the *pueblo*. He is also a new poet because he incites 'alegría' [happiness] as in his 'Oda a la alegría', where his old melancholic self looked at things with glasses on and he was 'mal aconsejado' [badly advised] by the 'antiguos poetas' [the old poets] (PN2 52), referring to his reading of the great dead like Rimbaud, Nerval etc. On his lover's mouth he placed a 'triste beso' (surely a reference to his *Veinte poemas de amor*). Neruda was also well aware of how critics read him in his new Communist phase as his new readers 'eat' his words. Critics are 'mudos' [dumb] or 'ciegos' [blind] or monarchical, or 'vestidos de cadáveres' [dressed as corpses] (PN2 83) and kick about in Marx's beard. Some critics were 'ingleses' [English], but all of them with their teeth and dictionaries and 'citas respetables' [respectable quotations] disputed 'mi pobre poesía / a las sencillas gentes / que la amaban' [my poor poetry from the simple people who loved it]. For Neruda, there is no space for a bourgeois critic; there should just be poets and readers. His original practice was to by-pass rationality and rational critics, and his novel way of reading poems was to voice them and make them immediate. 'Oda a la envidia' [Ode to envy] recounts his journey as a poet from the south, a 'muchacho / desterrado' [exiled lad], out to the Far East with its fevers and crowds, to become yet another poetic reworking of his own life. Despite all the envy, he writes 'para no morirme' [so as not to die]. 'Oda a la poesía' defines, yet again, his new art as different from his Rimbaudian style when he buried his eyes in puddles to see the stars. This was Rimbaud's conclusion to his 'Le bateau ivre': 'Si je désire une eau d'Europe, c'est la flache / Noire et froide où vers le crépuscule embaumé / un enfant accroupi plein de tristesses, lâche / Un bateau...' [If there is one water in Europe I want, it is the black cold pool where into the scented twilight a child squatting, full of sadness, launches a boat], a poignant self-portrait of early Neruda. Now poetry speaks with 'voz férrea' [iron voice], a reference to Stalin, man of steel; it is useful like flour or metal or bread or wine.[17] His new poetry will 'luchar cuerpo a cuerpo' [fight body to body] (PN2 199), an 'unusually public role' for a poet, according to De Costa.[18] Throughout this ode cycle, Neruda obsessively criticises himself, his earlier poetry.

[17] Rimbaud, *Oeuvres completes*, p. 69.
[18] De Costa, 1979, p. 163.

The better odes are not involved with redefinitions of the poet, but put the new poetics into practice, like 'Oda a la alcachofa' [ode to the artichoke]. The poet gives us a verbal and material description in a baroque mode (using metaphor) where the artichoke is a warrior, with a tender heart, a proud pomegranate who ends up in a basket in a market, in martial lines until bought by María. The poem ends 'escama por escama / desvestimos / la delicia / y comemos / la pacífica pasta / de su corazón verde' [leaf by leaf we undress the delight and we eat the peaceful paste of its green heart] (PN2 51). Neruda's greedy eulogy of common food implicitly mocks the *modernista* worship of French Haute Cuisine, champagne and roast beef. Food becomes a favoured topic. In his 'Oda al caldillo de congrio' [Ode to congrio broth] (a very Chilean dish), we get a recipe. Garlic is evoked in hyperbolic ways as 'ese marfil / precioso' [that precious ivory], its smell is 'su fragancia iracunda' [angry fragrance] (PN2 69); garlic in the 'cono sur' was loathed by the upper classes. Then add sliced onions and a tomato, fry until golden, throw in the 'camarones' [prawns] and add cream to the fish. You will then taste 'las esencias de Chile' and know heaven. The whole ode is baroque, tongue-in-cheek and light. Neruda's 'Oda a la cebolla' [ode to onion] (another enemy of the oligarchy) celebrates the onion growing underground with its 'vientre de rocío' [dew belly] (PN2 72), and is born like Aphrodite, like a magnolia, a planet, a 'redonda rosa de agua, / sobre / la mesa / de las pobres gentes' [a round rose of water on the table of the poor] (PN2 73). In a salad, onions are like 'granizo' [hail] and kill off the hunger of the 'jornalero en el duro camino' [day worker on the tough road]. More than celebrating things in a general way, Neruda celebrates the 'things' of the poor. From this premise, the onion excites his analogical libido. De Costa calls this ode 'highly conceptual' where the words are singled out as 'pure and simple'.[19] The onion for Neruda is more beautiful 'que un ave / de plumas cegadoras' [a bird with blinding feathers] (mocking the *modernista*'s peacocks). Robert Pring-Mill revealed how the poet came to his final version by studying the manuscript dated 31 December 1953, and detailing Neruda's self-editing process.[20] In his delightful 'Oda al tomate' [ode to the tomato], the poet heightened the sensuousness of the tomato (and the poet's greed): 'Tiene / luz propia, / majestad benigna' [It has its own light, benign majesty] (PN2 230), with a touch of humour: 'Debemos, por desgracia, / asesinarlo: / se hunde / el cuchillo / en su pulpa viviente' [we have to unfortunately assassinate it: you sink the knife in its living pulp]. The tomato is almost an excuse for verbal cleverness (Golden Age *conceptismo*) as it is for asserting his patriotic love for Chile, underlying all the odes: 'llena [su pulpa] las ensaladas / de Chile'

---

[19] De Costa, 1979, p. 171.
[20] Robert Pring-Mill, 'La elaboración de la cebolla', in Angel Flores (ed.), *Aproximaciones a Pablo Neruda*, pp. 229–41.

[its pulp fills the salads of Chile] (PN2 230). There are further odes to César Vallejo, to wood, to birds, to bread, to the sea etc.

The term that Neruda used to justify his work, as already noted, is 'sencillez' [simplicity]. And within this concept, his new poetry is excluded from the drawing rooms and cafés packed with 'los más exquisitos peder-astas' [with the most exquisite pederasts] (PN2 218), where we get a clearer sense of simple people, not only the poor (and his own roots in working-class poverty), but also the heterosexual (similar to his attack on 'Gidistas' earlier) as if pederasts 'complicate' and must be cast out of his 'society', like critics, the old poets, his literary enemies. De Costa sees this as shocking the reader 'with simplicity', what you could call a continuing avant-garde aim.[21]

Nuevas odas elementales, 1956

As in his first book of odes, the opening poem here defines Neruda's aesthetics against his earlier hermetic poetry and against all difficult poetry. The basic metaphor is the poem as a house (itself derived from Heidegger's notion of language as the house of the self). The poet's personal and social identity are now fixed ('Sé lo que soy / y adónde va mi canto' [I know who I am and where my song is going], PN2 259) and his house is poor and transparent. The opening assertion deliberately grates with André Breton's famous opening to his novel Nadja, 'Qui suis-je?', with its questioning of the self. Neruda's past verse reappears in the third stanza: 'Yo destroné la negra monarquía, / la cabellera inútil de los sueños' [I dethroned the black monarchy and useless hair of dreams], where 'negra monarquía' refers to the dominance of 'night' and the useless hair of dreams to all his Residencia cycle. That is, inner, subjective explorations are well over. His poetry is as useful – his new style of metaphorising – as a 'taza' [cup] or a 'herramienta' [tool] (PN2 260). These metaphors for the poem are a conceit for a poem is not an 'object' and does not make anything happen, as Auden once quipped. Again, the poet equally stresses his Chilean-ness. The odes that follow are ordered alphabetically.

The first is another paean to local Chilean foods, 'Oda al aceite' [Ode to olive oil] (the talismanic word 'Chile' reappears in countless odes). The olive is compared to a 'pezón' [nipple] and its oil to the 'llave celestial de la mayonesa' [celestial key to mayonnaise]. The word 'aceite' itself is pure Castilian (actu-ally, a Moorish word). This first ode, then, continues the humorous, verbally clever and patriotic song to the simple life of the Chilean working class. There are also countless references to the poet's rejected past version of

---

21 De Costa, 1979, p. 172.

being a poet. For example, in 'Oda al diccionario' [Ode to the dictionary], he reveals that once he despised dictionaries, thought words came direct from a 'Sinaí bramante' [a roaring Sinai], like surrealist automatic writing, and that he would reduce poetry to 'alquimia' [alchemy]; 'soy mago' [I'm a magician], he once boasted. These are obvious allusions to Rimbaud's 'Alchimie du verbe' and to his letters to his teachers about making himself a 'mage'. Neruda includes an 'Oda a Jean Arthur Rimbaud', talking to his photo as a child with twisted locks, half-closed eyes and bitter mouth, who, had he lived, would be like Neruda today. Rimbaud wandered the world, 'perdido, / desdichado' [lost, unhappy] (PN2 391), and was denied 'la sencillez', a house, wood, bread and bear. Capitalism condemned Rimbaud to 'hell'. Neruda confesses his own 'truth' as a poet who has joined a party: 'Ahora / no estarás / solitario' [now you would not be alone] (PN2 393). Neruda retains his identity with Rimbaud. This later CP-happy Neruda learnt the beauty of looking up words in the once-hated dictionaries: 'qué maravilla / pronunciar estas sílabas' [how marvellous to pronounce those syllables] (PN2 302). In his 'Oda a la gaviota' [Ode to a sea gull], he interrupts his celebration of the sea bird with 'soy / poeta / realista' [I'm a realistic poet] (PN2 330).

In this *Nuevas odas elementales* he included his 'Oda a Juan Tarrea' (1954), clearly the Spanish poet Juan Larrea, with 'tarrea and 'tarado' (idiot) almost punning. The ode exploits the invective that defines one aspect of Neruda's poetics. He accuses Larrea of 'robbing Andean tombs', then of hanging himself around Vallejo's neck, opening a shop 'de prólogos y epílogos' [of prologues and epilogues] (PN2 406). Tarrea has now discovered the New World. Neruda mocks him: 'No sabe nada / pero / nos enseña' [He doesn't know anything but he teaches us]. But what he teaches is a 'berenjal de vaguedades' and 'tontas teorías' [aubergine bed of vaguenesses / stupid theories]. Don't touch me Larrea, Neruda chants, leave our poets Darío and Vallejo alone. Stay away in Bilbao with your Caudillo (dictator Franco). When Larrea read this ode, he called it 'el golpe más bajo' [lowest blow] that he had ever received, and that he resented that his children might have read it.[22] Larrea then wrote his own critique of Neruda's *Alturas de Macchu Picchu*, already explored. What this ode and its reception reveal is how poetry can sting as well as sing.

---

[22] Juan Larrea, *Del surrealismo* ..., p. 122. See also David Bary, 'Sobre la "Oda a Juan Tarea"',*Cuadernos Americanos*, 159 (1968), pp. 197–214 and Emir Rodríguez Monegal, *El viajero inmóvil*, pp. 107–10.

Estravagario, 1958

With this long book of poems (343 pages in the first edition), Neruda relaxes
with his knowledge that the reader now knows him, his life, his loves, his
dislikes and his latest affair with Matilde Urrutia. He plays with this knowl-
edgeable and interested reader. Years later in 1973, he looked back on this
book and claimed that 'for its irreverence it is my most intimate book'.[23] Emir
Rodríguez Monegal concurred that it was 'maybe Neruda's most personal and
whimsical book, his major intimate revelation', but, I would add, it builds its
meanings on the way he has let readers know him through his poems.[24] Enrico
Mario Santí deemed it a return to an 'introspective vein', but really meant
autobiographical.[25] At a biographical level, the book chronicles a journey
the poet took with Matilde to the Far East, visiting many of the places that
he lived in while writing *Residencia en la tierra 1*. Poetically, he responds
to Nicanor Parra's *Poemas y antipoemas*, 1954, where the anti-poems can
be conceived of as anti-Neruda poems. In an interview with Mario Benedetti, Parra admitted: 'to be sincere, Neruda was always a problem for me,
a challenge, an obstacle' and labelled him 'that monster'.[26] Parra's implicit
critique of Neruda's poetry stresses a gallows humour constantly harping on
a vocabulary of tombs and death with a surrealist, even Dadaist sense of the
absurd. His poems have a narrative structure, and mock lyrical language, in
favour of colloquialisms and idiomatic phrases. Parra employs irony against
Neruda's more vatic pronouncements. But the opposition is not always that
clear, as Mario Rodríguez Fernández outlined, when he saw that Neruda's
poems 'Walking around' and 'Caballero solo' led into the later Parra.[27]

Neruda's title *Estravagario* is a neologism, like his earlier *Crespusculario*,
possibly parodying it (and himself). He tends to neologism only in titles. It
clearly suggests extravagance. As De Costa footnoted, the title appears once
in a poem as 'mi navegante estravagario', some hint at life's journey, at a
midlife reckoning.[28] In the word is also 'vagar', to wander, to travel, one
of the definitions of himself that he elaborated throughout his life. The first
edition, but not subsequent ones in the complete works, included illustrations
to each of the 68 poems from a nineteenth-century Mexican reading manual

23 Neruda, *Confieso*, p. 397: 'por su irreverencia es mi libro más íntimo'.

24 Rodríguez Monegal, *El vaijero inmóvil*, p. 289.

25 Enrico Mario Santí, 'Re-reading the Unknown Neruda', p. 186.

26 Mario Benedetti, *Los poetas comunicantes*, p. 52: 'para ser sincero, Neruda fue siempre
un problema para mí, un desafío, un obstáculo' ... 'ese monstruo'.

27 Mario Rodríguez Fernández, 'Nicanor Parra, destructor de mitos', in Angel Flores y
Dante Medina (compiladores), *Aproximaciones a la poesía de Nicanor Parra* (México DF:
EDUG, 1991), pp. 49–51.

28 De Costa, 1979, p. 183.

called *Libro de objetos ilustrados* and two full-page Jules Verne illustrations etc.

The opening poem mimics one of Apollinaire's 'calligrammes', with the one line rising towards the heaven it mocks. Playing with typography became one of Parra's trademarks, so Neruda was discreetly acknowledging him. When you turn the page, the poem reverts to its traditional form and a vague metaphoric meaning suggesting the need for imagination and natural fantasy. The book begins in earnest with 'Pido silencio' [I ask for silence], equally associated with Parra, always addressing his reader and asking for silence as in the 1962 poem 'Pido que se levante la sesión' [I ask that the session close]. Parra often employs the hectoring tone: 'Atención, señoras y señores, un momento de atención' [Attention, ladies and gentlemen, a moment of attention].[29] In Neruda's case, it is familiarity with his readers: 'Ahora me dejen tranquilo' [Now leave me in peace] (PN2 626). He mentions Matilde in his five requests and then states: 'sucede que soy y que sigo' [it happens that I am and I continue]. That use of 'sucede' echoes his famous *Residencia* poem 'Walking around', 'Sucede que me cansa de ser hombre'; Neruda knows his readers know his poems as he knows them. But contrary to that earlier poem, Neruda is solidly Pablo Neruda the poet, contented, travelling, and in love with Matidle: 'Nunca me sentí tan sonoro / nunca he tenido tantos besos' [I have never felt myself so sonorous, I have never had so many kisses] (PN2 627).

The better poems in this collection deal with his life in the late 1920s and early 1930s. In 'Regreso a una ciudad' [Return to a city] he searches for the 'loca' [mad woman] who loved him (Josie Bliss in Rangoon). But all traces of his past are 'cenizas' [ash], Quevedo's great term for the memory of sexual love still hurting and lingering. In one street he finds a house where he lived for 14 months: 'escribí desdichas' [I wrote unhappinesses]. That is his epitaph, all his *Residencia* poems are just 'desdichas' that echo Nerval. Yet another poem, then, surveys his past. By now, it is self-evident, one of Pablo Neruda's greatest themes is Pablo Neruda, he is his own creation. He realises that the past is dangerous: 'de repente / es una cárcel el pasado' [suddenly, the past is a prison] (PN2 633). In the poem 'El miedo' [fear], he turns this self-interest into an allegory. He is so well-known by 'todos', a term that opens five stanzas, that he yearns for privacy, locks himself away 'con mi más pérfido enemigo / Pablo Neruda' [with my most perfidious enemy, Pablo Neruda] (PN2 643). The created, public self as the enemy is Borgesian ('Borges y yo') and Baudelairian ('L'ennemi').

---

[29] Nicanor Parra, *Obra gruesa* (Santiago de Chile: Editorial Universitaria, 1969), pp. 90, 44.

Playing with his self-image is the theme of 'Parteogénesis', which again
opens with 'todos', his fame. He answers his public: 'Y entonces si me dejan
tranquilo / me voy a cambiar de persona' [and so if you leave me alone I
will change my persona] in order to be himself 'porque no sé hacer otra
cosa' [because I do not know what else to do]. That is, he can only be Pablo
Neruda, but not the one his readers know, another Pablo. His poems play
games with his readers' awareness of his life in verse. There are some lovely
poems that tease the reader about Neruda. 'No me pregunten' [Don't ask me]
ends with the poet asking his readers to knock on his vest to really understand
how little he understands about time: 'y veán cómo me palpita / un saco de
piedras oscuras' [and may you see how a jacket of obscure stone beats inside
me] (PN2 655). Is that a joke, or is that his imagistic way of confessing to
not-knowing? The poem 'Muchos somos' (We are many, so Whitmanesque)
concludes in a jokey muddling of identity:

> Mientras escribo estoy ausente
> y cuando vuelvo ya he partido:
> voy a ver si a las otras gentes
> les pasa lo que a mí me pasa,
> si son tantos como soy yo,
> si se parecen a sí mismos
> y cuando lo haya averiguado
> voy a aprender tan bien las cosas
> que para explicar mis problemas
> les hablaré de geografía. (PN2 658)

> [While I write I am absent and when I return I have already left;
> I will go and see if the others experience what happens to me, if
> they are as many as I am, if they see themselves similarly and
> when I have found out I will learn things so well that to explain
> my problems I will talk of geography]

The last word 'geography' as key to identity is no joke, for Neruda's poetry
is grounded in his Chilean roots in Temuco, its wind and rain and shores etc.
The fine poem 'Galopando en el Sur' [Galloping in the south] explains his
identification with a horse (so much part of his poetic self-image), galloping
across the Malleco mountain range in the rain (PN2 677). If 'geography'
is part of Neruda's literary personality (creating itself on the page for his
readers), it also implies travel. The crucial poem 'Itinerario' occupies itself
with the status of memories. He questions his earlier self: 'Para qué me casé
en Batavia?' [Why did I marry in Batavia?] (PN2 687). His answer is because
he was an 'idiota puro y errante' [pure errant idiot]. This 'idiot' was also the
author of the *Residencia* cycle. His long days in Colombo are vanishing;
all that remains is 'la lluvia de Carahue' [rain in Carahue] (PN2 688). He

has no answers, except to return home, to Valparaíso. In 'Adiós a París', Neruda stated: 'Tengo tanto que hacer en Chile' [I have so much to do in Chile] (PN2 690), for the talismanic word Chile summarises roots, meaning, Neruda. He has become the national poet, 'El Poeta'. De Costa viewed this 'very personal book' as Neruda treating everything 'irreverently', mentioning Nicanor Parra, rival poet of Chile, as provoker.[30]

Cien sonetos de amor, 1959

Biographically, this book of formal love sonnets without rhyme, celebrates the poet's relationship with Matilde Urrutia. The collection has been popular with readers, an autumnal version of his teenager love poems. Neruda was a keen reader of Shakespeare's sonnets to his 'dark lady', and there is a homage therein especially concerning ageing and time passing (he bought a copy in Jakarta in 1930). For example, the closing of Shakespeare's sonnet 147: 'For I have sworn thee fair, and thought thee bright, / Who art as black as hell, as dark as night' becomes the gentler Nerudan version ending sonnet XLIX: 'Por eso canto al día y a la luna, / al mar, al tiempo, a todos los planetas, / a tu voz diurna y a tu piel nocturna' [For that I sing day and moon, sea, time, all the planets, your diurnal voice, your nocturnal skin] (PN2 885); both last conceits match 'dark as night' / 'piel nocturna'.[31] Another example is the topos of the beauty of the real woman as opposed to the ideal woman of the sonnet tradition (the muse). Shakespeare's sonnet 130 opens with a negative: 'My mistress' eyes are nothing like the sun; / Coral is far more red than her lips' red; / If snow be white, why then her breasts are dun', echoed in Neruda's sonnet XVII: 'No te amo como si fueras de sal, topacio / o flecha de claveles que propagan el fuego; / te amo como se aman ciertas cosas oscuras ...' [I don't love as if you were salt, topaz or arrow of carnations that propagate fire. I love you as one loves certain dark things] (PN2 864–5).

Writing sonnets, the formal challenge, can also be seen as a way to kindle creativity, as they were later for Robert Lowell in his *Notebook*, 1970. Neruda's sonnets are essentially private, an antidote to the politicised *Canto general* and sometimes (like sonnet XII) sensuous and erotic. Again, Neruda can be self-referential. Sonnet 1 plays with the same simile (tunnel) as poem 1 of *Veinte poemas de amor*: 'Oh nombre descubierto bajo una enredadera / como la puerta de un túnel desconocido / que comunica con la fragancia del mundo!' [Oh name found under a climbing plant like the door of an unknown tunnel that communicates the world's fragrance] (PN2 855), but is

---

30 De Costa, 1979, p. 179.
31 Shakespeare's *Sonnets* (Madrid: Turner, 2002), p. 155.

the complete opposite to 'Fui solo como un túnel' (PN1 179) and the sexual imagery of moss. Here the tunnel is her vagina hidden by creepers (not moss) and that leads to 'fragrance', a sensuous version of love not just lust. Neruda is clearly far 'happier' with Matilde.

The imagery can be very conventional and at times 'cursi' [kitsch], like the terrible line in sonnet VII, 'Oh amor, ahora olvidemos la estrella con espinas!' [Oh love, now let's forget the star with thorns] (PN2 859) and some seem like exercises in rhetoric (as many sonnets do anyhow), like sonnets X and XIII where the woman is compared to wheat, bread, grain in CP clichés. Neruda has made a special kind of shorthand of terms that are his, such as 'rocío', 'pan', 'paloma', 'miel' [dew, bread, dove, honey], that verge on hackneyed commonplaces. But most moving is Neruda's continuing exploration of geography and love (his poor roots), especially in sonnet XXXI, 'Con laureles del Sur y orégano de Lota' [With laurels of the South and Lota marjoram], where the second stanza runs:

> Eres, como el que te ama, de las provincias verdes:
> de allá trajimos barro que nos corre en la sangre,
> en la ciudad andamos, como tantos, perdidos,
> temerosos de que cierren el mercado (PN2 873)

> [You are, like the one who loves you, from the green provinces, from there we brought the mud that runs in our veins, in the city we walk, like many, lost, scared that the market will close]

7

Post-1960s' poetry:
from *Plenos poderes* to *La rosa separada*

Post-1960s' poetry

The constant and massive output of Neruda's last decade until his death in 1973 from cancer, and then his eight posthumous collections, all prepared by the poet, constitute a critical challenge. These books consolidate his world status and his awareness of his readership. He had won the Nobel Prize in 1971 and represented the 'poet' in the eyes of most Latin Americans. He is perhaps the most translated poet in Spanish ever (see my Appendix). His themes all related to his public self, even the love poems are 'public', avidly read by thousands.

The collection *Plenos poderes* (cleverly rendered as *Fully Empowered* by Alastair Reid) appeared with Losada in 1962, and was perhaps his most 'abigarrados' [varied], claimed Loyola.[1] A normally hostile critic, Mario Benedetti, praised this book as an 'austere book, without concessions, of settling scores with himself, is one of the most authentic and valuable books Neruda has written'.[2] The poems are genuinely circumstantial, and can be read against his biography (his travels, his friends, his houses etc.). I take the title as a confession of the ageing poet's contented self-awareness, his 'dicha' [happiness] (PN2 1096), his boast that: 'Estoy contento con tantos deberes' [I am content with so many duties] (PN2 1132). As is usually the case, the opening poem is directed at alerting the reader to the poems that follow. 'Deber del poeta' [Poet's duty] tells the reader trapped in work to listen to the sea. We have here a therapeutic version of art that opens out the listener's imagination:

> *A quien no escucha el mar en este viernes*
> *por la mañana, a quien adentro de algo,*
> *casa, oficina, fábrica o mujer,*
> *o calle o mina o seco calabozo;*

[1] H. Loyola, PN2 1393.
[2] Mario Benedetti, *Letras del continente mestizo*, p. 65: 'libro austero, sin concesiones, de ajuste consigo mismo, es de lo más auténtica y valiosa que ha escrito Neruda'.

> *a éste yo acudo y sin hablar ni ver*
> *llego y abro la puerta del encierro*
> *y un sin fin se oye vago en la insistencia ...* (PN2 1091)

[To whoever is not listening to the sea this Friday morning, to whoever inside something, house, office, factory or woman or street or mine or dry jail; to him I rush and without speaking or looking I arrive and open the locked door and an endlessness can be heard vague in its insistence][3]

One constant of Neruda's art has been the 'ear', to listen to the sound of nature, the ocean and the inner sea: 'y el mar palpita, muere y continúa' (PN2 1091). This is the great rhythm of being, of life. Neruda's verse, his sentences, their very sound capture this tidal to-and-fro. No anguished soul-searching, rather the poet fully aware of his gifts, that emphatic 'yo' of the fifth line. The poet's duty is to preserve the sea's lament in his mind, for sea and freedom talk with the 'corazón oscuro' [dark heart] (the last words of the poem and possibly literal not metaphorical). Neruda's nature-based poetics are frankly Romantic. His 'duty' no different from John Keats's in his sensuous poem 'On the Sea', which opens: 'It keeps eternal whisperings around / Desolate shores, and its mighty swell / Gluts twice ten thousand caverns ...' for the poet to shake his reader awake with 'Oh ye! Whose ears are dinned with uproar rude, / Or fed too much with cloying melody – to sit and listen to the sea.'[4] The poet's task is to cure sick minds, to free workers from mind-numbing chores.

As Loyola noted, Neruda's verse autobiography *Memorial de Isla Negra* appeared in five volumes in 1964 as a sixtieth birthday present to himself. A poet's need to revise his poet's life is a natural urge. Neruda's public is sufficiently interested in 'Neruda' to warrant this self-inspection from the vantage-point of old age, like William Wordsworth's *The Prelude*, or later, Octavio Paz's *Pasado en claro*, 1975. The title enshrines the place where Neruda chose to live out his old age and his death; as is well known, it was not an island, but a village on Chile's ocean shore. He had surveyed his own past many times before in verse like the section 'Yo soy' [I am] in the *Canto general*; he will do so in prose with his ten pieces published in Brazil in 1962 and then his posthumous *Confieso que he vivido*, 1974 [Memoirs]. In many individual poems, he has turned against his earlier, dark self, revising his poetry against the turbulent dreams of the 1920s and 1930s. He has always been revisionist, and his life is shaped by who he is at the present moment of writing (a Communist Party stalwart). In fact, he refers back to himself rather

---

3   Alastair Reid has 'vibration' for 'sin fin', which reads and sounds just right.
4   John Keats, *Selected Poems*, edited with an Introduction and Notes by John Barnard (Harmondsworth: Penguin, 1988), p. 24.

than to other poets, so that readers may learn how he is changing, and that he owes little to his reading or to culture. All his post-1950s work assumes a reader who does not need to have read much else but Neruda before.

The first volume, covering the years from 1904 to 1921, is the most sequentially autobiographical. The first poem naturally deals with birth in Parral. The second moves to Temuco, associated with the rain of the Chilean south. Nature in his poetry was never benign; weather was inclement, cold, relentless. The home smelt of wood. The third poem deals with his step-mother ('La mamadre') and then his father ('Mi pobre padre duro' [My poor hard father]). The poems are clear, almost narrative, playful and emotional. We then get the poet's sexual awakening with the plain title and short-lined 'El sexo', an incident where two girl cousins seduced him by showing him 'un minúsculo / nido / de avecilla salvaje' [a minuscule nest of a little wild bird] (PN2 1154), hinting at a young girl's vagina, and then inspect his 'primer hombrecito' [first little man] (or penis). From then on the poet had discovered the electric flower of desire (given less space in his posthumous prose memoirs). Finally, in his awakening, there is poetry itself, which came from 'invierno o río' [winter or river], but not from words in books. It was a natural mystery, like the wind: 'mi corazón se desató en el viento' [my heart let itself go in the wind] (PN2 1156). Wind, of course, is a traditional symbol of inspiration. Because in 1962 he was ensconced in the Party, his vision of his earlier self fits his new-found state. That is, 'La injusticia' [Injustice], a title of a poem about his early loneliness and misery, becomes his early understanding of the suffering of others, when in reality Neruda at that age and stage was self-involved and self-exploring. His present obviously tampers with his past.

Reading books was Neruda's escape from his background and timid personality. In 'Los libros', he enumerates the 'libros / devorados, devoradores' [devoured devouring books] (PN2 1169), retaining his distinctive digestive metaphor for his way of reading. Authors are associated with taste ('Nietzsche, con olor a membrillos' [with a smell of quince]), and Gorky and Victor Hugo are also named. The sole Latin American book cited is Jorge Isaacs's *María* 'que nos hizo llorar de puros' [that made us cry as pure ones] (PN2 1169).

These reminiscing poems also evoke his collections of poems. 'La pensión de la calle Maruri' can be read alongside *Crespusculario*, with its section citing this same street. The student Neruda's loneliness is foregrounded: 'Soy prisionero con la puerta abierta, / con el mundo abierto, / soy estudiante triste perdido en el crepúsculo, / y subo hacia la sopa de fideos / y bajo hasta la cama y hasta el día siguiente' [I am a prisoner with the door open, with the world open, I am a sad lost student in the twilight and I climb to the pasta soup and go down stairs to bed and so on to the next day] (PN2 1172). The following poems in section II evoke the women behind his *Veinte poemas*

(Terusa / Rosaura, but still in 1964 not their real names), his 'muchacha de mis sueños' [girl of my dreams] (PN2 1173). His two long nostalgic poems about his first love do not repeat his earlier imagery, melancholy and joy, despite the 'cabellera de helechos, / pubis mojado' [fern hair, damp pubis]. At one time, the poet's past erotic acts become so vivid that he switches to the present tense, 'te abrazo, / te condeno, / te muero' [I embrace you, condemn you, die you] (PN2 1186–7), the last verb twisted out of its normal use by association with sexual orgasm. In these poems, he places his women in actual Chile. In fact, ageing is the primal experience (rivers, time passing) of these moving poems. In his essay on Milton, T. S. Eliot pondered the ageing of a poet, deciding that few poets experienced emotions as they had when young. He added:

> It requires, indeed, an exceptional honesty and courage to face the change. Most men either cling to the experiences of youth, so that their writing becomes an insincere mimicry of their earliest work, or they leave their passion behind and write only from the head, with a hollow and wasted virtuosity.[5]

Neruda's struggle with ageing was to become self-referential and revise his past.

The poem 'Primeros viajes' [First journeys], apparently straightforwardly autobiographical, touches on one of the great early drives in his poetry – the need to travel to become a poet. He evokes himself as 'infinito', alluding to his *tentativa del hombre infinito*, as someone who believed in 'la torre sumergida' [the buried tower] (PN2 1193), that sexual act of plunging inwards. He had perforated his darkness, had become the 'deshabitado' 'en los ay del amor' [deserted one, in the ohs of love], and was a skinny as a skeleton. He did not know languages (but he was learning French), and, a key line about his early work and reading, 'no sabía leer sino leerme' [I didn't know how to read but read myself], which is not quite the truth as he read plenty. But he would soon discover that the world was not the self. Nobody came when he called: 'aquella cita había terminado: / nunca más, nunca más, decía el cuervo' [that appointment had ended, never more never more, said the raven] (PN2 1193), Poe's 'The Raven' and its cry of 'Nevermore' concurs about not finding truth solipsistically. The poems enumerate the travels: Paris in 1927 was smoke and café chats for 'el fuego se había ido de París' [fire had left Paris] and Singapore and opium, and Rangoon. But Josie Bliss is not named, just described as 'un amor desmedido y desterrado' [an excessive and exiling love] (PN2 1198). He met 'her' in the port of Martabán: 'Era mi amor que yo no conocía' [she was my love I didn't know]. He sat next to her and just

---

5   T. S. Eliot, *Selected Essays*, pp. 188–91.

wanted 'mujer' [woman]. And they both gave into 'el placer amargo de los desesperados' [bitter pleasure of the despairing]. Again, this is his interpretation from 1962, for in the actual poems of the late 1920s there was no bitterness, no despair, just a seeking for sexual 'treasure' and liberating poetry. CP political correctness had biased his memories.

Book III, 'El fuego cruel' [The cruel fire], opens with the Spanish Civil War, another crisis moment for Neruda's poetry. In 1964 Franco still ruled, so Neruda naturally reverted to insult over the death of his poet-friends Lorca and Hernández; the poet spits, insults the 'sotanas' [cassocks] evoked in his *España en el corazón*. The poet recalls saving 2000 Republicans by having them transported to Chile in the *Winnipeg*, where poem and history overlap.[6] In the poem 'Los míos' [mine], Neruda reminds his readers of one of his most famous lines: 'Yo dije: A ver la sangre! / Vengan a ver la sangre de la guerra!' [I said: To see blood, Come and see the blood of war] (PN2 1219) from his earlier 'Explico algunas cosas', the poem that registered the enforced change in his aesthetics.

Then, finally, Josie Bliss appears in two poems with her name in the title (already referred to); she is the 'furiosa', the 'iracunda' [irate], and he has returned to Rangoon looking for her after the war. He never found out what happened to her. Did she die and was she buried in the Irrawaddy river? He fled the city, but she won by torturing his memory ('Josie Bliss me alcanzó revolviendo / mi amor y su martirio' [Josie Bliss reached me, stirring up my love and martyrdom], PN2 1235). With 'tus pies desnudos' (Neruda had highlighted her bare feet 35 years before), her 'rencor de puñal' [dagger rancour], as told in 'Tango del viudo', she was 'abandonada de mi amor' [abandoned by my love] as if she was the 'desdichada' of Nerval's sonnet. Here, at last, Neruda confessed to the truth about Josie Bliss, his discarded Beatriz.

Section IV deals with roots and Chile and does not tie in so closely with Neruda's own chronology. But travels (to Mexico, for example) and women still enter ('De tanto amar y andar salen los libros' [from so much loving and walking emerge the books], PN2 1292). Neruda sings to Delia, another of his abandoned muses as he outlines his recovery of his 'patria' Chile. Section V is what Charles Tomlinson called the 'ideological climax' of the collection over Khrushchev's shocking revelations about Stalin for CP members like Neruda.[7] In a speech on 25 February 1956 at the 20th Congress of the Communist Party Khrushchev described Stalin as capricious and despotic. Examples from a terrible litany: in 1937 and 1938, 98 of the 139 members of the Central Committee were shot on Stalin's orders; 750,000 people were executed between 1934 and 1953; 18 million people passed through camps

---

6   See Diego Carcedo, *Neruda y el barco de la esperanza* (Madrid: Editorial Temas de Hoy, 2006).
7   Charles Tomlinson, 'Overdoing the Generosity', p. 286.

and some 6 million died in the 1933 famine following forced collectivisation.[8] Neruda does not recant and continues to assert his CP ideals: 'Somos la plata pura de la tierra' [we are the pure silver of the earth]; a 'politics of a dismal crudity', said Tomlinson. Stalin, that 'ingeniero del amor' [engineer of love], had turned into a tyrant without Neruda being critically aware. Loyola has no notes on these poems from section V. To take one example of what was known about Stalin in Latin America, Octavio Paz had published in *Sur* in March 1951 a denunciation of Stalin's crimes, following revelations by David Rousset in Paris.[9] Though published in Buenos Aires, *Sur* was read continent-wide. Neruda simply turned a blind eye. This political issue is the hardest question to resolve when reading Neruda's post-1960s poems. At the same time as his long poem on Khrushchev's revelations, Neruda wrote sensuous and amusing poems about the market in Valparaíso and its abundance of foods in his odes tradition. Take cheese:

> Cuidado con el queso!
> No vino aquí sólo para venderse:
> Vino a mostrar el don de su materia,
> Su inocencia compacta,
> El espesor materno
> De su geología. (PN2 1313)

> [Watch out with the cheese! It did not come here to sell itself. It came to show the gift of matter, its compact innocence, the maternal thickness of its geology]

Memorial de la Isla Negra is about the poet himself, and that includes his dogmatic politics. We can read him in the way that he presented himself or as one of his enemies, but seduced every now and then by a poem, by its sounds, by its surprises. Somehow his capacious 'ego' attracts his readers, but most especially in his love poems. However, he was not alone in his reactions to Khrushchev, and he spoke for many of his fellow-travelling readers, equally willing to ignore. But first and foremost, he sang of himself, and that confident self was projected into the poems.[10] The most acute comments about his Stalinism come from a review by Enrico Mario Santí. He contrasted Loyola's volume of the complete works 'Nerudiana dispersa' with Schidlowsky's two volumes of documents, calculating that some 200 pieces were excluded by

[8]   Cited in Aileen Kelly, 'A Great Russian Prophet', *New York Review of Books*, 3 November 2005, pp. 63–6.

[9]   See my translation, with notes, of Octavio Paz's *Itinerary* (London: Menard Press, 1999), pp. 69–72.

[10] See Luis F. González-Cruz, *Pablo Neruda y el Memorial de Isla Negra* (Miami: Ediciones Universal, 1975), for a detailed reading of the whole collection.

Loyola. Santí criticised Loyola's deliberate choice to proscribe such documents as 'deshonesto' [dishonest]. He alleged, rightly, that reading these documents made him feel like 'blushing with shame' over Neruda's 'estalinismo crónico' [chronic Stalinism], and referred to several negated documents like one proving that Neruda obtained a visa for the Mexican muralist painter Siqueiros after he had tried to murder Trotsky in Mexico City.[11]

La rosa separada, 1974

Published in a limited edition in 1972, *La rosa separada* was conceived as the first of eight books that Neruda seemed to write concurrently to celebrate his seventieth birthday. The other seven were posthumous. He had prepared them all for press except for *El mar y las campanas* [The sea and bells]. In the years of the Allende government (1970–73), Neruda was asked to be Chile's ambassador in Paris and was ill with cancer. In interviews (with Rita Guibert, for example), he reiterated that he no longer saw himself as a political poet, more a love poet. Since the Khrushchev revelations in 1956, he seems to have retired from public avowals without ever withdrawing from the Party. Did he ever privately acknowledge Stalin's monstrous tyranny? Was living in far-off Chile an excuse for not feeling part of the Soviet experiment? The whole issue of his Party activities and how or whether they pollute his poetry is extremely tricky to deal with as a critic. The standard response seems to be that despite his Party adherence, Neruda continued to write, every now and then, astonishing poetry. You could go further, though, and claim that all his work from 1945 onwards falls from its dazzling heights because he had relinquished a crucial part of his poetic responsibilities to the Party. By quelling his anxieties and resolving his doubts, he also lost his poetic acumen. In his memoirs Neruda takes up the accusation of his Stalinism:

> Many have believed me to be a convinced Stalinist. Fascists and reactionaries have painted me as a lyrical exegetist of Stalin. Nothing of this specially irritates me. All conclusions become possible in such a devilishly confused period.[12]

Yet, he could not deny that he deeply admired the early Stalin – 'defensor titánico de la revolución rusa' [titanic defender of the Russian Revolution]

---

[11] Enrico Mario Santí, 'Rostro y rastro de Pablo Neruda', *Estudios Públicos*, pp. 285–7.

[12] Pablo Neruda, *Confieso*, p. 426: 'Muchos me han creído un convencido staliniano. Fascistas y reaccionarios me han pintado como un exégeta lírico de Stalin. Nada de esto me irrita en especial. Todas las conclusiones se hacen posibles en una época diabólicamente confusa.'

and victor over the Nazi forces with the Red Army. Adam Feinstein quoted Arthur Miller's characterising Neruda's Stalinism as a 'nearly religious loyalty to the dream Russia' and reminded us that Neruda finally admitted to a French journalist in September 1971, 'je me suis trompé' [I was wrong].[13] In 1974 his posthumous collection *Elegía* was published, originally titled as *Elegía de Moscú*, according to Loyola (who omits any mention of Stalin).[14] There are nostalgic poems to the city and people like Lenin, Mayakovsky, Ehrenburg and Stalin, about whom we can read: 'Luego, adentro de Stalin / entran a vivir Dios y el Demonio, / se instalaron en su alma. / Aquel sagaz, tranquilo georgiano, / conocedor del vino y muchas cosas, / aquel capitán claro de su pueblo ...' [Then inside Stalin God and Devil enter to live and install themselves in his soul. That wise, quiet Georgian, expert in wine and many things, that clear captain of his people] (PN3 774). He might have been a schizoid with a split personality or worse, the most ruthless killer of the twentieth century, but for Neruda he remained the Captain, a lover of wine. Loyalty blinded him in his participation in what Martin Amis called 'the great intellectual abasement'.[15]

What did Neruda gain from Communist Party membership from 1945 onwards? At a deep level, the Party solved existentialist problems; it also found him new friends (Aragon, Eluard, Picasso, Ehrenburg etc.). It gave him years of travel and prizes and adulation; it also kept his deep rebelliousness alive (it was often dangerous in the 1950s being a card-carrying member). It also handed him a political role in Chile as senator. It kept him close to his working-class roots, with new 'readers' and 'listeners' to his poetry. This relocation of his readers and associating working-class readers with 'gente sencilla' [simple people] is at the core of his later work. Was this condescending? Charles Tomlinson felt that 'Neruda does not really trust us as readers' and that he had become 'the village explainer, thus reducing us all to a role of purely passive and loving acceptance'.[16] The 'passive' accusation is interesting for it does not allow development or complication and confirms a Romantic view of the working class. Tomlinson's notion of 'loving acceptance' is crucial for here Neruda identified with the public persona he created of himself in his work, 'el Poeta'. Neruda said that reading his poem aloud in La Vega Central (a market in Santiago) was 'el hecho más importante de mi carrera literaria' [the most important deed in my literary career] (PN5 931), where the workers clapped and cried on hearing him read aloud.

Robert Pring-Mill wrote a fine tribute to the later Neruda in 1975 without touching on Stalinism or the CP issues. His detailed, biographic approach

---

13 Adam Feinstein, *Pablo Neruda*, pp. 343, 377.
14 Loyola, PN3, p. 1006.
15 Martin Amis, *Koba the Dread*, p. 38.
16 Charles Tomlinson, 'Latin America Betrayed', p. 6.

saw the publication in 1958 of *Extravagario* as ushering in 'the return to introspection'.[17] Another critic, Jaime Alazraki, also saw this date as Neruda's 'retorno al yo' [return to the ego].[18] Pring-Mill argued for reading the last works as those of an old man, especially through the poem 'Con Quevedo, en primavera' [With Quevedo in spring] from *Jardín de invierno* [Winter garden], 1974, where the poet is 'obsessed with the disparity between the rebirth of fields and orchards and his own bleakness'. It might be tempting to compare Neruda's last collections with W. B. Yeats's late angry and erotic poems, or with Thomas Hardy's old man's verse; there might be a common ageing poet's concerns with death. However, my intention is to focus on the first of his eight collections, *La rosa separada*, and review his existential melancholy, and to explore further what Pring-Mill meant by 'bleakness' in a poet who for nearly thirty years had dealt with 'future' and 'happiness'.

Christopher Perriam developed Pring-Mill's insights in his book *The Late Poetry of Pablo Neruda*, 1989, where he explored Neruda's 'monstrously productive literary life' from *Extravagario*, 1958, onwards when the poet relied on his reputation with readers and played on self-referentiality. Perriam noted how Neruda seemed to revert to his Hispanic roots (Quevedo especially) as he approached death and how closely his poems follow his autobiography. He is acute on Neruda's 'mental geography' and how Neruda restored his 'effroi métaphysique' [metaphysical terror] after suppressing it for so many years. Perriam evoked these last books as the words of a man 'casually thinking aloud'.[19] A more typical response to the later bulk of work is Jaime Concha's 'Neruda, desde 1952'. Like many critics faced with such a prolific output, Concha touched on the challenge to find some unity behind 'this gigantic poetic organism'.[20] He linked three areas. The first was Neruda's ongoing 'cántico socialista' [socialist canticle]. Here Concha agreed with fellow critics like Alain Sicard and simply illustrated Neruda, without any critique. The second level is the autobiographical impulse (already touched on) and the third, Neruda's insistence on objects and things. I would add that if Neruda is readable over these years it is because his poetry escapes these categories, rather than incorporating them. That it is his sensuous imagination that counts, not his ideological coherency.

Neruda travelled to Easter Island with a TV crew in January 1971. The 'rosa' of the title, a conventional shorthand term that Neruda used throughout his work, refers to Easter Island being a far-flung outpost of his *patria* Chile.

17   Robert Pring-Mill, 'The Winter of Pablo Neruda', p. 1154.

18   Jaime Alazraki, 'Para una poética de la poesía póstuma de Pablo Neruda', *Simposio Pablo Neruda*, p. 48.

19   Perriam, *The Late Poetry of Pablo Neruda*, p. 119.

20   Jaime Concha, 'Neruda, desde 1952', in Angel Flores (ed.), *Nuevas aproximaciones a Pablo Neruda*, p. 199.

Robert Pring-Mill saw this 'pilgrimage' as a 'counterpart' to his climb up
Machu Picchu. If pilgrimage suggests seeking some kind of wisdom or
message, then the journeys could not be more different.

The collection opens with 'Introducción de mi tema' [Introduction to
my theme] in simple, direct language, naming the 'Isla de Pascua' [Easter
Island], the mysterious statues, the sea, clouds and stones. 'Piedra' [stone]
has been a key term in Neruda's later output, signifying ontological solidity.
He knows death approaches and that this new journey seeks something that
he has not lost. Out there he can 'recomienzo las vidas de mi vida' [recom-
mence the lives of my life], a Proustian search for lost time. Nobody else is
named, not the people, nor his companion. He appears alone, as is inevitably
the case when facing death. The 1973 Losada edition has no index and the
poems oscillate between 'los hombres' [men] and 'la isla' [island].

The first poem sets the tone for the collection. He is just another 'tourist'.
This elimination of being a 'special poet' is remarkable, for it has fed into
his poetry and reputation all his life. As a tourist, the epoch of Sindbad
the Sailor and Columbus and real discovery is over. People arrive sitting
and digesting in 'gansos inmensos de aluminio' [immense aluminium geese]
(14). Neruda is just another tourist: 'Muerte al romanticón' [Death to the
Romantic] (17): that augmentative 'ón' is a wonderful self-mocking. Poem
3, 'La isla', speaks in the third-person plural, Neruda and the tourists, asking
forgiveness to ancient Rapa Nui, 'patria sin voz' [fatherland without voice].
These 'parlanchines del mundo' [chatterboxes of the world] spit in its lava
and have come to question the 'silence', which throughout the collection
becomes the opposite of the tourists. He then develops a moving analogy
between the volcanic crater of Ranu Raraku and death. His striking visual
simile is 'como una iguana inmóvil, soñoliena, escondida' [lie an immobile,
dreamy, hidden iguana] (22). He has known volcanoes, but here he has come
up against 'el ombligo de la muerte' [the navel of death] (22). Death makes
him howl with terror; he would have thrown himself into that green fear,
the toothless crater mouth; he experiences a moment of 'terror / de la boca
lunaria' [terror from the lunar mouth] (23). It is an honest poem.

Poem 4 continues in the first-person plural. He is one with all humans:
'Somos culpables, somos pecadores' [we are guilty, we are sinners] (27),
and he lists jobs and people, no longer separating the working class from
its enemies (death as the great leveller). Under our clothes we have the 'la
misma piel sedienta' [the same thirsty skin] (28). His view of humanity has
lost its political frame of the simple, good peasants against the capitalist
tyrants. Fear of imminent death has widened his focus.

Another crucial noun, 'viento' [wind], is explored here. He associated
wind with his childhood in Temuco, and with becoming a poet; its archetypal
sense links it with respiration and inspiration. He refers to 'el viento genital',
the 'Dios Viento' on the island. He has travelled to 'interrogar / a las estatuas

interrogadoras' [question the questioning statues] (40), sculpted by the wind. He is just another of life's 'desengañados' [deceived], that famous Quevedan cry, who rediscover their 'soledad' and 'oscuridad' (54). The poet, just another tourist, remember, has seen 'un vacío oceánico' [oceanic emptiness] and asked 'una pobre pregunta / con mil contestaciones de labios desdeñosos' [a poor question with a thousand answers of scornful lips] (70). As they leave Easter Island, he breaks out in English, 'too much for me!' (74). Adam Feinstein argued that this new misanthropy had a biographic source, partly 'fuelled by Neruda's unhappiness at the interruption of his love affair' and his friction with his wife Matilde.[21] But it is also a self-reckoning.

Poem 16 summarises his view of himself, and his fellow travellers (and all of us). It is one long sentence:

> El fatigado, el huérfano
> de las multitudes, el yo,
> el triturado, el del cemento,
> el apátrida de los restauranes repletos,
> el que quería irse más lejos, siempre,
> no sabía qué hacer en la isla, quería
> y no quería quedarse o volver,
> el vacilante, el híbrido, el enredado en sí mismo
> aquí no tuvo sitio: la rectitud de piedra,
> la mirada infinita del prisma de granito,
> la soledad redonda lo expulsaron:
> se fue con sus tristezas a otra parte,
> regresó a sus natales agonías,
> a las indecisiones del frío y del verano. (77–78)

> [The weary one, the orphan of the crowds, the ego, the crushed one, the cement one, the unpatriotic one of the full restaurant, the one who wanted to go far, always, didn't know what to do on the island, wanted and didn't want to stay or return, the hesitating one, the hybrid, the caught up in himself, had no place here: the rectitude of stone, the infinite look of the granite prism, the round loneliness, expelled him: he went with his sorrows elsewhere, returned to his native agonies, the indecisions of the cold and of summer]

It is an acute facing of the self as part of the herd, for the poem is a self-portrait. From this confession, we move back to the island. Poem 17 is a shortened version of the verbless description of Macchu Picchu that opens 'Oh torre de la luz, triste hermosura ...' [oh tower of light, sad beauty] (81).

---

[21] Feinstein, *Pablo Neruda*, p. 374.

Back home on mainland Chile, he confessed that he felt a coward, unable to stay and live on the island of 'la última pureza' [ultimate purity] (90):

> Como todos miré y abandoné asustado
> la limpia claridad de la mitología,
> las estatuas rodeadas por el silencio azul. (90)

> [Like all I looked and abandoned, scared, the clean clarity of mythology, the statues surrounded by blue silence]

So the lesson learnt on Easter Island was that 'blue silence'. I would like to think that 'azul' kept its Darío analogy of hope from his collection *Azul* of 1888 published in Chile, of that Mallarmean 'Fuir! là-bas fuir!', into the 'azure', for Neruda had been restored to his provincial Temucan roots: 'yo, poeta oscuro, recibí el beso de piedra en mi frente / y se purificaron mis congojas' [I, obscure poet, I received the stone kiss on my forehead and my worries were purified] (97). He had started as an 'obscure' poet in every sense (dark, unknown) and now, nearing death, was returning to being one. Then the poet slips back to love, the 'rosa secreta' [secret rose] with its sexual connotations, as if his journey has confirmed his love for his woman as well as a hopelessness about the future of mankind. This reads as too conventional. For the nugget Neruda found on the Chilean island was personal love and poetry in a foul world where people would kill, spit on, smash that beautiful balance of breathing 'basados en la verdad de la piedra y del viento' [based on the truth of stone and wind] (106). The poet concluded his confessional poem about the ancient keys to meaning and life, and the 'cien miradas de piedra que miran hacia adentro / y hacia la eternidad del horizonte' [hundred stares of stone that look inside and towards the eternity of the horizon] (110). His mythological and telluric sense that man is a shadow and that the real gods look inside and out to space is moving. What is new is that he no longer divides humankind into good and bad, and continues to view nature as the source of all. Pring-Mill noticed a further difference with the 'triumphant mood' of his Macchu Picchu poem. His outsider position (just another tourist) meant that 'there is no way of getting through to the long-forgotten race which carved the statues, whose blank eyes shut him out'.[22]

Interestingly, Neruda had written about Easter Island in 1948 in his *Canto general* in the poem 'Rapa Nui' (PN1 773), evoking the 'roca religiosa' [religious rock], with the statues as 'centinelas' [sentries] and the 'silencio' of the 'eternidad de las espumas' [eternity of foam] (that linking of religion, silence and eternity recall Pascal's 'Le silence éternel de ces espaces infinis

---

22 Pring-Mill, 'The Winter of Pablo Neruda', p. 1155.

m'effraie').[23] The poet spoke through one of the statues' builders, as he had done in his Machu Picchu poem and defined his view of art: 'Nada quieren decir, nada quisieron / sino nacer con todo su volumen de arena, / subsistir destinadas al tiempo silencioso' [they mean nothing and wanted nothing but be born with all their volume of sand, to subsist destined to silent time] (PN1 774). Neruda's thinking is reduced to the verb 'nacer', to be born into the pulse or throb of life, not into intellectualising meaning. The third 1948 poem about Easter Island is a love poem, with a premonition that death is 'mirando / el Océano' [looking at the ocean] (PN1 777). Love is 'el movimiento del mar que nos rodea' [movement of sea surrounding us], where 'mar' shifts into 'amar' and that verb 'rodear' conveys an erotic charge and no longer a threat as it was in his *Residencias*. Rain, ocean, silence, sea and rain are all images of that greater being without meaning. In rain and sea the individual is submerged into the infinite as a release of personality, that 'nada' that the poet had experienced as relief in the 1930s. The poem ends affirming the palpitations of life:

> deja mi mano entre tus pechos para que palpite
> al mismo tiempo que tus pezones mojados en la lluvia.

> [Leave my hand between your breasts so that it may throb at the same time as your nipples soaked in the rain]

In his later poems, there are many elegies for dead writer friends. For Neruda, reading a book was akin to meeting the poet, and knowing a poet was to have read his books without reading them. The metaphor uniting these experiences is that of deep intimacy not usually associated with the barriers of social intercourse or textual reading. For example, his long poem to 'Oliverio Girondo' in *Fin de mundo* [End of world], 1969, reverts to his Buenos Aires days (1933), with Argentina's most informed surrealist poet, outsider to the *Sur* group, and enemy to Jorge Luis Borges (as well as husband to Norah Lange). Girondo had died in 1967. His house on calle Suipacha was centre to countless extravagant parties. Neruda pays tribute to his 'vida insurrecta' [insurrectionary life] (PN5 427), to his 'fogonazo' [explosion], to his 'insolencia matutina' [morning insolence]. Girondo was not political, but was an 'iconoclasta desenfrenado' [wild iconoclast] (PN5 428). Girondo broke the spell that Sully Prudhomme and Europe in general had on Latin Americans with his 'espuelas del tango' [tango spurs], and stayed and lived in Buenos Aires: 'De todos los muertos que amé / eres el único viviente' [of all the dead I loved, you're the only one alive]. Neruda also writes poems to Vallejo, to René Crevel, to Whitman and Ercilla, and often cites Quevedo. Indeed, Alain

---

[23] Blaise Pascal, *Pensées et opuscules* (Paris: Hachette, 1935), p. 52.

Sicard touched on how Quevedo's example best evokes Neruda's last works: 'el desengaño que nos enseña la necesidad de modificar la perspectiva' [the disappointment that teaches us the need to modify our perspective].[24] But more than anything, Neruda did not decrease his productivity. From *Arte de pájaros*, 1966 to *El mar y las campanas*, 1973, there are 886 pages in his *Obras completas*. As Pring-Mill noted, in the poem '[No hay mucho que contar]' [There's not much to tell], titled from the first line and from *El mar y sus campanas*, Neruda alludes to his earlier *Residencia en la tierra* when he writes: 'Debo decir: aquí estoy, / esto no me pasó y esto sucede' [I should say: here am I, this did not happen and that did] (PN3 921). This answers his poem 'No hay olvido (Sonata)', which famously opened with 'Si me preguntáis en dónde he estado / debo decir "Sucede"' [If you ask me where I have been I should say 'it happens'] (PN1 343). His late poem ends simply in the present tense: 'Aquí está lo que tengo, lo que debo, / oigan la cuenta, el cuento y el sonido. / Así cada mañana de mi vida / traigo del sueño otro sueño' [Here's what I have, what I owe, listen to the count, the story and the sound. Thus every morning of my life I bring from my dream another dream] (PN3 921). The directness of this language, and one reference, reminded me of Antonio Machado's 'Retrato' [Portrait], 1907, where he uses the verb 'debo' [I owe] about his death: 'Y al cabo, nada os debo: debéisme cuanto he escrito' [And at the end I owe you nothing; you owe me all I've written].[25] So at the end, Neruda recognised that dreams remain the source of his art, that art itself is another form of dreaming (very similar to Borges's view of art), and that what really counts in poetry is 'sound'. Neruda is a great poet of the twentieth century because he consciously worked with dreams and sounds through reading and writing poetry to restore their primacy as the matter of art and thought, but it only remained at the core of his calling until the mid-1940s.

[24] Alain Sicard, 'Soledad, muerte y conciencia histórica en la poesía reciente de Pablo Neruda', p. 164.
[25] Antonio Machado, *Obras. Poesía y prosa*, p. 136.

Appendix 1

Pablo Neruda (1904–73): A Chronology

1904
Pablo Neruda was born on 12 July as Ricardo Eliecer Neftalí Reyes Basoalto (he was known as Neftalí Reyes) in Parral (meaning vine arbour) in central Chile. His mother died of TB two months after his birth, on 14 September.

1906
His train guard father remarried in Temuco where Neruda was brought up by a step-mother he nicknamed Mamadre.

1910
The family settled in Temuco. The geography of the area, with its forests, wind, rain and Pacific coast, imbued Neruda's sensibility and poetry. As an adolescent, he was very shy, skinny, solitary and an omnivorous reader. He went to the Liceo de Niños. He wrote vividly of these years in his posthumous memoirs, *Confieso que he vivido. Memorias*, 1974.

1917
Published his first piece (in prose) titled 'Entusiasmo y perseverancia'.

1919
Gabriela Mistral, Chile's earlier Nobel Prize winner in 1945, appointed head of the Liceo de Niñas in Temuco. She encouraged him to read Russian fiction.

1920
He began using the *nom de plume* Pablo Neruda on a school exercise book (see text for more on this choice).

1921
In March, travelled to Santiago de Chile to study to be a teacher of French at the Instituto Pedagógico, but never finished his degree. There are references in poems to his boarding house on Calle Maruri, 513.

1922
T. S. Eliot published *The Waste Land*, James Joyce *Ulysses* and César Vallejo *Trilce*.

1923
Published his first book of poems, *Crepusculario*.

1924

Published his *Veinte poemas de amor y una canción desesperada*. Over these Santiago years, he lived as a poet and associated with anarchists and their magazine *Claridad*. Neruda protected his lovers' identity, first by calling the two (at least) women of his poems Marisol and Marisombra; then, post-humously, biographers linked them to Teresa Vázquez and Albertina Rosa Azócar, the great love of his early life. In fact, in 1932, he still hoped to elope with her, though both were married. André Breton published the collectively signed first surrealist manifesto in Paris.

1925

Accompanied his friend Rubén Azócar on a teaching post to Ancud on Chiloe island, some 1100 kilometres south of Santiago. Started writing the early poems of *Residencia en la tierra*.

1926

Published *tentativa del hombre infinito* and his sole and short novel, *El habit-ante y su esperanza*.

1927

In June, won an honorary consular post in Rangoon, Burma (then part of the British Empire, today renamed Yangon in Myanmar). He travelled there by boat, with a friend, Alvaro Hinojosa, via Buenos Aires where he met Borges and Xul Solar, and then on to Lisbon and by land to Madrid and Paris. On 1 August from Marseille, took a boat to the Far East. He arrived in Singapore in October and then Rangoon, where he lived on Dalhousie Street. He met his most important lover and muse, the Burmese Josie Bliss. He visited Calcutta between November and December.

1928

Transferred to Colombo, Ceylon (Sri Lanka) where he lived by the sea in Wellawatta (today a suburb of Colombo) with a servant and a mongoose.

1929

Wall Street Crash.

1930

Transferred in June from Colombo to Singapore and then Batavia (today Djakarta) in Java, Indonesia where he met and then married on 6 December 1930 his first wife, known as 'Maruca', the Dutch-speaking Maria Antonieta Hagenaar. Their daughter Malva Marina was born in Madrid with hydro-cephalus in 1934 (she would die in 1942). Mayakovsky committed suicide.

1931

Ship back to Chile with wife and daughter, a seventy-five-day journey. Arrived in Puerto Montt on 18 April. Vicente Huidobro published *Altazor*.

1932

Second edition of *Veinte poemas*.

1933

Published the belated *El hondero entusiasta*, written in 1924, and the first volume of *Residencia en la tierra*. Transferred to Buenos Aires on 28 August, where he lived on the twentieth floor on Avenida Corrientes, near the Bajo. He met Federico García Lorca on 13 October. They gave a radio broadcast on Rubén Darío on 28 October and a composed a book together. He celebrated Lorca with an ode in 1935. He also met the Argentine poet Oliverio Girondo and his wife Norah Lange, the poet Raúl González Tuñón and the Chilean writer María Luisa Bombal, who became close friends. German Reichstag set on fire.

1934

Left Buenos Aires on 5 May, appointed Consul in Barcelona.

1935

Appointed Consul General in Madrid in February 1935. He lived in what he called La Casa de las Flores (on calle de Rodríguez San Pedro), close friend to Spain's great '1927' poets such as Rafael Alberti, Vicente Aleixandre, Miguel Hernández etc. He met his second wife, a politicised Argentine and sister-in-law to the late writer Ricardo Güiraldes called Delia del Carril, nicknamed 'la hormiga' [ant] or 'hormiguita' [little ant], some twenty years older than himself. Published first and second volumes of *Residencia en la tierra* in Madrid. He edited the poetry magazine *Caballo verde para la poesía*, first number in October.

1936

In July, outbreak of Spanish Civil War as General Franco toppled the elected government. He edited *Poetas del mundo defienden al Pueblo español* with Nancy Cunard. Lorca murdered in Granada in August. First book on Neruda by Arturo Aldunate Phillips. As Franco's troops approached Madrid on 7 November, Neruda abandoned Spain.

1937

On 26 April Guernica bombed by Germans. In Paris, met César Vallejo. Helped organise the congresses of artists and writers against fascism held in Madrid, Barcelona and Valencia in early July, with writers from Louis Aragon and Octavio Paz to Stephen Spender invited. Arrived back in Chile on 12 October with Delia. Published his angry war poems *España en el corazón* in Santiago. Created the Chilean Alianza de Intelectuales on 7 November and was its first president. The Chilean government of Arturo Alessandri veered towards a pro-Axis line.

1938

Read his Spanish poems aloud at La Vega central market in Santiago, an epiphanic moment in his life as a poet. His father died and then his stepmother months later. The Popular Front won the elections and President Aguirre Cerda sent Neruda back to Europe.

1939

Before the Second World War broke out in September, he went to Paris as Consul for Spanish Emigration, aiding refugees fleeing Franco's dictatorship, which finally controlled Spain from 19 May. Chartered the ship *Winnipeg*, which took 2000 Republicans to Chile. Lived in Valparaíso. Bought stone house in Isla Negra.

1940

Nazi–Soviet pact on 29 September. In August, travelled as Consul General to Mexico City and remained until 1943. Made friends with the muralists Diego Rivera and David Alfaro Siqueiros and adopted their view of Latin American history. He helped David Alfaro Siqueiros escape arrest for attempting to assassinate Trotsky in May 1940, then in exile in Mexico City, by giving him a Chilean passport. Siqueiros illustrated the first edition of *Canto general*. Trotsky murdered by Ramón Mercader on 20 August, four days after Neruda's arrival. Amado Alonso published his excellent book on Neruda in Buenos Aires.

1942

Miguel Hernández died in Alicante prison on 28 March.

1943

Finally married Delia in Tetecala, Mexico. On his way home to Chile from Mexico in October, climbed the Incan fortress of Machu Picchu.

1944

Received Chile's Premio Municipal de Poesía. 8 May Germany surrendered.

1945

On 8 July he finally joined the Chilean Communist Party. On 4 March, elected to the Senate for the northern mining regions of Tarapacá and Antofagasta. Received the Premio Nacional de Poesía in May. Published *Alturas de Macchu Picchu*. 6 August, atomic bomb dropped on Hiroshima; Japan surrendered.

1946

Won the Order of the Aztec Eagle from the Mexican government. González Videla won Chilean elections of 4 September, with Neruda's Communist

Party backing. On 28 December legally adopted name Pablo Neruda. Cold War politics permeates his actions and thoughts.

1947

Published in Buenos Aires his *Tercera residencia*, which includes his Spanish Civil War poems and his love poem of 1934, 'Las furias y las penas'. Attacked the Chilean president in his *Carta íntima para millones de hombres* in a Caracas newspaper, *El Nacional*, on 27 November.

1948

Communist Party outlawed in Chile. As a senator on 6 January gave a speech 'Yo acuso', naming 628 people detained in a concentration camp in Pisagua, which led to President González Videla ordering his arrest. His house was burnt down and he sought diplomatic refuge in the Mexican embassy. He went underground, but continued to write poems for his *Canto general*.

1949

Crossed the Andes incognito as an ornithologist, with a beard, on horse-back in March, via San Martín de los Andes and then Buenos Aires. He travelled to Paris in disguise on the passport of Guatemalan writer Miguel Angel Asturias. Visited Russia for the first time in June where he met Stalin. In Mexico City met Matilde and restarted an affair that began in 1946. Mao Tse-tung proclaimed People's Republic of China.

1950

Published his vast rewriting of Latin American history as *Canto general*. Won the World Peace Prize with Pablo Picasso and Paul Robeson.

1951

Toured Italy, stayed on Capri with his lover and later third wife, Matilde Urrutia.

1951

Visited Mao's China for the first time.

1952

Publishes *Los versos del capitán* about his new love, but anonymously. In August, returned to Chile after three years and five months of exile and settled in his Isla Negra house by the sea.

1953

Won the Stalin Peace Prize (later renamed Lenin Peace Prize). Stalin died. Started building La Chascona in Santiago for Matilde.

1954

Donated his library and shell collection to the Universidad de Chile. Published *Odas elementales* and *Las uvas y el viento*.

1955

Separated from Delia del Carril.

1956

On 25 February at the 20th Congress of the Russian Communist Party, Khrushchev revealed horrors behind Stalin's dictatorship. Invasion of Hungary on 4 November.

1957

His first *Obras completas* published in Buenos Aires by Losada. In Buenos Aires he was arrested on 11 April and briefly imprisoned in the Penitenciaría Nacional. Visited Ceylon for a Peace Conference, and on way to China with Matilde and Jorge Amado stopped at Rangoon, looking vainly for Josie Bliss. Then on to Moscow, where he would often travel as member of the Peace Prize committee.

1958

Published *Estravagario*.

1959

On 1 January, Fidel Castro and Che Guevara lead Cuban Revolution, ousting Batista. Published *Cien sonetos de amor*.

1960

Visited Cuba, and praised the Revolution in his *Canción de gesta*. Huge earthquake in Chile, destroying Puerto Saavedra.

1961

House-warming of his Valparaíso house, La Sebastiana. One million copies of *Veinte poemas* sold. Russian Yuri Gagarin completed first flight into space and back.

1962

Published *Plenos poderes*. Cuban missile crisis.

1964

Published *Memorial de Isla Negra*.

1965

Awarded D. Litt. at Oxford University.

1966

Travelled to New York for PEN meeting in June. Emir Rodríguez Monegal published first biography of Neruda. Married Matilde.

1967

Read at the London Poetry Festival on the South Bank. Showing of his sole play, *Fulgor y muerte de Joaquín Murieta*, about a bandit, in the university theatre in Santiago. Che Guevara assassinated in Bolivia.

1968

Prague invaded by Russia on 21 August. Two-volumed *Obras completas* out.

1970

Neruda campaigned for his friend Salvador Allende, who won the presidency as a socialist.

1971

In April appointed Chilean ambassador in Paris. Left Chile on 2 March, and lived there until ill health forced him to resign in 1972. Read poems in London in memory of J. D. Bernal. Visited Easter Island with a television team. Won the Nobel Prize in Literature on 21 October. *Veinte poemas de amor* sells 2,000,000 copies.

1972

Published *La rosa separada* in Paris about Easter Island.

1973

General Pinochet's violent coup of 11 September led to President Salvador Allende's suicide in the presidential palace. On 23 September, Neruda died of prostate cancer, his last words being 'me voy' [I'm off]. He could not be buried at Isla Negra, and so was lent a friend's niche. His body was transferred in May 1974 to Santiago's general cemetery. Three-volumed *Obras completas* published (3522 pages).

1992

With democracy restored, Neruda and Matilde's bodies (she died on 5 January 1985) reburied at Isla Negra.

1999

First of five volumes of his *Obras completas* published, with Hernán Loyola as general editor.

Sources: Pablo Neruda, *Confieso que he vivido. Memorias*, 1974; Matilde Urrutia, *Mi vida junto a Pablo Neruda (Memorias)*, 1976; Robert Pring-Mill, *A Poet for All Seasons*, 1993; Ilan Stavans (ed.), *The Poetry of Pablo Neruda*, 2003; Adam Feinstein, *Pablo Neruda. A Passion for Life*, 2004; Hernán Loyola, *Neruda. La biografía literaria*, 2006.

Appendix 2

Further Reading

Poetry

Begin with Neruda's memoirs, *Confieso que he vivido*, 1974. Equally stimulating is the correspondence with Héctor Eandi (ed. Aguirre, 1980).

A small anthology of the best of Neruda's poetry would include poems 1, 13, 15, 17 and 20 from the *Veinte poemas*; 'Galope muerto', 'Tango del viudo', 'Arte poética', 'Sonata y destrucciones', 'Walking around', 'Caballero solo', 'Agua sexual', 'Oda a Federico García Lorca' and 'No hay olvido (Sonata)' from *Residencia en la tierra I* and *II*; 'Explico algunas cosas' and 'Las furias y las penas' from *Tercera residencia*; 'Alturas de Macchu Picchu' and 'La arena traicionada' from *Canto general*; 'Oda a la alcachofa' and 'Oda a la cebolla' from *Odas elementales*.

Best available text with translations is Stavans, 2003.

Critics

In English, begin with Feinstein's biography; the best critics are Manuel Durán and Margery Safir, 1981, René de Costa, 1979, Robert Pring-Mill, 1975, Enrico Mario Santí, 1982, Christopher Perriam, 1989 and Dominic Moran, 2006 (full details in the Bibliography). Best interview in English, Rita Guibert, *Paris Review*, 51, 1971.

In Spanish, there are many biographies, from the chatty Jorge Edwards, 1990, to the most complete, Loyola, 2006. I still like Emir Rodríguez Monegal's mix of literary criticism and biography, 1966. For literary criticism in Spanish, consult the classic book on Neruda by Amado Alonso, 1940. The views of Saúl Yurkievich, Jaime Concha and Hernán Loyola (see Bibliography) are always well-considered. The essays edited by Flores, 1974 and 1987, and by Schopf, 2003, are excellent as surveys of critical approaches.

Appendix 3

Neruda in English (books only)[1]

There is a list of Neruda in English in Ilan Stavans's 2003 anthology, pp. 946–9. As far as I know, the first single poem translated into English was by Andrew Boyd for Grigson's *New Verse* in 1936, commented on in the text. Neruda then appeared in Dudley Fitts's *Anthology of Contemporary Latin-American Poetry* (Norfolk: New Directions, 1942), with H. R. Hays's version of 'Walking around' (also commented on in the text) and Fitts's of 'Ritual of my legs' as the first poems into American English. Neruda was also a translator himself, as noted, from his earliest days, starting with Baudelaire, Rilke, France and then on to William Blake's 'Las hijas de Albion' and 'El viajero mental' for Bergamín's magazine *Cruz y Raya* in 1934. He also translated Joyce's poems and Shakespeare's *Romeo and Juliet*, and later, a book on Romanian poets.

Selected Poems of Pablo Neruda, translated by Angel Flores (New York: Peter Pauper Press, 1944). From *Residencia en la tierra*, 1935.

Residence on Earth and Other Poems, bilingual, translated by Angel Flores (New York: Norfolk, CT, 1946; New York: Gordian Press, 1976). From *Residencia en la tierra*, 1935.

Tres cantos materiales / Three Material Songs, translated by Angel Flores (New York: East River Editions, 1948). From *Residencia en la tierra*, 1935.

Alturas de Macchu Picchu, translated by Angel Flores in Whit Burnett (ed.), *The World's Best* (New York: Dial Press, 1950). *Alturas de Macchu Picchu*, 1946.

Let the Rail-Splitter Awake and Other Poems, translated by Joseph M. Bernstein (New York: Masses and Mainstream, 1951; with an introduction by Christopher Perriam, London: Journeyman, 1988). From *Canto general*, 1950.

Thirty Poems of Love and Exile, translated by Kenneth Rexroth (San Francisco: City Lights Books, 1956). From *Veinte poemas de amor y una canción desesperada*, 1924.

Twenty Love Poems based on the Spanish of Pablo Neruda, translated by Christopher Logue in *Songs* (London: Hutchinson, 1959). From *Veinte poemas de amor y una canción desesperada*, 1924.

The Elementary Odes. A Selection, translated by Carlos Lozano (New York: Las Americas, 1961). *Odas elementales*, 1954.

---

[1] Translations are listed chronologically.

Selected Poems, translated and edited by Ben Belitt (New York: Grove Press, 1961).

Residence on Earth, translated by Clayton Eshleman (San Francisco: Amber House Press, 1962). *Residencia en la tierra*, 1935.

Bestiary / bestiario, translated by Elsa Neuberger (New York: Harcourt Brace & World, 1965). *Bestiario*, 1958.

The Heights of Macchu Picchu, bilingual, translated by Nathaniel Tarn. Preface by Robert Pring-Mill (London: Cape, 1966; New York: Farrar, Straus & Giroux, 1967). *Alturas de Macchu Picchu*, 1946.

We are Many, bilingual, translated by Alastair Reid (London: Cape Goliard, 1967; New York: Grossman, 1968).

Twenty Poems of Pablo Neruda, bilingual, translated by James Wright and Robert Bly (Madison, MN: Sixties Press, 1967; London: Rapp & Whiting, 1968).

Twenty Love Poems and a Song of Despair, translated by W. S. Merwin (London: Cape, 1969; New York: Grossman, 1971; Harmondsworth: Penguin Books, 1976). *Veinte poemas de amor y una canción desesperada*, 1924.

The Early Poems, translated by David Ossman and Carlos Hagen (New York: New Rivers Press, 1969).

Pablo Neruda: a New Decade. Poems 1958–1967, translated and edited by Ben Belitt and Alastair Reid (New York: Grove Press, 1969).

Selected Poems, edited by Nathaniel Tarn and translated by Anthony Kerrigan, W. S. Merwin, Alastair Reid and Nathaniel Tarn (London: Cape, 1970; New York: Delacorte Press, 1972; Harmondsworth: Penguin Books, 1975).

Neruda and Vallejo: Selected Poems, bilingual, edited by Robert Bly and translated by Robert Bly, John Knoepfle and James Wright (Boston: Beacon Press, 1971).

The Captain's Verses, translated by Donald Walsh (New York: New Directions, 1972). *Los versos del capitán*, 1953.

Splendor and Death of Joaquín Murieta, translated by Ben Belitt (New York: Farrar, Straus & Giroux, 1972; London: Alcove Press, 1973). *Fulgor y muerte de Joaquín Murieta*, 1967.

Extravagaria, translated by Alastair Reid (London: Cape, 1972; New York: Farrar, Straus & Giroux, 1974). *Estravagario*, 1958.

New Poems, 1968–1970, translated by Ben Belitt and Alastair Reid (New York: Grove Press, 1972).

Residence on Earth, translated by Donald Walsh (New York: New Directions, 1973; London: Souvenir Press, 1976). *Residencia en la tierra*, 1935 and 1947.

Five Decades. A Selection. Poems 1925–1970, translated by Ben Belitt (New York: Grove Press, 1974).

Veinte poemas de amor y una canción desesperada. Una interpretación en inglés / Twenty Poems of Love and a Sad Song of Hopelessness. A Rendition in English by Giovanni Previtali (Santa Rosa, CA: Plumtree Press, 1974).

Fully Empowered, translated by Alastair Reid (New York: Farrar, Straus & Giroux, 1975; London: Condor Books / Souvenir Press, 1976). *Plenos poderes*, 1962.

Song of Protest, translated and introduced by Miguel Algarín (New York: William Morrow, 1976). *Canción de gesta*, 1960.

Memoirs, translated by Hardie St Martin (New York: Farrar, Straus & Giroux, 1976; London: Souvenir Press, 1976; Harmondsworth: Penguin Books, 1989). From *Confieso que he vivido. Memorias*, 1974.

Incitement to Nixonicide and Praise for the Chilean Revolution, translated by Steve Kowit (Houston, TX: Quixote Press, 1977). *Incitación al Nixonicidio y alabanza de la revolución chilena*, 1973.

A Call for the Destruction of Nixon and Praise for the Chilean Revolution, translated by Teresa Anderson (Cambridge, MA: West End Press, 1980).

The Heights of Macchu Picchu, translated by John Felstiner in *Translating Neruda. The Way to Macchu Picchu* (Palo Alto, CA: Stanford University Press, 1980). *Alturas de Macchu Picchu*, 1946.

Isla Negra; a Notebook, bilingual, translated by Alastair Reid (New York: Farrar, Straus & Giroux, 1981; London: Souvenir Press, 1982). *Memorial de Isla Negra*, 1964.

Skystones, translated by Ben Belitt (Easthampton, MA: Emanon Press, 1981). *Las piedras del cielo*, 1971.

Selections: Poems from Canto General, translated by J. C. R. Greene (Isle of Skye: Aquila Publishing, 1982). *Canto general*, 1950.

Passions and Impressions, edited by Matilde Neruda and Miguel Otero Silva, translated by Margaret Sayers Peden (New York: Farrar, Straus & Giroux, 1983). *Para nacer he nacido*, 1978.

Still Another Day, translated by William O'Daly (Port Townsend, WA: Copper Canyon Press, 1984). *Aún*, 1969.

Eight Odes, translated by Ken Norris (Ste Anne de Bellevue, Québec: The Muses' Company, 1984).

Art of Birds, translated by Jack Schmitt (Austin: University of Texas Press, 1985). *Arte de pájaros*, 1966.

The Separate Rose, translated by William O'Daly (Port Townsend, WA: Copper Canyon Press, 1985). *La rosa separada*, 1972.

One Hundred Love Sonnets / Cien sonetos de amor, bilingual, translated by Stephen Tapscott (Austin: University of Texas Press, 1986). *Cien sonetos de amor*, 1960.

Winter Garden, translated by William O'Daly (Port Townsend, WA: Copper Canyon Press, 1986). *Jardín de invierno*, 1974.

The Stones of Chile, translated by Dennis Maloney (Fredonia, NY: White Pine Press, 1986). *Las piedras de Chile*, 1961.

The Heights of Macchu Picchu, translated by David Young (Boston, MA: Songs Before Zero Press, 1986). *Alturas de Macchu Picchu*, 1946.

Stones of the Sky, translated by James Nolan (Port Townsend, WA: Copper Canyon Press, 1988). *Las piedras del cielo*, 1971.

The Sea and the Bells, translated by William O'Daly (Port Townsend, WA: Copper Canyon Press, 1988). *El mar y las campanas*, 1973.

The House at Isla Negra, translated by Dennis Maloney and Clark M. Zlotchew (Fredonia, NY: White Pine Press, 1988).

Late and Posthumous Poems: 1968–1974, translated and edited by Ben Belitt. Introduction by Manuel Durán (New York: Grove Press, 1988).

Selected Odes of Pablo Neruda, translated with an introduction by Margaret Sayers Peden (Berkeley: University of California Press, 1990; publ. as *Elemental Odes*, London: Libris, 1991).

Selected Poems, translated by Anthony Kerrigan (New York: Mariner Books, 1990).

The Yellow Heart, translated by William O'Daly (Port Townsend, WA: Copper Canyon Press, 1990). *El corazón amarillo*, 1974.

The House in the Sand, translated by Dennis Maloney and Clark M. Zlotchew (Minneapolis, MN: Milkweed Editions, 1990). *Una casa en la arena*, 1966.

Canto General, translated by Jack Schmitt. Introduction by Roberto González Echevarría (Berkeley: University of California Press, 1991).

The Book of Questions, translated by William O'Daly (Port Townsend, WA: Copper Canyon Press, 1991). *Libro de las preguntas*, 1974.

Spain in the Heart: Hymn to the Glories of the People at War, translated by Richard Schaaf (Washington, DC: Azul Editions, 1993). *España en el corazón*, 1937.

The Captain's Verses, bilingual, translated with introduction by Brian Cole (London: Anvil Press Poetry, 1994). *Los versos del capitán*, 1952.

Odes to Common Things, bilingual, translated by Ferris Cook and Ken Krabbenhoft (Boston, MA: Bulfinch Press, 1994).

Neruda's Garden: an Anthology of Odes, bilingual, translated by Maria Jacketti (Pittsburgh: Latin American Literary Review Press, 1995).

Love. Pablo Neruda. Poems, translated by Stephen Tapscott, W. S. Merwin, Alastair Reid, Nathaniel Tarn, Ken Krabbenhoft and Donald Walsh (London: The Harvill Press, 1995).

Maremoto: Seaquake, translated by Maria Jacketti and Dennis Maloney (Fredonia, NY: White Pine Press, 1995). *Maremoto*, 1970.

Odes to Opposites, translated by Ken Krabbenhoft and illustrated by Ferris (Boston, MA: Little, Brown & Company, 1995).

Ceremonial Songs / Cantos ceremoniales, translated by Maria Jacketti (Pittsburgh: Latin American Review Press, 1996). *Cantos ceremoniales*, 1961.

Full Woman, Fleshly Apple, Hot Moon: Selected Poems of Pablo Neruda, translated by Stephen Mitchell (New York: HarperCollins, 1997).

Pablo Neruda and Nicanor Parra Face to Face: a Bilingual and Critical Edition of their Speeches, translated and edited by Marlene Gottlieb (Lampeter, Wales: Edward Mellen Press, 1997). From *Discursos*, 1962.

Epic Song, translated by Richard Schanf (Falls Church, VA: Azul Editions, 1998). *Canción de gesta*, 1960.

Machu Picchu, translated by Stephen Kessler, photographs by Barty Brukoff and prologue by Isabel Allende (Boston, MA: Bulfinch Press, 2001). *Alturas de Macchu Picchu*, 1946.

The Poetry of Pablo Neruda, various translators and edited, with an Introduction by Ilan Stavans (New York: Farrar, Straus & Giroux, 2003).

On the Blue Shore of Silence: Poems of the Sea, translations by Alastair Reid, illustrated by Mary Heebner and afterword by Antontio Skármeta (New York: Rayo, 2003).

The Essential Neruda: Selected Poems, edited by Mark Eisner and translated by Lawrence Ferlinghetti, Robert Hass, Stephen Mitchell, Alastair Reid, Forrest Gander, Stephen Kessler and Mark Eisner (San Francisco: City Lights Books, 2004).

Spain in Our Hearts: España en el corazón, translated by Donald Walsh (New York: New Directions, 2004).

BIBLIOGRAPHY

Primary sources are ordered chronologically, secondary sources alphabetically according to author.

Bibliographies

Loyola, Hernán, 'La obra de Pablo Neruda: Guía bibliográfica', Pablo Neruda, *Obras completas* (Buenos Aires: Losada, 1973), pp. 911–1106.
Santí, Enrico Mario, 'Fuentes para el conocimiento de Pablo Neruda' [Bibliography 1967–1974] *Simposio Pablo Neruda. Actas* (New York: University of Southern Carolina / Las Américas, 1975), 276 items listed.
Becco, Horacio Jorge, *Pablo Neruda. Bibliografía* (Buenos Aires: Casa Pardo, 1975). 1057 entries listed.
Woodbridge, Hensley C. and David S. Zubatsky, *Pablo Neruda. An Annotated Bibliography of Biographical and Critical Studies* (New York and London: Garland Publishing, 1988). 2374 entries listed.
Robert Pring-Mill, *A Poet for All Seasons*, Exhibition of Nerudiana at the Taylor Institution, Oxford, 1993.
Pérez López, María Ángeles, 'Revisión bibliográfica sobre Pablo Neruda. Última década', *Insula* 690 (junio 2004), pp. 15–18.
Neruda Concordance on <www.spsu.edu/sis/nuhfer-hatten/webconcordances/neruda>
Fundación Neruda on <www.fundacionneruda.org/home.htm>
Neruda criticism on <www.neruda.uchile.cl/critica>

Poetry

Veinte poemas de amor y una canción desesperada (Santiago: Nascimento, 1924).
tentativa del hombre infinito (Santiago: Nascimento, 1926).
Residencia en la tierra I and *Residencia en la tierra II* (Madrid: Cruz y Raya, 1935).
Canto general, fly leaf illustrated by Diego Rivera and end leaf by David Alfaro Siqueiros (México DF: no publisher [subscription edition], 1950).
Poemas, 'Pablo Neruda', pp. 5–7 (Buenos Aires: Editorial Fundamentos, 1952).

Antología esencial, selección, prólogo de Hernán Loyola (Buenos Aires: Losada, 1971).

La rosa separada (Buenos Aires: Losada, 1973).

A Basic Anthology. Selection and Introduction by Robert Pring-Mill (Oxford: The Dolphin Book Co. Ltd: 1975).

Residencia en la tierra, edición de Hernán Loyola (Madrid: Cátedra, 1987).

Poemas de amor de Pablo Neruda, selección y prólogo de Oscar Hahn (Santiago de Chile: Editorial Universitaria, 1994).

Cuadernos de Temuco, edición y prólogo de Víctor Farías (Barcelona: Editorial Seix Barral, 1997).

Obras completas I. De 'Crepusculario' a 'Las uvas y el viento', 1923–1954. Edición y notas de Hernán Loyola. Introducción general de Saúl Yurkievich. Prólogo de Enrico Mario Santí (Barcelona: Galaxia Gutenberg, 1999).

Obras completas II. De 'Odas elementales' a 'Memorial de Isla Negra', 1954–1964. Edición y notas de Hernán Loyola. Prólogo de Saúl Yurkievich (Barcelona: Galaxia Gutenberg, 1999).

Obras completas III. De 'Arte de pájaros' a 'El mar y las campanas', 1966–1973. Edición y notas de Hernán Loyola. Prólogo de Joaquín Marco. (Barcelona: Galaxia Gutenberg, 2000).

Obras completas IV. Nerudiana dispersa 1, 1915–1964. Edición de Hernán Loyola (Barcelona: Galaxia Gutenberg, 2001).

Obras completas IV. Nerudiana dispersa II, 1922–1973. Edición de Hernán Loyola (Barcelona: Galaxia Gutenberg, 2002).

Veinte poemas de amor y una canción desesperada, edited with an introduction, critical analysis, notes and vocabulary by Dominic Moran (Manchester: Manchester University Press, 2007).

Nerudiana

Homenaje a Pablo Neruda (Madrid: Plutarco, 1935).

Neruda, Pablo (editor), *Caballo verde para la poesía*, n. 1, octubre 1935; n. 2 noviembre 1935; n. 3 diciembre 1935; n. 4, enero 1936.

Neruda, Pablo, 'Federico García Lorca', in Prados, Emilio, *Homenaje al poeta García Lorca contra su muerte. Selección de sus obras* (Valencia: Ediciones Españolas, 1937), pp. 43–9.

Neruda, Pablo and Parra, Nicanor, *Discursos* (Santiago: Nascimento, 1962).

Neruda, Pablo, 'J.E.', in Juan Emar, *Diez* (Santiago: Editorial Universitaria, 1970).

Neruda, Pablo, 'The Art of Poetry XIV', interview with Rita Guibert, *Paris Review*, no. 51 (Winter 1971), pp. 149–75.

Neruda, Pablo, 'Pablo Neruda se confiesa', *Siempre*, n. 954, 6 de octubre 1971, p. 36.

Neruda, Pablo, *Confieso que he vivido. Memorias* (Buenos Aires: Losada, 1974).

Fernández Larraía, Sergio (ed.), *Cartas de amor de Pablo Neruda* (Buenos Aires: Editorial Tucumán / Ediciones Marymar, 1975).

Neruda, Pablo, *Para nacer he nacido* (Barcelona: Editorial Seix Barral, 1978).

Neruda, Pablo, *Cartas a Laura*, estudio preliminar de Hugo Montes (Madrid: Ediciones Cultura Hispánica, 1978).

Aguirre, Margarita, *Pablo Neruda / Héctor Eandi. Correspondencia durante 'Residenca en la tierra'* (Buenos Aires: Editorial Sudamericana, 1980).

Neruda, Pablo, *Canto General*, translated by Jack Schmitt, introduction by Roberto González Echevarría (Los Angeles: University of California Press, 1991).

Stavans, Ilan (ed.), *The Poetry of Pablo Neruda* (New York: Farrar, Straus & Giroux, 2003).

Neruda, Pablo, *Epistolario viajero (1927–1973)*, selección, estudio preliminar y notas de Abraham Quezada Vergara (Santiago: RIL Editores, 2004).

Neruda, Pablo, *Habla Neruda. Memorias imposibles de corregir*. Compilación de Roberto Silva Bijit (Santiago: Catalonia, 2004).

Neruda, Pablo, *Yo respondo con mi obra. Conferencias, discursos, cartas, declaraciones (1932–1959)*, edición de Perdo Gutiérrez Revuelta y Manuel J. Gutiérrez (Salamanca: Ediciones Universidad de Salamanca, 2004).

Cordal, Alfredo, 'Mi entrevista con Pablo Neruda', *Qué*, marzo–abril 2005, pp. 16–18.

Neruda, Pablo por él mismo, *Alturas de Macchu Picchu*. Texto completo (Buenos Aires: AMB Discografía, no date).

Secondary sources

Aguirre, Margarita, *Las vidas de Pablo Neruda* (Santiago de Chile: Empresa Editora Zig-Zag, 1967).

Alazraki, Jaime, *Poética y poesía de Pablo Neruda* (New York: Las Américas, 1965).

—— 'La estructura de la oda elemental', in Angel Flores (ed.), *Nuevas aproximaciones a Pablo Neruda*, pp. 223–8.

Alberti, Rafael, *La arboleda perdida. Libros I y II de memorias* (Barcelona: Editorial Seix Barral, 1971).

—— *Sobre los ángeles* (Madrid: Turner Libros, 1994).

Allende, Isabel, *Mi país inventado* (Buenos Aires: Sudamericana, 2003).

Alonso, Amado, *Poesía y estilo de Pablo Neruda: interpretación de una poesía hermética* [1940] (Madrid: Gredos, 1997).

Alonso, J. M., 'Neftalí Ricardo Reyes invents Pablo Neruda', *Review 72*, Winter 1971 / Spring 1972, pp. 33–8.

Amis, Martin, *Koba the Dread* (London: Vintage, 2003).

Anderson Imbert, Enrique, 'La prosa vanguardista de Neruda', in *Simposio Pablo Neruda*, 1975.

Anon., 'Tarnished Tarn', *The Times Literary Supplement*, 16 March 1967, p. 220.

Anon., *The Song of Roland*, translated by Dorothy L. Sayers (Harmondsworth: Penguin, 1960).

Apollinaire, Guillaume, *Alcools* (Paris: Gallimard, 1980).

Bataille, Georges, *L'érotisme* (Paris: Minuit, 1957).

Baudelaire, Charles, *Les Fleurs du mal* (Paris: Editions de Cluny, 1941).

—— *Mon coeur mis à nu* (Paris: Librarie Générale Française, 1972).

—— *Petits poëmes en prose* (Paris: Nouvelle Revue Française, 1973).

Beckett, Samuel, *Proust* (London: John Calder, 1931).

Bécquer, Gustavo Adolfo, *Rimas* (Madrid: Anaya, 1964).

Bell, Julian, 'The Cunning of Francis Bacon', *New York Review of Books*, 10 May 2007, pp. 4–8.

Bellini, Giuseppe, *Quevedo y la poesía hispanoamericana del siglo XX: Vallejo, Carrera Andrade, Paz, Neruda, Borges* (New York: Eliseo Torres & Sons [1967], 1976).

Benedetti, Mario, 'Vallejo y Neruda: dos modos de influir', in *Letras del continente mestizo* (Montevideo: Arca, 1967), pp. 62–6.

Bernardin de Saint-Pierre, Jacques-Henri, *Journey to Mauritius*, translated, with an introduction, by Jason Wilson (Oxford: Signal Books, 2002).

Blake, William, *Complete Writings* (London: Oxford University Press, 1969).

Bloom, Harold, *The Western Canon. The Books and School of the Ages* (London: Macmillan, 1995).

Bly, Robert, 'On Pablo Neruda', *London Magazine*, no. 4, July 1968, pp. 24–35.

Bonnefoy, Yves, *Rimbaud par lui-même* (Paris: Editions du Seuil, 1970).

Bowra, C. M., *Poetry and Politics, 1900–1960* (Cambridge: Cambridge University Press, 1966).

Breton, André, 'Les mots sans rides', in *Les pas perdus* (Paris: Gallimard, 1949).

—— *Entretiens* (Paris: Gallimard, 1952).

—— *Manifestes du surréalisme* (Paris: Jean-Jacques Pauvert Éditeur, 1962).

—— *Nadja* (Paris: Gallimard, 1964).

Brown, Norman O., *Love's Body* (New York: Vintage Books, 1966).

Butlin, Martin, *William Blake* (London: Tate Gallery, 1978).

Cage, John, *Silence* (Cambridge, MA: MIT Press, 1970).

Charpier, Jacques and Seghers, Pierre, *L'Art poétique* (Paris: Seghers, 1956).

Chisholm, Anne, *Nancy Cunard* (London: Sidgwick & Jackson, 1979).

Cohen, J. M., *Poetry of this Age* (London: Hutchinson, 1966).

Coleridge, Samuel Taylor, *Biographia Literaria* (London: Dent, 1967).

Concha, Jaime, 'Interpretación de *Residencia en la tierra* de Pablo Neruda', *Atenea*, pp. 41–81.

—— *Neruda (1904–1936)* (Santiago: Editorial Universitaria, 1972).

—— 'Neruda, desde 1952', in Angel Flores (ed.), *Nuevas aproximaciones a Pablo Neruda*, pp. 199–222.

Cortázar, Julio, 'Neruda', in *Obra crítica 3*, edición de Saúl Sosnowski (Madrid: Alfaguara, 1983).

Cortínez, Carlos, 'Caballo de los sueños', in Angel Flores (ed.), *Nuevas aproximaciones a Pablo Neruda*, pp. 101–12.

Costa, René de, *En pos de Huidobro* (Santiago: Editorial Universitaria, 1978).

—— *The Poetry of Pablo Neruda* (Cambridge, MA: Harvard University Press, 1979).

—— 'El Neruda de Huidobro', in Angel Flores (ed.), *Nuevas aproximaciones a Pablo Neruda*, pp. 273–9.

Cunningham, Valentine (ed.), *The Penguin Book of Spanish Civil War Verse* (Harmondsworth: Penguin, 1980).

Dante Alighieri, *La Divina Commedia, Inferno. Purgatorio. Paradiso* (London: J. M. Dent, 1933).

—— *Hell*, translated, annotated and introduced by Steve Ellis (London: Vintage, 1994).

Darío, Rubén, *Los raros* (Buenos Aires; Espasa-Calpe, 1952).

—— *Prosas profanas* (Madrid: Espasa-Calpe, 1964).

—— *Cantos de vida y esperanza, los cisnes y otros poemas*, edición de Francisco J. Díez de Revenga (Salamanca: Ediciones Almar, 2001).

Deacon, Terence, *The Symbolic Species. The Co-evolution of Language and the Human Brain* (Harmondsworth: Penguin, 1997).

Deutscher, I., *Stalin. A Political Biography* (London: Oxford University Press, 1949).

Díez-Canedo, Enrique, *La poesía francesa del romanticismo al superrealismo* (Buenos Aires: Losada, 1945). [Updating of the 1913 anthology.]

Dodsworth, Martin, 'Words and Music', *The Guardian*, 23 April 1975, p. 16.

Drabble, Margaret (ed.), *The Oxford Companion to English Literature* (Oxford: Oxford University Press, 2000).

Ducasse, Isidore, Comte de Lautréamont, *Oeuvres complètes* (Paris: Gallimard, 1973).

Durán, Manuel and Safir, Margery, *Earth Tones: the Poetry of Pablo Neruda* (Bloomington: Indiana University Press, 1981).

Edwards, Jorge, 'Un adiós a muchas cosas', in A. Fontaine, *Estudios Públicos*, pp. 291–6.

Eliot, T. S., *The Use of Poetry and the Use of Criticism* [1933], (London: Faber, 1954).

—— *Collected Poems, 1909–1962* (London: Faber & Faber, 1963).

—— *Selected Essays*, edited by J. Hayward (Harmondsworth: Penguin, 1965).

Ellis, Keith, 'La búsqueda infructuosa en *Veinte poemas de amor y una canción desesperada*', in Flores, Angel (ed.), *Nuevas aproximaciones*, pp. 53–62.

Eshleman, Clayton, 'In Defense of Poetry', *Review 72*, Winter 1971 / Spring 1972, pp. 39–47.

—— *Companion Spider. Essay* (Middletown, CT: Wesleyan University Press, 2001).

Espronceda, José de, *Obras poéticas 1* (Madrid: Espasa-Calpe, 1952).

Feinstein, Adam, *Pablo Neruda. A Passion for Life* (London: Bloomsbury, 2004).

Felstiner, John, *Translating Neruda. The Way to Macchu Picchu* (Stanford: Stanford University Press, 1980).

Fitts, Dudley, reprint of 1967 *The New York Times Book Review*, in *Review 68*, p. 25.

Flores, Angel (ed.), *Aproximaciones a Pablo Neruda* (Barcelona: Ocnos, 1974).

—— *Nuevas aproximaciones a Pablo Neruda* (México DF: Fondo de Cultura Económica, 1987).

Fontaine, Arturo, ' "Entrada a la Madera": un comentario', in Fontaine (ed.), Special number on Neruda of *Estudios Públicos*, n. 94, 2004, pp. 71–108.

Forster, Merlin, *An Index to Mexican Literary Periodicals* (New York: The Scarecrow Press, 1966).

Fowlie, Wallace, *Age of Surrealism* (Bloomington: Indiana University Press, 1963 [1950]).

—— *Rimbaud and Jim Morrison. The Rebel as Poet* (Durham, NC: Duke University Press, 1993).

Fraser, G. S., 'The Man', *Adam*, March–April 1948, pp. 2–3.

—— *News from South America* (London: The Harvill Press, 1949).

Fromm, Erich, *The Art of Loving* (New York: Harper & Row, 1956).

García, Alvaro, *Poesía sin estatua. Ser y no ser en poética* (Valencia: Pre-textos, 2005).

García Lorca, Federico, *Obra completa* (Madrid, Aguilar, 1963).

—— *Dibujos*, ed. Mario Hernández (Madrid: Ministerio de Asuntos Exteriores de España, 19??).

García Méndez, Javier, *Diez calas en el hacer de la poesía de Pablo Neruda. Residencia en la tierra y Canto general* (Rennes: Presses Universitaires de Rennes, 2001).

Gibson, Robert, *Modern French Poets on Poetry. An Anthology arranged and annotated* (Cambridge: Cambridge University Press, 1961).

Gobello, José, *Nuevo diccionario lunfardo* (Buenos Aires: Corregidor, 1991).

Gonzalez, Mike and Treece, David, *The Gathering of Voices. The Twentieth-Century Poetry of Latin America* (London: Verso, 1992).

González-Cruz, Luis F., *Neruda. De Tentativa a la totalidad* (Madrid: Ediciones Abra, 1979).

Graves, Robert, *The Greek Myths*, 2 vols (Harmondsworth: Penguin Books, 1955).

Green, André and Kohon, Gregorio, *Love and its Vicissitudes* (London: Routledge, 2005).

Grigson, Geoffrey (ed.), *New Verse* (London: Faber & Faber, 1939).

Guerra Cunningham, Lucía, '*El habitante y su esperanza* de Pablo Neruda: primer exponente vanguardista en la novela chilena', in *Texto e ideología en la narrativa chilena* (Minneapolis, MN: The Prisma Institute, 1987), pp. 83–99.

Gullón, Ricardo, 'Relaciones Pablo Neruda – Juan Ramón Jiménez', *Hispanic Review*, 39, April 1971, pp. 141–66.

Hamburger, Michael, *The Truth of Poetry. Tensions in Modern Poetry from Baudelaire to the 1960s* (London: Weidenfeld & Nicolson, 1969).

Hamsun, Knut, *Pan* [1894], translated by James W. McFarlane (New York: Bard Books, 1975).

—— *Hunger*, translated by Robert Bly, with an introduction by Isaac Bashevis Singer, 'Knut Hamsun, Artist of Skepticism' (London: Duckworth, 1967).

Hart, Stephen M. (ed), '*¡No pasarán!' Art, Literature and the Spanish Civil War* (London: Tamesis, 1988).

Heaney, Seamus, *The Government of the Tongue* (London: Faber & Faber, 1988).

Hidalgo, Alberto, Huidobro, Vicente and Borges, Jorge Luis (eds), *Indice de la nueva poesía americana* (Buenos Aires: Sociedad de Publicaciones El Inca, 1926).

Hobson, J. Allan, *Dreaming. An Introduction to the Science of Sleep* (Oxford: Oxford University Press, 2002).

Homer, *The Odyssey*, translated by E. V. Rieu (Harmondsworth: Penguin Books, 1971).

Huidobro, Vicente, *Obras completas* (Santiago de Chile: Editorial Zig-Zag, 1964).

Joyce, James, *Ulysses* (London: The Bodley Head, 1967).

Kadir, Djelal, 'Neruda and Whitman: Short-circuiting the Body Electric', *Pacific Coast Philology*, 8 (April 1973), pp. 16–22.

Karpf, Annie, *The Human Voice. The Story of a Remarkable Talent* (London: Bloomsbury, 2006).

Kelly, Alice, 'Why They Believed in Stalin', *New York Review of Books*, 26 April 2007, pp. 58–62.

Kipling, Rudyard, *Selected Poems*, edited by Craig Raine (Harmondsworth: Penguin Books, 1992).

Kristal, Efraín, 'Introduction', César Vallejo, *The Complete Poetry*, a bilingual edition, edited and translated by Clayton Eshleman, with a foreword by Mario Vargas Llosa and a chronology by Stephen M. Hart (Berkeley: University of California Press, 2007).

Larrea, Juan, *Del surrealismo a Machupicchu* (México DF: Joaquín Mortiz, 1967).

Lawrence, D. H., *Women in Love* [1921] (London: Heinemann, 1945).

—— *Lady Chatterley's Lover,* [1928] (Harmondsworth: Penguin, 1993).

—— *Love Poems* (London: Studio Vista, 1958).

—— *The Complete Poems*, with an introduction and notes by David Ellis (Ware: Wordsworth Poetry Library, 2002).

Lewis, Norman, *Golden Earth. Travels in Burma* (London: Cape, 1954).

Lihn, Enrique, 'Momentos esenciales de la poesía chilena', *Panorama de la literatura latinoamericana* (Madrid: Editorial Fundamentos, 1971), pp. 246–57.

Longo, Teresa (ed.), *Pablo Neruda and the U.S. Culture Industry* (New York: Routledge, 2002).

López Velarde, Ramón, *Obras*, edición de José Luis Martínez (México: Fondo de Cultura Económica, 1979).

Loveluck, Juan and Lévy Isaac, Jack (eds), *Simposio Pablo Neruda. Actas* (New York: University of South Carolina / Las Américas, 1975).

—— 'El navío de Eros: *Veinte poemas de amor … Número nueve*', in *Simposio Pablo Neruda*, 1975.

—— 'Neruda ante la poesía hispanoamericana', *Revista Casa Silva*, 4, enero 1991, pp. 63–73.

Loyola, Hernán, *Ser y morir en Pablo Neruda* (Santiago, 1967).

—— *Neruda. La biografía literaria. 1 La formación de un poeta (1904–1932)* (Santiago de Chile: Editorial Planeta Chilena, 2006).

Lugones, Leopoldo, *Obras poéticas completas* (Madrid: Aguilar, 1974).

Machado, Antonio, *Obras. Poesía y prosa,* edición reunida por Aurora de Albornoz y Guillermo de Torre (Buenos Aires: Editorial Losada, 1973).

MacNeice, Louis, *The Strings are False. An Unfinished Autobiography* (London: Faber, 1965).

Mallarmé, Stéphane, *Oeuvres complètes* (Paris: Gallimard, 1945).

Melis, Antonio, 'Neruda y la poesía hispanoamericana: una presencia polémica', in Schopf (comp.), *Neruda comentado*, pp. 17–56.

Méndez-Ramírez, Hugo, *Neruda's Ekphrastic Experience. Mural Art and* Canto general (Lewisburg, PA: Associated Universities Press, 1999).

Milán, Eduardo, *Una cierta mirada. Crónica de poesía* (México DF: Juan Pablo Editor / Universidad Autónoma Metropolitana, 1989).

Mistral, Gabriela, 'Recado sobre Pablo Neruda', in Schopf (comp.), *Neruda comentado*, pp. 179–84 and reproduced in *Nerudiana*, no. 1, agosto de 2006, pp. 19–21.

Molina, Enrique, 'Neruda de siempre', *La Nación*, 21 de diciembre 1973, pp. 1, 8.

Morris, Jan [James], *Pax Britannica. The Climax of an Empire* (Harmondsworth: Penguin, 1982).

Neira, Julio, 'De Pablo Neruda a José María Souvirón, una carta inédita', *Insula*, 694, octubre 2004, pp. 19–20.

Nerval, Gérard de, *Aurélia ou le rêve et la vie*, édition établie par Jean Richer (Paris: Minard, 1965).

—— *Les Chimères*, bilingual edition, translated by William Stone (London: Menard Press, 1999).

—— *Poesía*, versión, prólogo y notas de Alejandro Bekes (Córdoba, Argentina: Ediciones del Copista, 2004).

The New Encyclopedia of Poetry and Poetics, edited by Alex Preminger and T. V. F. Brogan (Princeton: Princeton University Press, 1993).

Núñez-Faraco, Humberto, *Borges and Dante. Echoes of a Literary Friendship* (Bern: Peter Lang, 2006).

Ocampo, Victoria, *Tagore en las barrancas de San Isidro* [1961] (Buenos Aires: Ediciones Fundación Sur, 1983).

Olivares, Edmundo B., *Pablo Neruda: los caminos de Oriente. Tras las huellas del poeta itinerante (1927–1933)* (Santiago: LOM Ediciones, 2000).

—— *Pablo Neruda: los caminos del mundo. Tras las huellas del poeta itinerante II (1933–1939)* (Santiago: LOM Ediciones, 2001).

Orwell, George, *Inside the Whale and Other Essays* (Harmondsworth: Penguin, 1981).

Oses, Darío, 'Pablo Neruda bibliófilo y lector, el amor por la vida y el amor por los libros', *Atenea*, 489, 2004, pp. 51–62.

Osuna, Rafael, *Pablo Neruda y Nancy Cunard (Les poètes du Monde défendent le peuple espagnol)* (Madrid: Editorial Orígenes, 1987).

Ovid, *The Erotic Poems*, translated with an introduction and notes by Peter Green (Harmondsworth: Penguin, 1982).

Nicanor Parra, *Obra gruesa* (Santiago de Chile: Editorial Universitaria, 1969).

Paseyro, Ricardo, 'The Dead World of Pablo Neruda', *TriQuarterly*, no. 15 (Spring 1969), pp. 203–27. Translated as *Le Mythe Neruda* (Paris: L'Herne [1958], 1965).

Paz, Octavio, 'Pablo Neruda en el corazón', *Ruta*, n. 4, 15 de septiembre de 1938, pp. 25–33.

—— *Poemas (1935–1975)* (Barcelona: Editorial Seix Barral, 1979).

—— *Sombras de obras* (Barcelona: Seix Barral, 1983).

—— *La llama doble. Amor y erotismo* (Barcelona: Seix Barral, 1993).

—— *Obra completa 1* (Barcelona: Galaxia Gutenberg, 1994).

Perriam, Christopher, 'Metaphorical *Machismo*: Neruda's Love Poetry', *Forum for Modern Language Studies*, 24 (1988), pp. 58–77.

—— *The Late Poetry of Pablo Neruda* (Oxford: The Dolphin Book Co. Ltd, 1989).

—— 'Re-reading Neruda's *Veinte Poemas de Amor y Una Canción Desesperada*', *Bulletin of Hispanic Studies*, LXXV (1998), pp. 93–108.

Phillips, Adam, *Terrors and Experts* (London: Faber, 1995).

Piglia, Ricardo, *Formas breves* (Buenos Aires: Anagrama, 2005).

Pinker, Steven, *The Language Instinct* (Harmondsworth: Penguin, 1994).

Plato, *The Symposium*, translated by W. Hamilton (Harmondsworth: Penguin, 1951).

Poe, Edgar Allan, *The Portable Edgar Allan Poe*, selected and edited with an introduction and notes by Philip Van Doren Stern (New York: The Viking Press, 1945).

Poniatowska, Elena, *Octavio Paz. Las palabras del árbol* (Barcelona: Plaza y Janés, 1998).

Pring-Mill, Robert, 'La elaboración de la cebolla', in Flores (ed.), *Aproximaciones a Pablo Neruda*, pp. 229–41.

—— 'Introduction', Pablo Neruda, *A Basic Anthology* (Oxford: The Dolphin Book Co. Ltd, 1975), pp. xv–lxxix.

—— 'The Winter of Pablo Neruda', *Times Literary Supplement*, 3 October 1975, pp. 1154–6.

—— *A Poet for all Seasons* (Oxford, 1993).

Quevedo, Francisco, *Antología poética*, dispuesta y prologada por R. Esteban Scarpa (Madrid: Espasa-Calpe, 1959).

Radhakkrishnan, S. (ed.), *The Dhammapada* (Oxford: Oxford University Press, 2005).

Reid, Alastair, 'Climbing Macchu Picchu', *The New York Review of Books*, 5 November 1981, pp. 54–5.

Rich, Adrienne, *Adrienne Rich's Poetry and Prose*, selected and edited by Barbara Charlesworth Gelpi and Albert Gelpi (New York: W. W. Norton, 1993).

Riess, Frank, *The Word and the Stone. Language and Imagery in Neruda's* Canto general (Oxford: Oxford University Press, 1972).

Rimbaud, Arthur, *Oeuvres complètes*, édition établie, présentée et annotée par Antoine Adam (Paris: Gallimard, 1972).

Rodman, Selden, *South America of the Poets* (Carbondale: Southern Illinois University Press, 1970).

Rodríguez Fernandez, Mario, '*Reunión bajo las nuevas banderas* o de la conversión poética de Pablo Neruda', in Flores (ed.), *Aproximaciones a Pablo Neruda*, pp.149–64.

Rodríguez Monegal, Emir, *El viajero inmóvil. Introducción a Pablo Neruda* (Buenos Aires: Editorial Losada, 1966).

—— and González Echeverría, Roberto, 'El surrealismo es uno', in: *Convergencias / divergencias / incidencias* (Barcelona: Tusquets Editor, 1973).

Rougemont, Denis de, *Passion and Society*, translated by Montgomery Belgion (London: Faber [1939], 1962).

Rowe, William, 'Latin American Poetry', in John King (ed.), *Companion to Modern Latin American Culture* (Cambridge: Cambridge University Press, 2004), pp. 136–70.

Salas, Horacio, *El tango* (Buenos Aires: Planeta, 1995).

Salerno, Nicolás, 'Alone y Neruda', in Fontaine, *Estudios Públicos*, pp. 297–389.

Salmon, Russell and Lessage, Julia, 'Stones and Birds: Consistency and Change in the Poetry of Pablo Neruda', *Hispania*, 60, 2 (May 1977), pp. 224–41.

Sanhueza, Leonardo, compilación y prólogo, *El bacalao. Diatribas antinerudianas y otros textos* (Santiago: Ediciones B Chile, 2004).

Santí, Enrico Mario, 'Re-reading the Unknown Neruda', *Latin American Research Review,* 1977, pp. 185–92.

—— *Pablo Neruda. The Poetics of Prophecy* (Ithaca: Cornell University Press, 1982).

—— 'Politics, Literature and the Intellectual in Latin America', *Salmagundi,* 82–3, Spring–Summer 1989, pp. 92–110.

—— 'Rostro y rastro de Pablo Neruda', in Fontaine, *Estudios Públicos*, pp. 279–289.

Schidlowsky, David, *Las furias y las penas Pablo Neruda y su tiempo*, 2 vols (Berlin: Wissenschaflicher Verlag, 2003).

Schopf, Federico, *Del vanguardismo a la antipoesía. Ensayos sobre la poesía en Chile* (Santiago de Chile: LOM Ediciones, 2000).

—— (compilador), *Neruda comentado* (Santiago: Editorial Sudamericana, 2003).

Shaw, Donald, ' "Ebrio de trementina": Another View', in Round, Nicholas and Walters, Gareth (eds), *Readings in Spanish and Portuguese Poetry for Geoffrey Connell* (Glasgow: University of Glasgow Department of Hispanic Studies, 1985), pp. 235–46.

Sicard, Alain, 'Soledad, muerte y conciencia histórica en la poesía reciente de Pablo Neruda', in Loveluck and Lévy Isaac (eds), *Simposio Pablo Neruda*.

—— *El pensamiento poético de Pablo Neruda* (Madrid: Gredos, 1981).

Silva Castro, Raúl, *Pablo Neruda* (Santiago: Editorial Universitaria, 1964).

Starkie, Enid, 'Rimbaud in England', *Adam*, 244–6, 1954, pp. 2–9.

Steiner, George, *Extraterritorial* (London: Faber, 1972).

Suárez, Eulogio, *Neruda total* (Santiago: Editorial América Morena, 1994).

Sucre, Guillermo, 'Canto general de Pablo Neruda', *Vuelta*, 4, marzo 1977, pp. 36–7.

Tagore, Rabindranath, *Gitanjali*, with an introduction by W. B. Yeats (London: Macmillan, 1913).

—— *The Gardener*, translated by the author from the original Bengali (London: Macmillan, 1931).

Teitelboim, Volodia, *Neruda* (Madrid: Meridión, 1984).

Tomlinson, Charles, 'Overdoing the Generosity', *Times Literary Supplement*, 25 March 1983, p. 286.

—— 'Latin America Betrayed', *Times Literary Supplement*, 28 June 1991, pp. 5–6.

Unamuno, Miguel de, *Antología poética* (Madrid: Espasa-Calpe, 1959).

Urrutia, Matilde, *Mi vida junto a Pablo Neruda (Memorias)* (Santiago: Seix Barral, 1986).

Valdivieso, Jaime, 'Neruda: misión y poesía', in *Realidad y ficción en Latinoamérica* (México DF: Mortiz, 1975), pp. 93–106.

Vallejo, César, *Contra el secreto profesional* (Lima: Mosca Azul Editores, 1973).

—— *El arte y la revolución* (Lima: Mosca Azul Editores, 1973).

—— *Poesías completas*, edición crítica y exegética de Juan Larrea (Barcelona: Barral Editores, 1978).

—— *Obras completas*, tomo 2, Artículos y crónicas (1918–1939). Desde Europa. Recopilación, prólogo, notas y documentación por Jorge Puccinelli (Lima: Biblioteca Clásicos del Perú, 1987).

Vargas Llosa, Mario, *Diccionario del amante de América Latina* (Barcelona: Paidós, 2006).

Verlaine, Paul, *Oeuvres poétiques Complètes*, texte établi et annoté par Y.-G. Le Dantec (Paris: Gallimard, 1962).

—— *Selected Poems*, edited and translated by Martin Sorrell (Oxford: Oxford University Press, 1999).

Villaurrutia, Xavier, *Obras* (México DF: Fondo de Cultura Económica, 1966).

Watkins, Vernon, 'For Whom does a Poet Write?', *Temenos*, 1, 1981, pp. 93–6.

Whitman, Walt, *Leaves of Grass*, with an introduction by Gay Wilson Allen (New York: New American Library, 1958).

Williams, Hugo, 'Freelance', *Times Literary Supplement*, 25 February 2000, p. 16.

Wilson, Jason, *Darío, Borges, Neruda and the Ancient Quarrel between Poets and Philosophers* (London: Institute of Latin American Studies, 2000).

—— 'In the Translator's Workshop', *Poetry London*, Summer 2002, pp. 30–2.

—— 'Spanish American Surrealist Poetry' in Robert Havard (ed.), *A Companion to Spanish Surrealism* (London: Boydell & Brewer / Tamesis Books, 2004).

—— *Jorge Luis Borges* (London: Reaktion, 2006).

Wood, Michael, 'The Poetry of Neruda', *The New York Review of Books*, 3 October 1974, pp. 8–11.

Wordsworth, William, *Selected Poems* (Oxford: Oxford University Press, 1950).

Wright, James, reprint of review from *Poetry*, June 1968, in *Review 68*, 1969, p. 29.

Yeats, W. B., *Collected Poems* (London: Macmillan, 1961).

Yudin, Florence L., 'The Dialectical Failure in Neruda's "Las furias y las penas"', *Hispania*, 68 (March 1985), pp. 55–62.

Yurkievich, Saúl, *Fundadores de la nueva poesía latinoamericana* (Barcelona: Seix Barral, 1973).

—— 'Pablo Neruda: persona, palabra y mundo', in Pablo Neruda, *Obras completas 1* (Barcelona: Galaxia Gutenberg / Círculo de Lectores, 1999), pp. 9–79.

Zerán, Faride, *La guerrilla literaria. Huidobro, de Rokha, Neruda* (Santiago: Editorial Sudamericana, 1997).

INDEX